THE YEAR BOOK OF WORLD AFFAIRS 1983

VOLUME 37

Editors:

GEORGE W. KEETON

AND

GEORG SCHWARZENBERGER

Managing Editor:

C. G. BURNHAM

THE YEAR BOOK

OF

WORLD AFFAIRS
1983

Published under the auspices of
THE LONDON INSTITUTE OF WORLD AFFAIRS

WESTVIEW PRESS

Boulder, Colorado

All editorial communications should be addressed to the
Managing Editor, 9 Boswell Drive, Ickleford,
Hitchin, Hertfordshire, SG5 3YB, England

Published in Great Britain in 1983 by
Stevens & Sons Limited of
11 New Fetter Lane, London
Computerset by
Promenade Graphics Ltd., Cheltenham
Printed in Great Britain by
Page Bros. (Norwich) Ltd.

Published in the United States of America in 1983 by
Westview Press, Inc.
5500 Central Avenue
Boulder, Colorado 80301
Frederick A. Praeger, President and Publisher

Library of Congress Catalog Card Number 47–29156

ISBN 0 86531–519–1

CONTENTS

v

TRENDS AND EVENTS

THIS annual survey is intended to serve three purposes:

(1) With every additional volume of the *Year Book*, it becomes increasingly difficult for new readers to derive the fullest benefit from the material available in earlier volumes. This survey brings together references to themes examined in the past which have particular current relevance.

(2) The specific object of an annual publication is to make possible analyses in a wider perspective and on the basis of more mature reflection than may be possible in a quarterly or monthly journal. Thus, it is not the object of this *Year Book* to provide instant information on current issues of world affairs. Yet, international affairs have a stereotyped and, largely, repetitive character, so that, frequently a "new" happening, or "modern" development has been anticipated in one or more of the earlier volumes of the *Year Book. Trends and Events* provides evidence of some such continuity as may be traced over a span of years. An illustration is provided by J. Daniel's paper, *Conflict of Sovereignties in the Antarctic* (3 Y.B.W.A. 1949).

(3) References to earlier contributions also offer readers an opportunity to judge for themselves the adequacy of the conceptual and systematic frameworks chosen or taken for granted in the papers selected:

(A) ARMS CONTROL AND DISARMAMENT

Boyle, Sir Dermott: *Thoughts on the Nuclear Deterrent* (16 Y.B.W.A. 1962)

Bull, H.: *Two Kinds of Arms Control* (17 *ibid*. 1963)

Coffey, J.I.: *The Limitation of Strategic Armaments* (26 *ibid*. 1972)

Curle, A.: *Peace Studies* (30 *ibid*. 1976)

Dinstein, Y.: *Another Step in Codifying the Laws of War* (28 *ibid*. 1974)

Garnett, J.C.: *The Concept of War* (30 *ibid*. 1976)

James, A.: *Recent Developments in United Nations Peace-Keeping* (31 *ibid*. 1977)

Keohane, D.: *Hegemony and Nuclear Non-proliferation* (35 *ibid*. 1981)

Lee, R.: *Safeguards Against Nuclear Proliferation* (23 *ibid*. 1969)

Mitchell, C.R.: *Peace-Keeping: The Police Function* (30 *ibid*. 1976)

1

Ranger, R.: *Arms Control in Theory and in Practic* (31 *ibid.* 1977)
Schwarzenberger, G.: *The Law of Armed Conflict: A Civilised Interlude?* (28 *ibid.* 1974)
Young, W. and Elizabeth: *Disarmament Now: Catching Up with Crucé* (36 *ibid.* 1982)

(B) Crises and Survival

Bell, C.: *Crises and Survival* (36 Y.B.W.A. 1982)
Burnham, C.G.: *Czechoslovakia: Thirty Years After Munich* (23 *ibid.* 1969)
Joynt, C.B.: *The Anatomy of Crises* (28 *ibid.* 1974)
Nicholson, M.: *Catastrophe Theory and International Relations* (35 *ibid.* 1981)
Strange, S.: *Cuba and After* (17 *ibid.* 1963)
——: *Suez and After* (11 *ibid.* 1957)

(C) The World Environment

Auburn, F.M.: *The Antarctic Environment* (35 Y.B.W.A. 1981)
Brown, E.D.: *Deep-Sea Mining: The Legal Régime of Inner Space* (22 *ibid.* 1968)
Cheng, B.: *The 1968 Astronauts' Agreement* (23 *ibid.* 1969)
Dickstein, H.L.: *International Law and the Environment: Evolving Concepts* (26 *ibid.* 1972)
Dimbleby, G.W.: *Restoring the Ecological Balance* (23 *ibid.* 1969)
Falk, R.A.: *The Logic of State Sovereignty Versus the Requirements of World Order* (27 *ibid.* 1973)
Gorinsky, C.: *Cultures in Conflict: Amerindians in New Societies* (24 *ibid.* 1970)
Grebinik, E.: *Population Problems of Underdeveloped Countries* (12 *ibid.* 1958)
Hambro, E.: *The Human Environment: Stockholm and After* (28 *ibid.* 1974)
Heskie, F.: *Forestry as an International Problem* (4 *ibid.* 1950)
Johnson, D.H.N.: *The Geneva Conference on the Law of the Sea* (13 *ibid.* 1959)
Kalmus, H.: *Living Together Without Man* (25 *ibid.* 1971)
Penman, H.L.: *The International Hydrological Decade* (26 *ibid.* 1972)
Schwarzenberger, G.: *Trends in the Law of the Sea* (33 *ibid.* 1979)
Shaw, C.A.: *Dilemmas of Super-Growth* (30 *ibid.* 1976)
Zemaneck, K.: *The United Nations and the Law of Outer Space* (20 *ibid.* 1965)
Zuckerman, Lord: *The Risks of a No-Risk Society* (34 *ibid.* 1980)

(D) THE ENERGY EQUATION

Beenstock, M.: *OPEC and the World Economy* (36 Y.B.W.A. 1982)

Brown, E.D.: *Deep-Sea Mining: The Legal Régime of "Inner Space"* (22 ibid. 1968)

——: *The Anglo-French Continental Shelf Case* (33 ibid. 1979)

Frankel, J.: *The Anglo-Iranian Dispute* (6 ibid. 1952)

Nieburg, H.L.: *The International Atomic Energy Agency: A Critical Approach* (19 ibid. 1965)

Odell, P.R.: *The International Oil Companies in the New World Oil Market* (32 ibid. 1978)

Penrose, E.: *Monopoly and Competition in the International Petroleum Industry* (19 ibid. 1964)

Shaw, C.A.: *Energy and a New World Economic Order* (36 ibid. 1982)

(E) EUROPEAN SECURITY

1. East European Security

Bettany, A.G.: *Czechoslovakia Between East and West* (1 Y.B.W.A. 1947)

Burnham, C.G.: *Czechoslovakia: Thirty Years After Munich* (23 ibid. 1969)

Ginsburgs, G.: *Socialist Internationalism and State Sovereignty* (25 ibid. 1971)

——: *The Constitutional Foundations of the "Socialist Commonwealth"* (27 ibid. 1973)

Remington, R.A.: *The Warsaw Pact* (27 ibid. 1973)

Seton-Watson, H.: *Eastern Europe* (3 ibid. 1973)

——: *Eastern Europe Since Stalin* (11 ibid. 1957)

2. West European Security

Richardson, J.L.: *Two Theories of Western European Defence* (11 Y.B.W.A. 1957)

Schmidt, H.: *New Tasks for the Atlantic Alliance* (29 ibid. 1975)

Strange, Susan: *Strains on NATO* (10 ibid. 1956)

Williams, G.: *European Defence in the 1970s* (27 ibid. 1973)

3. German Security

Bonn, M.J.: *The Demise of the Adenauer Era* (18 Y.B.W.A. 1964)

Burmeister, W.: *The Struggle for Germany* (7 ibid. 1953)

——: *Brandt's Eastern Policy* (27 ibid. 1973)

Joetze, G.: *The Legal Nature of the Trade Agreements between West and East Germany* (16 ibid. 1962)

Morgan, R.P.: *The Scope of German Foreign Policy* (20 ibid. 1966)

(F) LATIN AMERICA IN FERMENT

Ball, M.M.: *Recent Developments in Inter-American Relations* (3 Y.B.W.A. 1949)

Berner, M.F.C.: *The Panama Canal and Future United Stated Hemisphere Policy* (34 *ibid*. 1980)

Blakemore, H.: *Chile: Continuity and Change* (27 *ibid*. 1973)

Carnegie, A.R.: *The Law of Commonwealth Caribbean Regionalism: Legal Aspects* (33 *ibid*. 1979)

Crossley, J.C.: *Agrarian Reform in Latin America* (17 *ibid*. 1963)

Ferns, H.S.: *Argentina in Travail* (29 *ibid*. 1975)

Gorinsky, C.: *Cultures in Conflict: Amerindians in New Societies* (24 *ibid*. 1970)

Graber, D.A.: *United States Intervention in Latin America* (16 *ibid*. 1962)

Hilton, R.: *Castrophobia in the United States* (18 *ibid*. 1964)

Hutchinson, G.W.: *The Coup in Chile* (29 *ibid*. 1975)

Milensky, E.S.: *The Cartagena Agreement: In Transition* (33 *ibid*. 1979)

Nelson, L.D.M.: *The Andean Common Market* (29 *ibid*. 1975)

O'Shaughnessy, H.: *Christian Democratic Upsurge in Latin America* (21 *ibid*. 1967)

Parkinson, F.: *The Alliance for Progress* (18 *ibid*. 1964)

——: *Santo Domingo and After* (20 *ibid*. 1966)

——: *International Economic Integration in Latin America and the Caribbean* (31 *ibid*. 1977)

Rubin, A.P.: *The Panama Canal Treaties: Locks on the Barn Door* (35 *ibid*. 1981)

Salera, V.: *Economic Relations between the United States and Latin America* (14 *ibid*. 1960)

Strange, S.: *Cuba and After* (17 *ibid*. 1956)

Tannenbaum, F.: *The Continuing Ferment in Latin America* (10 *ibid*. 1956)

Whitaker, A.P.: *The Organisation of American States* (13 *ibid*. 1959)

Wood, B.: *The Organisation of American States* (33 *ibid*. 1979)

(G) INTERNATIONAL LAW

1. Armed Conflict

Dinstein, Y.: *Another Step in Codifying the Laws of War* (28 Y.B.W.A. 1974)

——: *The New Geneva Protocols* (33 *ibid*. 1979)

Radojkovic, M.: *Les Armes Nucléaires et Le Droit International* (16 *ibid*. 1962)

Schwarzenberger, G.: *Present-Day Relevance of the Hague Peace System 1899–1979* (34 *ibid.* 1980)
——: *The Law of Armed Conflict: A Civilised Interlude?* (28 *ibid.* 1974)

2. *Comparative Aspects and Jurisprudence*
Bredima, Anna: *Comparative Law in the Court of Justice of the European Communities* (32 *ibid.* 1978)
Butler, W.E.: *Eastern European Approaches to International Law* (26 *ibid.* 1972)
——: *Methodological Innovation in Soviet International Legal Doctrine* (32 *ibid.* 1978)
Connelly, A.M.: *The History of International Law in a Comparative Approach* (32 *ibid.* 1978)
Lapenna, I.: *International Law Viewed through Soviet Eyes* (15 *ibid.* 1971)
——: *The Soviet Concept of Socialist International Law* (29 *ibid.* 1975)
Schapiro, L.B.: *The Soviet Concept of International Law* (2 *ibid.* 1948)
Schwarzenberger, G.: *Equity in International Law* (26 *ibid.* 1972)
Watson, J.S.: *A Realistic Jurisprudence of International Law* (34 *ibid.* 1980)

3. *Economic Aspects*
Joetze, G.: *The Legal Nature of the Trade Agreements between East and West Germany* (16 *ibid.* 1962)
Kojanec, G.: *Recent Developments in the Law of State Contracts* (24 *ibid.* 1974)
O'Keefe, P.J.: *The International Centre for the Settlement of Investment Disputes* (34 *ibid.* 1980)
Seidl-Hohenveldern, I.: *Multinational Enterprises and the International Law of the Future* (29 *ibid.* 1975)
——: *The Impact of State Trading on Classical International Law* (16 *ibid.* 1962)

4. *Equality and Discrimination in International Economic Law*
Goldsmith, P. and Sonderekötter, F.: *The European Communities* (28 *ibid.* 1974)
——: *The European Communities and the Wider World* (29 *ibid.* 1975)
Kaplan, G.G.: *The UNCTAD Scheme for Generalised Preferences* (26 *ibid.* 1972)

Ramcharan, B.G.: *Development and International Economic Co-operation* (35 *ibid.* 1981)
——: *The Commonwealth Preferential System* (26 *ibid.* 1972)
——: *The Council for Mutual Economic Assistance* (34 *ibid.* 1980)
——: *The UN Regional Economic Commissions* (32 *ibid.* 1978)
Schwarzenberger, G.: *Equality and Discrimination in International Economic Law: Introduction to the Series* (25 *ibid.* 1971)
Stoiber, C.: *The Multinational Enterprise* (31 *ibid.* 1977)
Sutton, A.: *Trends in Regulation of International Trade in Textiles* (31 *ibid.* 1977)

5. Inner and Outer Space
Brown, E.D.: *Deep-Sea Mining: The Legal Régime of "Inner Space"* (22 *ibid.* 1968)
——: *The Anglo-French Continental Shelf Case* (33 *ibid.* 1979)
Dickstein, H.L.: *International Law and the Environment* (26 *ibid.* 1972)
Johnson, D.H.N.: *The Geneva Conference on the Law of the Sea* (13 *ibid.* 1959)
Schwarzenberger, G.: *Trends in the Law of the Sea* (33 *ibid.* 1979)
Zemanek, K.: *The United Nations and the Law of Outer Space* (19 *ibid.* 1965)

6. Institutional Aspects
Cheng, B.: *The First Twenty Years of the International Court of Justice* (20 *ibid.* 1966)
Engel, S.: *The Changing Charter of the United Nations* (7 *ibid.* 1953)
Hambro, E.: *The International Court of Justice* (3 *ibid.* 1949)
Johnson, D.H.N.: *International Arbitration Back in Favour?* (34 *ibid.* 1980)
Prott, L.V.: *The Future of the International Court of Justice* (33 *ibid.* 1979)
Ramcharan, B.G.: *The International Law Commission* (29 *ibid.* 1975)
Rosenne, S.: *Relations Between Governments and the International Las Commission* (19 *ibid.* 1965)
Schwarzenberger, G.: *The Judicial Corps of the International Court of Justice* (36 *ibid.* 1982)
——: *The Problem of Functional Incompatibilities before the International Courts* (27 *ibid.* 1973)
Yturriaga, J.A. de: *Non-Self Governing Territories: The Law and Practice of the United Nations* (18 *ibid.* 1964)

7. Inter-Disciplinary Aspects
Corbett, P.E.: *Law and Society in the Relations of States* (4 *ibid.* 1950)
Kimminich, O.: *International Relations and International Law* (27 *ibid.* 1973)
Schwarzenberger, G.: *Civitas Maxima?* (29 *ibid.* 1975)
——: *Détente and International Law* (35 *ibid.* 1981)
——: *International Law and Society* (1 *ibid.* 1947)
——: *Neo-Barbarism and International Law* (22 *ibid.* 1968)
——: *The Frontiers of International Law* (6 *ibid.* 1952)
Vallat, Sir Francis: *International Law—A Forward Look* (18 *ibid.* 1964)
Yuen-Li Liang: *Methods for the Encouragement of Progressive Development of International Law and its Codification* (18 *ibid.* 1948)

(H) INTERNATIONAL ORDER

Aaronson, M.: *Political Aspects of International Drug Control* (9 Y.B.W.A. 1955)
Beloff, M.: *Problems of International Government* (8 *ibid.* 1954)
Falk, R.A.: *The Decline of International Order: Normative Regression and Geographical Maelstrom* (36 *ibid.* 1982)
——: *The Logic of State Sovereignty Versus the Requirements of World Order* (27 *ibid.* 1965)
Rostow, E.V.: *The Politics of Force: Analysis and Prognosis* (36 *ibid.* 1982)
Vincent, R.J.: *The Factor of Culture in the Global International Order* (34 *ibid.* 1980)
——: *The Idea of Concert and International Order* (29 *ibid.* 1975)
Yalem, R.J.: *The Concept of World Order* (29 *ibid.* 1975)

(I) AUTHORITY AND DISSENT

1. Dissent
Glazov, Y.: *Dissent in Post-Stalinist Russia* (35 Y.B.W.A. 1981)
Roberts, A.: *Civil Resistance as a Technique in International Relations* (24 *ibid.* 1970)
Szamuely, T.: *Student Revolt in East West* (24 *ibid.* 1970)

2. Human Rights
Franck, T.: *"Congressional Imperialism" and Human-Rights Policy* (35 *ibid.* 1981)
Hermens, F.A.: *Return to Democratic Government* (32 *ibid.* 1978)
Honig, F.: *Criminal Justice in Germany Today* (5 *ibid.* 1951)

Loescher, G.D.: *Human Rights and the Helsinki-Belgrade Process* (35 *ibid.* 1981)
Martin, A.: *Human Rights and World Politics* (5 *ibid.* 1951)
Reoch, R.: *"Disappearances" and the International Protection of Human Rights* (36 *ibid.* 1982)
Rubin, A.P.: *The Hostages Incident: The United States and Iran* (36 *ibid.* 1982)
Vickers, Dame Joan: *Missing Persons* (28 *ibid.* 1974)

3. Civil Strife
Duncanson, D.: *Dilemmas of Defence Against National Liberation* (34 *ibid.* 1980)
Foot, M.R.D.: *Resistance, War and Revolution* (31 *ibid.* 1977)
Mitchell, C.R.: *External Involvement in Civil Strife: The Case of Chad* (26 *ibid.* 1972)
Roberts, A.: *Civil Resistance as a Technique in International Relations* (23 *ibid.* 1970)
Shearman, H.: *Conflict in Northern Ireland* (24 *ibid.* 1970)
——: *Conflict in Northern Ireland* (36 *ibid.* 1982)

4. Terrorism
Duncanson, D.: *Dilemmas of Defence Against National Liberation* (34 *ibid.* 1980)
Kittrie, N.N.: *Reconciling the Irreconcilable: The Quest for International Agreement over Political Crime and Terrorism* (32 *ibid.* 1978)
Smith, W.H.: *International Terrorism: A Political Analysis* (31 *ibid.* 1977)

(J) World Portraits

Bonn, M.J.: *American Statesmen* (5 Y.B.W.A. 1951)
——: *The Demise of the Adenauer Era* (18 *ibid.* 1973)
Burmeister, W.: *Brandt's Opening to the East* (27 *ibid.* 1973)
Criddle, B.J.: *Valéry Giscard d'Estaing* (34 *ibid.* 1980)
Hilton, R.: *Castrophobia in the United States* (18 *ibid.* 1964)
James, A.: *U Thant and His Critics* (26 *ibid.* 1964)
Nicholas, H.G.: *The Nixon Line* (25 *ibid.* 1971)
Pickles, D.: *France Under General de Gaulle* (16 *ibid.* 1962)
Sceats, R.: *The Continuity of French Policy* (26 *ibid.* 1972)
Tinker, H.: *Indira Gandhi: Autocratic Democrat* (33 *ibid.* 1979)
Vincent, R.J.: *Kissinger's System of Foreign Policy* (31 *ibid.* 1977)

It may also be helpful to remind readers of the Cumulative Index to Volumes 1 to 25 in the 1971 Volume of the *Year Book of World Affairs—Managing Ed.*, Y.B.W.A.

THE AGEING OF DETERRENCE

By

JOHN DOWNEY

OVER the past two or three years there has been a marked revival of the public debate about defence and a resurgence of anti-nuclear protest throughout the West. The idea of military deterrence as the best or only way to keep the peace of the world has never been short of critics, but it now seems to be suffering its greatest crisis of confidence since the early 1950s.

This is a very divisive conflict of opinion since it forces what appears to be a choice between moral values and national loyalties. In Great Britain and West Germany, and long since in the smaller NATO nations, it has reached the level of party political decision, threatening the whole Western defensive position. This is partly because, as in all public debates, there is much confusion between ends and means, in this case between defence in principle and the possession of nuclear weapons as one of its mainstays. Consequently many people among the great majority who still believe in defence, but who are justly alarmed by nuclear weapons, may lend their support unwittingly to those who do not believe in any defence at all or who do not want the West to defend itself against the East.

In such an emotional and politicised debate there is inevitably much emphasis on whether present defence policies *should* be maintained, to the neglect of whether they *can* be. The second question depends fairly heavily on economic trends which have received all too little attention even from experts. This paper attempts to summarise the economic position as concisely as possible and relate it to the other strains within the Western Alliance.

The picture which emerges strengthens the instinctive view now taken by a large majority that, although the military confrontation is unavoidable and must be supported, it cannot remain stable indefinitely and therefore major initiatives are needed to reduce its tempo and its dangers. It is shown that this groundswell of opinion coincides with an acceleration in the rising cost of defence, leaving governments with lessening time for manoeuvre. It is argued that our failure to react sooner to this convergence is due to narrow defence thinking at national level and a declining sense of direction in wider, Western councils. New standards of Allied strategic management are needed to face the long expected period of maximum danger which the confrontation is now entering.

I—ENDS AND MEANS

In most respects the role of armed force in international affairs in the nuclear age obeys the same logic as in earlier days. Most nations profess that their sole reason for arming is to exercise the ancient right of sovereign States to protect their political and territorial independence. Real intentions may come under suspicion by virtue of the matrix of buffer zones and alliances which have been created, but these things are not new in principle. Nor does the current emphasis on deterrence make it a new strategy: "force in being" as it used to be called has many precedents. Even today's weapon systems and concepts of operation owe their development to long-established trends. Military technology has always sought to find more decisive and cheaper ways of waging war, as for example in trying out naval blockade and air bombing in the two World Wars as alternatives to lengthy and costly land campaigns. Nuclear weapons were developed initially for similar reasons and were used against Japan for precisely those ends.

But what is new is that nuclear weapons have now become so abundant that their actual use would almost certainly nullify the whole purpose of defence by causing huge and widespread destruction. Consequently, wherever the major nuclear Powers face each other directly the concept of using military force to *prevent* war has been promoted to a position of supreme importance. Armed forces exist and are developed as if they were still usable, but in fact their primary external role has become static; they have come to be seen as "forces in being" to an extent never previously envisaged. Moreover, as will be argued in Section II, this has resulted in a further profound change, a revolution in the economics of defence. On close inspection, therefore, defence in the nuclear age is on very different terms indeed from those of any earlier period.

An accidental or even a deliberate outbreak of hostilities can, of course, never be discounted. Therefore the central operational problem for strategists and armed forces in the East-West confrontation is to know what level of resistance can be offered without pushing the enemy, or being pushed by him, across the nuclear threshold. An even more difficult question is whether this is a Rubicon which, once crossed, can ever be re-crossed. The extreme uncertainty surrounding these judgments has led to a doctrine usually referred to as *flexible response*. The basis of this is that an attack should be met initially at its own level, the scale of conflict being raised as slowly as possible so that the attacker may be made to see reason and desist. The doctrine thereby provides a framework within which separate but co-ordinated roles may be assigned first to conventional forces, then to theatre nuclear weapons, and finally to systems for strategic nuclear bombardment.

Flexible response demands reasonable balances between and within the two sides in both nuclear and conventional forces. The nuclear arsenals on both sides are now so massive that it is widely accepted that exact parity is not essential. According to the International Institute for Strategic Studies, the United States has some 9,000 deliverable warheads in the strategic category and the Soviet Union over 7,000.[1] In the shorter range categories the proportions are reversed in favour of the Soviet Union, the total being more than 50,000,[2] making the grand total about 66,000. However, it is important to our later discussion to note that reaching these huge totals has not brought development or manufacture to an end, mainly because both sides fear that countermeasures may endanger the survival of the delivery systems or the warheads themselves.

In the conventional sector there is a serious imbalance between East and West as a result of a long decline in Western numbers. Moreover, in the opinion of the International Institute for Strategic Studies, the West has also "largely lost the technical edge which allowed NATO to believe that quality could substitute for numbers."[3] In the event of war this particular form of imbalance would lower the nuclear threshold since the West would be unable to resist a Soviet advance without early resort to theatre nuclear weapons. This is unsatisfactory both politically and militarily since it puts the West in a position from whence it is known in advance that it would probably be the side to initiate nuclear war. Any delay in making the awesome political decisions required could open the way to a rapid Soviet conquest of all or part of Western Europe.

There are also less obvious consequences of imbalance. Any tendency for nuclear arsenals on both sides to grow at the expense of conventional forces would lower the nuclear threshold generally since it would be more difficult to contain even accidental incidents, especially if they occurred, as is likely, as the result of a tense political situation. Moreover, since effort must still be devoted to nuclear development, the larger the nuclear sector the more its cost in maintenance and development is likely to deny spending on conventional forces.

---

[1] *The Military Balance 1981–1982*: IISS, London.
[2] F. Barnaby, "The Strategic Balance," in this *Year Book*, Vol. 34 (1980), pp. 41–59.
[3] *The Military Balance 1981–1982*: IISS, London.

It is therefore all important to any judgment of the long term stability of deterrence strategy to know whether the imbalances which already exist are the result of trends which may continue. This is what we shall now examine.

II—The New Economics of Defence

From the earliest times until the present nuclear era the rhythm of defence preparation has been cyclic; in quiet times nations have always dropped their guard in the knowledge that, if war threatened, effort could be quickly mobilised. This principle was essential to pre-industrial society in which manpower had to be used to the full on the land. But even the two World Wars of the twentieth century were prepared for and conducted on the same lines; indeed it is imbedded in the consciousness of Britons and Frenchmen, and no doubt in Russian minds also, that they allowed their military preparedness to become too low before 1914 and before 1939. All the same, although Russia fell in 1917 and France in 1940, the less well prepared but fundamentally stronger side was able to win both wars eventually because the speed of events allowed it time to muster its strength.

The circumstances of defence today are entirely different. A new major war in the industrial world would consume existing military resources very quickly and, if nuclear weapons were used, all forces and all their sources of re-equipment might be destroyed in a matter of weeks or less. Even if for one reason or another the tempo was restrained, the complexity of modern weapons systems is such that replacements, let alone new developments, could not be produced on any scale of numbers approaching that of the past. This has profound consequences economically since it means that the distinction between war and peace is much less sharp than hitherto. Defence can no longer be funded at low peacetime levels with a view to huge expansion in war: the funding required at all times is now approaching levels previously attained only in war.

This change has to be seen in the context of the changed role for armed forces, that of preventing rather than fighting nuclear war. Forces which exist mainly to prevent war must be constantly available at high states of readiness. The nuclear forces have to be at immediate readiness. Thus much else is changed. More or less the complete order of battle must always be in the shop window, so to speak. Nations still count on some trained reserves, but raising and equipping great citizen armies, as in 1914 to 1916 and 1939 to 1941, is now out of the question. Nor is it any longer possible to rely on mobilising scientific backing only when war threatens; large scale government research and development (R and D) is needed in peace in order to sustain the constant competitive development of weapons and tactics. Perhaps most important of all, the cost of defence can no longer be minimised when it is unpopular, leaving the greatest burden to be imposed only during the fervour of war: the public must now be ready to pay a high premium at all times as an insurance against war itself.

It has become increasingly clear over the past 30 years that this insurance premium rises at a rate higher than ordinary prices; there is, in other words, a form of special defence inflation. The reason for this lies in the fact that although a long military confrontation is not a new phenomenon, it now takes place in a climate of high technology which *is* historically new and is uniquely fertile and self propagating. Every military development quickly leads to ideas for a successor or a counter measure and neither side can afford to forgo these further steps for too long for fear of imbalance. As the confrontation becomes more sophisticated militarily, the greater the dangers of being outflanked technologically.

Each side therefore compares its armaments with those of its potential enemy in terms of both quantity and quality. Quantitative imbalance will certainly be a spur to renewed effort, especially for reasons of political prestige or national or allied confidence. However, an even greater incentive is any disparity in quality because that might destroy the whole quantitative balance at a stroke. The most striking example is in the nuclear sector where, as we have seen, the two super-Powers alone already possess something like sixty or seventy thousand warheads, the equivalent or about one million Hiroshima bombs or over three tons of TNT for every man, woman and child on earth. And yet nuclear research and development continues at full stretch on both sides in order to prevent one side reaching a position where, mainly by superior penetration and evasion, it could annihilate its opponent before he could reply.

Each new generation of weapons is usually more complicated than its predecessor and therefore more costly and takes longer to design, develop and produce despite the speed at which new ideas are spawned. This has always been the trend, but the intensity of the military confrontation today means that defence (including much space exploration) has become the main sponsor of new technology, forcing its pace. This is the main reason why military cost inflation exceeds ordinary inflation. Whereas in the civil sphere new technologies often cheapen products by raising productivity, this is rarely so in military products where the prime aim is nearly always to increase effectiveness.

The results of all this can be illustrated by the rising cost of the main classes of weapon systems since the 1960s, *i.e.* in the course of introducing one or two generations. In real terms, tank prices have roughly doubled, naval vessel prices have risen three times, tactical aircraft four times and anti-aircraft weapons about eight times. These increases reflect, in the main, the huge cost of research and development. The SIPRI *Yearbook* for 1981 quotes as an example that in 1975, in the United States, R and D averaged 43 per cent. of the output value of military products compared with an average of 2.3 per cent. for civil products.[4]

It is difficult to see the situation just outlined as less than a revolution in defence economy, almost comparable in significance to the nuclear revolution from which it mainly stems. If defence preparation can no longer be cycled according to the likelihood of war, and if technology continues to proliferate, it seems that the cost of defence must accelerate throughout the forseeable future. This will have profound military and political consequences.

III—THE MILITARY CONSEQUENCES

The Strategic Survey 1980–1981[5] contained the following remark: " . . . the spiralling cost of modern weapons will soon exceed the funds available. . . . It will not be easy to maintain affordable and yet credible conventional forces in the 1980s." The Institute goes on to observe that the problem will be intensified if the West Europeans should wish to help the United States with her projected direct military involvement in the Middle East.

In fact the trend referred to has been evident for some years and has been illustrated nowhere better than in the British experience. The table (over) compares our defence expenditure over the 20 years since 1960 with force strengths (expenditure is shown at constant price indices, 1970 = 100).

In other words, whilst real defence expenditure rose by over a fifth, manpower fell by well over a third and combat units by nearly a third. This was despite heavy pruning of the "tail" which took place throughout the period, and its increasing civilianisation. Moreover, in that same period the United Kingdom withdrew from nearly all her extra-European military commitments where the cost of maintaining forces was, of course, higher than at home or on the Continent. Although the smaller forces of 1980 were much better armed than the larger forces of the earlier years, so also were the

---

[4] F. Barnaby (ed.), *World Armaments & Disarmament: SIPRI Yearbook 1981* Stockholm International Peace Research Institute.

[5] International Institute for Strategic Studies, London.

	1960	1966	1970	1975/6	1980
Expenditure	100.6		100	114.6	122
Manpower[1]	525.6	418.4	373	345	329.2
RN Ships[2]		198		149	130
Army Regts.[3]		132		114	109
RAF Sqns.[4]		98		65	62

Notes:
[1] Uniformed men and women; thousands.
[2] Down to and including minesweepers.
[3] Excluding Army Aviation.
[4] Including helicopter sqns, but not OCUs.
(Note also that National Service ended in 1958.)

Sources:
Statement on the Defence Estimates (Annual) HMSO
The Military Balance (Annual) International Institute for Strategic Studies

potential enemy's: therefore the general trend can only be seen as a fall in strength against a rise in cost.

Looking to the future it should be noted that in the 1981 Defence Debate in Parliament the present Government announced its intention of sharply increasing defence expenditure over the next few years in line with the 1979 NATO decision that all of its member nations would strive for a 3 per cent. per annum increase. However, this announcement was accompanied by plans for further force reductions, particularly in the Royal Navy whose role in the Eastlant Area will be curtailed as a result. This means that despite all the economies mentioned above and despite a steeper trend in spending, it will still be necessary to abandon our tradition of balanced land, sea and air strategies. This was partly as a result of the decision to modernise the British nuclear deterrent force. Therefore, all in all, the British experience underlines two of the dangerous tendencies identified earlier in this article, namely dwindling conventional forces and growing nuclear/conventional imbalance.

The record of other NATO forces over the same period shows similar trends. In the following table the *ratios* of manpower to spending for each quoted year have been reduced to common constant price indices and averaged. As will be seen the result is again a drop of roughly a third.

	1961	1967	1970	1973	1976	1979
US, UK, FGR and France	121	101	100	88	83.5	80
UK, FGR and France only	125	102.3	100	89.3	83.3	79.3

Figures for the Soviet bloc published in the West are only estimates and vary rather widely. However, they show clearly enough the same divergence between strength and spending. For example, in the Soviet Union itself military manpower has remained high, falling only a tenth or less over the past 20 years whilst spending has risen at an increasing rate (*e.g.* at about 1.5 per cent. compound since 1970). This has raised the proportion of GDP spent on defence to somewhere between 12 and 14 per cent. *i.e.* roughly twice the proportion for the United States or the United Kingdom and three to four times the average for most of NATO or, for that matter, the other Warsaw Pact Powers.[6]

These trends can only be seen as a process of diminishing returns for defence spending. Any nation which cannot accept rising (and probably, in the future, accelerating) defence budgets, must choose between dwindling numbers or growing obsolescence in her military equipment. For the reasons given earlier, the two super-Powers will be driven by their rivalry to reject both these options and accept rising cost. Moreover their striving for modernity is likely to give priority to the nuclear sector, so accentuating the tendency for imbalance with the conventional sector. A striking example occurred in the single year 1980–81 when the Soviet Union increased her number of strategic nuclear warheads from 6,000 to 7,000 by introducing multiple heads to existing delivery systems.[7] The cost of this must have been prodigious.

The effect on the lesser Powers will be to leave them further and further behind in modernity, particularly the West Europeans who do not have standardised equipment developed largely by their major partner, as does the Warsaw Pact. NATO is already markedly inferior to the Warsaw Pact in the numbers of certain crucial conventional weapons such as tanks and tactical aircraft. But

---

[6] *Military Balance 1981–1982*, International Institute of Strategic Studies, London.
[7] *The Military Balance 1981–1982*, International Institute of Strategic Studies, London.

quite apart from this there are growing gaps in both quantity and quality between the West Europeans and the United States. Whereas the latter is a first class military Power deploying all categories of major weapons systems on land, sea, in the air and in space, West European forces are confined mainly to land/air roles on the European Continent; and even there they lack many of the more advanced capabilities now needed. Although the United Kingdom and France still possess significant maritime and nuclear forces, both are finding these increasingly difficult to reconcile with adequate conventional strength in the land/air roles. These growing differences obviously strain an Alliance based on the complete political independence and nominal equality of its members.

In summary, after 30 years' experience of nuclear deterrence it is to be seen as a policy which still works but which, if it is to continue to do so, must become a commitment to ever rising cost. For some years past the Soviet Union has accepted the inroads thus made into other national needs and the United States has recently announced increases which will at least maintain the proportion of resources devoted to defence and may deny increases in other sectors. By contrast most European NATO nations have allowed the defence commitment to fall in relation to other spending: in other words they have tended to revert to pre-nuclear, cyclic defence funding, with the result that their force levels and military capabilities have declined sharply in relation to the super-Powers. They have also declined in relation to the Warsaw-Pact East Europeans who, although they have not in general spent more heavily, enjoy the military advantages of a more monolithic alliance.

For most of the past 30 years these incongruities have been masked by several factors—by the great economic and military power of the American partner, by the initial lead held by the Americans over the Soviets in nuclear and other technologies, and even when this was largely lost, by the inherent ability of nuclear deterrence to absorb a great deal of imbalance. Nevertheless the cracks are now beginning to show, first in the weakness of NATO's conventional forces compared with those in the East, secondly in the imbalance between Western conventional and nuclear power, and thirdly in the strains which these deficiencies and the need to rectify them impose on the Alliance.

IV—THE CONVERGENCE OF CIRCUMSTANCES

As mentioned earlier, there are already plans, agreed in 1979, to increase Western defence spending. However, these increases are unlikely to do more than slow down the long decline in conventional forces or, at best, arrest it. Moreover they coincide with a decline in world trade and in Western economic growth so that they are unlikely to be paid for without increasing the share of national incomes devoted to defence. The tensions which this will cause within the Western Alliance will be exacerbated by the fact that American re-armament will introduce yet more sophisticated systems which will leave the European partners further behind militarily and technologically, reducing their influence on the East-West dialogue. Already there is much dissent in Western Europe against the introduction of such items as the Cruise Missiles, Pershing II and the so-called Neutron Bomb, even although these items are developed and paid for by the Americans. As the military confrontation between the super-Powers moves into space, as it is now beginning to do, the Europeans will be further outclassed and their influence and pride further injured.

In retrospect it can be seen that the North Atlantic Treaty could never have developed into an alliance of equals without the West European unity originally foreseen in the Treaty of Rome. Although the combined wealth and resources of Western Europe are comparable with those of the United States, by remaining sovereign States, each with its own independent R and D and its own defence industry, and all competing for arms sales, the Europeans have remained second class military Powers. As a result NATO wastes at least a third and possibly nearly a half of its military potential compared with the more centralised and militarily standardised Warsaw Pact. But enthusiasm for West European unity seems past its peak on any grounds, least of all as a means of consolidating defence strategies which are becoming sources of public alarm and protest.

It is this rift in the Alliance as much as the growth of the nuclear arsenals which makes the anti-nuclear protest movement more deep seated and formidable than during its earlier manifestation in the 1950s. It now contains strong elements of anti-Americanism and anti-NATO sentiment and, most important of all, it is beginning to capture party political platforms in Western Europe, signalling the end of the consensus on defence policy hitherto existing between West European centre parties. The break up of the Alliance would leave Western Europe wide open to the East and to Soviet domination, possibly even to occupation. This would not preclude a continuing confrontation between the United States and the Soviet Union, indeed it might make it more bitter. Nor would nuclear proliferation necessarily come to an end: the two super-Powers could be tempted to further it in their competition for new allies to the South. The "red-is-better-than-dead" option is therefore by no

means a clear alternative to defence, as is so often suggested by the
unilateral disarmament movement.

The unilateral movement at its best (*i.e.* discounting the ulterior
political motives which it clearly includes) presents what is
essentially a moral argument demanding moral leadership within
the community of nations. But the sacrifices which the nations
taking this lead would be required to make would not be merely
unselfish as, for example, in putting down the old slave trade, or as
would be required if a nation withdrew from the modern arms trade.
The trend setters in this case would have to sacrifice the classic aims
of defence, not only exposing their people to the risk of physical
attack, but also offering up the hard won Western political heritage
as a whole. In exchange, as we have seen, there would be no certain
peace or protection from universal nuclear catastrophe.

Given a clear distinction of aims, public common sense could be
counted on to reject this lack of realism. But public protest
movements do not always define their aims clearly and sometimes
neglect to do so deliberately. The *multilateralist* movement certainly
commits this sin of omission and is the more formidable as a result.
It has become a broad church able to embrace a wide spectrum of
attitudes ranging from the political views of the centre-left to an
alliance of religious denominations. A groundswell of these proportions may become a force which cannot be ignored. An article in
October 1981 by *The Times* Religious Affairs Correspondent
comments specifically on the deliberate intention of one religious
group to blur the distinctions between unilateralism and multi-
lateralism, adding; "What matters, in (their) view, is to create such
a degree of public bother that the non-disarmament option becomes
closed, and the problem for governments is then how to make the
best of the remaining possibilities."[8]

The obvious danger in all this, however well intentioned, is that it
pressurises the West much more than the East. Nominally, the
movement might claim official support on both sides, since Eastern
and Western governments have both publicly professed interest in
arms reduction and, over the past 10 to 15 years, have signed or
discussed some 10 different sets of agreements relating to disarmament or arms control. But progress has always been painfully slow.
There are now signs of negotiation re-starting but the atmosphere is
not propitious. In the words of the IISS, " . . . super-Power
relations seem to be flawed by a fundamental and unresolved
difference between the two over what should be, in the 1980s, the
rules of the game."[9]

---

[8] C. Longley, "Two Sides to Death in a Nuclear War," *The Times*, October 19, 1981.
[9] *Strategic Survey 1980–1981*: International Institute of Strategic Studies, London.

Although Eastern government is much more immune to public opinion than Western, the East is clearly not without great problems. The burden of the arms competition is proportionately greater for the weaker Soviet Bloc economies and can only be met by denying social and economic progress severely. As events in Poland show, the contrived isolation of the East cannot insulate public awareness from the greater freedom and affluence of the West. In the view of the Institute of Strategic Studies these factors are so strong that time is no longer in the Soviet Union's favour in the 1980s and the central question for the West is how to cope with her now that "she is incapable of finding solutions to her increasing political problems, yet is in possession of unprecedented military power."[10]

But surely time is not on the Western side either. The West is stronger economically than the East but, because public opinion is more influential, cannot deploy its strength whenever necessary towards defence. Greater political freedom is also the source of the West's greater political stability—in the long run: but in the short run that freedom happens to be turned in directions which may weaken the West militarily *vis-à-vis* the East. It is therefore extremely difficult to foresee which side would outlast the other should they continue their military competition unabated to the point of exhaustion. Whatever the answer, the stresses created would certainly be extremely dangerous in a world possessed of enormous nuclear power. Undoubtedly, therefore, the proper question is not who can last the longer but whether the two sides can agree to restrain their mutual progress towards destruction whilst there is still time.

It is this question which the public instinct in the West has grasped ahead of its politicians. As a result Western governments are finding themselves cornered by circumstances. Public pressure for meaningful negotiation with the East is mounting at a time when the inflationary tendencies in the arms competition are becoming acute. Thus readiness to negotiate is fast becoming a condition of public support for the rising defence bill, whilst the ability to meet that bill is a standing condition of being able to negotiate from strength.

V—THE CASE FOR A GRAND STRATEGY

How have Western governments allowed themselves to come to this predicament? It is difficult to resist the view that it has been for want of what used to be called *grand strategy*; that is for lack of a well-defined sense of direction to which subordinate, military,

---

[10] *Ibid.*

diplomatic and domestic strategies can be related. Cynics may argue that grand strategies have never existed except when deduced by historians in retrospect. However, in the nuclear age, with the survival of civilisation at stake, exceptional standards of policy management are called for.

The West entered the post-1945 era with more strategic purpose and more inventive policies than are to be seen today. Western Europe was rebuilt with Marshall Aid; NATO was formed out of the determination to defend the post-war frontiers; there were quick reactions to the Berlin and Korean incidents; the West Europeans united sufficiently to form a new international structure, the EEC, inspired to a great extent by the vision of a new epoch in European history. The incentives lay in post-war desolation and Soviet antagonism whilst the energy and sense of direction were supplied largely by a newly victorious and confident United States. Since then American confidence has been undermined and her standing reduced by the long failure in Vietnam and by the internal crises of the Nixon era. Western Europe has been unable to supplement or replace American leadership, having lost its own early momentum towards some form of political union. As Harold Macmillan has implied, Europeans have been too engrossed in the price of butter to attend to what really matters, even to their own defence.

This is not to belittle achievements in the defence field. Western politicians might point out that, unlike the 1930s, the '50s, '60s and '70s have seen massive investments in defence and that, in NATO, we have a sophisticated military machine to show for it. In many ways NATO is unique as a supra-national, politico-military planning system. Moreover in the armed forces themselves professionalism is very high and in national defence ministries such things as operational analysis and the management of R and D have been greatly improved. There is therefore no comparison with the pre-war period when the Western partners were not only physically weaker than the Germans but behind them in some important areas of military thinking. Throughout most of the post-war period, and probably still, the West has led the East at the technical level.

But the ability to manage in detail the 30-year-old strategy of deterrence is not at all the same thing as the capacity to re-think it and broaden it when necessary. In fact the more elaborate management systems now in fashion have had rather the reverse effect in that they have institutionalised existing defence concepts, making it all the harder to see major limitations. It is characteristic of bureaucracies in all fields that they become pre-occupied with the details of relatively short term issues, particularly with budget snipping. Certainly Western defence machinery seems to have been insensitive to the broad economic trend outlined here, reacting to it with no more than a modest series of international weapon development projects. Had the fundamental nature of what is happening been better appreciated, defence needs might have had gtreater influence on political attitudes to European unity. Even now some lesser step towards joint procurement and NATO standardisation could no doubt be devised, but there is no sign of it. How much less likely is it that purely pragmatic defence management will produce policies commensurate with the even wider problem of declining public support?

It is true that the 1979 NATO decision to re-arm was accompanied by the resolve to negotiate as well—the so-called "two-track" policy. Since negotiation from strength is clearly the only realistic way forward, this seemed sound enough, even if decided remarkably late. However, we do not seem to be able to implement it cohesively. If Western voters had been clearly presented with a forthright policy of negotiation from strength, political parties out of power might have been less vulnerable to the disarmament lobby. In the United States both the Carter and Reagan Administrations have been criticised specifically for lacking coherent policies towards the Soviet Union and even the November 1981 "zero-option" initiative by President Reagan appears as an ad hoc reaction to anti-nuclear protest. As Edward Heath is reported to have told the European Parliament, there appears to be disarray which threatens " . . . the entire process of Western consultation on economic and defence matters."[11]

The situation therefore contrasts sadly with the strong sense of direction exemplified by post 1945 Euro-American initiatives like the creation of the Organisation for Economic Co-operation and Development (OECD) and NATO itself. At root the key to those earlier successes was psychological: they put hope in place of the despair engendered by post-war desolation and the threat of the early resumption of war. Hope is precisely what is required now to rally and unite the Western voter. At present he sees no refuge in the future other than an increasingly precarious balance between forces of almost limitless destructive power which will have to be provided at mounting cost, not only to domestic economies, but also to the detriment of the great unsolved North-South problem.

Hope might be provided by a coherent strategy which explicitly retains deterrence but equally clearly transcends it, aiming squarely at an agreed East-West security system for the North. There is, of

---

[11] *The Times*, November 19, 1981.

course, no certainty that such an agreement is possible. The spectrum of opinion on this ranges from the idealism of those who believe total mutual disarmament to be attainable to the view of some experts who find it implausible to disinvent nuclear weapons and who believe that some balance of nuclear power will always remain. This paper may have done something to show that a solution could lie between these extremes. The pressures on both East and West are now very great. Quite apart from the mutual fear of war, it is clear that the arms competition is crippling the Eastern economies whilst, in the West, it is dividing the body politic. Both sides must see in all this that there is limited time for agreement and that, as we have argued here, there is no certainty which has the least time. Therefore as time runs short each will desire efficient negotiation even if, earlier on, each exploits confusion in the other. It could be said, then, that both have an interest in clearer grand strategy, just as it has been in their common interest for over 30 years to manage deterrence on tacitly agreed lines.

THE REAGAN ADMINISTRATION AND AMERICA'S PURPOSE IN THE WORLD

By

R.J. VINCENT

THERE is no cause for alarm, it may be said, when a new American Secretary of State avers that the fundamental objective of the United States abroad should be "to help structure an international environment that is hospitable, at least, to the values that . . . Americans cherish."[1] This, it might be added, is a bland enough purpose, and might accurately describe the foreign-policy objective of any State in international society, insofar as it was capable of making any impact on its environment. But it is the kind of pronouncement that has a special resonance in American politics, because the United States was formed to preserve the values that Americans cherished, and her policy abroad as well as at home is legitimised by reference to these great purposes.[2] What are taken abroad merely to be the ritual noises of the American tribe about liberty and self-determination, have at home the solemn function of religious rites which is to re-dedicate the faithful to the purposes that bind them together. And it is not enough just to speak the words: some positive attachment to them needs also to be demonstrated. In this sense, the United States of America is not simply to be regarded as a State in a world of States, having the preoccupations that all States are bound to share. It is special. It needs to guard its unique institutions. And one way of guarding them is to do what it can to see that the rest of the world shares them. So within the world of States, the faction in which the United States belongs, in point of her purposes, is that made up of those who are deeply dissatisfied with the existing system: and the Soviet Union is a member of this group too. One of a number of things that the United States has in common with the Soviet Union is the discomfort of living with a revolutionary tradition.

---

[1] See, e.g. "A Foreign Policy Review," address to State Department Foreign Policy Conference June 2, 1981, in U.S. International Communications Agency official text, June 4, 1981.

[2] See Tracy B. Strong, "Taking the Rank with what is ours: American political thought, foreign policy and questions of rights," in Paula R. Newberg (ed.), *The Politics of Human Rights* (1981), pp. 33–64.

The dilemma of foreign policy for the country in this position is whether to attempt continually to export its institutions, which is a recipe for permanent conflict, or to be content with their success at home, which is a betrayal of the universal purpose in the achievement of which the revolution in one country is but a first step. It is with knowledge of this dilemma that the pundits await each new American administration. President Reagan was greeted as an ideologue, someone with a clear view of the values that the United States stood for, and a determination to defend them whenever and wherever they were under threat. The United States supported the freedom of the market place. This was natural, and normal. Communism was an aberration: it was "not a normal way of living for human beings."[3] The task of foreign policy was, then, to allow, and even to encourage, the natural to overcome the abnormal: "the West will not contain Communism, it will transcend Communism."[4] But Soviet military power had become formidable as Western strength and resolve had declined. The United States should take the lead in rebuilding Western strength, promoting solidarity among allies and even forming new alliances, and substantially increasing defence expenditure. Once these objectives were realised, then it might be profitable to parley with the Russians.

Negotiations from strength, liberation as well as mere containment: these were notions reminiscent of Dean Acheson and John Foster Dulles. And one of the themes for the interpretation of the Reagan Administration's foreign policy in its first year was that of a return to the simplicities of the Cold War: the Soviet Union was an adversary not an adversary-partner. But declamatory anti-communism has in fact provided for Reagan no clearer a guide than it did previously for Acheson and Dulles. Conviction, no matter how deeply held, cannot provide a detailed prescription for each new contingency. And inevitably, Reagan's foreign policy has already provided some nice examples of the confronting of faith by circumstance, such as the decision in November 1981 to offer to negotiate with the Soviet Union across the board of arms control well before the strength that was earlier insisted on had been established. The need to keep allies together upset the schedule in the approach to adversaries. And adjustment to the pressing needs of the moment rather undermined the procedural virtues which

---

[3] See President Reagan's address at the University of Notre Dame, *Daily Telegraph*, May 18, 1981.

[4] Reagan, White House Press Conference, June 16, 1981, in International Communication Agency official text, June 17, 1981.

Secretary-of-State Haig had taken as his text at the outset of the Administration. The requirements of consistency, reliability and balance if foreign policy were successfully to be managed were challenged not by any failure of will or execution on the part of the United States, but by unsettling circumstances beyond her control.[5]

This does not mean, as some might argue, that the idea of pursuing certain lofty purposes in foreign policy must be abandoned to the empire of circumstance. What it might mean, however, is that purposes of this kind must be worked out more carefully so as to include consideration of an international audience as well as a domestic one, so that, for example, the European left is considered as well as the American right. And for this more subtle account, strident anti-communism is insufficient. Not merely will it offend those who are already the enemies of the United States, but it is also likely to be obnoxious to that branch of liberal opinion which is inclined to think that not every issue in world politics can be forced into an East-West mould. In this regard, it is the narrowness and meanness of the Reagan view of America's place in the world that is striking. The gathering of military strength for the crusade against communism takes the justice of the cause and also of the means to its achievement for granted. There is little sensitivity either to the view that the Soviet threat is anything less than overwhelming, or to the notion that the balance of power must take account of more than mere military strength. Meanness is added to this narrowness in two ways. In the first place, the issue of human rights that so preoccupied the previous Administration has been dealt with with a certain Realist relish in which the smacking of lips has been so obvious as to be offensive to anyone who is inclined to take them at all seriously. The issue of human rights has been used by the Reagan Administration in a blatantly self-serving way: to excuse the shortcomings of right-wing régimes friendly to the United States, and to point out the weaknesses of totalitarian régimes, enemies of the United States. The second way in which meanness is added to narrowness is with regard to the matter of North-South relations. This is interpreted as really an East-West question about the relative value of market and command economies as models for development in the Third World. Again the treatment is blatantly self-serving and the Realism chilling: the celebration of private enterprise in the lectures to the Third World does not require the United States actually to do anything about the structural inequality

---

[5] For the "procedural virtues" see Alexander Haig, Confirmation Hearings, Senate Foreign Relations Committee, January 9, 1981, International Communication Agency official text, January 12, 1981.

of the globe, and the manner of her denial of any such commitment has been especially offensive to those least advantaged by the current world economic system.

Better a robust Realism, it might be argued, than the mealy-mouthed version in which homage is paid by vice to virtue. But this means that the United States, whose stand on these issues might make the most difference, is prepared to pass on the great questions of justice in contemporary international politics by supposing them merely to be a subordinate aspect of her relationship with the Soviet Union. America's purpose is reduced to confronting the purposes of a particular adversary. It is to an account of this doctrine, and the difficulties associated with it, that this paper is addressed.

I—THE ELEMENTS
OF REAGAN'S FOREIGN POLICY

When President Reagan looked forward to the transcendence of communism, it was Soviet communism that he had in mind. It was Moscow, he said, that would cheat and lie and commit any crime to promote world revolution.[6] So amid the talk of a new Cold War, within as well as about the Reagan Administration, there was at least a sense that the contest was limited to the Soviet Union and did not involve the "international communism" of the 1950s—an adversary the Americans had stalked to no avail. And from the State Department the line was less doctrinaire even about the Soviet Union alone, than that coming from other parts of the Administration. The problem for the 1980s, Secretary-of-State Haig argued, was that of coping with the military power of the Soviet Union which had been transformed since the Second World War from a capacity for continental defence to a capability to support an imperial foreign policy on a global scale.[7] The focus was to be on the Soviet Union not because of any ideological preoccupation, but because it was the greatest source of international security.[8] The threat was to be countered and Soviet military power managed.

Countering the threat involved, first, the rebuilding of Western strength which was perceived to have declined dramatically in relation to that of the Soviet Union during the previous decade or so. For this particular purpose, it mattered little that different parts of the Administration did not share a view of the nature of the

---

[6] *International Herald Tribune*, February 2, 1981.

[7] Haig Confirmation Hearings, January 9, 1981, International Communications Agency, January 12, 1981.

[8] Haig, speech to American Society of Newspaper Editors, April 24, 1981, International Communication Agency official text, April 27, 1981.

Soviet threat as a hostile Power or as a hostile ideology. And it was a task to which the Defense Department in particular attended with gusto. Defending the largest-ever increase in the defence budget, Secretary-of-Defense Weinberger, casting precision to the winds, declared: "We don't know what is enough, and if you don't spend enough you may never find out about it until too late."[9] Certainly nothing less than balance was thought to be enough, and the United States wanted all the weaponry the Soviet Union had got. In the case of strategic nuclear forces, the State Department added political arguments to the unsurprising insistence of the military on the capability to match every system in the opposing armoury. Testifying before the Senate Foreign Relations Committee, Secretary Haig stressed that these forces were not merely acquired for the purposes of deterrence, they also influenced the performance of the United States in the management of crises and in day-to-day diplomacy. They were the back-drop against which all foreign policy was conducted, and they affected the outcome of all significant decisions.[10] Arms transfers too had a new respectability. The rebuilding of Western strength involved the military capability of friends and allies as well as that of the United States, and there was nothing obnoxious about American aid either for this purpose or for the purposes of enhancing bilateral relations, supporting basing and access, and signalling commitment.[11]

Once the Soviet challenge was effectively countered, the next task was to manage Soviet power, and for this exercise Kissinger's old doctrine of linkage was resurrected. The old doctrine was that the way to deal with the communist world was to enmesh it in a network of relations with the Western world that would establish a pattern of common interests that it would be difficult to disrupt.[12] This was the détente between East and West. The West was to manage the détente and to provide for its continuation by manipulating the connections in the network: more trade, for example, and more credit, if more Soviet restraint of her allies in African affairs. The Reagan Administration had found less wrong with this theory than with its practice before their assumption of office. Détente had become a one-way street. It had come to mean restraint by the

---

[9] Caspar Weinberger, interview on NBC's "The Today Show," March 18, 1981, International Communication Agency official text, March 19, 1981.

[10] Testimony of November 4, 1981, International Communication Agency official text, November 5, 1981.

[11] Richard Burt, Director of the Bureau of Politico Military Affairs to sub-committee of House Foreign Affairs Committee, March 23, 1981, International Communication Agency official text, March 25, 1981.

[12] See my "Kissinger's System of Foreign Policy," in this *Year Book*, Vol.31 (1977), pp. 12–13.

United States, but not by the Soviet Union. The fact of linkage between one policy area and another had not been exploited by the United States. And "a policy of pretending that there is no linkage promotes reverse linkage. It ends up by saying that in order to preserve arms control, we have to tolerate Soviet aggression."[13] Linkages must be made to hold firm, and to allow management in the interests of the United States not of the Soviet Union. This marked off the more extreme elements of the Reagan Administration from Kissinger. Kissinger's concern had been to provide for the mutual advantage of the two super-Powers—to make the Soviet Union a satisfied Power. Weinberger's concern was that the Soviet Union was becoming too satisfied, that the West should take care not to make her stronger, not to allow trade to benefit a "potential aggressor."[14] So the Reagan chant of "I believe in linkage" had a quite different harmony from that of the Kissinger period.

But just as in the Kissinger period linkage was made to connect only when it seemed to suit a particular moment, so in the Reagan period doctrine has not been an infallible guide to practice. With regard to East-West relations, the continuing crisis in Poland has caused the less ideological State Department to become more so; while the perceived need to proceed with arms control talks has made the more ideological parts of the Administration less so. The pragmatism of the State Department which allowed it to see Soviet weaknesses as well as strengths, to countenance negotiation rather than fruitless confrontation, and to concede that not every issue in world politics was an East-West one,[15] has been confronted by the Polish crisis, and the result has been a toughening of the line. There has been no inclination to interpret events in Poland as chiefly a Polish affair, or to see General Jaruzelski as some in Europe have seen him as a Polish patriot rather than a Soviet puppet. And given Soviet involvement, there has been no talk, at any rate in public, of respecting a Soviet right to a predominant say in the affairs of Eastern Europe. Instead, with the imposition of sanctions on the Soviet Union as well as on Poland, the talk seems designed to enflame rather than calm: "The generals of this war against the Polish people are none other than those of the Polish régime itself, acting under the instigation and coercion of the Soviet Union. We

---

[13] Haig speech to Foreign Policy Association, New York, July 14, 1981, International Communication Agency official text, July 15, 1981.

[14] BBC, *File on 4,* August 12, 1981.

[15] See Deputy-Secretary-of-State William P. Clarke's address to the Austrian Foreign Policy Association, Vienna, June 24, 1981, International Communication Agency official text, July 26, 1981.

would be threatening the future peace of Europe if we ignored this dramatic attack on international principles."[16]

It was for this reason that Secretary Haig wished to have Poland monopolise the agenda at the talks scheduled to be on arms control with the Soviet Foreign-Minister Gromyko in January 1982. Yet even here, there was a reluctance to follow the logic of linkage and to break off the talks on arms control due to Soviet misbehaviour elsewhere. So that while Haig argued that relations between the Soviet Union and the West would be determined by Soviet conduct in the Polish crisis, he also said that the talks on intermediate range nuclear forces in Europe constituted "a very special category" of East-West relations to be continued under all "but the most exceptional circumstances."[17] This "special category" status seems to have come from the President's address of November 19, 1981, announcing the offer to negotiate with the Soviet Union on conventional, intermediate-range nuclear and strategic forces.[18] Whatever had led to this offer—the need to keep the NATO allies together, or the recognition that there were limits even on the American defence budget—it was a constraint on toughness over Poland. The wish by the Secretary of State seemingly to have his cake and eat it too, linkage but maybe not when negotiation on a particular matter was crucial, was then something imposed by circumstances, rather than a foolishness derived from lack of logic.

Attention, then, to but two issues—that of Poland and that of arms control—reveals the difficulty of maintaining coherence even among such apparently complementary goals as confronting the Soviet Union ideologically, building strength, and maintaining linkage. Behind the strong ideological line there is a willingness to compromise even on so basic an issue as the defence of Western Europe. The foundations of strength are barely laid before a willingness is declared to negotiate. And linkage might not hold in special circumstances. This is partly, as the sceptics have pointed out, the inevitable result of office. It is partly too because rhetoric about great purposes is not the same thing as a strategy for their achievement,[19] and if there is no such strategy there is no reason for surprise that the fall-back position is one of a rather banal pragmatism. In this regard the stress that there has been among the commentators on the spectacular differences of opinion between the

---

[16] Haig to the European Security Conference, *The Times*, February 10, 1982.
[17] International Communication Agency Report by Russell E. Dybrik, January 7, 1982.
[18] Text in *The Times*, November 19, 1981.
[19] This is the argument of Stanley Hoffmann in "Reagan Abroad," *New York Review of Books*, February 4, 1982.

Defense Department and the State Department, or the State Department and the White House, has been misplaced. What is surprising is that the disagreements have not been more frequent and more substantial.

However that may be, the argument of this paper is devoted to the "great purposes" that a strategy is designed to achieve rather than to the nature of the strategy itself. The concern of the next section is to show that United States' foreign policy has been impoverished from the outset of the Reagan incumbency by the failure to recognise as purposes of foreign policy certain liberal values which the United States has been accustomed to defend. Indeed, the very issues on which the Administration seems to regard its performance as a strength by virtue of benign neglect, are those on which many outsiders judge the United States to be negligent to a degree which seems to be wilfully offensive.

II—THE LIMITATIONS
OF REAGAN'S FOREIGN POLICY

Although the Reagan Administration has come to terms, in some respects, with the existence of the Soviet Union, the notion of her as, in the end, an implacable enemy has not changed. Confrontation with the adversary seems to be the natural Reagan style, rather than accommodation with an opponent with whom one nevertheless has something in common. Thus the dismissal of détente as a one-way street, strategic arms limitation as a dismal concession to Soviet interests, and even of trade with the Soviet Union as designed more to buttress communism than to assist Western manufacturers. Talk of this kind carries with it the danger of submerging what should be the overriding purpose of the relationship with the Soviet Union which is to find ways of avoiding any confrontation that might lead eventually to a strategic exchange between the two super-Powers. Whether these ways are called the method of peaceful co-existence as the Soviet Union prefers, or détente as used to be preferred in the West, they involve the super-Powers *together* in the attempt to make the world a safer rather than more dangerous place. In this enterprise the Soviet Union ought to appear as an equal, a State engaged in a joint attempt to manage the most dangerous aspects of international politics, rather than as a mere object of the confining attention of the United States. And it is in its having apparently lost sight of the partnership half of the adversary-partnership that the Reagan Administration is at its most worrying. When Secretary Haig declares that the United States has more than a right, a duty, to insist that the Soviet Union support a peaceful international order,[20] this is distressing not merely for its imperialist tone, but more for its failure to recognise that the other super-Power might have a different notion of what a peaceful international order consists in. Nor is posturing about the transcendence of communism likely to produce the situation in which the two super-Powers can begin to engage in the joint management of their relationship which might offer some prospect of stability within it.

This preoccupation with the adversarial aspect of the relationship with the Soviet Union has unfortunate implications outside that relationship as well as within it. This is partly because the Soviet Union is itself seen as an adversary everywhere, and not just within a sphere of influence, either by its active policy of intervention, or its support for international terrorism, or its conduct of war with the West by proxy.[21] And it is partly because if the Soviet Union is not thought itself to be directly implicated then it is nevertheless the beneficiary of instability. So one way or the other, the Soviet Union is at work against America's interest: in Poland through coercion of the régime, in El Salvador through the export of communism *via* proxies in Latin America, and in Iran through the communist Tudeh Party waiting to move in.[22] This interpretation of the world as an undifferentiated arena for the struggle between freedom and enslavement is what has prompted the cries of a return to the Cold War, and the dilemma it presents to policy is that either the threat is to be met wherever it shows itself (which is beyond the resources even of the United States) or some areas are to be treated as more crucial than others (which undermines the reliability of the United States as an ally). Better perhaps to start the analysis with the locality rather than imposing an external framework which itself induces the requisite answer.

Allies too might find the United States' obsession with the Soviet Union uncomfortable. The tough American line on Poland, especially after the imposition of martial law at the end of 1981, did not appeal immediately to all the NATO allies. This was partly a question of what each of them stood to lose. The American attitude to détente as something one should stop doing if it only benefited the other side, was not shared in Europe, and especially in Germany, where certain concrete gains had been derived from the relaxation of tension with the Soviet Union. So that when the United States urged solidarity among the allies, the Europeans

---

[20] Haig, address to American Society of Newspaper Editors, April 24, 1981, International Communication Agency official text, April 27, 1981.

[21] *Ibid.*

[22] Reagan interview with *U.S. News & World Report*, January 19, 1981, reprinted in International Communication Agency official text, January 13, 1981.

asked, in their view legitimately, solidarity against what and at whose cost. And when Americans pointed out the dangers of too deep a dependence on the Soviet Union, as they aid on the gas pipeline to connect Western Europe to Soviet supplies, Europeans might have felt entitled to refer to the enmeshment through linkage doctrine of an earlier administration. Again, on the not-unrelated issue of theatre nuclear force modernisation in Europe, American anxiety that Europeans should see the merits of an alliance strategy that was in fact a version of the American doctrine of flexible response against the Soviet Union, confronted a European wish not to frighten the neighbourhood super-Power at the same time as neither losing the more distant guarantor of their security, nor accepting its terms too slavishly. The primary European anxiety that the Americans might seek to insulate the United States from Europe if a nuclear exchange took place there brought a roar of disapproval from Assistant Secretary Eagleburger, who called it a "disgusting claim."[23]

To recap, it is suggested that the ideological blinkers of the Reagan Administration have forestalled any attempt to engage the Soviet Union in a managerial relationship in which the Soviet Union is a responsible equal, rather than a recalcitrant subordinate; they have made it difficult for the United States to take seriously the notion that there might be problems in international politics which do not have an East-West dimension; and they have led to trouble with allies who imagine anyway that their range of vision is broader. And as was suggested at the outset, it is this narrowness of purpose that weakens what might otherwise be the unexceptionable Reagan principles of strength and of linkage. Strength to build a balance of power on which, in Kissinger's once-favoured term, a structure of peace might be constructed is one thing. But strength upon strength because you never know how much you might need is quite another. Equally, the connection of one policy to another in a co-ordinated strategy towards the Soviet Union, and towards the wider world, is one thing, but the mindless repetition of the slogan of the indivisibility of linkage is quite another: it would imply what no foreign-policy maker could accept, that each issue is as important as every other.

The narrow anti-communism of the Reagan Administration also restricts its largeness of vision on two issues that have come in recent years to monopolise between them the debate about justice in international relations: human rights and distributive justice. On

---

[23] In speech to the North Atlantic Association, October 15, 1981, International Communication Agency official text, October 15, 1981.

human rights, Jeane Kirkpatrick set the tone for the new Administration with her criticism of the Carter years of 'continuous
self-abasement and apology to the Thirld World.''[24] The point, she
said, was to recognise that the bad was not as bad as the worst: a
"moderately repressive" pro-United States autocracy was preferable to a Cuba-backed insurgency in Latin American or Africa
aimed at integrating a country into the Soviet bloc.[25] In paler
language, Haig endorsed this view, and advised against excess of
zeal on human-rights questions.[26] In fact, the zeal when it came
derived from the opportunity to combine anti-communism with a
high line on human rights. "Human rights" said a State-Department
memorandum in November 1981 "is not something we tack on to
our foreign policy but its very purpose: the defence and promotion
of freedom."[27] And it was this that was used to legitimise the United
States' reaction to the imposition of martial law in Poland.

The difficulty from a purely prudential viewpoint with the defence
of moderate repression is that this might quite as easily lead towards
the worse totalitarian option as away from it: one way of promoting
revolution in any country is to have the United States support the
government of it. And the deeper difficulty with the use of human
rights as a stick with which to beat the Russians or the Polish
authorities, is that the high ground of principle is said to have been
abandoned, and the accusations of double-standards multiply as the
United States appears to tolerate abuse of human rights in
Guatemala, or Chile, or South Africa.[28] The Reagan Administration has a revealing if not altogether plausible response to this line
or attack—that of turning it on its head. Its first report on human
rights urged that an emphasis be put on ending 'the hypocrisy of
current double standards, discrimination against Latin American
countries and indifference to violations by the Soviet Union and its
communist allies.''[29]

The question of distributive justice gets shorter shrift than that of
human rights. Progress in the developing countries was taken by
Haig to be one of the four pillars of his foreign-policy structure
along with the solidarity of alliance, the defensive strength, and the
restraint of the Soviet Union that have already been discussed.[30]

---

[24] *The Sunday Times*, January 4, 1981.

[25] *The Sunday Telegraph*, January 11, 1981

[26] Nomination Hearings, January 12 and 13, 1981, International Communication Agency
official text, January 16, 1981.

[27] *The Times*, November 5, 1981.

[28] *The Times*, December 29, 1981.

[29] *The Times*, February 9, 1982.

[30] Haig to the American Bar Association, August 11, 1981, International Communication
Agency official text, August 12, 1981.

And the President himself spelled out what this progress consisted in.[31] It meant free people building free markets to ignite dynamic development for everyone. It meant understanding the real meaning of development based on the experience of the United States and other successful countries. And it meant engaging in practical measures of co-operation such as improving the climate for private investment. This celebration of private enterprise did not require the United States actually to do anything positive to assist development, but merely to release the productive machine of capitalism. Meanwhile the United States could benefit from stopping wasteful aid to the Third World. One of the most grotesque moments reported in Reagan's first year in office was the President being photographed in the White House Rose Garden receiving a magnified cheque for $28 million, representing the savings in foreign aid to 12 of the poorest countries.[32]

This lamentable political style, giving offence unnecessarily to a political constituency already sensitised by a reduction in aid, may, as many have said, simply bear witness to the domestic preoccupations of the Reagan Administration. More substantially, there is at least a good argument that the under-development of Third-World countries is the result of the operation of the market. And when many Third-World leaders believe this to be the case, the Reagan message of the magic of the market is unlikely to be well received. Moreover, if Third-World countries are anxious to obtain aid for the development of the infrastructure of their economies, a sector which even in the United States is largely in public ownership, then the advocacy of private enterprise seems misplaced if not hypocritical. Most importantly, in regard to the long-term interests of the United States itself, the mistake of the Reagan Administration in its attitude to the question of distributive justice is to turn the back of the United States on one of the central moral issues of contemporary world politics. Whether she likes it or not, the United States has the power to make a difference to the world on this question, even if only at the margin: obliviousness to it will alienate the United States from its environment and make the achievement of what Secretary Haig called "international civility" impossible.

CONCLUSIONS

Much of what may seem to an outsider to be the least pleasant aspects of United States foreign policy may actually be the

---

[31] Reagan to World Affairs Council, Philadelphia, October 15, 1981, International Communication Agency official text, October 16, 1981.
[32] *The Observer*, August 9, 1981.

consequence of American self-absorption: the tendency to treat "abroad" as something rather abstract invoked for a domestic purpose, rather than being a varied and complex environment with which the United States does actually have to come to terms. So the outsider's first wish for the future of the Reagan Administration might be that it should promote foreign policy up the order of importance, take it more seriously, and think more carefully about the external as well as the internal impact of policy pronouncements. This might reduce not merely the number of lapses in taste and style, but also the tendency to think, say, of Poland in terms of the Polish-Americans, the Soviet Union in terms of the dissidents' lobby and the Middle East in terms of the Jewish vote. The evidence of the first year in office was that while there was a good deal of sophisticated analysis of international affairs going on, showing itself mainly in State-Department speeches, this was not shaping policy at the highest level where there sometimes seems to be a crude know-nothingism on foreign affairs.

The second wish might be that the United States thought more systematically about what it wanted in the world, rather than negatively about what it did not want. The only coherence to be imputed to the Reagan foreign policy so far has been that which is provided by finding out what is thought to be in the interests of the Soviet Union and opposing it—in Poland, on arms control, in the Middle East, Africa and Latin America, and also in China—though friendliness with the People's Republic against the Soviet Union has been limited by the campaign pledge to support Taiwan. There is a depressing self-fulfilling prophecy aspect to this. The Soviet Union is the chief threat to international security, and the chief exploiter of instability. Insecurity and stability anywhere must either be caused by or be to the advantage of the Soviet Union. Therefore the policy of the United States anywhere must be to buttress the insecure and unstable against the Soviet Union. This is the trap of linkage which Kissinger sought to avoid by making a distinction between the commitments of the United States and her interests. And while Kissinger has attacked the Reagan Administration for its insufficiently fierce line on the Soviet Union,[33] the Kissinger-in-office might be a better guide than the Kissinger-in-search-of-it.

Not only does the preoccupation with obstructing the Soviet Union tend to pour East-West relations back into the mould of the Cold War, it also surrenders quite needlessly the initiative in international affairs to the Soviet Union, and emasculates constructive thought about issues in international relations that cannot be

---

[33] See articles in *The Times*, January 22 and 23, 1982.

viewed primarily in terms of the dispute between, in Reagan's terms, "freedom and compulsion."[34] The United States is a natural improver not a mere wrecker of the attempted improvements of others. And for this enterprise the starting-point is not to see what someone else is doing but to refer to one's own political tradition. The truths the United States holds to be self-evident are about the rights of all men, and not just of those who happen now to stand in the way of the Soviet Union. In this regard, the purposes contained in the demands for human rights, and for a new international economic order are closer, it may well be argued, to those of the founding fathers than is the impoverished anti-Sovietism of the Reagan Administration. And while it is no simple matter to translate the achievements of the American policy domestically into something recognisable as an "international civility," as the experience of the Carter Administration demonstrated, this is not a good reason for abandoning the endeavour. It has been the argument of this paper both that the United States should recognise how difficult it is to further the values for which it was established, *and* that it should continue the attempt. The Reagan Administration, by making those values the servant of the contest with the Soviet Union rather than the master, and by making every issue in international relations subordinate to the contest with the Soviet Union, has stunningly reduced the range of American power. For those whose instinct it is that the United States can be a force for good in the world, the Reagan Administration's interpretation of its purpose is a profound disappointment.

---

[34] Reagan to World Affairs Council, October 15, 1981, International Communication Agency official text, October 16, 1981.

UNITED STATES POLICY
TOWARDS ARMED REBELLION

By

ROBERT A. FRIEDLANDER

In his inaugural address delivered on January 20, 1981, President Ronald Reagan proclaimed a renewed American commitment to aid those friendly States subject to radical terrorist subversion or guerrilla attack both in the Western hemisphere and throughout the world. Asserting that Americans have never been unwilling to pay the price of freedom, the President went on to denounce all enemies of free societies and to promise "those neighbors and allies who share our freedom, [that] we will strengthen our historic ties and assure them of our support and firm commitment." He concluded with a clear if strident warning that henceforth, when American national security interests are at stake, the United States will not hesitate to act.

To dispel any lingering doubt as to the future intentions of the new Administration, exactly one week later Secretary of State Alexander Haig at his first press conference adopted a hard line in announcing that "[i]nternational terrorism will take the place of human rights in our concern because it is the ultimate abuse of human rights." The reason for this militant posture was Haig's strong belief that the prime target of terrorists everywhere, especially in Latin America, was the United States. It was only natural, therefore, that the Reagan leadership would select Central America as its first ideological battleground, since it uniformly believed that a worldwide Communist network was promoting insurgency and revolution throughout that region. Escalating terror-violence between leftist and rightist factions merely accentuated the determination of the new Republican Administration to do something quickly that would transform its bold language into some sort of identifiable action.

According to the Reaganites, the repudiated Carter policy-makers had guessed wrong on Iran and had guessed wrong on Nicaragua. The new incumbents had therefore resolved not to permit another misjudgment, given the severe injuries to American interests occasioned by previous Carter errors and indecision. Arguing that there exists a basic difference between authoritarian and totalitarian régimes, with the former favourable to United

39

States interests and hostile to Communist approaches, in two influential and widely-quoted articles Jeane Kirkpatrick (soon to become American Ambassador to the United States) accused the Carter Administration of literally fostering Marxist insurgency and Communist subversion in Latin America and the Caribbean.[1] To continue a hands-off posture, refraining from support of friendly governments who were threatened by growing radical insurgent movements, would result in an adverse domino effect. Or, in the words of one Reagan State Department spokesman: "I know that these guerrillas, these very individuals who are fighting today in El Salvador, if they win, are committed to fight tomorrow in Guatemala and the day after in Honduras. How far can we let them go on?"[2]

To many observers, either sympathetic or critical, the Reagan geopolitical vision reflected a conscious attempt to break loose from the political quagmire created by the Vietnam War. All three presidential administrations during the decade of the 1970s were trapped by prior history and confrontational politics. Vietnam had not only sapped the energies of the American people and seriously undermined presidential authority in the conduct of United States foreign relations, but it also came to be viewed as a symbol of the limits of American power in an increasingly chaotic world. President Reagan's dramatic anti-Communist rhetoric has sought to ignite the flames of patriotic renewal on the part of the American people and its Congress, and to rekindle a dedication to the cause of freedom everywhere that comprised the fundamental aims of American diplomacy for most of the post-Second World War generation. As with its domestic philosophy, Reaganism in international affairs wishes to revert to traditional values and to stress historic ideals. However, the Reagan Administration may well have embarked upon a quixotic quest, for history and tradition were wrested out of joint by the turbulent aftermath of the Second World War. American policy toward armed rebellion during the Cold War was, in truth, a major departure from the overall precedents of the past.

---

[1] J. Kirkpatrick, "Dictatorships and Double Standards," 68 *Commentary* (November 1979), pp. 34–45; J. Kirkpatrick, "U.S. Security & Latin America," 71 *Commentary* (January 1981), pp. 29–40.

[2] 97th Congress, First Session, U.S. Policy Toward El Salvador, *Hearings before the Subcommittee of Inter-American Affairs of the Committee on Foreign Affairs* (1981), p. 49. See, also, W. LeoGrande, "A Splendid Little War: Drawing the Line in El Salvador," 6 *International Security* (Summer 1981), p. 45, who quotes presidential candidate Ronald Reagan as stating: "We are the last domino."

I—INTERVENTION AND NON-INTERVENTION:
FROM THE FAREWELL ADDRESS
TO THE GOOD NEIGHBOUR POLICY

During the First Hague Peace Conference held at the end of the nineteenth century, the American delegation, in its announced reservation to the convention for the peaceful adjustment of international differences, made reference to America's "traditional policy of not intruding upon, interfering with, or entangling itself in the political questions or policy or internal administration of any foreign state. . . . "[3] For the entire 100-year-span of the constitutional republic stretching from the presidency of George Washington to that of William McKinley, American foreign policy rested theoretically upon the twin pillars of neutrality and non-intervention. Both concepts had their roots in Washington's famed Farewell Address of September 19, 1796, which warned against entangling alliances and advocated political neutrality. As several distinguished historians have carefully noted, Washington was actually proclaiming a policy of national sovereignty rather than abjuring the prospect of *any* future alliances, since he carefully left open the possibility of "temporary alliances for extraordinary emergencies." And he likewise was averring that the American continent should stand independent from European quarrels.[4]

In truth, within two decades of Washington's pronouncement, the United States became twice involved in European conflicts—once *de facto* (1798–1800) and once *de jure* (1812–1815). Yet the neutrality principle would in fact take hold, after those minimal departures, for an entire century. The commitment to non-intervention would remain a cherished American ideal until the Spanish–American War of 1898, although one may well argue that the controversial Monroe Doctrine (1823) provided theoretical justification for a policy of intervention whenever the United States believed its national interests to be threatened either by hemispheric upheaval or undue foreign influence.

Overt intervention by one sovereign State or combination of States in the domestic affairs of another was not violative of traditional international law. Indeed, the European Powers had been incited to take up arms against the First French Republic in 1792, and they again went to war together against France upon the

---

[3] Statement of July 25, 1899, quoted in J.B. Moore (ed.), *A Digest of International Law*, Vol. 6 (1906), p. 594, hereinafter cited as *Moore Digest*.

[4] *Cf.* S.F. Bemis, *American Foreign Policy and the Blessings of Liberty—and Other Essays* (1962); pp. 240–258; R.W. Leopold, *The Growth of American Foreign Policy: A History* (1962); pp. 19–21; J. W. Pratt, *A History of United States Foreign Policy*, 2nd ed. (1965), p. 45 fn.

return of Napoleon I from exile in 1814, making the French Emperor the first modern war criminal. The Quadruple Alliance (not to be confused with Czar Alexander I's Holy Alliance which was a mere statement of principle) intervened in the Revolutions of 1820 and 1830; Great Britain, France, and Russia (which eventually went to war over the issue) supported the successful Greek Rebellion in 1827–1829; the Eastern European Powers stifled the central European revolutions of 1848; and the Great Powers under British leadership put a lid on the explosive Near Eastern Question at the Congress of Berlin in 1878. Lord Palmerston even went so far as to declare in 1844, from a militant liberal perspective, "that if any nation should be found not fit for constitutional government, the best way to fit such a nation for it would be to give it to them."[4a] As the two Moroccan crises were to reveal (1905–1906 and 1908–1909), foreign intervention by larger Powers in the affairs of lesser politics continued up to the eve of the First World War. Unquestionably, the Austrian ultimatum to Serbia on July 23, 1914, was the very instrument (along with Princip's pistol) which unleased the mobilisations and war declarations causing the first world conflict.

When President James Monroe issued his annual message to Congress on December 2, 1823, the portion which came to be known as the Monroe Doctrine was specifically aimed at the Quadruple Alliance and its possible intervention against the rebel Latin-American colonies on behalf of their Spanish and Portuguese masters. (Incongruously, Monroe elsewhere in his message indicated a fervent support for Greek independence.) The first portion of the declaration repeated what had become by this time America's continuing commitment to non-intervention, and the latter part constituted a warning to Europe to do the same with respect to the Western Hemisphere. Although it was a unilateral proclamation by an American head of State, reinforced by no legislation or international agreement, the Monroe Doctrine was to become the third cardinal principle of American foreign policy, and certain publicists were later to assert that it had evolved into an international legal norm.

At first, during the 1830s and 1840s, and again at the time of the American Civil War, Great Britain and France pointedly ignored the Monroe declaration and intervened on several occasions in Latin America. The high point of foreign intervention was the French attempt to supplant the democratically elected government of Benito Juárez in Mexico with an Austrian prince, an undertaking which collapsed when France withdrew her forces in the wake of the

---

[4a] Quoted by R. J. Vincent, *Nonintervention and International Order* (1974), p. 95.

Northern triumph over the Confederacy. By the time of the Venezuelan boundary dispute of 1895–1896, and the Venezuelan blockade of 1902, the United States was willing to threaten war to achieve its national interests, and in both cases the intervening European governments backed off.

Ostensibly, American policy was guided throughout that century by the principle Secretary of State William Seward enunciated in 1867: "The Government of the United States does not assume to dictate the internal policy of other nations, or to make suggestions as to what their municipal laws should be or as to the manner in which they should be administered."[5] Actually, the United States did not hesitate to indicate its sympathies with revolutionary causes (such as Greek and Hungarian independence), though it is stretching the point to claim as one contemporary scholar has done, that "for much of its history, the United States was an example of revolutionary change and, indeed, a supporter of such change."[6]

The lure of manifest destiny as expressed in the "large policy" of Alfred Thayer Mahan, Theodore Roosevelt, Albert J. Beveridge, and Henry Cabot Lodge, infused an imperialist impulse into the Monroe Doctrine, and their interventionist legacy would continue until repudiated by the New Deal Good Neighbour Policy of Franklin D. Roosevelt. America's "splendid little war" with Spain in 1898 not only provided the springboard for the American rise to world power, but it also represented a transformation of the underlying assumptions of the Monroe Doctrine and the historic, if not altogether consistent, tradition of non-intervention. Cuba thus proved to be a significant watershed for the future of American foreign relations.

For several years prior to the blowing up of the battleship *Maine* in February 1898 and the Congressional Joint Resolution two months later which began the war with Spain, the ruthlessness of the Spanish response to the Cuban rebellion—led by General Valeriano Weyler, nicknamed "The Butcher"—attracted the attention and elicited the sympathy of the American people. Although Secretary of State Sherman was primarily concerned with the disruption of United States commercial and industrial ventures, President McKinley, reflecting public opinion, took a humanitarian approach which denounced Spain's oppression of the Cuban people as "unbearable to a Christian nation. . . . "[7] When the President finally sought Congressional approval for American intervention on April 11, 1898, his argument was based first on humanitarian

---

[5] Quoted by L.C. Green, *Law and Society* (1975), p. 293.

[6] G. Quester, "Consensus Lost," *Foreign Policy* Nr. 40 (Fall 1980), p. 19.

[7] Moore Digest, *op. cit.* in note 3 above, p. 193.

grounds and then on protection of American citizens, commerce, and national security. The Joint Resolution of April 20 unilaterally granted freedom and independence to Cuba, thus constituting in effect a declaration of war against imperial Spain.

Humanitarian intervention throughout the nineteenth century was in the process of becoming an international legal norm. Senator Spooner probably spoke for the Senate majority when he declared: "We intervene not for conquest, not for aggrandisement, not because of the Monroe Doctrine . . . we intervene for humanity's sake. . . . "[8] The problem was that although the United States intervened in the Cuban rebellion on grounds largely unrelated to Monroe Doctrine, the historical consequence of that intervention was to enlarge the sphere of Monroeism by causing the United States to assume the role of Policeman of the Caribbean.

Although historians generally date the first substantial expansion of the Monroe Doctrine in the twentieth century with the enunciation of the Roosevelt Corollary in 1904, the ever-widening scope of Monroe's declaration was pointedly articulated by President Theodore Roosevelt in his annual message of December 1901. The Monroe Doctrine, he wrote, remained the cardinal feature of American foreign policy. It was not intended to be hostile to Europe, so long as Europe did not aggrandise itself on Latin-American soil. Nor was it intended to enable one World State to seek the advantage of another. It was, however, a policy of hemispheric security, and if any State within or without the Western Hemisphere engaged in misconduct, the United States by implication would seek to punish the transgressor. The so-called Corollary message three years later merely confirmed established practice: "the adherence of the United States to the Monroe Doctrine may force the United States, however reluctantly . . . to the exercise of an international police power."

Roosevelt's flair for self-dramatisation led to his boast that "I took the Canal Zone," and thereby engendered an historical myth that continues to flourish. Despite the controversiality that continues to surround the series of events which led to the United States acquisition of the Panama Canal Zone, and the judgment of many historians that if Roosevelt did not directly aid in inciting the Panamanian rebellion, he at least acted in collusion with the rebels, a careful reading of all the historical evidence would indicate otherwise. The roughriding American President's actions were both morally straightforward and legally justified. He did not hide what

---

[8] Quoted by F.R. Dulles, *Prelude to World Power: American Diplomatic History, 1860–1900* (1965), p. 178.

he intended to do under the circumstances which were developing, and the United States carried out in full its treaty commitments, while simultaneously protecting its nationals and their property. But the illusion of United States interventionism became within a very short time far more significant than the reality. The United States appeared to have involved itself in a successful Central American armed rebellion with substantial benefits accruing to the intervenor. In this much misunderstood historical incident, the legacy overshadowed the original operative facts.

William Howard Taft, a stronger president than most realised, but who lacked the dynamism of his predecessor and his successor, set forth the justification for the dispatch of United States marines to Nicaragua in 1910 partly on the basis of protecting American citizens and their property (two Americans who had joined the rebel side were executed by the Nicaraguan dictator) and partly on the basis (a new precedent) that "the revolution represented the wishes of the majority of the Nicaraguan people."[9] Not only did this military intervention result in a change of régime, but the United States landed troops once again in 1912, this time at the request of a friendly Nicaraguan government. His last annual message to the Congress contained a rationale that would directly involve the United States for another two decades in Central American politics: "A nation enjoying our liberal institutions can not escape sympathy with a true popular movement and one so well justified."[10] Taft's version of Big Stick protectionism was to be continued by Woodrow Wilson, and the United States thus assumed, in fact if not in law, the controversial role of political arbiter of Central America and the Caribbean.

During his two terms in office, Woodrow Wilson authorised a half dozen unilateral armed incursions into Mexico, Nicaragua, Haiti, and the Dominican Republic. As was his custom, the intellectual president veiled his pragmatic actions with high-flown rhetoric. But even his stoutest defender is forced to concede that Wilson's Mexican policy basically symbolised "limited intervention and a violation of Mexican rights of self-determination."[11] The message sent out over Secretary of State Lansing's signature to almost every American embassy on November 24, 1913, in effect constituted an apologia for United States interference throughout Central America and the Caribbean: "The purpose of the United States is solely and

---

[9] Annual Message dated December 6, 1910, in J. Richardson (ed.), *A Compilation of the Messages and Papers of the Presidents*, Vol. 16 (1925), pp. 7500–7501.

[10] Annual Message dated December 3, 1912, in *ibid.* pp. 7773–7774.

[11] K. Clements, "Woodrow Wilson's Mexican Policy, 1913–1915," 4 *Diplomatic History* (Spring 1980), p. 125.

singly to secure peace and order in Central America by seeing to it that the processes of self-government there are not interrupted or set aside. . . . It is the purpose of the United States, therefore, to discredit and defeat such usurpations when they occur."[12] Not without reason did the distinguished American diplomatic historian, Samuel Flagg Bemis, who rarely criticised presidential statecraft, admit that Wilson's Latin American policy was an historic failure. It could not have been otherwise since it involved "complete control" of the internal and external affairs of several Central American and Caribbean countries.[13]

Perhaps the most notorious Wilsonian attitude and reaction towards armed rebellion involved the United States Siberian intervention, dating from August 1918 to April 1920. The entire episode constituted one of the more confusing and controversial incidents in the history of American foreign policy, and its impact upon Soviet-American relations has been felt right down to the present day. Whatever the specific motivation underlying Wilson's decision to intervene, and historians have differed over the exact cause, surrounding circumstances point to a pervasive fear on the part of Wilson and his advisers that the spectre of Bolshevism was threatening the very existence of European civilisation. Whether the initial rationale was based on an attempt to block potential Japanese control over Siberia, saving the Czech Legion, a combination of these factors, or primarily as a war measure to save Allied supplies and matériel, the justification for maintaining the Allied troops in Siberia was anti-Bolshevism pure and simple.

During the Paris Peace Conference of 1919, the wearied American President complained to his private secretary: "If the Bolsheviks get control of all central Europe, I don't see anything for us to do but take our blocks and go home—if we can get there."[14] Wilson's most influential adviser and collaborator, Colonel Edward M. House, was even more outspoken: "Bolshevism is gaining ground everywhere. . . . We are sitting upon an open powder magazine and someday a spark may ignite it. . . . [15] Wilson and his advisers, during the last stage of the war and the subsequent peace negotiations, had become almost paranoid in their obsession with the Bolshevik menace. This led not only to the abortive quasi-recognition of the Kolchak régime by May 1919, but also serves to explain the embarrassing domestic incident known as the Great Red

---

[12] Cited in A.S. Link and W.M. Leary, Jr. (eds.), *The Diplomacy of World Power: The United States, 1889–1920* (1970), p. 88.

[13] Bemis, *op. cit.* in note 4 above, pp. 390 and 395.

[14] Gilbert F. Close papers, abstract provided to the author by Helen Close McCann.

[15] Quoted by T.A. Bailey, *Woodrow Wilson and the Lost Peace* (1963), p. 119.

Scare of 1919–1920. Wilson desired to be known as the prophet of non-interference and the champion of self-determination, yet his actions continued to belie his ambitions, and the net result was to stimulate militant nationalism at the expense of regional and global co-operation, the League of Nations Covenant notwithstanding. The noted Sovietologist George Kennan goes so far as to question "whether Bolshevism would ever have prevailed throughout Russia had the Western governments not aided its progress to power by this ill-conceived interference" in Siberia.[16]

With reference to the post-war world, Woodrow Wilson devoutly believed that his League of Nations would become the price instrument of international change, but his vision was clouded and his hopes went largely unfulfilled. America retreated into normalcy and isolation in its global policies (with exceptions for the Washington Naval Conference and the Kellogg-Briand Pact). Likewise, Monroeism faded into swift decline, despite renewed armed intervention in Nicaragua beginning March 1927, and the sale of arms in 1924 and again in 1929 to Mexican governments threatened by rebellion. In the latter case, refusal by the United States to recognise the belligerency of the rebel party aided the collapse of the Mexican insurrection. Although the foundations for a meaningful Pan-American era of co-operation were being laid during the 1920s, the claim by former Secretary of State Charles Evans Hughes, at the Havana Conference on the Rights and Duties of States in the Event of Civil Strife, occurring in February 1928, that prior American intervention was merely an "interposition of a temporary character" for the internal good of the republic in question, was intended as a vindication of the T. Roosevelt-Taft-Wilson era. Its message spoke to the past. But its concerns looked to the future. Even so, the United States delegation signed the Havana Convention on February 20, 1928, and the Senate subsequently approved.

Publication by the United States government in 1930 of Under-secretary of State J. Reuben Clark's *Memorandum on the Monroe Doctrine*, prepared two years earlier, had the symbolic effect of repudiating the Doctrine as it had previously applied to Latin-American internal strife, the Roosevelt Corollary, the Wilsonian constitutional legitimacy test, and the maintenance of *de facto* Caribbean protectorates. When President Franklin D. Roosevelt introduced the phrase "good neighbour policy" via his Inaugural

---

[16] G.F. Kennan, *Russia and the West under Lenin and Stalin* (1962), p. 114. For a *contra* view, see A.S. Link, *Woodrow Wilson: Revolution, War and Peace* (1979), p. 12, who argues that Wilson alone prevented large-scale Anglo-French intervention in the Russian civil war.

and Pan-American addresses of spring 1933, he was merely restating an accomplished fact. F.D.R. and his Secretary of State, Cordell Hull, then shaped a new regional security system upon the concepts of mutual interest and collective defence, and for almost a generation they were able to substitute non-intervention, or non-interference, in place of Monroe's historic legacy. Moreover, until the outbreak of the Second World War, the new United States position on armed rebellion in the Western Hemisphere was simultaneously reflected in official American attitudes towards the darkening shadows of European crises.

II—THE SPANISH CIVIL WAR:
A TRADITION UPHELD

Born of revolution by the ballot on April 12, 1931, the Second Spanish Republic succumbed to revolution by the bullet on March 28, 1939. Spain's civil war broke out on July 17, 1936, and continued for two years, eight and one-half months. Often regarded by liberal commentators as the prelude to the Second World War, the Spanish conflict served as the great ideological battleground of the pre-war decade. It was in Spain, more than anywhere else, that the foreign policies and domestic politics of the appeasement years were fashioned in the crucible of diplomatic deadlock and military stalemate. In the words of novelist Arthur Koestler, "Spain caused the last twitch of Europe's dying conscience."[17]

Despite Administration misgivings, the United States Congress had already committed the United States, through the Neutrality Act of August 1935, to take the same position toward European affairs that President James Monroe wanted Europe to take in the Americas—namely, that of non-involvement. F.D.R. had wished for a more flexible document, and when the Ethiopian War commenced in October of that same year, he attempted to pursue "a bold neutrality policy," but the end result was a "disillusioning experience."[18] The lesson of Ethiopia was that neither Congress, nor the American people, nor even his own State Department advisers were willing to inject themselves in Europe's quarrels. The reverse side of Pan-Americanism at home was non-involvement abroad.

It is undeniably true that in his private communications with his

---

[17] A. Koestler, *The Invisible Writing* (1954), p. 326.
[18] See R. Dallek, *Franklin D. Roosevelt and American Foreign Policy, 1932–1945* (1979), pp. 101–121; R.A. Divine, *The Illusion of Neutrality* (1962), pp. 81–134; R. Friedlander, "New Light on the Anglo-American Reaction to the Ethiopian War, 1935–1936," 45 *Mid-America* (April 1963), pp. 115–125.

ambassadors and friends abroad, F.D.R. was knowledgeable, perspicacious, and even assertive, but he was also unwilling to risk any stronger course until the winds of war engulfed Poland in September 1939. Although there were clear signs of an impending disaster, none of the Western democratic Powers had foreseen the possibility of a Spanish military upheaval, and when it finally occurred, only France and the Soviet Union were sympathetic with the plight of the Second Republic.

The United States Department of State manifested a hostile attitude towards Republican Spain at the beginning of hostilities, and high echelon Department officials were strongly pro-Franco for the greater part of the war. Under-Secretary of State William Phillips, who although like his President was away from Washington when the war erupted, saw the conflict as being "between the Conservatives or so-called Rebels and the 'Popular Front' Government, which has in its fold Socialists, Communists and even Radicalists."[19] There is no indication either in the Roosevelt papers or any of his subordinates that at this time he favoured the Republican side. His position was probably best expressed by the personal sentiments of Interior Secretary Harold L. Ickes (who later became a fierce partisan of the Spanish Loyalists): "I could not conceive of any circumstances which would make me favor this country intervening in another war in Europe."[20]

A second Neutrality Act had been passed in 1936, but it dealt only with inter-State conflict and not with civil strife. This conundrum was emphasised by Under-Secretary of State Phillips in a cable dated August 7 sent to all United States consulates in Spain: "It is clear that our Neutrality Law with respect to embargo of arms, ammunition, and implements of war has no application in the present situation, since that applies only in the event of war between or among nations."[21] The temporary solution reached by the Roosevelt Administration was the imposition of a "moral embargo" against the export of arms and war matériel by American companies. It was designed to work in consonance with the European Non-Intervention Committee (N.I.C.) established by the five major European Powers which set up a "control system" surrounding the Spanish peninsula. Violations of the Non-Intervention

---

[19] William Phillips Diary, August 3, 1936, Vol. II, pp. 1617–1618, William Phillips Papers, Harvard University. The author is indebted to the late ambassador for permission to use his papers.

[20] H.L. Ickes, *The Secret Diary of Harold L. Ickes: The Inside Struggle, 1936–1939* (1954), p. 655.

[21] Department of State, *Foreign Relations of the United States: Diplomatic Papers, 1936*, Vol. II: *Europe* (1954), p. 471.

Agreement, however, began from its inception and continued throughout the remainder of the civil war. Italo-German assistance to the Spanish Rebels, and their recognition of the Franco régime on November 19, 1936 (considered interference by international law standards), made little difference with respect to the daily operation of the N.I.C.

Given these factors, it was no accident that the United States accepted without reservation the Additional Protocol Relative to Non-Intervention at the Buenos Aires Inter-American Conference for the Maintenance of Peace, held during December 1936. The Protocol declared as inadmissible direct or indirect intervention "in the internal or external affairs" of the signatories.[22] That principle was carried over to the Spanish civil war in the form of the Pittman Resolution of January 1937, by which the United States Congress specifically applied the Neutrality Act to Spain, just in time to prevent a shipment of American arms and munitions to the Spanish Republican government. General Franco was delighted, enthusiastically declaring: "President Roosevelt behaved in the manner of a true gentleman. His neutrality legislation . . . is a gesture we Nationalists shall never forget."[23] On May 1, 1937, another permanent Neutrality Act was signed by F.D.R., replacing the previous Act on its expiration date, and containing two new important provisions—a discretionary embargo power granted to the president in the occurrence of civil strife and a prohibition against the solicitation of war contributions, except in such ways as the president may choose to designate. The Neutrality Act was not further modified or moderated, until November 1939, when under the impact of the Second World War, the new legislation permitted a discretionary finding by either the chief executive or the Congress through a concurrent resolution. The mandatory provisions embodied in the three previous statutes were thereby repealed, and the Allies benefited accordingly.

Following the Austrian *Anschluss*, a growing public sentiment for repeal of the embargo legislation as it applied to Spain led Senator Gerald P. Nye to formally propose lifting the embargo and permitting the Loyalist government to purchase war material on a cash and carry basis (permitted by the May 1937 Neutrality Act). He did not succeed, although the Czechoslovakian crisis, the Munich conference, and the prolonged resistance of the Spanish Loyalists

---

[22] The leading authority on U.S. policy towards the Spanish conflict remarks that Secretary of State Hull's commitment to Pan-American unity "contributed to Washington's steadfast refusal to aid the Spanish Loyalists." R.P. Trania, *American Diplomacy and the Spanish Civil War* (1968).

[23] Quoted by F.J. Taylor, *The United States and the Spanish Civil War* (1956), p. 81.

against overwhelming odds, finally endendered an agonising re-appraisal by Roosevelt and his subordinates. Events outraced the Administration's internal deliberations, and despite a growing sympathy by F.D.R. for the Loyalist side, the Second Spanish Republic succumbed to military conquest at the end of March 1939.

Despite all expectations to the contrary, America's non-interference policy toward Spain had exactly the opposite effect of what the national interest required. One view goes so far as to argue that any decision to adhere to non-intervention is actually a form of intervention. Other commentators have charged that United States policy was part and parcel of the appeasement era, and that in the end, F.D.R. "even encouraged the aggression he so badly wished to prevent."[24] Roosevelt himself confessed that he had made a mistake in a farewell meeting with his former Ambassador to Republican Spain. Whatever the final historical verdict on America's role in the Spanish Civil War, United States neutrality was both consistent and traditional in its opposition to European entanglements. But the forthcoming global upheaval would put a dramatic end to this isolationist tradition.

III—THE GREEK CIVIL STRIFE: A NEW DEPARTURE

The United States entry into the Second World War was reluctant and belated, coming only after the Japanese surprise attack upon Pearl Harbour and the Italo-German war declarations. With the Soviet Union under invasion and Great Britain standing virtually alone against the Nazi juggernaut, the mantle of Allied leadership was literally thrust upon the United States. Unlike Woodrow Wilson, who sought to make the world safe for democracy, Franklin Roosevelt promised the American people at the onset of American participation to create a world "safe for our children."[25] As the war progressed, F.D.R.'s grand strategy encompassed many political objectives which had their origins in the Wilson era: a United Nations Organisation to replace the League of Nations; a trustee-ship system that would succeed the mandate supervision established by the League; a vigorous and expansive American role in world affairs; an end to colonial empires, particularly that of France; granting Great-Power status to Nationalist China; and a

---

[24] Dallek, *op. cit.* in note 18 above, p. 143.
[25] *Ibid.* p. 317.

strengthened Inter-American system within the United Nations framework.

From the dual perspective of history and international law, neither the Tehran nor Yalta agreements, which dealt with immediate priorities and contemporary realities, had as much impact upon the future of Europe and the world as the spring 1945 San Francisco Conference on organising the United Nations. The culmination of the San Francisco meeting was the promulgation in June of the United Nations Charter, a document that has had an enormous impact on the entire international legal process. Of particular importance for the future legality of third-party intervention with respect to internal strife was the wording of Article 2 (7), which established the domestic sovereign jurisdiction of member States: "Nothing in the present Charter shall authorise the United Nations to intervene in matters which are essentially within the domestic jurisdiction of any state. . . . " Interpretations vary as to the precise meaning of this section (it postulates a strong barrier to the application of human rights theory), but most commentators seem agreed that constraints placed on aid or assistance provided by outside States parties, unless requested by a legitimate government, are severe.

As soon as the Germans began to withdraw from the Greek peninsula during the autumn of 1944, Greece plunged into the turmoil of civil war. Unlike Spain, this time the banner of revolt was raised by the left against the centre-right, and the E.A.M./E.L.A.S. (Communist political and guerrilla organs) were quickly aided and abetted by Yugoslavia, Bulgaria, and Albania. At first, the United Kingdom intervened on behalf of the Greek monarchy, then persuaded King George II to withdraw in favour of a regency, and thus temporarily stabilised the political scene. However, the United Kingdom's resources were not equipped to maintain the level of assistance needed to maintain the new régime in power, and the new Labour government, which was neither willing nor able to continue pursuit of imperial commitments, finally removed its military forces at the beginning of 1947, after a third Communist uprising. Greece was again engulfed by civil strife, seemingly helpless to prevent an internal Communist takeover that was sustained by her unfriendly neighbours.

The Truman Administration, rudely awakened in the aftermath of Potsdam to the realities of the post-war world, looked on the vacuum created by British withdrawal from the Eastern Mediterranean as providing a direct threat to vital American interests. As early as September, 1946, Secretary of State James Byrnes had become convinced of the need to assist Greece and Turkey in their struggles for democratic survival.[26] An internal State Department memorandum, prepared the next month, predicted the possibility of "open civil war" with dire results for United States security, and it also raised the possibility of a replay of the Spanish conflict, with the victors in this instance being the "Communist-dominated Extreme Left."[27]

Small wonder, then, that momentum gradually built up within the Truman Administration for extending massive aid to the imperiled Greek government. One June 7, 1947, the Greek Ambassador to Washington visited the State Department and bluntly declared that the Greek régime was fighting for its life in a desperation struggle. He then submitted an *aide-mémoire* on behalf of his government which claimed that "Greece finds herself in a veritable state of war. . . . openly aimed at the suppression of Greece's independence." The culprit was not hard to identify, for the Soviet Union had blatantly manifested "undisguised designs against the very existence of Greece as an independent state."[28] The following week an American Economic Mission, created to assist the Greek government, left for Athens, and the Secretary of State's instructions, wired from Paris, identified the primary political objective of the United States: "Maintenance of the independence and integrity of Greece, specifically to keep Greece from falling into the Soviet orbit. . . . "[29] By the time of the United Kingdom's withdrawal from the Greek peninsula, American representatives on the scene were literally bombarding Washington with anguished pleas for help.

The die of intervention was firmly cast on March 12, 1947, in the form of President Harry Truman's special message to a joint session of Congress on the subject of Greece and Turkey, which he personally delivered, and which proclaimed the famed Truman Doctrine. Often taken as the formal declaration of the Cold War, Truman's message changed the history and direction of United States foreign policy. No longer was America going to insulate itself from European and world affairs, except as they affected its own national interests. For the post-war world, the traditions of the past were going to be set aside, since the United States had come to identify the preservation of freedom with its own security. In the

---

[26] See cable from Paris, dated September 24, 1946, in Department of State, *Foreign Relations of the United States*, Vol. VII: *The Near East and Africa* (1969), pp. 223–224, hereinafter cited as *Foreign Relations*.

[27] Memorandum Prepared in Office of Near Eastern and African Affairs, Washington D.C., October 21, 1946, in *ibid*. pp. 240–245.

[28] Henderson Memo, June 13, 1947, Washington D.C., in *Foreign Relations*, Vol. 5 (1971), pp. 195–196.

[29] Cable of July 11, 1947, in *ibid*. p. 219.

words of President Truman: "I believe that it must be the policy of the United States to support free peoples who are resisting attempted subjugation by armed minorities or by outside pressure."[30]

Truman had hinted at America's new departure in an earlier speech on foreign economic policy given at Baylor University, March 6, 1947, when he vigorously asserted: "Our people are united. . . . They are ready to assume their role of leadership. They are determined upon an international order in which peace and freedom shall endure." There is no question but that this represented a landmark departure in the history of United States foreign relations. The United States had consciously, and without reluctance, assumed post-war leadership in the anti-Communist West. To some historians the Truman Doctrine represented "intervention and entanglement on a heretofore unimagined scale."[31] To others it marked "the beginning of the third great American adventure into active world politics."[32] For better or for worse, the United States had now become the Gendarme of the Free World.

IV—The Vietnam Conflict:
Defeat and Disarray

Although it has been close to a decade since the conclusion of the Vietnam War, the effects of American involvement linger on within the United States body politic. Writing in the midst of the Carter years, one well-informed observer argued that "America is in the grip of a 'No more Vietnams' psychology which stands in sharp contrast to the spirit of active involvement in global affairs prevailing in the years following the Second World War; this fear of becoming entangled has led to a decline in the political influence of the United States."[33] Several years later, another scholarly analyst decried the "unravelling" of American power, hinting obliquely that there is a connection, however blurred, "that connects Saigon to Phnom Penh to Angola to Ethiopia to Aden to Tehran to Managua to Kabul, perhaps to something worse."[34] Referring to the Salvadorian policy of the Reagan Administration, a recent

---

[30] W.R. Reid (ed.), *Public Papers of the Presidents of the United States: Harry S. Truman, 1947* (1963), pp. 178–179. Truman also linked U.S. assistance to preserving the principles of the U.N. Charter. *Ibid*. p. 179.

[31] F.R. Dulles, *America's Rise to World Power, 1898–1954* (1954), p. 231.

[32] J.W. Wheeler-Bennett and A. Nicholls, *The Semblance of Peace: The Political Settlement after the Second World War* (1972), p. 566.

[33] G. Lewy, *America in Vietnam* (1978), p. 428.

[34] C. Horner, "America Five Years after Defeat," 69 *Commentary* (April 1980), p. 58.

political commentator concludes that the American public "has not recovered from a part of the Vietnam syndrome."[35]

Whatever the judgment of contemporary history on the meaning of the Vietnam tragedy, a careful reading of the historical record reveals that the United States did not plunge precipitately into the Vietnam maelstrom. It tripped under Eisenhower, stumbled under Kennedy, then fell under Johnson. Under Nixon, it finally picked up and ran away. Daniel Ellsberg, who leaked the Pentagon Papers to the United States press, and who was a prominent and vociferous critic of the war in its later years, denied that the Vietnam struggle was a civil war, calling it instead "a foreign aggression: Our aggression."[36] Henry Kissinger, on the other hand, maintains that the American commitment to South Vietnam began "in innocence, convinced that the cruel civil war represented the cutting edge of some global design."[37] The last French commander in Indochina, General Jean de Lattre de Tassigny, best summarised the Vietnam conundrum after his arrival in Saigon: "History has never been anything but illusions."[38]

The Vietnam war, especially in its American phase, engendered not only a national debate marred by bitter invective and mutual recrimination, but it also promoted among American legalists a disturbing reappraisal of the nature, processes, and prospects of contemporary international law (which played a minor role at best throughout the more than two decades of upheaval in Indochina). The resulting cacophony of legal argumentation resolved almost nothing, but it did reveal in full measure the strengths and weaknesses of the international legal system. If nothing else, Vietnam sadly demonstrated that although law is primarily a means of conflict resolution, statesmen and statecraft are often prisoners of events, and events have an embarrassing habit of outrunning legal remedies. The failure of American policy in Indochina was not as much the failure of international law as it was the limitations of human frailties and the volatile admixture of idealist impulses and mundane realities.

A respected scholar and defender of the American involvement in Vietnam has admitted in retrospect that the original decisions which led to intervention were based "on a misreading of the national interest. . . . "[39] Other academic opponents of American interven-

[35] R. Tucker, "Spoils of Defeat: Rationalizing Vietnam," 263 *Harper's* (November 1981), p. 88.

[36] D. Ellsberg, *Papers on the War* (1972), p. 33.

[37] H. Kissinger, *White House Years* (1979), p. 226.

[38] L. Bodard, *L'aventure: de Lattre et les Viets* (1967), p. 115.

[39] Lewy, *op. cit.* in note 33 above, p. 429.

tion in South-East Asia criticise the United States for failing to take
a realistic appraisal of ends and means, and for being indiscriminate
in the commitment of American power. The Kennedy and Johnson
Administrations were both foolish and disingenuous in seeking to
justify the American presence by talking of defending Western
democracy in the rice paddies and jungles of the Indochinese
peninsula. The decision to intervene, and the gradual escalation of
American forces occurred because both the Kennedy and Johnson
leadership believed that Vietnam had become, rightly or wrongly,
the testing ground of American military strength, diplomatic
influence, and treaty obligations. In that view, they were correct, for
American involvement, whatever the original motivation, had by its
very nature put United States credibility and prestige on the line.
The domino theory was a consequence—not a cause.

As the Second World War drew to a close, President Franklin
Roosevelt informed both the British Ambassador and Secretary of
State Hull that, in F.D.R.'s view, "Indo-China should not go back
to France but that it should be administered by an international
trusteeship."[40] This did not occur, and the United States a decade
later found itself confronted with a French plea for assistance at the
time of the siege of Dien Bien Phu. Contrary to popular
misconception, the Eisenhower Administration was prepared to
give aid and support if the British Commonwealth nations, the
Phillipines, and friendly South-East Asian countries also were
willing to participate. Eisenhower viewed this crisis as a challenge to
collective security, reminding Winston Churchill that "we failed to
halt Hirohito, Mussolini and Hitler by not acting in unity and in
time." The American President then added, ominously: "May it not
be that our nations have learned something from that lesson?"[41] At
that same time a secret recommendation of the National Security
Council proposed that "[i]t be United States policy to accept
nothing short of military victory in Indo-China."[42]

The French collapse occurred soon after, rendering the question
of American participation moot for the time being. The ensuing
1954 Geneva Declaration was a political rather than a legal
document, and, unfortunately, turned out to be ignored by both

---

[40] Memorandum dated January 24, 1944, in G. Porter (ed.), *Vietnam: A History in Documents* (1981), p. 6.

[41] D. Eisenhower, *Mandate for Change, 1953–1956* (1965), p. 420. *Cf.* similar remarks by President Lyndon B. Johnson in his press conference of July 28, 1965, and those of Dean Rusk in January of that same year. W.R. Reid (ed.), *Public Papers of the Presidents: Lyndon Johnson, 1965*, Vol. II (1966), p. 794; W. Cohen, *Dean Rusk* (1980), p. 247.

[42] Memorandum dated April 5, 1954, in N. Sheehan *et al.* (eds.), *The Pentagon Papers* (1971), p. 36.

sides as it suited their convenience. The United States was not a party to the Final Declaration, but officially indicated support for that settlement. In retrospect, no one was legally bound, since the agreement was neither treaty nor convention, but merely a statement of intent. By January 1955, American aid, matériel, and several hundred advisers had begun to flow slowly, but incrementally, to the Diem régime in South Vietnam. The turning point proved to be the inauguration of President John F. Kennedy, who once again reasserted the American claim to act as the guarantor and the protector of the free world: "Let every nation know. . . . that we shall pay any price, bear any burden, meet any hardship, support any friend, oppose any foe to assure the survival and the success of liberty."

This claim to the guardianship of the non-Communist world represented the broadest and most expansive statement on American involvement in global affairs since the inception of the American Republic. It was unrealistic and unsuccessful, and would result in the Americanisation of the Vietnam War. The final and largest phase of United States intervention, when it became in fact as well as in name an American conflict, occurred in April, 1965, as President Lyndon B. Johnson approved the use of ground troops in offensive operations. The so-called peace settlement arranged by Secretary of State Henry Kissinger, spelled out in the Act of Paris, signed on March 2, 1973, was merely a cosmetic face-saving gesture applied to an already lost cause. It demonstrated clearly and categorically the obvious ineffectiveness of international agreements in resolving military conflict and revolutionary violence. The United States was actually making the best of a bad business. South Vietnam by this time had nothing to negotiate, and the United States was preparing to depart in unseemly haste. The events of the next two years were merely a distasteful and embarrassing *dénouement*. In retrospect, the wounds left by the Vietnam conflict on the American political system were to heal slowly and painfully, and their impact on the course of United States foreign relations still lingers.

V—THE DOMINICAN REPUBLIC,
NICARAGUA, AND EL SALVADOR:
MONROEISM REDEFINED

Three years after the end of the Second World War and the formation of the United Nations, a regional security system was established in the Western hemisphere through the Charter of Bogotá (legitimated by Article 52 of the U.N. Charter) which created the Organisation of American States (OAS). The OAS was originally designed as a collective security organisation. Articles 15 and 16 of the Bogotá Charter denounced all forms of intervention by one State in the affairs of another, either direct or indirect, or any means of coercion, but the United States interpreted this language to stand for external threats rather than internal subversion. A State-Department memorandum of February 1960 linked Monroeism to those attempts by "extra-hemispheric powers to extend a political system, such as international communism, to any portion of the hemisphere."[43] The stage was therefore set for the United States-Dominican intervention.

During the four years following the May 1961 assassination of General Raphael Trujillo, who had ruled the Dominican Republic with an iron fist for more than three decades, eight changes of government rapidly occurred, and instability became commonplace. A new uprising began on April 24, 1965, but this time the United States was quickly drawn into the Dominican political vortex. Within a week the United States government landed four hundred marines in Santo Domingo, and that number soon increased to 20,000 American troops. By May 19, United States forces were openly fighting the remnants of the rebel faction on behalf of the governing military junta. Not until United States intervention had effectively determined the outcome of the rebellion did the Organisation of American States establish an Inter-American Peace Force and belatedly acquiesce in the already accomplished fact.[44]

The reasons for the Dominican intervention remain a source of great historical controversy, and the motivations of the Johnson Administration are still somewhat obscure. Initially, the Administration defended American action by referring to the need to protect American nationals "from violence in a situation of anarchy."[45] By May 2, however, the President had combined concern over American lives with the fear of Communist intervention. From then on, the official explanation of American motivations focused on the latter rationale, with the Administration proclaiming that its action had prevented "a forcible seizure of

---

[43] M. Whiteman (ed.), *Digest of International Law*, Vol. 5 (1965), pp. 409–410.

[44] President Johnson later offered the justification that the OAS Council "moved too slowly to permit a collective decision in the time available." L.B. Johnson, *The Vantage Point: Perspectives of the Presidency, 1963–1969* (1971), p. 202.

[45] Statement of Ambassador Ellsworth Bunker, quoted by V. Nanda, "The United States' Action in the 1965 Dominican Crisis: Impact on World Order—Part I," *Denver Law Journal*, Vol. 43 (Fall 1966), p. 460. President Johnson had voiced the fear that "American blood will run in the streets." Quoted by R.J. Barnet, *Intervention and Revolution: The United States in the Third World* (1968), p. 172.

power by the Communists."[46] The United States House of Representatives went so far as to pass a resolution denouncing Communist "intervention, domination, control, and colonisation . . . in the Western Hemisphere."[47]

Humanitarian intervention as a last resort, particularly on behalf of one's own nationals, is permissible in international law, depending upon the proportionality of the measures in question, the immediacy of the action taken, and the maintenance of both the territorial integrity and political sovereignty of the target State. All three of these elements arguably met the test in the Dominican episode, but the Johnson Administration's anti-Communist justification did not. Significantly, despite talk of a so-called Johnson Doctrine for the Caribbean, nothing of the sort emerged from the tangled events of April-May 1965. In fact, one prominent American historian claims the Dominican intervention "probably cost the Johnson Administration the vital support of the American foreign policy establishment" at a critical time during the Vietnam War.[48]

The missing piece in the Dominican puzzle may well be the Vietnam conflict, for if the American intervention in Santo Domingo had not only been successful, but also had been popular, public and private pressures building up over the Vietnam escalation might have diminished or even evaporated. It would not have been the first time that one foreign policy gamble was utilised to salvage another diplomatic disaster. Yet even if this was the intent, the end result was to still further undermine the Johnson Administration's credibility. United States policy towards armed rebellion in the 1960s was truly a losing proposition, for the United States sacrificed in prestige, strength, and influence far more than it could have won under the most advantageous circumstances.

Nearly a decade and a half later, another Democratic president found himself confronted with the conundrum presented by a Central American authoritarian régime of mildly repressive nature paralysed from the throes of progressive destabilisation. Ignoring the Sandanista rebel movement's propensity for committing acts of terror-violence, the Carter Administration fell victim in Nicaragua to its own human rights rhetoric. Anastasio Somoza was a dictator. Therefore, he was unacceptable to the human rights-orientated United States government. The Sandanista rebels were fighting a dictatorship. Thus, *ipso facto*, they had to become acceptable. As

---

[46] V. Nanda, "The United States' Action in the 1965 Dominican Crisis: Impact on World Order—Part II," 44 *Denver Law Journal* (Spring 1967), p. 229. *Cf.* also Johnson, *op. cit.* in note 44 above, p. 201.

[47] Quoted by Nanda, *ibid.*, p. 243.

[48] Cohen, *op. cit.* in note 41 above, p. 268.

illogical as this form of inverted reasoning was, the Carter Administration's long delay in taking any stand whatsoever is, in a diplomatic sense, almost incomprehensible. The lessons of Fidel Castro's Cuban triumph acquired so painfully two decades earlier were either ignored or forgotten, and the Carter non-feasance in Nicaragua was to be repeated again in Iran—with more disastrous results—during the fall of the Shah.

Whether or not the Carter Administration "brought down the Somoza régime," as United Nations Ambassador Jeane Kirkpatrick has charged,[49] and whether or not the Sandanista triumph symbolised a "U.S. loss of power in Central America,"[50] the fact remains that United States abandonment of Somoza, and its subsequent policy of non-intervention, actually constituted a negative interventionist posture. Possibly inept, certainly "dismal," the Carter Administration "consistently tried to fit a square peg of policy into the round hole of reality."[51] For the first time since the Panamanian revolution of 1903, the United States had backed the rebel side in Latin America, and by so doing had reversed its post-Second World War traditional stance. In the Spanish Civil War of 1936–1939, American neutrality had indirectly aided the Nationalist rebels. Thirty years after, at the height of the Sandanista crisis, American abstention during a critical juncture aided the rebel victory. The cost of that victory in terms of United States interests and security are still to be determined, but present indications are that the United States paid dearly for the Carter Administration's indecisive policy and unrealistic vision.

The Carter policy towards El Salvador was likewise that of indecision and tergiversation. Upon assuming office, it was as much by accident as by design that the Reagan Administration's initial pronouncements on terrorism became linked with the guerrilla war in El Salvador. Terrorism in the form of the Iranian hostage crisis had cost Jimmy Carter the American presidency. Ronald Reagan's campaign image of bold decisiveness greatly enhanced his electoral landslide victory. What could provide a better contrast between the ineffectual, hapless outgoing Administration and the vigorous, vigilant incoming Administration than a new direction in United States foreign policy? And what could be more dramatic than a successful revival of Monroeism?

El Salvador is physically small, military backwards, and of

---

[49] Kirkpatrick, "U.S. Security & Latin America," *op. cit.* in note 1 above, p. 36, emphasis omitted.

[50] R. Millett, "Central American Paralysis," *Foreign Policy*, Nr. 39 (Summer 1980), p. 101.

[51] W. LeoGrande, "The Revolution in Nicaragua: Another Cuba?," 58 *Foreign Affairs* (Fall 1979), p. 37.

arguable strategic importance, even if one accepts the Central American domino theory. It is relatively easy to account for large scale arms shipments from outside sources to the American continent, and this in turn made possible the United States decision to reassert once again its claim to be the defender of the hemisphere. For the first six months of the Reagan Administration, $35.5 million in military equipment was dispatched to the beleaguered El Salvador government, along with $144 million in economic aid and 54 military advisers. Additional funds and replacement advisers were requested by the State Department in the summer and autumn of 1981. As of this writing, the end is not yet in sight.

VI—THE UNITED STATES:
FREE-WORLD POLICEMAN OR CLAY COLOSSUS?

"We used to think that our neutrality was a wise thing, since it prevented us being dragged into danger by other people's policies; now we see it clearly as a lack of foresight and a source of weakness."[52] This statement by a representative of the ancient Greek city-State of Corcyra, seeking aid from the Athenian empire, could easily be attributed to every post-Second World War American president. The defeat of the Axis Powers by the Allied forces in 1945 put an end to America's isolationist impulse and reawakened its interventionist tendencies. With the onset of the Cold War, the United States enthusiastically assumed a global burden in the attempt to defend the frontiers of freedom against direct or indirect Communist encroachment. Although American determination momentarily faltered in Korea, not until Vietnam did the United States discard its Cold-War assumptions and retreat from the combative stance first undertaken by the Truman Administration in Greece and Turkey.

The Nixon Doctrine, inspired by the Vietnam debacle, mandated that the United States only helps those friendly governments who first help themselves either against foreign aggression or domestic subversion. The War Powers Act of 1973 and the Clark Amendment of 1976 were reactive measures adopted by the United States Congress to forestall future presidential commitments to besieged régimes seeking American military and economic support when threatened by internal or external conflict. The price of defending freedom throughout the globe became too dear, and the American

---

[52] Thucydides, *History of the Peloponnesian War*, trans. by R. Warner (1968), Chap. III, p. 31.

people were no longer willing, and perhaps unable, to sustain a policy of maximum strength for an indefinite period.

However, the resounding defeat of Jimmy Carter in the election of 1980 was interpreted by the incoming Reagan Administration as a vote for the reassertion of American power and prestige throughout the world. Encouraged by a resurgent domestic conservative movement which believed that the United States should not shirk the role of global policeman, the new United States government drew the line in El Salvador immediately upon assuming office. In the words of Secretary of State Alexander Haig, "had we done something less than we did in El Salvador, we might be facing another totalitarian régime there today."[53] Yet, the Administration's growing number of critics maintain that its hard-line military response to the guerrilla conflict in El Salvador "is the climatic proof of Washington's inability—or unwillingness—to understand the region. . . . "[54] Likewise, President Reagan's seeming pledge to defend the Saudi régime against internal enemies excited still more controversy.

"I recognise the administration's White Paper on El Salvador as a virtual reprint of the one I was involved with in 1965," declared Daniel Ellsberg at a Vietnam War symposium held in November 1981.[55] *New York Times* columnist James Reston maintains that the Reagan Administration prefers military solutions to political problems. But appearances can be deceiving, and this has often been the case in the history of American foreign policy. So far, the Reagan Administration's bark has been worse than its bite. "The truth, of course, is that the United States is both isolationist and interventionist, but one never knows which and when."[56]

Although El Salvador represents a return to the Monroeism of the past and to the traditional image of American foreign relations, the United States in the decade of the 1980s no longer carries the burdens, and no longer can maintain the obligations, of the Truman-Eisenhower-Kennedy era. If not a clay colossus, America is, nonetheless, a much-reduced image of its former self. The wounds of recent years have served to temper the confrontations of the present, and most likely they will limit the challenges of the future. If Lord Acton's dictum on power rings true, then a more restrained and temperate American nation will prove in the long run to be a more effective and influential global leader.

[53] 81 *Department of State Bulletin* (July 1981), p. 19.

[54] A. Riding, "The Sword and the Cross," *The New York Review of Books*, May 28, 1981, p. 8.

[55] *Fort Lauderdale News*, November 20, 1981, p. 6 A.

[56] L. Barzini, "The Americans: Why We Baffle the Europeans," 263 *Harper's* (December 1981), p. 82.

SANCTIONS AGAINST THE SOVIET UNION

THE AFGHAN EXPERIENCE

By

MARGARET DOXEY

THE introduction of some 85,000 Soviet troops into Afghanistan in late December 1979 was widely condemned by the international community. The Soviet justification that troops had been sent in response to an urgent request from the Afghanistan government threatened by external pressures from the United States, China and Pakistan was quite unconvincing and although the Soviet veto blocked action in the United Nations Security Council, strong disapproval was expressed at an emergency session of the General Assembly in January 1980.[1] Twenty-four Third-World countries sponsored a resolution calling for the complete withdrawal of all foreign troops from Afghanistan which carried by 104 votes to 18, with 18 abstentions.[2] Further evidence of Third-World disapproval came at a meeting of the Islamic Conference of Foreign Ministers in May 1980 which expressed deep concern over the continued Soviet military presence in Afghanistan. The West's reaction, which is the theme of this paper, was predictably condemnatory. Unfortunately, it proved impossible to co-ordinate an effective response in concert with Third-World countries, or even to present a united Western "front." The tone of statements by President Carter and other Administration spokesmen in Washington expressing surprise and shock at the Soviet military intervention might suggest that there was no time to prepare a measured response, although it can hardly be claimed that Soviet interest in Afghanistan had not been clearly demonstrated over a long period.

I—THE HISTORICAL PERSPECTIVE

Nineteenth-century Russo-British imperial rivalry over Afghanistan is well documented; Afghanistan's territorial integrity as a "buffer State," with British control of foreign policy was recognised in a

---

[1] G.A. Resolution ES–6/2. This was only the sixth occasion on which the Uniting for Peace procedure had been used.

[2] Angola, Cuba, Ethiopia and Mozambique supported the Soviet position; Romania was among the absentees.

treaty between the two imperial Powers in 1907. But independence from British hegemony in 1921 opened up the possibility of closer contacts between Afghanistan and its powerful northern neighbour, by then under Bolshevik rule, and a Soviet-Afghanistan Friendship Treaty was signed in that year. By 1924 Soviet technicians were helping to train the Afghanistan army and air force and an agreement for airfield construction by the Soviets was signed in 1927.

After the Second World War the United States alliance with Pakistan precluded close American relations with Afghanistan. There was persistent friction between Pakistan and Afghanistan and the former closed the border on several occasions. From 1953 onwards, the Afghanistan government extended and deepened its contacts with the Soviet Union and after Pakistan joined the Baghdad Pact in 1955 Afghanistan concluded a major arms deal with the Soviet Union worth $25m. From the 1950s onwards, though officially "non-aligned" in orientation, Afghanistan received military equipment, technical assistance, training and general economic advice from the Soviet Union, which provided an alternative outlet for trade and a source of oil when the Pakistan border was closed. As the British had discovered to their cost and humiliation in two Afghan campaigns in the nineteenth century, the remote and inaccessible nature of the country and the fierce fighting spirit of its people made it a hard nut to crack; better transportation routes and the development of air transport could facilitate foreign intervention as well as internal control, and Soviet assistance with highway and airfield construction was no doubt less than wholly altruistic.

One might argue that although the development of these ties suggested that Afghanistan non-alignment was vulnerable, its incorporation into the Soviet bloc was not inevitable. For a time, the United States was also active helping with road building in the south, though always inhibited by its ties with Pakistan from developing closer ties with Afghanistan. After April 1978, however, it was hardly possible to argue that Afghanistan had not moved very close to becoming a Soviet client in the full sense of the word. In that month, the government of President Daoud was overthrown and a Marxist government took power in Kabul, headed by Nur Mohammad Taraki. Taraki looked to Moscow for help in his struggle to suppress internal resistance—and received it. It has been estimated that there were about 350 Soviet advisors in Afghanistan following Taraki's installation as President; a year later there were at least a thousand. A 20-year Treaty of Friendship, Good Neighbourliness and Co–operation between the two countries was signed in Moscow in December 1978. The following September in continuing internal unrest, Taraki was killed and the former Prime Minister, Hafizullah Amin became President but unrest did not subside and Amin, in turn, died in the course of the Soviet military intervention in December. Babrak Karmal was brought back from exile in Eastern Europe to become the President of a State whose government could no longer present any semblance of independence from Moscow, although armed resistance to the Soviet-supported régime continues at the time of writing (Autumn 1981) to be a factor in the story.

As Soviet influence in Afghanistan built up in 1978 and 1979, a series of warnings against military intervention was issued by the Carter Administration in Washington, which makes it impossible to argue that no such possibility had been envisaged. Indeed, the revolution in Iran must surely have been perceived to enhance the Soviet Union's concerns about instability on its southern border. A pointed warning was issued in March 1979, a month after the United States ambassador to Kabul was killed while apparently being held by a terrorist group; other warnings came in August and September. When Soviet military intervention came in December it added considerably to the difficulties of President Carter, who was already immersed in the problems created by the seizure of the United States Embassy and diplomatic personnel in Tehran at the beginning of November; the Soviet government may have considered the timing of its venture more opportune on this account.

II—THE CALL FOR RESPONSE

The Soviet intervention compounded the foreign policy dilemmas faced by Washington. Neither the Iranian nor the Afghanistan crisis could be handled in isolation, without reference to the other, and both reinforced the American perception of the urgent need to restore the image of the United States as a super-Power which could neither be humiliated by a lesser Power (Iran) nor ignored by the other world Power (the Soviet Union)—or at least not with impunity. Response was necessary, and external support would add to impact and credibility. In both cases, therefore, the United States looked to its allies in Europe and elsewhere to join in condemnation and punishment. But both these crises presented some intractable problems in terms of determining an appropriate response, and as was to be clearly and embarrassingly revealed, there were different views among the allies of their political significance and of the kind of measures which would be helpful. Iran which under the Shah had been regarded as a bulwark of stability, pro-Western and outside the Arab camp, was in the throes of revolutionary upheaval led by fanatical Moslems who, at least for the time being, rejected conventional forms of international behaviour by holding United States diplomats as hostages and threatening them with trial and execution. Precipitate retaliatory action on the part of the United States would probably have resulted in the deaths of the hostages and could also have had the effect of further destabilising the whole area and of alienating moderate opinion in the Arab world—indeed of confirming Iranian accusations of United States interventionism. The challenge of Afghanistan on the other hand, involved the other world power and raised questions at the super-Power level of defining, or redefining, the limits of permissible intervention and "spheres of influence."

In the Cuba Missile Crisis it had been made clear that the United States was prepared, if necessary, to use force. While Soviet influence in Cuba might be tolerated—and perhaps would have to be if the United States were not itself prepared to mount a full scale invasion—Soviet missiles would not. Similarly, the status of West Berlin had been guaranteed by United States pledges during the Cold War, and the boundaries of Eastern and Western Europe had been finally accepted in the (Helsinki) Final Act following the Conference on Security and Co-operation in Europe (CSCE). The Soviet intervention in Afghanistan, in the words of then Secretary of State Muskie at a State Department briefing on June 4, 1980, was "the first direct intrusion of Soviet forces into combat outside of the countries Soviet forces occupied when the Second World War ended."[3]

If military intervention and occupation are indisputably more blatant violations of international standards of conduct laid down in the United Nations Charter than political manipulation or economic coercion, they are also harder to undo unless those opposing them are, themselves, willing to resort to force. This the United States was not willing to do, any more than it had felt able to challenge physically the Soviet interventions in Hungary in 1956 and Czechoslovakia in 1968. The price was too high.

There were two interpretations of the Soviet action, one of which identified it as part of a grand global expansionist strategy and the other as a more opportunistic and defensive response to a variety of factors such as concern about the Moslem revival on the borders of the Soviet empire; instability induced by the Iranian revolution

---

[3] U.S. Department of State, Washington D.C., *Current Policy*, Nr. 194, June 5, 1980, p. 1.

which had anti-Communist overtones; a chance to extend influence to the borders of Pakistan; the need to back up a client régime.[4] But from either perspective it was obvious that the presence of Soviet forces in Afghanistan could not be ignored. And the affront to Third-World susceptibilities could perhaps be capitalised on in the American response. Earlier adventures by Cuban forces acting as Soviet proxies in Africa (in Angola, Ethiopia/Somalia and South Yemen) were hardly welcome to the United States, but the presence of Soviet forces in Afghanistan was obviously seen in a more serious light, partly because of the *direct* involvement of Soviet forces but also, no doubt, because of what had gone before. Enough was enough and this was too much, particularly in an area close to the Persian Gulf where the United States and its allies have vital interests. It scarcely needs to be repeated here that oil supplies are the basis of these interests: some 25 per cent. of United States' imports of oil, 66 per cent. of Western Europe's and 75 per cent. of Japan's come from the Gulf area.

The purpose of this paper is specifically to examine the West's direct response to the Afghanistan crisis, and particularly the short-term measures adopted by the United States, which took the lead in imposing penalties; the paper does not attempt to deal with the longer term and far-reaching security issues which were raised, in terms either of what Secretary of State Muskie called "the wider balance" or of the more local defence of the Gulf in western interests.[5] President Carter stated categorically in his State of the Union message on January 23, 1980 that "an attempt by any outside forces to gain control of the Gulf region will be regarded as an assault on the vital interests of the United States and will be repelled by any means necessary including force." This was certainly a clear signal, reinforcing National Security Adviser Brzezinski's earlier comment that the United States would use armed force if necessary to preserve Pakistan's independence under the 1959 defence agreement between the two countries. But threats of future military action by the United States which might or might not deter any further expansion of Soviet influence in South West Asia, coupled with reappraisals of global stability and NATO's defences and the organisation of a rapid deployment force were all future-oriented. What was to be done to chastise the Soviet Union for its virtual occupation of Afghanistan?

---

[4] These opposing views of the nature of the threat are well set out in *NATO after Afghanistan*: a Report prepared for the U.S. House of Representatives Committee on Foreign Affairs, U.S. Government Printing Office, Washington D.C., October 27, 1980.

[5] It should be noted that if the United States is to do more in the Gulf area, other NATO members may have to assume additional defence responsibilities in Europe.

III—Penalties

The United States did not hesitate long before taking unilateral action to express its disapproval. On January 3 President Carter asked the Senate to postpone its debate on ratification of the SALT II agreement, signed the previous June 7, and the following day, in an address to the nation, he announced a series of diplomatic, cultural and commercial penalties which would be imposed on the Soviet Union, inviting allied governments to take similar action.

These measures covered areas in which economic and cultural relations with the Soviet Union had been developing in the period of détente and comprised the following: (i) Closing the United States consulate in Kiev and the suspension of cultural and scientific exchanges. (ii) The withdrawal of Soviet fishing privileges in United States waters. (iii) Embargoes on exports: (a) a ban on the export of 17 million tons of grain for animal consumption under order from the Soviet Union. This amount was additional to the 6.8 million tons of grain sold annually to the Soviet Union in terms of the agreement between the two countries dated October 20, 1975 which was not affected; (b) a ban on the provision or exchange of high technology items and a more rigorous set of criteria to govern exceptions; (iv) A boycott of the 1980 Summer Olympic Games: President Carter threatened that the United States would not participate in the Olympic Summer Games, scheduled to be held in Moscow in July 1980, if the Soviet Union did not withdraw its forces from Afghanistan by February 20, 1980.

Secretary of State Muskie and other official United States spokesmen emphasised that although the Soviet behaviour was illegal in terms of the United Nations Charter, the United States was not breaking legal agreements with the Soviet Union by taking any of these steps. They were unfriendly acts, certainly, intended to demonstrate disapproval and show the Soviet Union that it must pay a price for violating international norms, but they were not presented as international sanctions authorised by the United Nations, or any other international body.

The response of President Brezhnev to these announcements, and to the support offered with varying degrees of enthusiasm and/or reluctance by United States allies (see below) was that the Soviet forces would be withdrawn from Afghanistan when outside interference ceased; in March the Carter Administration announced that it would not only limit the export of high technology items, but industrial know-how. Oil equipment could be exported but not technology or expertise which would allow the Soviet Union to develop its own equipment.

At the same time as these pressures were being organised against the Soviet Union, the United States—and its allies to a lesser extent—were taking punitive measures against Iran, official United Nations sanctions having been vetoed by the Soviet Union. In April the abortive United States rescue attempt (Desert One) was mounted. The Iranian crisis was not resolved until the hostages were released, after mediation by Algeria, in January 1981, on the day of President Reagan's inauguration.

Those who have made a close study of sanctions and economic coercion have always made the point that the extent of the deprivation imposed on the target depends—on the one hand—on its need for, or dependence on, the items it is denied and on its ability to find other sources of supply, and—on the other hand—on the competence of the sanctioning Power(s) to close off these sources of supply. If the commodities or services under embargo can be dispensed with, the target will simply do without; if the same commodities or services are available domestically or from other external sources, or have ready substitutes, no great hardship will be experienced. A comprehensive collective effort is therefore of the essence if maximum direct impact is to be achieved, and in all cases of sanctions this has proved extremely difficult to organise. Not only are export embargoes unwelcome to exporting interests in the sanctioning States, but opportunities to gain new markets and to make profits are not to be despised particularly in times of economic hardship, so that third States who either view the "offence" as less heinous, or who are not prepared to suffer commercial loss for moral principles, may step in to supply embargoed items and so undermine the whole effort. Moreover, export and import embargoes are extremely difficult to enforce; smuggling and evasion have been rife in all cases where sanctions have been attempted.

The United States measures against the Soviet Union were announced unilaterally and allies were urged to support them *ex post facto*. In an analysis of the grain embargo, Joseph Hajda notes that consultations *within* the United States bureaucracy did not meet the criteria set by the United States Export Administration Act of 1979 which requires "affected industries" to be consulted before embargoes are imposed for political reasons.[6] Nor had there been consultation with allies and there was no united front. While it is true that the United States response came only a week or so after the Soviet military intervention, there had been a Marxist government in Kabul for some eighteen months, during which plans could

---

[6] J. Hajda, "The Soviet Grain Embargo," *Survival*, November/December 1980, p. 254.

have been made on a collective basis. Instead, the Western alliance was all too obviously in disarray.[7]

Only the United Kingdom government stood firmly behind the United States and its response to the call for collective pressure on the Soviet Union came on January 24 in the form of support from Mrs. Thatcher's government for the withdrawal of the Olympic Games from Moscow (discussed further below), the termination of preferential credit arrangements for the Soviet Union, the curtailment of Ministerial contacts and cultural exchanges and a tighter application of the COCOM rules for the transfer of sensitive technology to the Soviet Union. Other European allies were less enthusiastic. France announced that it associated itself with the condemnation expressed by its allies but would pursue an independent policy and President Giscard d'Estaing even carried on with his plan to meet Mr. Brezhnev in Warsaw in May 1980 and was criticised for doing so in the American press. The West German government cancelled high technology exports and put pressure on its national Olympic Committee to boycott the summer games, but at the EEC Foreign Ministers' meeting on January 15, there was no agreement to take specific counter-measures against the Soviet Union but only to cancel the food aid programme for Afghanistan and to help Afghan refugees with emergency aid. It was also agreed in principle that agricultural exports should not directly or indirectly be substituted for the grain sales embargoed by the United States. The NATO Council meeting in January also failed to agree on comprehensive "sanctions" or to support the United States-British call to boycott the Olympics. At the EEC Foreign Ministers' meeting in February, Lord Carrington, the British Foreign Secretary proposed that Afghanistan should be neutralised—a proposal still being explored in late 1981.

In Asia, the Australian and New Zealand governments reduced contacts with the Soviets and supported the Olympic boycott, while Japan associated itself with the boycott and also with the denial of high technology and export credits.

Willingness to take strong measures against the Soviet Union was noticeably lacking in Western Europe and the reasons were obvious. The United States itself does not want to be drawn into a head-on confrontation with the Soviet Union which would pose a choice between escalation into likely conflict or backing down with a serious loss of face, but it can sustain a halt to or temporary reversal of détente with less immediate and obvious harm to its interests than

---

[7] *Cf.* The Canadian Prime Minister's comment in London in June 1981 that reactions to Afghanistan were "absolutely chaotic," *Daily Telegraph*, June 17, 1981.

can Western Europe. A return to the deep freeze of the worst years of the Cold War would be most unwelcome to the European Powers who have to live on the same continent as the Soviet Union and worry about its massive conventional and nuclear capability and who are concerned to preserve and develop closer relations with Eastern Europe. For West Germany particularly, détente and super-Power arms limitation are priorities. Moreover, East-West trade and other economic links proliferated in the 1970s and the Soviet Union, Poland and other East European countries have received liberal credits from the West. Nor is the dependence all one-way; West Germany now imports large amounts of natural gas from the Soviet Union. Severing these connections would be very costly for both sdes. Scepticism about the *usefulness* of the penalties was also widely expressed. It is worth looking more closely at the grain embargo, the ban on technology transfers and the Olympic boycott to assess their impact.

(a) *The Grain Embargo*

Soviet dependence on imported grain is unquestioned, although it varies in intensity according to the size of the domestic harvest. A total embargo on exports from all possible sources of supply would be most unwelcome to the Soviet government, but it would also be extremely difficult to organise given the export potential of countries in various parts of the world: Australia, Canada, Argentina, and West European countries. However, in this instance, the United States itself did not propose to interfere with its basic five-year grain pact with the Soviet Union; but only to ban the export of an additional 17 million tons which the Soviets wanted. Denial of this extra amount could represent a deprivation for the Soviet economy, forcing cattle to be slaughtered because of shortage of feed, but only if the shortfall could not be made up from other suppliers. Hence it was very important for the Carter Administration to have wide and firm support from other exporting countries if the measures were to have any impact on the Soviet Union whether practical or symbolic. For while the symbolic impact of embargoes and boycotts is not necessarily directly proportional to their practical impact, there is clearly some connection. If no hardship is experienced by the target as a result of the severance of links of one kind or another, one might conclude that verbal condemnation through official pronouncements made unilaterally or in concert would do just as well. Penalties which are announced but not implemented or which turn out to be "blessings in disguise" because they spur inventiveness and self-sufficiency at the practical level and/or patriotic fervour at the emotional level, are even less useful.

A meeting was held in Washington on January 12, 1980 of representatives from other major grain suppliers—Argentina, Australia, Canada and the EEC members—with the object of ensuring that grain sales to the Soviet Union would be held at existing levels: *i.e.* no other supplier would make up the shortfall induced by the United States embargoes. But the meeting did not produce an impressive show of solidarity. Australia, Canada and the EEC countries agreed to keep their sales to "normal" levels and not to replace directly or indirectly the grain denied by the United States to the Soviet Union. The Minister of State at the Foreign and Commonwealth Office told the House of Commons Committee on Foreign Affairs that this could also cover "things bought as substitutes."[8] But Argentina stated plainly that it would not control sales of grain by destination[9] and it was therefore open to the Soviet Union, from the outset, to make up its imports by buying from Argentina, which it proceeded to do in massive amounts. Hajda gives figures showing that in terms of a long term agreement between the Soviet Union and Argentina, signed on July 10, 1980, Argentina agreed to supply 22.5 million tons of corn, sorghum and soyabeans over a five year period and undertook " . . . a massive shift of her grain from traditional markets to the Soviet Union, selling . . . at premium prices and letting the United States export companies and other suppliers sell in markets that previously were Argentina's."[10] The Soviet Union which in 1972–73 had demonstrated impressive commercial skills in buying up 13.7 million tons of grain from United States suppliers at bargain prices[11] also bought a cereal-based animal feed mix from EEC sources in 1980 which was not included in the list of items to be held "at normal levels" because the Soviets had not previously purchased it. Ironically, it appears that this particular feed mix is assisted by export subsidies to make it competitive in world markets.[12] For other purchases, the Soviet Union had to pay premium prices which did impose an

[8] See 5th Report from the Foreign Affairs Committee, Session 1979–80: *Afghanistan: the Soviet Invasion and its Consequences for British Foreign Policy*, House of Commons Paper Nr. 745, July 30, 1980. Evidence p. 14.

[9] Hajda, *loc. cit.* in note 6 above, p. 255.

[10] *Ibid.* p. 256.

[11] The so-called "Great Grain Robbery"—see the book of that title by J. Trager (1975). Henry Kissinger comments in his memoirs that "the U.S. government was simply not organized at that time to supervise or even monitor private grain sales as a foreign policy matter." *The White House Years* (1979), pp. 1269–70.

[12] See report in the (Toronto) *Globe and Mail*, October 30, 1980.

additional cost.[13] Friction also developed between the United States and its allies over the Canadian and Australian complaint that by concluding a massive wheat deal with China (details of which were announced in October 1980) the United States had broken its pledge not to invade the traditional markets of other suppliers to make up its lost grain sales to the Soviet Union. There were also accusations in Western Europe that the United States itself was not observing the embargo.[14]

Experience with this grain embargo not only confirms doubts about the problems of organising collective sanctions but also about the efficacy of food as a weapon.[15] Oil can be a good commodity for embargo, particularly by the Arab members of OPEC, because of the concentration of supply in relatively few areas, non-perishability and the lack of substitutes for certain uses, notably transportation. Food, in contrast, comes in a great variety of forms; perishability can be a problem; shortage and surplus cannot be predicted with certainty. Moreover, the international ramifications and activities of the leading international grain companies are relatively impenetrable as Dan Morgan found in researching his book *The Merchants of Grain*[16]: and these companies handle over 90 per cent. of United States exports of wheat, corn, oats and sorghum and most non-governmental Australian, Canadian and EEC exports. One of the largest, Cargill Inc., announced in June 1980 that it had been permitted to resume the sale of foreign grain to the Soviet Union.[17] Presumably the other multinational grain handlers enjoyed the same latitude.

The United States farmers' lobby was strongly opposed to the grain embargo from the outset; in June 1980 a group of senators from the farm belt introduced a Bill to rescind it, claiming that the United States was suffering severely while the Soviet Union was hardly affected. During his election campaign, which ran through much of 1980, Mr. Reagan promised to lift the embargo if he became President. In January 1981, he was faced with a difficulty in reconciling this promise with his declared and hostile attitude to the Soviet Union as the main fomenter of world instability by the direct

---

[13] See *The Economist*, March 15, 1980, which reported that the Soviet Union paid 20 per cent. above U.S. prices for Argentinian maize and Canadian wheat, barley and oats (pp. 36–7).

[14] See reports in the (Toronto) *Globe and Mail*, October 29, 1980 and the *Manchester Guardian Weekly*, November 2, 1980.

[15] See M. Doxey, "Food and Fuel as International Sanctions," XXXVI *International Journal*, Nr. 2, Spring 1981, pp. 311–334; R. Paarlberg, "Food, Oil and Coercive Resource Power," *International Security*, Vol. III, Fall 1978, pp. 3–19.

[16] Harmondsworth, Middlesex, 1980.

[17] See report in the *Daily Telegraph*, June 21, 1980.

sponsorship of international terrorism. However, in April the grain embargo was duly lifted and in the summer of 1981 talks began between the United States and the Soviet Union to draw up a new long-term grain agreement to replace the 1975 pact; in October the United States agreed to triple the amount of grain it would sell to the Soviet Union in 1981–82 to a total of 23 million metric tons.

(b) *Technology Transfers*

A ban on the transfer of technology and knowhow for which the Soviet Union had already shown a keen appetite might be seen as an innovative and effective penalty in that it is directly related to a specific vulnerability. But like commodity embargoes, it suffers from serious limitations: there is the same problem of alternative sources, in this case of information and knowledge, and in due course the Soviets can no doubt develop their own technology. They can also resort to espionage to obtain information. Refusing technology transfers can be expected to do no more than delay Soviet industrial progress; it cannot prevent it.[18]

Controls on trade in strategic goods with Communist countries date from the early days of the Cold War. The Co-ordinating Committee (COCOM), consisting of all NATO members except Iceland and with the later addition of Japan, has operated on a confidential basis to control and monitor this trade since 1949.[19] Three international lists covering atomic energy items (which includes reactors), munitions and military equipment of all kinds, and industrial items remain in existence, although they have been considerably reduced since the 1960s and the West European countries have been very keen to narrow the scope of embargoed items in order to facilitate East-West trade in Europe in which they have a major interest. Exceptions to the embargoes can be authorised by COCOM on a consensus basis but members can also bypass the COCOM procedures and issue their own licences. Members maintain their own national lists and control is exercised at the national level.

Quite apart from the general division of opinion between the United States and West European countries on the classification of dual-purpose items which can have military as well as industrial uses, with the presumption on the United States side being that security should have a very broad definition while the West

---

[18] A point made strongly in the House of Commons Foreign Affairs Committee *Report*, *loc. cit.* in note 8 above, p. xxxi.

[19] See G. Adler Karlsson, *Western Economic Warfare 1947–1967: a Case Study in Foreign Economic Policy* (1968); G.K. Bertsch, "U.S. Export Controls: the 1970s and Beyond," 15 *Journal of World Trade Law*, Nr. 1, January-February 1981, pp. 67–82.

Europeans generally prefer that military uses should be very clear before items are classified as prohibited, there is the problem that the COCOM partners have not been able to agree on a definition of strategic technology.[20] This is hardly surprising: there can be no arbitrary separation of technology which is for military purposes from that related to peaceful industrial uses. Moreover, it is extremely difficult to judge the economic impact of denying or providing technology, because it still has to be used productively. If it enables resources to be exploited, as with gas and oil drilling technology, is this to be considered as strengthening the military capability of the recipient or merely as releasing resources which could otherwise not be productively utilised?

Soviet interest in oil and gas extraction technology relates directly to reserves in remote parts of the Soviet Union which cannot be brought into production with existing Soviet technology and equipment. President Carter added oil and gas extraction technology to the United States Control List in 1978. But the argument can be made that preventing the development of these Siberian resources is hardly in Western interests. The Soviet Union is still a net exporter of oil, but if levels of consumption at home and in the Eastern European countries continue to rise, this situation could change; if their own Siberian fields are not developed the Soviets might have to look for new external sources of supply from areas on which the West depends. CIA studies have predicted the Soviet bloc will become a net importer of oil before 1985. There is already export of natural gas from Afghanistan to the Soviet Union, and Iranian oil fields are an obvious source for Soviet imports; even if one does not take the worst view and see the Gulf States as threatened.

The whole question of the development of Soviet natural gas reserves in Siberia has now become an issue between the United States and the European allies, particularly West Germany. The Reagan Administration is concerned about the extent of dependence on the Soviet Union which would follow the development of the gas fields and the construction of pipelines across Europe. The wells and the pipeline would be built with Western technology financed by low interest loans and repaid in the form of gas delivered at commercial prices. Some estimates are that West Germany would eventually receive 30 per cent. of its total energy requirements from this source. The issue illustrates the difficulties presented by hindrance—for political reasons—of trade and invest-

---

[20] See J.R. McIntyre and R.T. Cupitt, "East-West Strategic Trade Control: Crumbling Consensus?," 25 *Survey*, Nr. 2, Spring 1980, p. 106.

ment which bring employment and profit for Western capitalist interests.

(c) *The Olympic Boycott*

The United States attempt to instigate a full scale boycott of the Olympic Games in Moscow was the third prong of its short-term response to the Soviet intervention in Afghanistan, the other two being the postponement of SALT II and the economic measures discussed above. Unfortunately, the organisation of the Olympic boycott became a long drawn out and highly publicised wrangle between governments and sporting associations at the national and international level and the overall impression was not of pressure on the Soviet Union but of defiance of governments by sporting associations and of pressure on American allies from the United States Administration—thus exposing strains and fissures in the Western alliance. As noted earlier, President Carter proposed that the Games should be moved, postponed or cancelled if the Soviets were not out of Afghanistan by the end of February, and the British government supported this stand. But no such withdrawal took place and in April the United States Olympic Committee reluctantly voted to boycott the Games unless the President determined by the end of May that the boycott was no longer in the national interest. The decision of the United States Administration to oppose the holding of the Games in Moscow was bitterly opposed by the International Olympic Committee (IOC), headed by Lord Killanin; however, he was told in Washington on May 15 that it was final. On the same day, under pressure from their government, the West German Olympic Committee voted by 59 to 40 to boycott the games, but the British Olympic Committee decided to participate— which they did without government approval or support. The deadline for acceptance of invitations to participate in the Olympics was May 24, 1980, and by then the Japanese had also decided to stay away; the IOC announced on May 27 that 85 countries had accepted invitations, 29 had declined, 27 had failed to reply and four were barred from taking part.[21]

While the absence of athletes from the United States and other countries which participated in the boycott certainly made a gap in the proceedings at Moscow, the boycott was obviously limited in nature and correspondingly limited in impact.

---

[21] The number of countries which failed to join the boycott was about 60, including France, Greece and Iceland. Seven countries which participated in the Games boycotted the opening parade.

IV—THE EFFECTS OF THE PENALTIES

In categorising the benefits which might be expected to accrue to those resorting to sanctions or other punitive measures, one can make an analytical distinction between their practical and symbolic value. In terms of impact on the target, there is the possibility that a set of sanctions could be selected and imposed (or merely threatened) which would bring an end to the offending act within a reasonably short period of time (or deter its commission). Military sanctions are the most likely to achieve this result, although they can bring grave problems in their own wake; economic, political and cultural penalties have not generally proved so efficacious. The effect is not just a function of the impact of the measures—how much deprivation and hardship they cause—but also of the value which the target places on the policy which has attracted condemnation. The Arab oil embargoes which threatened fuel supplies to West Europe and Japan brought obvious shifts in foreign policy orientation from these countries but for them a pro-Arab, or a less pro-Israeli foreign policy was not too hard to initiate.

The abandonment of a core value will not be so readily achieved as a result of external pressure, as United Nations members found in applying sanctions to Rhodesia where whites were determined to hold on to their supremacist position. In the case of the Soviet Union and Afghanistan, a military intervention of such magnitude might be assumed to be a carefully thought-out policy designed to meet a serious problem; a certain amount of censure was no doubt expected, though perhaps not as much as was actually forthcoming, particularly from the Third World. Nobody in the West expected that the Soviets would withdraw from Afghanistan because of the measures adopted in retaliation; the most that was hoped for was that they would make continuation of the occupation more costly. They constituted a kind of fine for international misbehaviour, and also signalled a warning that further interventions would not be tolerated. Secretary of State Muskie stated quite plainly that the United States measures were intended "to demonstrate that aggression bears a price and to deter any further adventures in the region or elsewhere."[22] But the penalties discussed in this paper were not only designed to convey to the Soviet government and people the disapproval which had already been expressed in fora such as the United Nations General Assembly. They were also directed to audiences at home and in the rest of the world. As far as the Soviet government was concerned, it may have already written

---

[22] *Current Policy* cited in note 3 above, p.1.

off the SALT II treaty and the other measures were not of vital consequence. But one of the arguments used a great deal in connection with the Olympic boycott was that the Soviet people would understand that athletes from other countries were staying away because they disapproved of what was happening in Afghanistan. The problem here was not only the limited scope of the boycott, but also that the Soviet government could present its own account of the absences from the Games through its controlled media. And the only too obvious hesitancies and refusals to go along with the boycott further detracted from its value.

There seem to be good grounds for concluding that the Carter Administration's response to Afghanistan, as to Iran, was to a very considerable extent designed for United States domestic consumption, with the object of demonstrating to the American people that their interests were being upheld and that the United States was still a super-Power who could hold its rival in check. It can also be argued that the measures chosen, while not cost-free for the United States, minimised any hardship for United States producers and exporters, while West European governments' reluctance to support the United States reflected the heavier costs which would fall on them. Moreover, in an election year it was important for the President, standing for re-election, to present a convincing picture of firmness, particularly as United States foreign policy seemed to have become weak and vacillating over the previous years.

The fall of the Shah, the seizure of the Tehran embassy and the capture of American diplomats represented a particularly humiliating series of reverses for the United States. Questions were being asked not only about the credibility of the United States itself, but also about the support which it could expect and to which it felt entitled from its allies in Europe and elsewhere. Neither the Iranian nor the Afghanistan crisis produced a a unified allied response. In the case of Iran, where only the Soviet veto prevented a Security Council resolution ordering United Nations sanctions, the EEC Foreign Ministers did not agree to implement sanctions until May. Western countries did not close their embassies in Tehran and imposed very weak measures. For instance, the United Kingdom, which generally gives strong support to the United States, banned new exporters from doing business with Iran but contracts in process of execution and extensions of previous orders were not affected. Implementation was also very weak: exporters were on their honour to declare that their exports were not embargoed. A licensing system was considered too cumbersome and too expensive. A Foreign and Commonwealth Office memorandum to the Parliamentary Foreign Affairs Committee stated the official British position that the sanctions were to show Iran that she could not expect full economic co-operation with the West so long as she defied international law by detaining the hostages.[23] The British Parliament declined to make these limited restraints on trade with Iran retroactive to November 4, the date when the United States embassy was seized, and was clearly reluctant to get involved in sanctions at all. But as Douglas Hurd, Minister of State at the Foreign and Commonwealth Office reported in evidence to the Committee, the alternative was not to do nothing but "to go back to the President of the United States and slap him in the face."[24]

V—LESSONS FOR THE ALLIANCE

With the benefit of hindsight, one can argue that the United States should have closed its embassy in Tehran to prevent its seizure by militants. One can also argue that a firmer posture might have deterred the Soviet Union from military action in Afghanistan. Whether this would have happened depends on the value the Soviets placed on Afghanistan and the dangers they saw in continuing internal instability in that country. If it was already seen as a client and as an important addition to the Soviet bloc, the invasion might have come anyway. The Soviets had been building links there for decades; Chinese interest was viewed with suspicion, Moslem fundamentalism with apprehension. And it was probably safe to calculate that the Western response would be ineffectual, if vociferous. This is not to deny the importance for the United States of re-examining its strategy for countering Soviet threats—particularly if Afghanistan was to be a springboard for further adventures. The "loss" of Iran and the weakness, authoritarianism and nuclear aspirations of Pakistan represented a serious deterioration in the United States position in the area. But given the hostility to the United States in the Arab and Islamic world, and the very weak political base it has there, it might have been better to have planned and delivered a more measured response to the Soviet action. Overstatement of the extent of the danger, which President Carter described as the most serious since the Second World War, and over-hasty offers of aid to Pakistan which were spurned by General Zia as being inadequate,[25] detracted from the credibility of the United States posture. And although it was reasonable to expect support from United States allies in Western Europe and Japan,

---

[23] *Report* cited in note 8 above, p. 194.
[24] *Ibid.* p. 203.
[25] Although in September 1981, Pakistan did accept military assistance from the United States.

who benefit from United States security protection and are vitally dependent on Middle East oil, recent experience should have shown the need for prior consultation and suggested that there would be reluctance to embark on costly policies which would not produce worthwhile results. The 1973–74 Arab oil embargoes had revealed all too clearly the possibilities of disunity in the Western ranks.

Thus the effect on the Soviet Union and on world public opinion of the United States and allied penalties imposed after Afghanistan was largely dissipated by a combination of ineffectiveness and inter-allied argument. As far as the Olympics were concerned, the public wrangling between allies, between the IOC and governments, and between national committees and their governments was most unseemly and resulted in the loss of any major propaganda advantage. As noted above, the limited grain embargo was largely circumvented, and the ban on technology transfers of doubtful efficacy and possibly harmful to Western interests in respect of delaying Soviet oil and gas exploitation. There was obviously no political will, even in the United States, to attempt a full scale embargo on trade with the Soviet Union.

The question may be raised whether dignified Western condemnation, echoing the censure resolutions passed by the UN General Assembly at its emergency and regular sessions in 1980 would not have been adequate as "chastisement," coupled with intense concentration on better strategic planning for the defence of Western interests, particularly in the Persian Gulf, and firm warnings to the Soviet leadership about the dangers of further Soviet expansionism. This would have avoided exposing the strains in the Western alliance and charges that the penalties were largely meaningless. But if a range of penalties, however weak, was needed to satisfy United States domestic opinion and give a sense of strong government for as long as media attention was focused on that particular crisis,[26] then perhaps the United States response to Afghanistan was adequate and the allies half-hearted—and in some cases equivocal—support of less consequence. Scaled-down objectives can make scaled-down results look more like success than failure, although the attendant costs, particularly in terms of alliance unity, should not be overlooked.

---

[26] In June 1980 Mr. Muskie was exhorting the media to continue to pay attention, noting prophetically that "if the Soviet struggle in Afghanistan continues for the two-three year period for which they now seem to be preparing their people . . . the public perception of the significance . . . of the Soviet invasion will fade here, in Europe and elsewhere around the globe. . . . " *Current Policy*, cited in note 3 above, p. 2.

KURT WALDHEIM:

DIPLOMATS' DIPLOMAT

By

ALAN JAMES

"Is Dr. Kurt Waldheim the best man for the job?" This was how *The Times* began its first leading article on the day following his appointment as United Nations Secretary-General. By so doing the paper answered its own question, and underlined it by continuing, "The question is drowned by sighs of relief that the United Nations did, after all, at the eleventh hour agree on someone to succeed U Thant."[1] In a not dissimilar vein a leading American news magazine observed that the United Nations "had settled for what it could get."[2] But what it had got, according to one disappointed delegate, was "an Austrian U Thant."[3] This was bad news indeed, given the widespread view that what the United Nations needed was a different type of personality at the top.[4]

Ten years later Waldheim was still very recognisably the man who had received such an unenthusiastic reception in 1971. His style seemed not to have altered a jot. His period of office had been steadily unspectacular. But now relatively little criticism was heard. Unlike the situation at the end of Thant's decade as Secretary-General, there was no general sense of relief that his term would soon be up. Indeed, powerful backers sought his re-election. Why was this?

Luck, undoubtedly, provides part of the answer in that Waldheim had been spared the sort of crises which were bound to involve him in serious controversy. Additionally, there appeared to have been some alteration in view as to what might reasonably be expected of a United Nations Secretary-General. Waldheim in 1981 was more acceptable than a decade earlier, and he himself may have had a hand in inducing this change. For his disposition and approach, the member States gradually realised, were very suitable for the job. He had given satisfaction, winning that imprecise but enormously

---

[1] *The Times*, December 23, 1971.
[2] *Newsweek*, January 3, 1972.
[3] *Ibid.*
[4] See this writer's "U Thant and His Critics," in this *Year Book*, Vol. 26 (1972), pp. 43–64.

important term of approbation: sound. He had shown himself to be a diplomat's diplomat.

I—ARRIVAL

It was always Waldheim's ambition to be a diplomat. After leaving school in 1936 and then doing his compulsory military service (in a cavalry regiment: riding remains his favourite recreation) he registered at the Vienna Consular Academy. At the same time he became a law student at the University. The Second World War intervened and, drafted into the German army, he was wounded on the eastern front. This led to his discharge and he was able to resume his studies. In 1944 he obtained his doctorate in law and in the next year joined Austria's diplomatic service.

His rise was rapid. By 1958, at the age of 39, he was Ambassador to Canada. Subsequently he held the posts of Director-General for Political Affairs in Austria's Foreign Ministry and Ambassador to the United Nations. In 1968 he became Foreign Minister. Three years later he was a candidate for the Austrian Presidency, standing as an independent, but with the endorsement of the more conservative of Austria's two main political parties. He was unsuccessful, but this enabled him to run in a different kind of election.

The office of the United Nations Secretary-General is filled by the General Assembly, where all member States are equally represented. But the initiative rests with the 15–member Security Council which has to recommend a name. This means that the Council's five permanent members—the United Kingdom, China, France, the Soviet Union, and the United States—all have to agree, as any of them can veto an undesirable candidate. In 1971 the Soviet Union was said to favour a further term for Thant. But others, Thant not least, showed no enthusiasm for this idea. By contrast Waldheim was most interested and let the fact be known, albeit in a typically discreet way. His country, however, saw no need for circumspection and vigorously espoused his cause.

The going was not smooth. Waldheim was well known at the United Nations (since 1955 he had attended every annual session of the General Assembly), and was regarded as quiet, reserved, reasonable, and moderate. These, however, were not the qualities which were being generally looked for. Britain and America favoured Max Jakobson of Finland, seeing him as forceful and independently-minded. Other candidates were the Swede, Gunnar Jarring, and the Argentinian, Carlos de Royas. When the voting took place in private Council meetings Jarring soon dropped out of the running. The other three each obtained enough numerical support, but all fell foul of someone's veto. The Soviet Union was known to be against Jakobson: he had written an "unfriendly" book on the Russo-Finnish War, and also had a Jewish father. China, whose seat had just been transferred to the rightful owner, was said to be against the appointment of a European. And it may be that de Royas aroused European apprehensions about United States influence over a Latin American: Deadlock. Emergency plans were made to bring the Assembly back into session after Christmas. But over a weekend France persuaded China, according to one report, to withdraw her veto on Waldheim, and on December 21, 1971, his 53rd birthday, he was nominated as Secretary-General. One non-permanent Council member voted against him, and three members abstained, including, it was said, the United Kingdom. On the next day the Assembly appointed him to the customary five-year term by acclamation.

II—ATTITUDES

By going for "a diplomat of the old school, polished and courteous, a bit stiff and formal, but always correct,"[5] the United Nations was at least playing safe. This Secretary-General was most unlikely to misunderstand his position or the nature of the Organisation whose administrative head he was now to become. He would, indeed, have a role to play, and would have to stand up for the United Nations and its decisions. But abrasive hectoring was not to be expected from him, nor was he likely to forget that in essence the United Nations was a collection of sovereign States. They were the paymasters and he, ultimately, was their piper. He might be allowed or even encouraged to provide appropriate embellishments, but only in keeping with the general tune which they called.

If any reassurance was needed on this point it was soon forthcoming and often repeated over the next 10 years. For in his many speeches[6] Waldheim made it abundantly clear that his picture of the world was and remained basically that of the foreign offices of the member States. He was quick off the mark in reminding audiences that the United Nations was not a super-State and that what it could do was limited to what its members could agree upon. He spoke of the Security Council as a safety valve; he urged a pragmatic approach to the United Nations work; he encouraged quiet diplomacy. All this could not but have had the members nodding in approval.

Something which, on the face of it, might have caused them some

---

[5] The description of an acquaintance, *The Times*, December 22, 1971.
[6] Reported in the monthly *U.N. Chronicle*.

concern was Waldheim's sensitivity to the frequently-encountered forecast and charge that he is too passive and responsive, the typical faceless diplomat. Sometimes he has tried to take the sting out of the accusation by arguing that "one shouldn't follow examples in politics . . . You have to be your own personality,"[7] or by admitting, "I know I'm colourless."[8] More usually, however, he has been at pains to deny the charge of passivity, asserting that "All those who have ever worked with me know how false it is."[9] Perhaps he has protested a bit too much. In any event, he has also emphasised that the Secretary-General must know the limits within which he has to work, so that States have not been denied sleep by the thought that he might try to demonstrate his activist claims in an alarming way.

One characteristic of Waldheim's incumbency has been his insistence on the need to uphold the dignity of the United Nations and of his own office. No Hammarskjöldian-like economy class travel for him! But he has kept a firm grip on reality. Naturally, he has to display some measure of optimism in face of the world's troubles: this is virtually an obligation of his office. He must, too, touch his cap to the various orthodoxies of the day. But he has also both warned against over-optimism and underlined the need for a sense of proportion. As he told one dramatically-inclined questioner, "We are not at the brink of doom. . . . We should avoid hysteria. We need calm and, certainly, firmness . . . coupled with restraint."[10]

III—CONTACTS

"Calm," "restraint": the words epitomise the man. Conservative clothes covering a very long, thin frame, his matching angular head more often than not, it seems, inclined downwards to give respectful ear to someone more voluble than he. What does he really think about it all? He is too practised at the game to reveal that. Sometimes, however, the photographs show a small and possibly mischievous smile—Konrad Adenauer crossed with Danny Kaye, perhaps—and Viennese are after all said to take a lighter view of life than their linguistic brethren to the north. Certainly Waldheim has a sense of humour and can be a splendid guest. But when on duty all the traditional diplomatic qualities are to the fore. Thus it is not just in his attitudes that Waldheim has shown himself to be sound. He

---

[7] E. Lax, "One Man's World," XVI *Pegasus*, 1979, p. 19.
[8] *Newsweek*, December 8, 1975.
[9] *The Times*, January 4, 1972.
[10] XVII *U.N. Chronicle* Nr. 2 (March 1980), p. 48.

has also given satisfaction in the way he has conducted himself on the job.

The job, for him, seems synonymous with travel. From the first he was on the move and, apart from early September to late December (when the General Assembly is in annual session) he appears hardly to stop. No issue of the monthly *U.N. Chronicle* seems complete without a "Secretary-General visits six countries" story. Heads of State and prime ministers are called upon as a matter of course. He is received by the Pope (which must be particularly satisfying for a Roman Catholic). Intergovernmental organisations are addressed. When back at base there is a steady stream of official visitors to his door. He also has engagements with non-official bodies. And the media must be attended to.

Especially in view of the exacting nature of this schedule, it would not have been hard even for a skilled diplomat sometimes to give inadvertent offence, whether by remark or demeanour. And once, on arriving in Jerusalem, Waldheim did put his foot in it (although not in respect of his hosts) by saying how glad he was to be in Israel's capital.[11] But this kind of blunder has been very exceptional, and it is to Waldheim's credit that he has so seldom put a foot wrong. It goes a long way towards explaining why he has gone down so well in such a touchy context as the society of States.

This is not to say that Waldheim refuses ever to upset a member State. In 1972 he spoke out very strongly against the reported bombing by the United States of North Vietnamese dykes. This caused President Nixon to say that the Secretary-General, "like his predecessor" had joined "many well-intentioned and naïve people . . . "[12] in denouncing the United States while ignoring the havoc wrought in South Vietnam by the Northern invaders. But, as Waldheim had probably calculated, the incident did no lasting harm. And in 1981 the outgoing American President and the incoming Secretary of State both came strongly to his support after critical allegations were made regarding certain of his negotiations over the American hostages in Iran.

It was also in 1981 that Waldheim braved Prime Minister Begin's wrath by condemning Israel's attack on Iraq's nuclear reactor, although here too, given the nature of the act and the identity of the perpetrator, he was on safe ground. And by identifying himself with the United Nations anti-South African posture Waldheim has in no way endangered his standing and influence.

Condemnation, however, is not Waldheim's style. Rather he

---

[11] K. Waldheim, *The Challenge of Peace* (1980), pp. 8–9.
[12] *London Weekly Summary* (U.N. Information Centre), WS/72/31.

emphasises the importance of negotiation, no matter how hopeless the prospect seems, and of keeping in touch. This last he has certainly done, and he has linked it with the possibility of the United Nations playing an ameliorative role. His argument is that the willingness of States to turn to the Secretary-General as a go-between at a time of difficulty or crisis depends partly on their confidence in his impartiality and reliability, and that this is something he can help to instil by frequent personal contacts. Too much should not be made of this claim. But Waldheim's ability to exercise his good offices does seem to have been assisted by the fact that, partly in consequence of his indefatigable travelling, he is generally thought to be reliable. Unexciting, maybe, but reliable. Sound.

IV—GOOD OFFICES

There are a variety of ways in which Waldheim has come to exercise a mediatory influence. Sometimes he is specifically asked to do so by the General Assembly or Security Council, as in 1972 when he visited South Africa to talk about the future of Namibia. Three years later he was asked to negotiate with those involved in the dispute over Western Sahara. In 1979 his attention was directed to the American hostages in Tehran. And throughout his period of office he has been deeply involved in the Cyprus problem. He may have to pass a lot of the work on such issues over to a special representative, who can give them his full attention, and the United Nations political organs from time to time ask him to appoint such a person, as in the conflict between Iran and Iraq in 1974 and over East Timor in 1975. In 1980 the Council welcomed his appointment of a special representative to Iran and Iraq. It may be assumed, though, that the Secretary-General keeps closely in touch with the development of the mediatory process.

Waldheim has made it clear that if the Council is stymied he will see if he can move things forward. It was in this context that he sent a representative to the Middle East in 1976, and launched a peace initiative of his own in respect of that area in 1977. Occasionally, he has tried to prod the Council into action, as in 1976 in respect of the Lebanon and in 1979 over the seizure of America's Tehran Embassy. In this last case the Secretary-General based himself on the power given him under Article 99 of the United Nations Charter—only the second time in the United Nations history that it had been formally invoked. A rather different kind of initiative was that of 1972 when, at his suggestion, the Assembly put the problem of international terrorism on its agenda.

Often Waldheim is approached directly by the parties to a

dispute, or they respond positively to his quiet offers of help. A good deal of this activity may not yet be on the public record, but instances of it which are include Hanoi's 1972 appeal for help in arranging a cease-fire and, eight years later, the now unified Vietnam's request for his good offices over the problem which had arisen with Thailand over Kampuchea. He has had discussions about Chad, a hand in the ending of at least two aircraft hijackings, and in 1977 secured the release, at Christmas time, of eight French nationals who had been held in Western Sahara by the Polisario guerrillas. In an uncharacteristic theatrical move, Waldheim himself travelled with them to Paris.

In this last case Waldheim cited humanitarian considerations as the ground for his intervention. By so doing—and it appears to happen quite often—he mobilises the prestige of his office while dissociating his Organisation from action for which it has no authority or which it would find politically embarrassing. By the same tokens the States concerned usually have no desire for their contacts with Waldheim to be given publicity, so little is known about such matters. But there is no doubt about the pleasure it gives him that, "Many times, through personal intervention, I was able to save a human life, even free whole groups of people from persecution."[13]

V—PEACE-KEEPING

In exercising his good offices Waldheim has not overstepped the limits of acceptable action and has thus once again demonstrated his suitability for the job. This is, however, the type of activity on which surefootedness might be expected of him. Situations which are potentially much more difficult for a Secretary-General are those where the United Nations is involved in a bigger way. For then the Organisation's possible impact is correspondingly large, and the context within which it is operating is, almost by definition, of high political sensitivity. It is no coincidence that Waldheim's predecessors all ran into serious trouble on such matters. Trygve Lie became *persona non grata* with the Soviet Union over Korea; Hammarskjöld was subject to considerable abuse from the same source on account of the Congo operation; and many members lost confidence in Thant following his withdrawal of the United Nations Emergency Force from Egypt. Evidently peace-keeping is a graveyard for the reputations of Secretaries-General.

Under Waldheim there has, relatively speaking, been no shortage

---

[13] Waldheim, *op. cit.* in note 11 above, p. 1.

of such operations.[14] But they have not caused him to fall out
seriously with anyone. Partly this is the result of good fortune, in
that he has not been confronted with the type of situation which is
tailor-made for a Secretary-General's undoing. But on the other
hand it is definitely not the case that he has come through unscathed
because nothing more has been required of him than routine
administration. There have been numerous pitfalls along the way
which have been negotiated with considerable skill. Nor is it the
case that Waldheim has avoided dissension by failing to grasp
opportunities. For, although it appears hitherto not to have
attracted public comment, Waldheim has certainly been responsible
for a few telling moves and may reasonably be suspected of having
had a hand in several others. Thus he has lived up to the tradition
already set for his office in respect of peace-keeping operations
while also staying on good terms with his constituency. It would be
unreasonable to ask for more.

(a) *U.N. Truce Supervision Organisation (Untso)*

When Waldheim became Secretary-General Untso was playing
only a token role on the Israeli-Lebanese border on account of
Israel's lack of co-operation. However, in March 1972, following a
request from Lebanon, the Security Council asked him to increase
the number of observers on the Lebanese side. This was done,
accompanied by the establishment of three observation posts.
During the next six years the reports of these observers were made
public, thus sharpening the focus of the international community on
this increasingly-tense region.

It might be that Waldheim had some part in Lebanon's request
for the strengthening of Untso. Certainly he was responsible for the
continuation of the observer operation on the Israeli-Syrian front
after the October (or Yom Kippur) War of 1973. Untso had been
operational here prior to the War, but the cease-fire line which
emerged from it was not identical with the preceding one. On his
own initiative Waldheim entered into discussions with the parties
and, with their agreement, adjusted the observation arrangement to
the new situation. No one objected to his having done so.

Initially the United Nations had recourse to Untso to watch over
the 1973 cease-fire between Egypt and Israel, but this was
specifically called for by the Security Council on the basis of a joint
Soviet-American draft resolution. Perhaps he contributed to their
proposal. Be that as it may, it is very probable that he was intimately

---

[14] See this writer's "Recent Developments in U.N. Peace-Keeping," in this *Year Book*,
Vol. 31 (1977), pp. 75–97.

involved in the defusing of a potentially-hazardous situation which immediately developed. For it was at this juncture, when there was threatening Soviet talk about the need of the beleaguered Egyptian forces for help that, out of the blue, three dozen Soviet officers got off a plane at Cairo. Quickly and quietly they were integrated into Untso, the Americans hastening to bring their existing eight observers in the Organisation up to the same number. It was the Soviet Union's peace-keeping debut.

(b) *The Second U.N. Emergency Force (Unef II)*

As it turned out Untso was speedily replaced as the overseer of the Egyptian-Israeli cease-fire (although it continued to play a subordinate role). For on October 25, 1973, the Security Council set up Unef II. Waldheim immediately arranged to bring in some contingents from the United Nations force in Cyprus. Within 24 hours they were on their way and a provisional headquarters had been set up. This quick response is on the record, and gives Waldheim much satisfaction. What is not yet public knowledge, however, is the origin of the idea, put to the Council by its non-aligned members, that a United Nations Force should once again stand between Israel and Egypt. It might be that Waldheim had once again been at work behind the scenes.

Certainly he was responsible for a very important development which affected not only Unef II but also the later peace-keeping operations of the seventies. It concerned their financing. The refusal of some members, notably the Soviet Union and France, to help pay for the United Nations early operations led to a crisis for the whole Organisation in the mid-sixties. An accompanying consequence was that the operations established at that time were financed on a voluntary basis, which was highly unsatisfactory and continues to have serious repercussions. When, however, Waldheim, as asked, proposed terms of reference for Unef II, he included a paragraph stating that "the costs of the Force shall be considered as expenses of the Organisation to be borne by the members."[15] The whole report was adopted without debate.

Thus on paper the United Nations was back to a sound financial basis for its peace-keeping operations, and the credit for leading it there is Waldheim's. In practice things have not been quite as straightforward, as some members have refused to pay for all or part of the Organisation's peace-keeping expenses. But things are a lot better than they might have been.

---

[15] U.N. Document S/11052/Rev.1.

With the creation of the United Nations Disengagement Observer Force (Undof) for the Syrian-Israeli front in May 1974, Waldheim had little to do. The parties were brought to agreement through a round of Kissingerian diplomacy and the disengagement scheme was closely modelled on the one which he had secured earlier in the year between Egypt and Israel. Nonetheless, the Secretary-General made a valuable contribution to the pacification of the area by the smooth and efficient way in which Undof was set up and administered. As Kissinger himself came to realise, the United Nations was an exceedingly useful organisation to have on hand.

Something else for which Waldheim was not responsible—which for him was just as well—was the withdrawal of Unef II in July 1979. Angered by the Egyptian-Israeli peace treaty which had been signed in March, under which Unef II was to have important functions, the Soviet Union made it clear that she would veto its continuation. The matter was not taken to a public confrontation of this sort, and Unef II quietly expired. Waldheim did, however, manage to salvage something and thus add to his credit. For, having failed to get Israeli agreement to a continuing role in the area for the military observers of Untso (which would not have required a Council decision), he nonetheless ensured, by arrangement with Egypt, that Untso would continue to be represented there. In this way the United Nations maintains a token presence and is thus ready for immediate activity and expansion as the future demands.

(c) *The U.N. Force in Cyprus (Unficyp)*

The United Nations had sent a Force to Cyprus in 1964 in consequence of fighting between the two communities making up that State, the Greek Cypriots and the minority Turkish-Cypriots. Its task was to try to prevent further conflict and help to restore orderly and normal conditions. In the first of these tasks it proved very successful but the accompanying political talks made no real progress towards the solution of the basic problem. Then, in a double burst of fighting in July and August 1974, forces from Turkey took over the northern third of the country. It was during the first of these rounds that Waldheim made some bold moves regarding the control of Cyprus' main airport at Nicosia.

The Turks were most anxious to capture this prestige target and pushed to its perimeter fence. The United Nations Force thereupon spoke with the local commanders and persuaded them to let the United Nations take over the Airport which was declared a United-Nations protected area. The idea was that of Unficyp's Commander but received Waldheim's approval. Then, however, it emerged that the Turkish local commander was adjudged, by furious superiors, to have exceeded his authority. Fighting was resumed in the vicinity of the Airport and it looked as if the Turks intended to try to turn the United Nations out. Strong messages passed from the Secretary-General to Turkey, and the United Nations troops at the Airport were reinforced. Word was also passed along to the British, who held two bases on the island, and the Royal Air Force strength there was notably reinforced. Within 24 hours Turkey was announcing that without prejudice to her contention as to the legality of the United Nations presence at Nicosia Airport, she would not attempt to assume possession "by force . . . or other means of coercion."[16] In this manner Waldheim placed a very jaunty feather in the United Nations cap.[17]

The Secretary-General's response to the Cyprus crisis is also worthy of note in another and more general way. As has been indicated, Unficyp's mandate related to intercommunal tension and fighting within a single State. Now, in 1974, that State was effectively partitioned by Turkey, a clear line of division being established—the so-called Attila line. Thus Unficyp found itself in a quite different situation from that which had previously existed. Instead of an internal situation with international ramifications it was faced, *de facto*, with an international problem. One possible and perfectly legitimate response for Waldheim would have been to announce that the Force had no authority to operate in the new circumstances and ask the Security Council whether it wished to give Unficyp a new mandate.

The Council might well have responded positively but it was spared the necessity of having to try. For Waldheim simply carried on, securing the consent of the parties to an adjustment of the role of the United Nations peace-keepers to the new situation. In this way he effectively turned Unficyp from a law and order force, spread throughout the island, into a barrier force—one which interposed itself along and watched over the demarcation line between the two formerly-warring sides. It was, he said, a "pragmatic" response to ensure Unficyp's "effective functioning." A formal adjustment of its role would have to await "political negotiations."[18] No one took it upon themselves to complain about the Secretary-General's action. Nor has anyone tried, at the six-monthly renewal of Unficyp's life, to improve the correspondence

---

[16] XI *U.N. Monthly Chronicle*, Nr. 8 (August/September 1974), p. 32.

[17] For help with this paragraph I am indebted to Brigadier (retired) F.R. Henn who, at the time of the incident which it discusses, was Unficyp's Chief of Staff. See also, F.R. Henn, "Guidelines for Peacekeeping—Another View," *The British Army Review*, April, 1981. Brigadier Henn is preparing a book on his experiences in Cyprus.

[18] XI *U.N. Monthly Chronicle*, Nr. 9 (October 1974), p. 25.

between its mandate and the situation on the ground. Waldheim and his peace-keepers were awake. Sleeping dogs were allowed to lie.

(d) *The U.N. Interim Force in Lebanon (Unifil)*

Unifil is the third major peace-keeping operation to have been set up during Waldheim's incumbency. It was established in March 1978 following Israel's invasion of southern Lebanon and was intended to oversee an Israeli withdrawal and help the Lebanese Government to re-establish its authority in the area. Alas for such formal intentions! Israel did depart within a few months but left the border zone in control of Christian militias who, hand-in-glove with Israel, just refused to make way for the United Nations. To the immediate north of Unifil, and also in the area it occupies, were Palestinian guerrillas. Both groups were well armed, trigger-happy, and swashbuckling in their approach to life in general and the United Nations in particular. Further north again were various warring Lebanese groups and a Syrian army of occupation. In Beirut the so-called Government watched impotently over it all. Hammarskjöld is reported to have said of the Congo, "it isn't even anarchy."[19] One wonders what he would have felt about Lebanon.

Hammarskjöld rather rushed into the Congo. Having a better idea of what he would be faced with Waldheim did not encourage the idea of a United Nations force for Lebanon. But the major Powers saw it as a way of persuading Israel to get out of a situation which might otherwise have had very unhappy repercussions, and so the Security Council quickly gave its orders. The Secretary-General was ready for action and was then left to get on with administering the Force in a context which, in both military and diplomatic terms, was exceedingly frustrating and dangerous. Waldheim coped. This brought him little praise. But, more important, he avoided serious brickbats. He was fortunate, in that the situation neither polarised the Council's permanent members nor became critical on the ground. But he also made his own considerable contribution in the shape of patience and skill. Once again, therefore, he gave satisfaction.

VI—RESPONSE

To say that a man has given satisfaction does not have a very positive ring. It implies that a job had been done adequately; that there has been no cause for complaint. But it does not suggest that he has aroused much enthusiasm. This is in fact the sort of response

---

[19] A.L. Garshon, *The Last Days of Dag Hammarskjöld* (1963), p. 39.

which Waldheim elicited. Whether it is regarded as an acceptable level of performance depends on one's assessment of what can be achieved. Some feel that a United Nations Secretary-General should do better, usually citing Hammarskjöld as the criterion. One commentator, for example, discussing the "spectre of war" in the Middle East said (although he did go on to qualify it) that "A Hammarskjöld, one is tempted to think, would have intervened by now."[20] Such remarks fail to take sufficient account of the fact that although Hammarskjöld was a brilliant man he was able to take advantage of an unusual conjunction of circumstances.[21] It might be thought that at the official level there would be a greater understanding of the contextual limitations within which Waldheim had to operate, and greater appreciation of what he had done. But one rarely gets much by way of thanks from institutions. And after five years Waldheim found that the way to a second term of office—a reasonable expectation for a Secretary-General who has not blotted his copybook—was by no means free of obstacles.

Waldheim was quickly into the lists, announcing early in October 1976 that he would regard it as "a privilege and an honour"[22] to continue for a second term. However, Mexico responded by announcing that her about-to-retire President, Luis Echeverria, was also a candidate. His case was pushed hard, and was helped by the belief that China did not want the Secretary-Generalship to continue in European hands. Then the interest of the current President of the General Assembly, Shirley Amerasinghe of Sri Lanka, was announced, though he quickly added that he saw himself as a candidate only if the Council could not agree. Even then he would only let his name go forward it it "will be accepted by consensus and not put to a vote."[23]

In the event it was Waldheim versus Echeverria. The Mexican was behind on the first Security Council secret ballot, but Waldheim was at this stage vetoed by China. However, the veto was then dropped, Waldheim got the necessary majority in the Council, and in the Assembly was reappointed by acclamation.

It is very probable that most members thought it would be unreasonable to deny Waldheim a second term and that it was this,

---

[20] P. Calvocoressi, *The Sunday Times*, May 13, 1981.

[21] For this writer's views about the periodical controversies regarding the U.N. Secretary-General see note 4 above and "The Role of the Secretary-General of the United Nations in International Relations," 1 *International Relations* Nr. 12 (October 1959); "Neutral Men and Neutral Action," 2 *International Relations* Nr. 4 (October 1961); "The Soviet Troika Proposals," 17 *The World Today* Nr. 9 (September 1961) (reprinted in 3 *Survival* Nr. 6 (November-December 1961); and 'Why Dag's name no longer casts a spell," *The Times*, September 14, 1981.

[22] *London Weekly Summary* (U.N. Information Centre), W5/76/42.

[23] *The Times*, November 17, 1976.

rather than any more positive feeling, which resulted in his re-election. But it was also to be expected that by the end of his second term the general view would be that it was time for him to bow out gracefully. A change after 10 years might be thought to be desirable in principle. Waldheim had not exactly set the world alight. And after three Europeans and one Asian many would be thinking that a non-European in the job would be no bad thing.

However, no less so internationally than elsewhere, it is always rash to be too sure about the future. And as 1981 progressed the view gained ground that perhaps Waldheim should be kept on for an unprecedented third term. Without doubt part of this feeling stemmed from the problem of agreeing on another man, particularly at a time when relations between the major Powers had markedly deteriorated. Another part of it must have reflected the fact that although a West European (and a conservatively-minded one to boot), Waldheim had had considerable success in identifying himself very closely with the attitudes and policies regularly endorsed by the General Assembly. Even the invariable use of his academic title might have helped in the qualifications-minded Third World. (Hammarskjöld, no less a doctor, was always a mister.)

Additionally, however, there does seem to have been a change of attitude in recent years to the Secretary-Generalship of the United Nations. Increasingly States seem to have realised that to serve more than 150 masters is no easy task; that initiatives on the part of the Secretary-General which are both striking and generally acceptable are going to be uncommon; and that a good deal of his most fruitful activity will take place behind the scenes. What is needed, therefore, is a man who moves skilfully at this last level; who is willing, when necessary, to act on his own; but who recognises the limits within which he must operate and does not find them unduly frustrating. Thus in a sense the wheel has come full circle. For the first Secretary-General of the League of Nations, Sir Eric Drummond, was a man very much along these lines.[24] This is not to say that the wheel will now stand still. But at the end of 1981 the job specification was looking more and more like a call for a person in the Waldheim mould. Why then not Waldheim himself?

Ater 10 years it might have been expected that Waldheim would have been more than ready to step down. But this proved inaccurate. Hints that he was willing to carry on were dropped in the most discreet way but in the trade were instantly recognisable. Some

[24] See J. Barros, *Office Without Power. Secretary-General Sir Eric Drummond 1919–1933* (1979), *passim,* and especially pp. 397–402. See also the contribution by Barros in R. Jordan (ed.) *Dag Hammarskjöld Revisited: The U.N. Secretary-General as a Force in World Politics* (1982).

observers saw the publication of a selection of his speeches in book form,[25] in addition to the English version of *The Challenge of Peace*, as part of a campaign. And at a press conference prior to the opening of the 1981 General Assembly he came clean, announcing that if asked he would "consider it a duty and an honour to accept."[26]

VII—DÉNOUEMENT

But it was not to be. Both the United States and the Soviet Union gave Waldheim strong support, and France and the United Kingdom were also in his favour. But the Organisation of African Unity had already endorsed the candidature of Tanzania's Foreign Minister, Salim Salim, who received further backing not just from the Non-Aligned Movement but also from China. For six weeks it was a two-horse race, but neither was able to reach the finishing line. Waldheim was always ahead and in sight of the winning post, but throughout the Security Council's 16 secret ballots was consistently vetoed by China who, this time, stuck to her view that the next Secretary-General should come from the Third World. And in those ballots where Salim obtained the necessary minimum of nine Council votes he was regularly defeated by an American veto.

Early in December, therefore, Waldheim announced his withdrawal. A few days later Salim followed suit, having failed in a last effort to persuade the United States to lift her veto. Immediately there was a rush of nine Third World candidates to the starting line. Two then decided that the course was too formidable, but seven set off. Four were Spanish-speaking Latin Americans from Argentina, Colombia, Ecuador, and Peru; another from South America was the Guyanan Secretary-General of the Commonwealth; the sixth was from the Philippines (another Spanish-speaking country); and the seventh was the Iranian-born Sadruddin Aga Khan, former United Nations High Commissioner for Refugees. The last-named got the necessary nine votes but received a negative vote from one of the Council's permanent members. Five others did not even get the required numerical majority. But the remaining candidate cleared both hurdles and herefore received the Council's accolade. He was Javier Perez de Cuellar of Peru, a 61-year-old career diplomat who had also served for two years as the Secretary-General's Special Representative in Cyprus and for two further years in the United Nations Secretariat as Under-Secretary-General

---

[25] K. Waldheim, *Building the Future Order* (1980), ed. R. L. Schiffer.
[26] *The Times*, September 11, 1981.

for Special Political Affairs. His name was passed on to the General Assembly where it was approved by acclamation.

Waldheim, therefore, retired from the United Nations scene. But perhaps the most salient characteristic of Perez de Cuellar is that he is very much in the Waldheim mould. One newspaper reported that he was so anxious to avoid giving offence that he "is expected to be even less innovative"[27] than his predecessor. Another commented on his "conspicuous modesty" and his "grey, two-dimensional"[28] aspect. A third referred to his "self-effacing discretion."[29] It appears, therefore, that the Waldheim type of Secretary-Generalship will continue. This will be no bad thing for the United Nations. For, given the nature of the Organisation, people of the Waldheim and Perez de Cuellar sort are most likely to succeed at the head of its Secretariat. They may not have the thrust and flamboyance which some say the United Nations needs. But they are the most it can bear—while also having the experience to rise, if required, to the needs of the hour. In short, diplomats' diplomats.

WESTERN EUROPE AND JAPAN

By

WOLF MENDL

BEYOND stating the obvious, it seems far-fetched to suppose that the shared interests of Japan and the major States of Western Europe might lead to the establishment of a European-Japanese nexus, bringing a wholly new influence to bear on world politics. But then, few would have thought immediately after the October War that the Camp David agreement was a *realistic* prospect within five years. It is, indeed, hazardous to venture any guess about future configurations in a rapidly changing international system, just as it is foolish to rely on historical experience to be the only guide in policy-making.

The one thing it seems safe to predict is that the pace of change in the international scene will continue in the 1980s and may possibly accelerate. Consider a few of the outstanding events of the past decade alone: The American *rapprochement* with China, Egypt's switch into the Western camp, the succession of oil "crises" and their impact on the world economy, the Iranian and the wider Islamic revolutions, the Soviet occupation of Afghanistan. These changes are forcing a re-examination and readjustment of established concepts which provide the frame of reference for those charged with the task of making policy.[1]

It is against such a background that this essay attempts to examine whether European and Japanese interests, in spite of differences and conflicts between them, are converging and whether they might not form the basis for common policies and what shape such policies might take.

I—DIFFERENT ENVIRONMENTS

Western Europe and Japan are located at opposite ends of the Eurasian landmass. Western Europe is at least half a continent or—more precisely—of a continental peninsula, whereas Japan is a group of islands whose nearest point is more than 100 miles from the Asian mainland. The other geographical feature which sets them apart from each other is the great distance between them. It takes

---

[1] For an example of this kind of forced reappraisal of policy objectives, see M. Nacht, *The War in Vietnam: the Influence of Concepts on Policy* (ACIS Working Paper Nr. 26, Los Angeles, University of California, Centre for International and Strategic Affairs, July 1980).

longer to fly from Tokyo to Los Angeles than from Tokyo to London, but there is only water between Japan and the United States while there is a vast amount of land between Japan and Europe, divided among a host of States ranging in size and political importance from great powers to tiny principalities.

This brings one to the difference in their geo-strategic contexts. Europe is dominated by a bipolar alliance structure, with a few neutral States in between providing convenient meeting places for the interminable negotiations which seek to regulate this system. The cohesion of the two alliances may be more apparent than real, but each is dominated by a super-Power, though for somewhat different reasons. The West European States regard the American presence as essential for their security whereas the Soviet Union regards the East European States as essential for its security.

In East Asia there is a much more complex system of alliances. The Japanese-American security treaty imposes a limited liability on Japan; the United States has undertaken to come to the assistance of Japan if it is attacked, Japan does not have a reciprocal obligation except when American forces stationed within Japan are attacked by a third party.[2] The restraint on Japan's commitment stems from the provisions of the Japanese Constitution and strong resistance to any substantial change in Japan's post-war defence policy.[3] The United States has other bilateral security arrangements in the region, with South Korea and the Philippines, and a multilateral treaty with Australia and New Zealand—the ANZUS Pact. None of the Asian partners of the United States has an obligation to come to the aid of any other Asian State and thus there is no equivalent to the Atlantic Alliance.

In the past few years, however, there has been a noticeable trend towards bloc-building in East Asia. The Association of East Asian Nations (ASEAN), originally a loose economic grouping with an interest in establishing a regional order, has since the mid-1970s assumed an increasingly political character as a bloc of States opposed to a Vietnamese dominated group of States in Indochina.[4] While the United States, with the Vietnam experience fresh in mind, has kept discreetly in the background, China has stepped forward as the big friend of ASEAN, even though its friendship is

---

[2] Treaty of Mutual Co-operation and Security between the United States and Japan, January 19, 1960, Article V. Martin E. Weinstein, *Japan's Postwar Defence Policy, 1947–1968* (1971), pp. 139–41.

[3] Wolf Mendl, "The Japanese Constitution and Japan's Security Policy," 7 *Millennium: Journal of International Studies* (1978), pp. 36–51.

[4] Michael Leifer, *Conflict and Regional Order in South-East Asia* (London, The International Institute for Strategic Studies, 1980, Adelphi Paper No. 162).

suspect to at least some of the members. Through its Treaty of Friendship and Co–operation, the Soviet Union has an alliance with Vietnam but it has failed to overcome the resistance of the East European States to the inclusion of non-European States in the Warsaw Pact and its extension to military exigencies outside Europe.[5]

The drawing closer together of the United States and China; the sale by the Americans of military-related equipment to China; the Sino-Japanese Treaty of Peace and Friendship and the busy traffic of people and goods in both directions across the East China Sea; American and Chinese encouragement of greater Japanese defence efforts; all point to an emerging American-Chinese-Japanese alliance system.

Such, then, are the appearances in East Asia: A Soviet/ Indochinese/Mongolian alliance structure versus an American/ Chinese/Japanese/ASEAN/ANZUS alliance structure. But here again appearances obscure realities. Japan has some way to go psychologically and materially before it would be ready to enter into security commitments which extend beyond its national territory and the surrounding seas. The States of ASEAN are not agreed on what constitutes the major threat to their region. Depending on distance from Vietnam and the place of the overseas Chinese in their societies, some fear China more than Vietnam. In Korea, the potential flashpoint of the region, the Chinese find themselves uneasily alongside the Soviet Union in official support of North Korea, while the United States and Japan are lined up behind the South though not perhaps from an identical perspective. There is plenty of scope for crossed diplomacies on both sides of the dividing line, as illustrated by the informal contacts of South Koreans with Russians and Chinese, and unofficial Japanese interest in the North.

The European members of the Atlantic Alliance also have different perspectives of international problems from those of the United States and do not always agree among themselves, but they are grouped in an alliance structure more than 30 years old and formed at a time of a shared and acute perception of the Soviet threat. It will take a greater jolt than the Soviet invasion of Afghanistan to propel Asian States into a similar kind of alliance.

The historical and cultural context is a third factor of difference in the situation of Europe and Japan. The United States, after all, was a society spawned by Europe. It has developed a distinctive culture

---

[5] A. Ross Johnson, *The Warsaw Pact: Soviet Military Policy in Eastern Europe* (Santa Monica, Calif., The Rand Corporation, July 1981), p. 36. For the text of the Treaty between the Soviet Union and Vietnam, see XXI. *Survival* (1979), pp. 40–41.

over the centuries but it is still very closely bound to Europe. The cross-fertilisation of ideas, practices, and life-styles is intense, especially between the British Isles and the United States.

Japan, by contrast, can trace its association with the United States back to the middle of the last century. The relationship has passed through periods of warmth and periods of extreme hostility. However much the Japanese have admired and emulated the achievements of the United States and the "West" in general, their cultural home is in Asia and its sinic civilisation. Americans and Europeans, and they include Russians, are "outsiders." The Japanese have always regarded themselves as being rather special and separate from the rest of the world, but in their view of outsiders they have distinguished between those who are both physically and culturally their kinsmen and those, like Europeans, Indians, or Africans, with whom they have no such relationship.

To a large extent, the above comments must be regarded as a description of the past and one of the remarkable changes taking place today is the rapid obliteration of these kinds of distinction under the impact of mass communications and other technological features of our age. The younger people of Japan are more familiar with the ways of thinking and life-styles common to all advanced technological societies than with the traditional culture of East Asia. That does not mean that Japan has lost its unique social structures and the behavioural norms which flow from them. It is only that the Japanese now identify their political and economic system as being more Western than anything else. This, on the other hand, does not imply a lessening of the sense of national exclusivity. On the contrary, there are some signs that nationalist sentiment is on the increase with a corresponding desire to stress rather than minimise the *Japanese* "role" in the world.

The real differences between Japan and Western Europe that have been enumerated so far have to be set against equally real common features in their contemporary situation and outlook.

II—COMMON FEATURES AND SHARED INTERESTS

Both the West European States and Japan depend on the United States for their basic security against the Soviet Union. Without some tangible evidence of the American "guarantee" they would feel helpless and exposed to Soviet political and military pressures. The much maligned Finns have been remarkably successful in resisting absorption into the Soviet bloc and in retaining their own brand of liberal democracy during the past 36 years *without* any such guarantee, though no doubt they have benefited from the existence of a strong but neutral Sweden in their rear. However, the Finns would not deny that they have preserved their independence at the price of giving Soviet interests special consideration. Over the issue of Afghanistan, for instance, their hearts were surely on the side of the overwhelming majority of the United Nations which condemned the Soviet invasion, but they abstained when it came to voting.

This is precisely the situation that West Europeans and Japanese want to avoid. Hence the fear of "Finlandisation"—a concept which is both unjust and insulting to the Finns—in both regions. When the Japanese foreign minister reported to his colleagues that Mr Kosygin had suggested to him in the spring of 1977 that Soviet-Japanese relations should be modelled on those between the Soviet Union and Finland, his colleagues were reported to have been speechless with indignation.[6]

The sense of military impotence against the Soviet Union varies to some extent. The West Europeans might feel helpless in the face of overwhelming Soviet superiority in conventional arms but they do, at least, have indigenous nuclear deterrent forces. The credibility of the British and French deterrents—in spite of what the French might claim about the independence of their nuclear forces—rests on their role as "alternative centres of decision" which complicate the Russian calculus over the risks of a major nuclear conflict involving the United States. Without the American factor, the small nuclear forces in West Europe would hardly be credible as the decision to use them would amount to a decision to commit national suicide.

The Japanese have no nuclear weapons at their disposal but the Soviet military and naval threat is attenuated by the presence of American forces in Japan and the existence of a Chinese "deterrent." Furthermore, Soviet military dispositions in East Asia are primarily directed against China. In the last analysis, however, Soviet strategy in Asia is determined by perceptions of the relative importance of the European and East Asian theatres and the dangers of an American involvement on both fronts.

Europe and Japan, therefore, have a shared interest in making sure that the United States retains a presence in their respective regions as the ultimate deterrent against the Soviet Union. On the other hand, they have a strong common interest in maintaining if not friendly then at least businesslike relationships with it. The Americans can afford to regard the Soviet Union solely as a security problem and to adapt their policies accordingly. They consider economic co-operation with the Russians as a concession for détente and the good behaviour of the Soviet Union, a view related to the

---

[6] *The Guardian*, July 28, 1977.

doctrine of linkage as spelled out by Henry Kissinger.[7] Hence they have preferred short-term agreements, subject to renegotiation at regular intervals. It is easier to make an instrument of pressure or punishment out of the annual sale of grain than out of an arrangement for the supply of energy as a return on investment.

For the Europeans, however, economic co-operation is the consequence of détente. They have entered into it as a long-term commitment, as in the 25-year agreement for economic co-operation between West Germany and the Soviet Union, signed in May 1978. Co-operation over the exploitation and supply of sources of energy has been the crucial feature of the economic relations between East and West in Europe because of its strategic significance and the binding nature of such agreements. Within five years, from 1973 to 1978, the supply of Western capital goods for the development of energy resources in the Soviet Union increased fivefold.[8]

Already, substantial supplies of natural gas are being fed into the West European grid from the Soviet Union. The West, including Japan, is providing pipes and pumps for the transport of supplies from the Siberian fields to the European consumer.[9] On the other hand, Japanese interest in the development of the Soviet Far East is stagnant although there exist a number of co-operative ventures, mainly in the coal and timber industries and in the offshore prospecting for natural gas. The economic interest has been overtaken by interest in Chinese development which, too, is in the doldrums but is being pursued for long-term strategic reasons with active encouragement from the Japanese government.

Apart from purely economic motives such as need (natural gas for Europe, coal, lumber, and fishery resources for Japan) and the desire to beat one's competitors, there are political and strategic reasons for cultivating relations with the Soviet Union. They include interest in assisting Soviet economic development in order to increase the stability of Europe. Poland's troubles are due not only to the mismanagement of the Polish economy but to the inability of the Soviet Union to sustain it in the way in which the United States sustained the Western economies in the 1940s.

[7] Henry Kissinger, *The White House Years* (1979), pp. 129–130.

[8] Friedemann Müller, "Das Energieproblem der Sowjetunion," 36 *Europa Archiv* (1981), pp. 87–96.

[9] On June 3, 1981, it was announced that Japan's Export-Import Bank would provide credits to enable Japanese steelmakers to export large diameter steel tubes and compressors for the construction of a 4,300 km. pipeline to transport natural gas from Western Siberia to Western Europe. The decision was taken in response to pressure from business circles, alarmed that European competitors were capturing orders with the assistance of export credits from their governments. *The Japan Times Weekly*, June 6, 1981.

There is another argument that encourages collaboration because it might help to diminish the temptations of military adventures. If the West does not help the Russians to develop their enormous resources of oil and coal, which are found in remote regions subject to severe climatic conditions, then the Soviet Union will be tempted to gain control of Middle East oil. Furthermore, if the Russians are thrown largely on their own devices, they will be encouraged in continuing with their siege economy and relying on military power, the only strong card in their hands.

Against this, there is the view that economic aid to the Soviet Union, in whatever form, only helps in building up its military and strategic power and will not divert the attention of the leadership inwards. A society so tightly controlled and dominated by an aggressive totalitarian ideology will always give priority to defence and there are many indications that the Soviet Union is not content to catch up with the United States but aims to overtake it. This last is the prevailing opinion in the United States, although some economic interests run counter to it, as witness the pressures from the farmers of the prairie belt to ease the grain embargo. Europeans and Japanese, while fearful of Soviet military power, lean towards the former view. In Europe there is the added concern to avoid any destabilisation in the East European countries which would not only invite Soviet military intervention but greatly increase the tensions on the continent. The dangers of such a sequence of events are deemed to be so great that the Western countries, including Japan, supply food and massive credits to Poland.

On the whole, the American view is more detached. Physical distance from Russia and a global perspective incline the United States to seeing Western Europe and Japan as pieces, very important pieces indeed, on the chessboard of global power politics. China, Australia, Israel, Eygpt, South Africa, and the States of Latin America are also important pieces; all to be co-ordinated and moved in the game against the Soviet Union and its pieces. The States of Western Europe and Japan recognise the American perspective, but as regional Powers see their primary interest in maintaining a careful balance between the requirements of security and the need to live peacefully alongside the Soviet Union.

Because of their regionalism and their fear that conflict in distant parts may spread to their own neighbourhood through the application of the doctrine of linkage, Western Europe and Japan find themselves increasingly at cross-purposes with the United States in other parts of the world. In the Middle East they are moving towards recognition of the PLO and are exploring an alternative route to peace from the one charted at Camp David. In Central

America and the Caribbean there is a notable reluctance to support United States action over El Salvador and Cuba. The French have been most outspoken so far, but other governments share their view privately. The Japanese have been least in evidence but their rapidly expanding relations with Mexico may soon bring them into conflict with American policies in the region. Over Southern Africa there is growing disquiet that American support for the Republic of South Africa is playing into the hands of the extremists and undermining the more moderate and independent-minded régimes in the region.

In the Third World, therefore, we can trace another common interest to prevent super-Power rivalry from curtailing the independence and flexibility of States. This interest is complex because it has various roots. Anxiety about American policy in the Middle East stems from fears over oil supplies on which the Japanese and the continental European States are so much more dependent than the United States. This fear prompted the Japanese to move away from unconditional adherence to the American position at the time of the first "oil crisis" in 1973. Another element is the fear of being drawn into a conflict with the Russians in some remote part which will then have unwelcome repercussions nearer home. Trouble over Pakistan, for instance, leading to retaliation against West Berlin. Finally, there is the worry that the exacerbation of super-Power rivalry elsewhere in the world will distract American attention from Europe and East Asia. The despatch of a carrier task force from each of the Sixth and Seventh Fleets to the Indian Ocean and Gulf areas in January 1980 is an illustration of this point. To all these long-standing concerns must be added a European and Japanese reluctance to share the ideological fundamentalism of the present American Administration. Where President Reagan and his associates tend to divide States into the pro– and anti-communist camps, though for strategic reasons accept China as "pro-Western," the Europeans and Japanese prefer to see an infinite variety of *nuances* and shades, even among avowed communist States.

As a consequence of shared perceptions, the bases for European-Japanese co-operation seem to exist, but how sound are such foundations?

III—European-Japanese Relations

There are two great obstacles in the way of a fruitful development of relations between Japan and the countries of Western Europe: economic friction and cultural inhibitions. Both are more serious on the European side than on that of Japan.

Nothing need be said here about the problems of their economic relations. This is the only aspect of Euro-Japanese relations that receives any serious attention in the European press and is the subject of much scholarly attention.[10] Unless the friction can be overcome there is little prospect of any new development in the relationship between Europe and Japan. On the contrary, economic conflict will spill over into political conflict and may have a serious impact on Japan's current orientation towards the West. If there is anything the Japanese fear most, it is being isolated. Any hint of Europeans and Americans ganging up against them will set the Japanese to thinking about alternatives to their present associations.

The problem is that the main initiative for an improvement in the relationship must come from Japan. Various steps taken to rectify the trade imbalance have had little effect so far, appearing to Europeans (and Americans) as tardy and grudging responses to strong pressure from the beleaguered trading partners. Curbs on exports, import promotion, including the liberalisation of the import régime, and investment in European industries will not earn good will unless they are seen as positive and effective measures and not as reluctant concessions.

However sincere they may be in wanting to improve the unbalanced trade relations, the Japanese are handicapped by the poor image they have among Europeans generally. Attitudes to Japan vary widely from country to country and among interested groups within a country, but for most Europeans Japan is simply not on the politico-strategic horizon. When European statesmen and politicians urge Japan to do more for Western defence, they do so because they want to free American resources for use elsewhere, because it might divert more Soviet forces to the east, thus taking some pressure off Europe, and because in their hearts they hope that more defence spending will divert Japanese resources away from the export drive.

The eurocentric view of the world dies hard and is reinforced by American and Soviet emphases on the importance of Europe in the global balance of power. Hence there remains an underlying feeling that Japan is on the fringe of things. Strangely, Europeans are inclined to pay more attention to China and regard it as one of the world's major Powers; a view certainly not shared by the Chinese themselves nor warranted by China's economic development or military strength, in spite of a limited nuclear capability.

If the Europeans are inclined to be uninterested in or unfriendly to Japan, the same cannot be said the other way round. Since the middle of the last century the Japanese have looked to the West as a model and a source of inspiration. Even though they have surpassed

---

[10] See for example, L. Tsoukalis and M. White (eds.), *Japan and Western Europe: Conflict and Cooperation* (1982).

the Europeans in economic performance, they retain today a deep respect for European culture and civilisation. They have the added quality of being a very curious people, always willing to learn and adapt to changing circumstances. Their ethnocentrism is of a different kind.

Two and a half centuries of isolation and no experience of intensive inter-mingling with other peoples have left their mark on Japanese attitudes and thinking. One consequence has been a weak, if not wholly absent, element of universalism in their philosophical tradition. The isolation has long since broken down and today Japanese are to be found in every part of the world, but outsiders still find it difficult to penetrate Japanese society. Its homogeneity remains unbroken. While the European countries are becoming multiracial societies, there is no sign that Japan is moving in that direction. National traits, therefore, continue to be important inhibitory factors in Japan's relations with the outside world.

Europeans and Japanese must overcome such cultural and psychological barriers before they can develop an effective partnership. A growing familiarity with each other's cultures and the rise of a generation whose minds are uncluttered by the stereotypes and prejudices formed during the inter-war and Second World War years will facilitate this process. So will a convergence of political and strategic interests, once the worst economic friction is removed.

There is, however, a third and rather different obstacle to the development of closer relations between Western Europe and Japan. In terms of foreign policy, "Europe" hardly exists. One really has to talk of British, French, or German policy, and so on. The period of crisis which began with the seizure of American hostages in Iran (November 1979) and continued with the Soviet invasion of Afghanistan (December 24, 1979), saw an attempt to formulate a common European policy, to which Japan attached itself loosely. Since then, there have been European initiatives in the Middle East. But apart from that, the response of the West European States to particular events has been more often one of disarray than co-ordination. A particularly glaring example was the competition between President Giscard d'Estaing and Chancellor Schmidt in establishing a dialogue with the Russians in the spring of 1980.

For the Japanese, then, there have been few opportunities for a dialogue with "Europe" other than over the vexed issue of the bilateral trading relationship with EEC. Where there has been an attempt to formulate a response for the whole of EEC, as at the Luxembourg meeting in April 1980, which considered the crises affecting Iran and Afghanistan, it is significant that the Japanese were in attendance, if only in the ante-chamber. More recently, Japan has sought a closer co-ordination with the European Powers over policy towards Poland.

IV—EUROPE'S AND JAPAN'S CHOICES

The drift of world politics and especially the policies of the two super-Powers is towards the construction of two competing alliance systems. A similar drift occurred in the late 1940s and in the 1950s but was arrested; first, because of the emergence of the non-aligned movement in the mid-fifties and then by the emergence of new centres of influence and power which ushered in the period of so-called multi-polarity or polycentrism. Moreover, Soviet power in this earlier period was confined to the Eurasian landmass and could only be exercised effectively on the periphery of Russia's borders. The United States pursued a global policy of containment but was in practice the leader of a number of separate and isolated alliances.

The intervening period of the 1960s and 1970s created the conditions which have given a new dimension to the current phase of super-Power confrontation. The Soviet Union has achieved a rough strategic parity with the United States and has broken out of its periphery, acquiring client States in all the continents. The United States is no longer capable or willing to act as the world's sole "policeman." Its principal friends include one State, Japan, which is beginning to rival its economic power and another group of States linked in the European Community, which has the potential to become an economic and political giant.

In these circumstances, the two super-Powers have an interest in dragooning their friends into a solid phalanx of opposition against each other. Such a trend is potentially very dangerous because the logic of bipolar confrontation leads to a trial of strength which, under present conditions, would mean a contest for world domination—all the more serious because, unlike the period of the Cold War, the two principal contestants appear to be more or less evenly matched this time.

If this analysis is correct, one can envisage three possible responses by Europe and Japan. The first would be an unequivocal incorporation into a new bipolar system. The second would be a move in the opposite direction, marked by a gradual withdrawal from association with the United States into neutralist and third force policies. A third response, situated somewhere between the other two, might be the creation of strong buffer zones at the western and eastern extremities of the Soviet empire.

Judging from her public utterances, the first option of unequivocal association with the United States, could be described as the

Thatcher line. This is only logical if one accepts the current drift in world politics. Faced with a simple choice between the United States and the Soviet Union, Europeans and Japanese must throw in their lot with the Americans. Their value systems, their cultural and emotional ties with the United States, their global interests, their current policies, and their threat perceptions would dictate it.

The opposite course is not wholly unthinkable either. There are elements in Western Europe and Japan which have always opposed the American connection, only they would call it "domination." They are not confined to the communists and left-wing socialists of those countries. Indeed, Labour governments in Great Britain and socialist governments in France, especially since the inauguration of President Mitterand, have displayed greater enthusiasm for the Atlantic Alliance than their conservative opponents.

Gaullist-style nationalism, the partly open and partly hidden nationalism of the Japanese right, the nationalism of Enoch Powell and the populist little-Englander attitude of large sections of the Labour Party, German ambivalence stemming from a unique geo-political situation in the heart of Europe, are all potent forces which would loosen the ties with the United States, though their policies might be full of contradictions and irreconcilable objectives.

A general move away from the United States might take various forms. It could lead to the promotion of alternative structures, such as a West European bloc and a Sino-Japanese bloc, both of which are already in an embryonic state. The formation of a European-Japanese "alliance" is a less likely prospect for the reasons discussed above. On the other hand, a distancing from the United States might lead to strict neutralism of the kind previously practised by countries such as Switzerland and Sweden within the European system. Non-aligned policies, such as those practised by India under Nehru, might also have their appeal.

In between the response of incorporation into an American-led global alliance and the response of cutting loose from the United States, there lies the third response of creating buffer zones.

Martin Wight has described a buffer zone as "a region occupied by one or more weaker powers between two or more stronger powers."[11] While each of the stronger Powers has an interest in preventing such a zone from falling under the influence of the other(s), it will in turn seek to keep the zone neutral or, if it has the strength, try to extend its control over it.

Wight goes on to say that buffer States can be divided into "trimmers," "neutrals," and "satellites" and he defines as follows:

[11] Martin Wight, *Power Politics*, edited by Hedley Bull and Carsten Holbraad (1979), p. 160.

"Trimmers are states whose policy is prudently to play off their mighty neighbours against one another: the most famous of European trimmers was the Duchy of Savoy, which earned thereby first a kingdom and then the hegemony of United Italy; the neutralist states today are of their number. Neutral are states without an active foreign policy at all; their hope is to lie low and escape notice. Satellites are states whose foreign policy is controlled by another power."[12]

Wight's description of buffer zones and of the behaviour of States included in them would not necessarily apply to the pursuit of buffer zone policies by the West European States and Japan. They would not be trimmers because of their fundamental and positive allegiance to the "West." Nor would they be neutralist or non-aligned (a concept which Wight either did not know or chose to ignore) for the same reason. They would not be neutral because their foreign policies would be very active indeed and their size and general importance would hardly enable them to "lie low and escape notice." Nor could Japan and the major States of Western Europe be described as satellites by any stretch of the imagination. The unquestioned acceptance of American leadership in their foreign policies, if it ever existed, is a thing of the past.

The objectives behind the creation of buffer zones would be to provide for security against Soviet pressures and thus to retain some clearly defined link with the United States; to reassure the Soviet Union that the States of the zone would respect its security interests, harboured no aggressive designs and would not allow themselves to be used as a springboard for aggression; and to provide new openings for relations with the Third World which are presently bedevilled by super-Power rivalries.

The most difficult task would be to persuade the two super-Powers that such objectives are not against their interests and to devise the kind of measures that would give body to the idea and not leave it as an expression of empty aspirations.

The existing alliance structures limit both European and Japanese commitments and thus provide safeguards against their being involved in a global alliance, but the Americans would have to be convinced that European and Japanese policy initiatives and their refusal to take a rigidly confrontational attitude towards the Soviet Union would not undermine "Western" security. A continued American presence in Europe and East Asia seems essential but it might be reduced and less provocative (as seen by the Soviet Union), with clearly defined missions, although the regions must

---

[12] *Ibid.*

continue to be covered by the central strategic balance. Europeans and Japanese would, as a consequence, have to shoulder a greater responsibility for the security of their "zones."

The Russians would have to be convinced that the buffer zone was neither a threat nor an opportunity for infiltration and eventual domination. The burden of proof would rest with the States of the zones. As long as their societies are vigorous and cohesive communities there would be little opportunity for Soviet intervention. All the evidence of Soviet behaviour points to a great concern for Russia's security, caution in the use of military force, and a readiness to seize opportunities for expansion provided by a country's domestic problems. In the long run, effective economic and social policies are more important than military measures to ensure security against Soviet pressure. The Soviet 'threat" in Europe is greater when a country is bitterly divided against itself and when economic conditions create frustration and despair among large sections of society.

Independent and co-ordinated European and Japanese policies in the Third World would strike a responsive chord in many countries which resent the imperialism of the super-Powers and would welcome the opportunity to turn to third parties for assistance and support. Furthermore, such policies would help to arrest the process whereby every social and revolutionary upheaval in a developing country is turned into a zero-sum game between the super-Powers.

It is easier to envisage the emergence of a buffer zone in Europe, more difficult in East Asia where Japan by itself cannot constitute such a zone. Its creation with the inclusion of China, Korea, and ASEAN seems to be a remote possibility. However, events and developments in that region have moved so fast in the past decade that the idea may not be so fanciful after all.

V—Co-operation Between Europe and Japan

The preceding discussion has suggested that Western Europe and Japan, in spite of important differences, share several basic objectives: a continuation of the security relationship with the United States; a desire for a satisfactory *modus vivendi* with the Soviet Union; and a refusal to become entangled in the global rivalry of the super-Powers—indeed, a certain interest in preventing the spread of that rivalry into the Third World. How far can they be expected to co-ordinate their policies in pursuit of those shared objectives?

When considering the structures within which West European

and Japanese collaboration could be developed, there are several models from which to choose. One, the alliance model, has to be ruled out from the start for three reasons: first, there is the simple fact of geography; next, constitutional and political constraints within Japan make it impossible and undesirable; thirdly, we are far from the kind of unity in Western Europe which would make the concept of a European-Japanese "alliance" a feasible proposition.

Therefore, the association would have to take the form of some sort of procedures for consultations. It could be an institutionalised encounter between foreign ministers, interspersed with less frequent summit meetings. This would merely be an extension of the current bilateral meetings between Japan and the various European States. Alternatively, the consultation could follow the United Nations caucus model, making it a special feature at the annual meetings of the General Assembly. This would have the advantage of avoiding further pressures on the already crowded timetables of busy foreign ministers since they normally attend the General Assembly in the autumn. A different and more structured form of consultation would be the establishment of a small secretariat, similar to the Commonwealth or ASEAN secretariats, which would handle the machinery of consultation all the year round.

The great advantage of this last arrangement would be a more thorough and wide-ranging association than could be provided by very short periodic meetings of senior ministers. Such a secretariat would handle political, economic, and cultural business of common concern at lower levels on a day-to-day basis and develop a thickening web of contacts between Europe and Japan. One further benefit would be the opportunity for European and Japanese officials to become more familiar with each others outlook and methods of work. Cultural and linguistic barriers are still serious impediments to achieving the kind of easy intercourse that exists between Europeans and Americans.

In the economic field, the Europeans already have machinery which enables them to speak with one voice and it might be possible to relate it to a structure of Euro-Japanese consultation. It would be different in the political field where each state jealously guards its liberty. It is likely, therefore, that within a developing European-Japanese dialogue, Japan will find itself working more closely at the beginning with one of the West European States than with others.

The obvious candidate for this role would be the Federal Republic of Germany. The two countries have a great deal in common. Their historical background has interesting parallels; both have broken with their militaristic past and each has achieved phenomenal economic success in spite of very limited natural resources.[13] The potential for a convergence of German and Japanese interests has already won some recognition, as can be noticed from the visit of the Federal Minister of Defence, Herr Apel, to Japan in March 1980[14] and the meeting of Chancellor Schmidt and Mr. Ohira, following the funeral of Marshal Tito.[15]

Japan and the Federal Republic of Germany are the most important friends of the United States and have a particular interest in maintaining the security relationship with it. Because of their economic strength and growing influence in the world, the two countries are likely to seek a more independent role within this context. Both have compelling reasons for creating zones of stability and peace within their regions, which would serve to inhibit Soviet expansion and lay the foundations for good neighbourly relations with the Russians. Their geographical location makes them natural cores of buffer zones. German leadership in the pursuit of détente in Europe and Japanese ties with China and ASEAN may be the pointers to such a development.

---

[13] Arnulf Baring und Masamori Sase (eds.), *Zwei Zaghafte Riesen? Deutschland und Japan seit 1945* (1977).

[14] *Frankfurter Allgemeine Zeitung*, March 22, 25, 26, April 2, 1980; *Süddeutsche Zeitung*, March 25, 1980.

[15] *The Japan Times Weekly*, May 17, 1980.

THEATRE-NUCLEAR FORCES

By

PAUL BUTEUX

AMONG the more politically salient issues on the current agenda of the Atlantic Alliance are those flowing from the December 1979 decision to modernise the American long-range theatre nuclear forces (LRTNF) deployed in Western Europe in support of the North Atlantic Treaty Organisation (NATO). This decision, to deploy 108 *Pershing II* launchers in the Federal Republic of Germany and 464 ground-launched cruise missiles (GLCMs) in the Federal Republic, the United Kingdom, Italy and, with significant reservations, in the Netherlands and Belgium, was accompanied by further decisions to undertake a parallel arms control initiative concerning longer-range nuclear weapons in the European theatre and to reduce the NATO tactical nuclear stockpile by 1,000 warheads. These decisions were but the latest examples of alliance concern with the impact of technological, political and strategic change on its theatre nuclear arsenal. In one way or another, ever since the early 1970s the allies had been giving consideration to the possibility of modernising theatre nuclear forces, and a number of measures had been undertaken already. These included steps to increase the security of the weapons deployed in Europe; improvements in their command, contol and communications; and a trend, particularly among the short-range battlefield weapons, towards lower-yield warheads in order to reduce the collateral damage that would be associated with their use. Now, with the decision to deploy their new long-range theatre nuclear weapons, the allies were responding to what many saw as a particular threat to Western security: the development by the Soviet Union of the *Backfire* bomber and the SS–20 mobile Intermediate-Range Ballistic Missile (IRBM) which, together, considerably augmented Soviet "Euro-strategic" capabilities.

I—SHIFTS IN THE STRATEGIC BALANCE

The political and strategic context of these decisions was determined by widespread perceptions that adverse changes had occurred in the Alliance's strategic environment. Parity at the strategic level, together with shifts in the military balance in the European theatre, combined to challenge the premises on which the present strategic posture of the alliance is based. The military build-up of the Warsaw Pact in recent years led to suggestions that the alliance could no longer implement its declared strategy; improvements in the Warsaw Pact's conventional forces challenged the ability of NATO to offer a "stalwart" conventional defence, and improvements in the Soviet Union's theatre nuclear forces threatened NATO's own nuclear posture. The increase in the number and technical capability of Soviet battlefield nuclear weapons, when coupled with the deployment of new long-range "Eurostrategic" systems, has eliminated the basis for any alliance claim to superiority at the theatre nuclear level. As a result, there is concern that the Soviet Union is close to neutralising NATO's tactical nuclear options under the alliance strategic concept of flexible response.

The SS–20 has attracted particular attention since it gave the Soviet Union a significantly increased capability against targets throughout Western Europe. NATO references to the existence of the missile had appeared as early as 1975, and by 1977 the operational deployment of the new missile by the Soviet Union was believed to be imminent. It was in this year that the first formal alliance consideration was given to the possibility of a specific NATO response. At the May 1977, North Atlantic summit in London, agreement was reached on the need for a long term defence programme. Subsequently, in order to implement the programme, 10 areas were selected for special attention and task forces were established to deal with each one. Task Force 10 was concerned with theatre nuclear force modernisation, and the responsibility for developing proposals in this area was entrusted to the Nuclear Planning Group as the existing alliance body with special responsibilities for consultation on alliance nuclear policy.

In the ensuing debate which the resulting modernisation proposals generated, a great deal of attention has been given to the strategic rationale for the new deployments and to their implications for arms control and East-West relations generally. However, less attention has been given to the impact of the modernisation decision on the way in which the allies consult and seek agreement on questions of nuclear policy. In the past, when nuclear issues have become highly salient and controversial, quite apart from their political effect, they have had structural and institutional impact on the alliance system as well. Such has been the case with respect to LRTNF modernisation: the alliance has established new institutions to deal with it, and has modified the existing means for consultation on nuclear policy. In addition, it is clear that a degree of structural adaptation on the part of the alliance will take place if the institutional response is inadequate for dealing with the political stresses that theatre nuclear force modernisation has created.

II—Institutional Adaptation

The Nuclear Planning Group itself has its origins in an earlier period of alliance history in which nuclear issues were also prominent, between the launching of "Sputnik" by the Soviet Union in 1957 and the adoption by the NATO Council of flexible response in 1967. Then, as now, a combination of technological, strategic and political factors undermined the existing alliance consensus on nuclear policy, and seemed to many to threaten the foundations of the American nuclear guarantee. Again—then as now—there was concern that from the perspective of NATO adverse changes in the strategic balance had taken place. Among the resulting changes that took place in the alliance, clearly one of the most significant was the withdrawal of France, in dissent from the direction of American policy, from the integrated military commands. There was also, however, a more general allied concern with American policy, and this had found expression in demands for a greater say in the determination of the nuclear strategy of the alliance. Originally, this led to a series of "hardware" proposals by which the allies sought greater control over nuclear weapons through some means of nuclear sharing. The last of these proposals to receive any considerable alliance attention was the American plan for a multilateral force (MLF) of *Polaris* missiles to be mounted on surface ships which would be jointly manned, owned and controlled by those allies wishing to participate. The collapse of this scheme, which attracted a considerable degree of allied attention between 1963 and 1965, opened the way for an alternative approach to the problem of associating the allies with nuclear policy: that of improving, through institutional innovation and the greater exchange of information, the degree of consultation that took place between the United States and its allies on nuclear issues.[1]

A Special Committee on Defence Ministers was set up under the chairmanship of Robert McNamara to examine ways in which consultation on the possible use of nuclear weapons might be improved and the participation of interest allies in the process of nuclear planning might be extended. The recommendations of the Special Committee led to the creation in December 1966 of two new

---

[1] For accounts of the alliance debate on nuclear strategy in this period, see H.A. Kissinger, *The Troubled Partnership* (1965); J.L. Richardson, *Germany and the Atlantic Alliance* (1966); R. Hunter, *Security in Europe* (revised edition), (1972). An excellent account of the MLF proposal is to be found in J.D. Steinbrunner, *The Cybernetic Theory of Decision* (1974).

alliance bodies at the ministerial level: a Nuclear Defence Affairs Committee (NDAC) and, nominally subordinate to it, a Nuclear Planning Group (NPG). The NDAC was to act as a plenary body for all the allies interested in greater consultation on nuclear planning and policy-making, and would receive reports from the Nuclear Planning Group (NPG).

The United Kingdom, the Federal Republic of Germany, Italy and the United States were to be permanent members of the NPG, and three or four members of the NDAC would serve in rotation. As originally constituted, all members of the alliance with the exceptions of France, Iceland and Luxembourg were members of the NDAC, but until the June 1980 meeting of the NPG in Bodö in Norway, Portugal never attended a full ministerial meeting of the Group. From virtually the beginning of its existence, the NDAC was redundant, serving only to act as a "rubber-stamp" for papers generated by the NPG which, in any case, went to full meetings of the Defence Planning Committee. With the development of the Staff Group, drawn from the permanent delegations of all the allies participating in the NPG, the NDAC simply served to identify those allies wishing to take part in some way in the process of nuclear consultation; it served no consultative purpose itself. Although never formally dissolved, today, with the ending of rotation and the full participation of all the allies with the exception of France and Iceland, the NDAC has to all intents and purposes ceased to function as a distinct alliance body.[2]

In the late 1960s, as American strategic planning became more and more affected by the doctrine of mutual assured destruction, and as military planning in Europe reflected the concept of flexible response, a degree of strategic disconnection occurred between the strategy governing the central deterrent forces of the United States and that governing NATO forces in Europe. Although American spokesmen pointed out that mutual assured destruction was essentially a planning tool for determining strategic force requirements; nonetheless, towards the end of the McNamara era, American posture statements were more concerned with spelling-out the basis of second-strike effectiveness in approaching conditions of parity than they were with demonstrating how an extended deterrent commitment was to be maintained under the same circumstances. As a result, questions concerning the role of theatre nuclear weapons in alliance strategy became more insistent and,

---

[2] Apart from general references in NATO literature, little has been written about the Nuclear Planning Group. My own book-length study is forthcoming. A still useful description of the NPG can be found in Robert M. Krone, "NATO Nuclear Policy-Making," in J.P. Lovell and P.S. Kronenberg (eds.), *New Civil-Military Relations* (1974), pp. 193–228.

somewhat ironically in view of McNamara's earlier scepticism concerning the value of such weapons, the place of theatre nuclear weapons in the overall strategic posture of the alliance became more prominent. Thus, from the beginning of its existence, consultation about the strategy governing the alliance's theatre nuclear forces, and about the conditions and circumstances that might govern their use, became a central preoccupation of the Nuclear Planning Group. In consequence it was natural that the NPG should be charged with examining the role of theatre nuclear forces in NATO strategy within the context of the long term defence programme.

III—THE HLG AND SCG

At American urging, the Nuclear Planning Group departed from its previous practice and set up a "High Level Group" of senior officials primarily drawn from the Defence ministries of the various allies taking part. Representation on the new body was at a level senior to that usually found in NPG meetings at the Staff Group level, and it was hoped by this means to give it an urgency and authority that it might not have otherwise. Authorisation for the creation of the High Level Group (HLG) was given in October 1977 at the Bari ministerial meeting of the NPG where, in addition to examining the role of theatre nuclear forces in NATO strategy, it was given the task also of examining the implications of recent Soviet theatre nuclear force deployments, the need for NATO theatre nuclear force modernisation, and the technical, military and political implications of alternative NATO theatre nuclear force postures.[3]

From the beginning of its work, the HLG concerned itself almost exclusively with the broad question of LRTNF modernisation and, after undertaking a general survey of the implications of new technologies for theatre nuclear weapons, immediately became concerned with the possibilities and implications of introducing a modernised force of long-range weapons into the alliance's nuclear arsenal. Eighteen months later, in April 1979, the High Level Group was in a position to report to the full NPG at Homestead Air Force Base in Florida on the guidelines that should govern any decision to deploy new longer range nuclear forces in the European theatre.[4] By now, the United States, as well as the United Kingdom

---

[3] North Atlantic Assembly: Military Committee. *General Report on the Security of the Alliance: The Role of Nuclear Weapons*. (K.G. de Vries; Rapporteur), October 1979.

[4] *The Modernization of NATO's Long-Range Theatre Nuclear Forces*. Report prepared for the Subcommittee on Europe and the Middle East of the Committee on Foreign Affairs, U.S. House of Representatives, by the Foreign Affairs and National Defense Division, Congressional Research Service, Library of Congress, December 31, 1980. p. 20.

and the Federal Republic of Germany, were pushing for a decision by the end of the year, and to this end the HLG was instructed to prepare a further report containing specific proposals concerning the composition of any modernised force of LRTNF that the alliance might deploy.

The imminence of a positive decision of modernisation had the effect of focusing wide-ranging doubts and uncertainties among the European allies about the consequences of deploying new theatre nuclear weapons in Europe. Not only was there substantial opposition in a number of allied countries (which already had found expression in the revival of unilateralist and neutralist sentiment that accompanied the "neutron bomb" debate in the spring of 1978), but there were concerns also that LRTNF modernisation alone might exacerbate the nuclear arms race in Europe and lead to no net gain in allied security. Consequently, the Germans, who had done more than any other ally to raise the LRTNF question in the first place, proposed that the alliance establish a "Special Group" to examine the possibilities of arms control in this area and to study the arms implications of any modernisation proposal. The Special Group was to work in parallel with the High Level Group and was to produce a report outlining the basis for an arms control initiative that could be undertaken along with a decision on LRTNF modernisation.

Hence the "dual track" nature of the December 1979 decisions on modernisation, and hence also the decision to continue the existence of the Special Group in the form of the Special Consultative Group (SCG). The purpose of the Special Consultative Group was to produce follow-up studies based on its report to the Special Meeting of Foreign and Defence Ministers, but it was also understood that a further task of the SCG would be to act as a potential conduit between the United States and its allies once bilateral negotiations with the Soviet Union involving theatre nuclear weapons got under way. It had been assumed when the Special Group was preparing its report that these would take place within the framework of the future SALT negotiations. The failure of the Carter Administration to secure the ratification of the SALT II treaty and the policy of its successor in seeking revisions to it confounded the premises on which a number of allied governments had accepted the modernisation package. In the view of some representatives of the non-nuclear allies, ratification of SALT II had been a condition of their acceptance of the LRTNF deployments.[5]

---

[5] See *Western Security Issues: European Perspectives*; testimony of European representatives to the North Atlantic Assembly before the Subcommittees on International Security and Scientific Affairs and on Europe and the Middle East of the Committee of Foreign Affairs, House of Representatives, September 12, 1979, pp. 3–33.

Certainly, by itself, the December 1979 decisions in no way disposed of the question of LRTNF modernisation or of the issues underlying it, and the uncertainties over the future of SALT did nothing subsequently to make the implementation of the modernisation decision any easier. Anyway, some indication of how the SCG might function as a means of expressing allied interests in any arms control negotiations involving theatre nuclear weapons can be found in the way in the SCG has monitored the Soviet-American contacts established in Geneva in the fall of 1980 on the subject of theatre nuclear force arms control.

Along with the reconstitution of the Special Group as the Special Consultative Group, it was also decided that the High Level Group should continue in being in order to examine the impact of the new deployments on the balance of roles and systems in NATO's nuclear armoury as a whole. Although the two bodies had been charged with essentially technical tasks, together they have also served the political function of helping build and sustain an alliance consensus sufficient to allow implementation of the modernisation decision to take place. Like the circumstances in which the Nuclear Planning Group was originally created, consultation has again become a primary means by which the allies attempt to reconcile their differences over nuclear policy and maintain a degree of cohesion sufficient for their political purposes. However, unlike the earlier period when the allies of the United States sought greater access to and influence on American strategic policy, now they seek an effective voice in American arms control policy too. This, in turn, arises from attempts by the Americans to reconcile the conditions under which their extended deterrent commitment operates in Europe with the changing strategic balance.

IV—REVISIONS IN STRATEGIC DOCTRINE

The explicit recognition of strategic parity in the first SALT agreements in 1972 underscored the fact that the United States could no longer base its extended deterrent commitment to Europe on the supposed superiority of its strategic forces. With the subsequent disappearance of any plausible claim to theatre nuclear superiority on the part of NATO as well, it also became clear that the American strategic commitment could not be based on theatre superiority either. As a consequence, the disconnection that emerged during the 1960s between the strategy governing theatre nuclear weapons and the central strategic forces of the United States became a serious impediment to the continued credibility of the alliance's strategic posture; and, as on the earlier occasion when alliance strategy and strategic reality became sufficiently disjoined to threaten the military basis of allied security, so the United States has initiated changes in strategic doctrine. One purpose of the revised strategic targeting instructions contained in Carter's Presidential Directive 59 and what Secretary of Defense Brown called the "countervailing strategy" has been to strengthen the connection between the concepts governing strategic and theatre nuclear weapons. By increasing the targeting flexibility of United States strategic forces, the revised American strategy hopes to strengthen deterrence against less than all-out attacks on either the United States or its allies, and by so doing restore the escalatory link between theatre and strategic nuclear forces.

The revised doctrine gives far greater attention to the problems of extended deterrence than had been the case under assured destruction, and it is in how the new targeting arrangements reinforce the extended deterrent commitment that the implications for Western Europe of the revised doctrine lie. Even without offering a full exposition of the countervailing strategy and the objectives of P.D. 59, it is clear that much greater flexibility and capacity for sustained operations is being sought from strategic forces.[6] This objective has been complicated, however, by the perception that existing trends in the Soviet-American strategic balance threaten the integrity of American land-based missile forces. Hence, there is the urgency being given to the MX missile programme and, more generally, to the upgrading of other elements in the United States strategic triad by means of the ALCM and Trident.

Strictly speaking, the proposed LRTNF deployments should be seen as a separate if parallel development to that occurring with respect to strategic forces. On the other hand, although they will not be integrated into the "Single Integrated Operations Plan" (SIOP) of the American Joint Chiefs of Staff, but will be targeted in accordance with SACEUR's general strike plan, they nonetheless add to the range of choice available to an American President in the event of nuclear escalation in Europe. They provide a capability that is intermediate between battlefield and strategic weapons, and increase the threat to Soviet targets provided by "grey-area" theatre nuclear forces. Any contribution LRTNF make to effective deterrence in Europe will continue to rest, however, ultimately on their link with American strategic weapons, for the scale of the planned

---

[6] A clear statement of the "countervailing strategy" and its relationship to P.D. 59 can be found in the *Report of the Secretary of Defense, Harold Brown, to the Congress on the FY 1982 Budget, FY 1983 Authorization Request and FY 1982–1986* Defense Programs, January 19, 1981, pp. 38–45. See also, W. Slocombe, "The Countervailing Strategy", *International Security*, 5, 4, Spring 1981, pp. 18–27.

deployments is not sufficient to establish any autonomous "Euro-strategic" balance. Nevertheless, the planned deployments will create the possibility of an additional threshold between theatre and strategic nuclear weapons. In essence, the countervailing strategy attempts to extend the ideas of flexible response more fully into American strategic targeting options; but, in turn, it should be noted also that the deployment of modernised LRTNF makes possible the implementation of a countervailing strategy at the theatre level.

The shifts in the strategic balance, and the recognition of these shifts in United States strategic thinking, have had their impact on the theatre balance as well. A state of affairs considered satisfactory under one set of strategic conditions may no longer be considered so when those conditions change. A lot of the pressure since the early 1970s for theatre force modernisation can be seen in this light. As deterrence in Europe has come to rest increasingly on the plausibility of invoking flexible options at the theatre level, then in American eyes at least the adequacy of the alliance's theatre nuclear forces has been called into question. In the past, the Americans, by and large, have justified the threat to escalate in terms of securing some kind of military or bargaining advantage. Even though this advantage might be temporary only, it would, in their view, increase the chance of exercising some kind of control over the conflict and allow for the possibility of crisis-management after hostilities had occurred. However, in the present situation it is difficult to see any process of escalation operating to the alliance's advantage.

In contrast, European attitudes have tended to see the threat of escalation as increasing the risk of a general nuclear war which would be disastrous for everyone, and which it is assumed the Soviet Union would wish to avoid as much as anyone else. The presence of nuclear weapons in the alliance, together with the possession of an escalation doctrine governing their use, creates a risk of such unacceptable escalation. In effect, the Europeans and the Americans have two different interpretations of flexible response, but it is now doubtful how much longer the Europeans can credibly insist on their preferred interpretation. Not ony is it increasingly unlikely that escalation would work to the alliance's advantage, but there is a clear American interest in controlling such escalation before it reaches the stage of a strategic exchange. Inevitably the "gap" between theatre and strategic forces has widened, and the proposed deployment of modernised LRTNF is but a symptom of this fact. Thus fears have been raised both in Western Europe and elsewhere that the new LRTNF will "decouple" European securiy for American strategic forces. But it is not so much that these forces are themselves "decoupling" in effect, as that decoupling has already occurred and that their deployment is a means of maintaining some degree of extended American strategic commitment to Europe in circumstances in which the original basis of the commitment has been undermined.

In some sense, the application of the countervailing strategy to Western Europe would conform to the existing alliance consensus about the meaning of flexible response. The United States and the European allies can agree that the purpose of the alliance's military posture should be to convince the adversary that there is no prospect of victory at whatever the level of conflict. However, on those points on which the United States and its allies differ, the deployment of modernised LRTNF will make it easier for the United States to insist upon its own interpretation of flexible response. Other changes in the theatre nuclear arsenal that have occurred since the early 1970s have also had the same effect by increasing the ability of the United States to exercise control over the release and use of the NATO nuclear arsenal in a more discriminating fashion. These changes in themselves are not something to which the European allies are hostile, but, like the deployment of LRTNF, they do provide the United States with additional barriers to escalation to the strategic level. In the event of a nuclear war being fought in Europe, there is an increased possibility of the United States being able to conduct it without recourse to its strategic arsenal. It is this prospect of the alliance's deterrent posture resting increasingly on the ability to conduct a nuclear war in Europe that the European allies find so disturbing. The decision of the Reagan Administration to go one step farther than that of its predecessor and go ahead with the manufacture and stockpiling of enhanced radiation weapons (the "neutron bomb") simply confirms for many what is seen as a trend towards a nuclear war-fighting posture on the part of the United States.

It should be noted that, as such, the countervailing strategy is one that has been developed to govern the strategic forces of the United States, and no formal attempt has been made yet to seek formal revisions in alliance strategy. Nevertheless, the cumulative effect of changes in the theatre arsenal and in United States strategic doctrine has been to bring about *de facto* changes in NATO's strategic posture. Whether or not formal revisions in MC 14/3 (the basic Military Committee document on flexible response) are sought, the political impact on the shift in the alliance's nuclear posture is already apparent. Nuclear issues are far more salient than they have been in the alliance for many years and raise questions as to how successfully and in what ways the alliance will adapt to this situation.

V—The Limits of Consultation

As already indicated, one familiar means has already emerged: namely, the attempt to ensure adequate consultation through institutional innovation. The High Level Group and the Special Consultative Group both represent institutional responses to the problems created for the alliance as a whole, and for individual allies in particular, by LRTNF modernisation. In immediate terms, this institutional adaptation was successful. A modernisation package was agreed along with the associated arms control proposal, and follow-up consultation and planning has taken place. That the allies have been able to take decisions in this field is testimony to the effectiveness of consultation as practised in the alliance. On the other hand, given the degree of domestic opposition that has been aroused in many NATO countries, as well as the strength of the diplomatic and propaganda campaign that the Soviet Union has mounted against the alliance's LRTNF plans, doubts must arise as to whether the proposed deployments will in fact take place. The alliance consensus that underlay the modernisation decision was a fragile one, and it will require skilful and sympathetic alliance diplomacy if it is to be maintained.

In fact, the December 1979 decision and the consultative mechanisms by which it was brought about, illustrate an important political point about the processes of consultation in the alliance on such politically sensitive issues as those surrounding nuclear weapons. This is that it is far easier to secure agreement on the technical requirements of alliance security at the official level, or, indeed, at the level of defence ministers in a specialised forum such as the Nuclear Planning Group, than it is to implement these decisions within the context of broader political considerations. The continuing debate and doubts about the LRTNF decision demonstrate something of the limits of consultation as a means of dealing with contentious issues of alliance policy.

However effective they may be at one level of alliance interaction, by themselves, such elaborations of alliance consultative mechanisms as the High Level Group and Special Consultative Group are inadequate to the task of maintaining a politically effective alliance consensus on nuclear policy. Within the context of the changed strategic environment, and on the basis of the earlier alliance experience under conditions of strategic change, further adaptations in the pattern of alliance relationships can be expected. The changes in the theatre nuclear arsenal that have already occurred, and the changes planned in connection with the decision to deploy modernised LRTNF, represent, in their way, adaptations as well. Until the question of the deployment of enhanced radiation weapons arose, these changes had been relatively non-controversial. This was partly due to the fact that the changes were evolutionary and, in themselves, had little impact on the character of the nuclear arsenal, and partly because, for these reasons, the change attracted little political attention. The "neutron bomb" issue, and now the decision on LRTNF, have had the effect of dramatising the cumulative impact of the modernisation that has already been undertaken and of highlighting the implications of further changes. More importantly, the issue of theatre nuclear force modernisation has sensitised the allies at the highest levels to the political implications of the strategic changes that have been taking place.

In the past, one important function of the strategic doctrine governing theatre nuclear weapons has been to reconcile the different interests of the allies with the particular military posture that the alliance adopted. It has also served to provide a rationale for the purpose and military function of theatre nuclear forces. Now, the changes in the nuclear arsenal not only reflect changes in the strategic environment which call into question the previously accepted rationale for theatre nuclear forces, but themselves challenge accepted alliance strategic doctrine. It is not so much that the concept of flexible response no longer has validity, as that the means for implementing it are changing, and that it can no longer hold out for the alliance the prospect of some kind of diplomatic and crisis bargaining leverage as when it rested on a notion of NATO theatre nuclear superiority. Instead, under conditions of parity, the function of theatre nuclear forces becomes that of denying the possibility of bargaining advantage to the adversary. What is required in order to achieve this goal has become a source of allied differences: whether it is necessary that the posture should be based on a war-fighting capability, or whether nuclear weapons should be seen as enhancing deterrence by the very risk of escalation that their presence generates.

Even if it is accepted that an unmodernised arsenal in conditions of parity has a reduced deterrent credibility, allied differences can asise over what is necessary to restore deterrence sufficiently for perceived political and security needs. In the case of the planned modernisation of LRTNF, the numbers and planned deployments represent a compromise between the view that these weapons should have a clear military purpose which in turn would strengthen deterrence, and those who see any deterrent value they possess as resting simply on their countering Soviet systems for which otherwise the alliance would have no equivalent.

It is differences such as these that must be accommodated within the framework of flexible response. On the basis of past experience, the extent to which the concept will continue to function effectively in its present or some modified form can be seen also as a function of structural and political development in the alliance. In the end, flexible response became accepted as the basic strategic concept informing the nuclear posture of the alliance after France withdrew from the integrated command structure. The French action, both in itself, and in its consequences for alliance functioning, constituted a major structural change in NATO. French interests and aspirations, which of course went beyond differences with the Americans over nuclear strategy, in the end could not be accommodated within the existing alliance structure. By the same token, the acceptance by the other allies of a revised alliance strategy was made possible by the structural changes brought about by the French actions. The question thus arises of what kinds of structural change might the alliance undergo in response to current tensions over nuclear weapons.

VI—The Implications of Modernisation

One possibility, to which German policy has been particularly sensitive, is that the allies may break ranks over modernisation. From the initial states of allied consideration of the question, the Germans insisted that any decision be unanimous and that deployment be shared by other countries involved on the Central Front. A major factor behind these concerns was the fear that if deployment was not shared by other continental allies, Germany might be singled-out as having a special status in connection with LRTNF. This would be incompatible with a long standing German policy, for not only would it run counter to Germany's broader security objectives, but would imperil the Federal Republic's relationship with the Soviet Union. Germany was also concerned, however, that there not appear two classes of ally as a result of modernisation: those that were in some way associated with LRTNF and those that were not. The fact that a small percentage of the costs of the modernisation programme is to be borne by infrastructure funds is symbolic of this concern.

There have always been different classes of ally in terms of their relationship to nuclear weapons. There are those like France and the United Kingdom who possess their own nuclear forces; others who are prepared to host nuclear forces and who, in some cases, have nuclear-capable forces of their own, and still others, like the Norwegians and the Danes, who will not accept nuclear weapons on their territory in peacetime. Nevertheless, all accept that the military posture of the alliance is based on nuclear weapons and, with the exception of France, all currently pay lip-service to the strategy underlying that nuclear posture.

As it happened, some of the allies were extremely reluctant to go along with the December 1979 decision, and a failure on the part of a number of the allies to carry through with it would not simply undermine the basis of that decision, but would also reveal the break-up of the alliance's strategic consensus. One result might be, despite the intentions of German policy, the *de facto* emergence of a two-tier alliance with respect to nuclear weapons. One tier would consist of those allies that supported modernisation and the strategy that governed it; the other tier, those that did not. If a development of this kind were to come about, then it would be expected that attitudes towards LRTNF would spill-over and affect policies towards theatre nuclear weapons generally (again, European reactions to the American decision to produce enhanced radiation weapons illustrate this point), and one might see the development of a nuclear and non-nuclear alliance, but still within the framework of NATO. For example, the recent revival of interest in Scandinavia in a Nordic nuclear free zone is perhaps a straw in the wind. The LRTNF issue has thus placed additional stress on a consensus that already has been challenged by strategic change. It is for this reason that looking beyond the basically pragmatic rationale that has been provided by offical spokesmen for the new deployments, it can be appreciated that the LRTNF decision has a significance beyond any military or, indeed, any particular strategic purposes that modernised LRTNF might serve.

In addition to showing a marked capacity for institutional adaptation, NATO has shown over the years a considerable ability to make political adjustments. If it turns out that modernised LRTNF cannot be accommodated within the existing strategic consensus, then it can be expected that a search for some other formula will be mounted. As in the past, this will be conditioned by political considerations that extend beyond a narrow interpretation of the conditions of allied security. Given the impact of parity, one can expect that the allies will link any revised strategic posture with alternative approaches to the problem of European security. Arms control is seen by many as one such means, and the parallel arms control proposal that was adopted as part of the December 1979 package was a crucial element in securing allied agreement to LRTNF modernisation. But the prospects for successful arms control in this area are at best unclear, and the linkage of arms control and modernisation may, in the end, turn out to have negative consequences. Given the fragility of the consensus on which the modernisation decision was based, rather than strengthening alliance resolve to push ahead with modernisation, failure to make progress on the arms control side may make actual deployment more difficult. The Soviet Union, through its own response to the NATO initiative on LRTNF arms control, is in a good position to affect allied policies on modernisation.

The strategic changes of the 1960s were accompanied by a formal alliance commitment to détente, and the normalisation of East-West relations that flowed from that commitment can be understood as a political response to a situation in which security had been affected by military and strategic change. Similarly, today, the course of East-West relations is also bound-up with changes in these areas; though, clearly, the political context of security in contemporary Europe is affected by more than perceived shifts in the military balance. Perceptions of security and views of what constitutes an appropriate security policy, are affected by actions and events independently of the military balance. For example, allied differences over the security implications of events in Afghanistan and Poland were more immediate in their political impact than was the decision to modernise LRTNF. The consequences of the LRTNF decision on the structure of European security will be, then, the result of an interaction between political, strategic and military factors.

The greatest scope for autonomous action on the part of the European allies lies in the political realm, and it can be expected that they will continue to expand this area of autonomy. Not the least of the diplomatic challenges facing the alliance in connection with TNF modernisation is that of limiting allied differences over détente. If Western Europe and the United States move too far apart on the question of relations with the Soviet Union then modernisation will be in jeopardy. One very important reason why this will be so, is that the deployment of new LRTNF will reinforce further American dominance of NATO strategy. The new deployments highlight the tensions in an alliance in which the European members are insistent on their own automony while strategic developments reinforce their military dependence of the United States. The renewed interest in some kind of European defence identity is a sympton of these tensions, as is the increased political significance of French and British nuclear forces. The political conditions for a European nuclear force may not exist, but from the perspectives of Western Europe, at least the nuclear capabilities of the United Kingdom and France are in some sense European, and hold-out the prospect of some alternative to complete strategic dependence on the United States.

Whatever the final outcome of the LRTNF decision, it can be

expected that there will be renewed attempts to seek European solutions to European security problems. Nonetheless, all West European governments so far have recognised that such policies must operate within the context of the super-Power relationship, and the final outcome of the modernisation decision will depend to a considerable extent on whether Soviet-American relations can get back on track. In as much as they do, then the stresses generated by modernisation will be minimised.

POWER POLITICS
IN INDOCHINA

By

G.D. LOESCHER

IN the long-term context of the politics of power in Indochina, the French Indochina War of 1946–54, the Laotian Civil War of 1960–62, the American Indochina War of 1960–73, and the revival of conflict in Indochina at the turn of the 1970s appear to be mere phases of a prolonged struggle for control of the peninsula, involving both external and regional Powers. This paper examines the sources of regional conflict, both historical and contemporary, the interests and roles of States outside and within the region and, in light of the region's power structure, the prospects for peace in Indochina.

I—SOURCES OF CONFLICT

The principal sources of conflict in Indochina in the early 1980s are the Sino-Vietnamese conflict and the unresolved issue of the political identity and external affiliation of Kampuchea. These two problems are linked in that any political solution in Kampuchea depends not only on finding an acceptable head of government in Phnom Penh but also on reconciling the interests of China and Vietnam.

There is an almost irresistable temptation to see in the major armed clashes which have taken place in Indochina since the late 1970s a confirmation of past historical patterns. For over two thousand years Sino-Vietnamese relations have been characterised not only by long periods of Vietnamese tutelage and cultural affinity but also by deep-seated ethnic enmity. Likewise, Vietnam and Kampuchea have been rivals or enemies for three hundred years. Such historical patterns cannot be easily dismissed in any discussion of the contemporary situation.

The Sino-Vietnamese conflict has deep and long-lasting roots. Although Vietnamese language, literature, religion and political and social organisation were all heavily influenced by the Chinese model, traditional inter-State relations were marked by considerable conflict and tension.[1] Vietnam's mistrust of China's motives are

---

[1] A. Woodside, "Peking and Hanoi: Anatomy of a Revolutionary Partnership," 24 *International Journal*, (1968–69), p. 66.

rooted in a history of repeated invasions from the north and long periods of Chinese domination. From the second century BC to the tenth century AD, northern Vietman formed part of the Chinese empire and throughout this period there were frequent uprisings against Chinese rule. In 939 AD the Vietnamese successfully ended direct Chinese rule, but in 1406, Ming dynasty troops invaded Vietnam and made it once more a Chinese province. Popular resistance to Chinese rule quickly grew up and Vietnamese defenders forced the Chinese army to withdraw in 1427. Yet another Chinese expeditionary force, the last before the imposition of French rule in Indochina in the nineteenth century, was defeated in 1789. In the modern era, Chinese Kuomintang troops occupied northern Vietnam from August 1945 to March 1946 as part of the process of supervising the Japanese surrender in Southeast Asia. Like the earlier occupations, the Chinese presence proved to be extremely unpopular with the Vietnamese.[2] Throughout history, relations between China and Vietnam have been characterised by rivalry between a major regional Power and a smaller country determined to assert its independence and its own regional role.

The division between Vietnam and Kampuchea is also deep and lasting, and few modern Kampuchean politicians are likely to forget the long record of Vietnamese colonialism in their country. Kampuchea's small population and its geographical and political position in the Indochinese region have long left it vulnerable to stronger neighbours. Indeed, Kampuchea has been characterised as "a state possessing a small population sandwiched between two neighbours each of which has populations several times greater."[3] As numerous scholars have pointed out, geography is also a crucial factor in both a cultural and a geopolitical sense.[4] The border between Vietnam and Kampuchea serves as the boundary between the Indic and Sinic cultures and as such, Kampuchea has historically been a buffer between Vietnam and Thailand. Thus it is not surprising that over the centuries both Thailand and Vietnam have absorbed areas formerly under Kampuchean rule. Although subject to invasion or intrigue by its neighbours, there was an essential difference in the way Kampuchea perceived the two. Whereas

---

[2] B. Burton, "Contending Explanations of the 1979 Sino-Vietnamese War," 34 *International Journal* (1979), pp. 701–703. For a general historical treatment of the Kuomingtang occupation, see K.C. Chen, *Vietnam and China, 1938–1954* (1969).

[3] For a fuller discussion of these historical factors see: M. Osborne, "Can Kampuchea Survive?" 10 *Asia Pacific Community* (1979), pp. 45–57, and "Kampuchea and Vietnam: A Historical Perspective," 9 *Pacific Community* 1978, pp. 249–263.

[4] *Ibid.* and W.S. Turley and J. Race, "The Third Indochina War," 41 *Foreign Policy*, (1980), pp. 92–116.

Kampuchea and Thailand shared a broadly common culture, Kampuchea's Indian-influenced world view clashed with Vietnam's strongly Chinese-influenced views. Kampuchea viewed the Vietnamese as domineering, alien and determined to absorb their nation. The Vietnamese, in turn, traditionally viewed Kampuchea as a land of barbarians which needed to be "civilised" or "Vietnamised."[5] Indeed, in 1834, the Vietnamese Nguyen dynasty tried to swallow Kampuchea entirely and convert it into a Vietnamese military colony with a Vietnamese general stationed in Phnom Penh.

Despite repeated attempts to dismember it, Kampuchea managed to survive as an independent entity. French colonisation of Indochina in the nineteenth century forced the historic patterns of conflict into abeyance. While colonial rule arrested direct Vietnamese expansion, French policy accelerated the process by which the Vietnamese obtained a dominant position in Kampuchea's economy and administration. With French encouragement, large numbers of Vietnamese farmers, fishermen and artisans migrated into Kampuchea and France employed Vietnamese in the lower ranks of its administration in Kampuchea.

The defeat of France by Japan in Asia during the Second World War recreated throughout Indochina a situation of tension which the colonial period had concealed but left unchanged. In an attempt to contain the rise of Vietnamese nationalism and repossess Indochina, the French opened military hostilities in 1945. 1949 was a pivotal year, the year of triumph for the Chinese Communists, which had immediate implications for the military balance in Vietnam and for the transformation of the French Indochina War into an American-supported anti-communist struggle. Over the next quarter of a century, the United States committed itself militarily and politically to maintaining non-communist régimes in Indochina. During the 1950s, the American containment policy in Asia prevented or delayed the rise of open tensions among the members of the Soviet camp and the Democratic Republic of Vietnam (DRV) depended both on China and the Soviet Union for military, economic and technological aid. However, with the onset of open Sino-Soviet antagonism from the early 1960s, the Indochina conflict became more complex. Hanoi could ill afford to offend either sponsor unduly and therefore attempted to steer an independent course with regard to Sino-Soviet rivalry and was able to capitalise on Sino-Soviet differences to meet its aid requirements.

---

[5] A. Woodside, "Nationalism and Poverty in the Breakdown of Sino-Vietnamese Relations," 52 *Pacific Affairs* (1979), p. 385.

By the late 1960s, however, the strategic priorities of the major external Powers had begun to shift. United States policymakers were searching for ways to extricate themselves from Vietnam with the smallest loss of American prestige. To effect such a situation, the United States pursued a diplomacy with China and the Soviet Union to ensure that the DRV's position was relatively weak and its patrons were neutralised. After the Soviet invasion of Czechoslovakia in 1968 and the escalation of Sino-Soviet tension during the summer of 1969, China came to view the Soviet Union, and not the United States, as its chief external threat. The implication of this new strategic priority was profound. In order to limit the growing power and influence of the Soviet Union, Chinese policy had to be adapted to enable a tactical accommodation to be made with the United States. In particular, Peking had to drop its opposition to a negotiated settlement in Vietnam. The Soviet Union, on the other hand, was motivated by its desire to strengthen its leverage in East-West negotiations over strategic arms, trade and European security, to limit the developing Sino-American rapprochement and to compete with the Chinese for influence in Indochina as American military dominance in the area receded. Thus, although Sino-Soviet antagonism still ruled out any overt co-operation in the termination of the war, Moscow, and to a lesser extent Peking, had an incentive by the early 1970s to assist the Americans in persuading Hanoi to negotiate a compromise settlement. In the process, Hanoi which for many years had benefited from Sino-Soviet competition for assistance against the United States was under pressure to reach a settlement which would be acceptable to the Americans but would enable the communists to continue their political struggle in South Vietnam under favourable conditions.[6]

The 1973 Paris Accords set the seal on American withdrawal from Indochina but it did not provide a countervailing withdrawal of support to the DRV by their Soviet and Chinese allies. In the wake of the Watergate scandal, a judgment was made in Moscow and perhaps in Peking that the Nixon Administration was fatally weakened and that the resumption of large-scale military assistance to the DRV would no longer imperil détente. The subsequent triumph of communism in Indochina in 1975, however, did not lead to any unity in policy, nor to the appeasement of the age-old hostility between Vietnam and Kampuchea. When the war came to

---

[6] The 1973 settlement was seen by the DRV as an interim step forward and as one victory along the road to a final outcome. A.E. Goodman, "Ending the Conflict in Vietnam: Expectations in Hanoi and Saigon," 16 *Orbis* (1972), pp. 633–639. See also: G. Porter, *A Peace Denied: The U.S., Vietnam and The Paris Agreement* (1975).

an end, the Khmer Rouge, like Kampuchean leaders of the past, faced the foreign policy dilemma of how to maintain the existence of their small weak State against the potential threat of their more powerful and traditionally hostile neighbour. Vietnam and Kampuchea were unable to overcome differences of political identity and interest and the two communist States found themselves almost immediately at war with each other. Kampuchea adopted an anti-Vietnamese international line and the two countries engaged in armed skirmishes along their common border. By 1977 the low level friction between the two States rapidly escalated into full-scale border incursions.

Simultaneously, there occurred a fundamental realignment in the international politics of Indochina. The ending of the military conflict in 1975 removed any remaining restraints on the communist Powers imposed by the need for solidarity with the DRV during the war. "United States imperialism" was no longer enemy number one of Hanoi, Peking and Moscow, and rivalry for power and influence among the three communist States became more pronounced. The Soviet Union stepped up its involvement in Indochina in order to exert increasing influence over Vietnam and to promote a net of "collective security" to contain China. Peking, in turn, tried to encourage Southeast Asian States to collaborate with each other and with the United States to oppose Soviet and Vietnamese expansion. The Soviet Union and China became the external patrons of Vietnam and Kampuchea respectively and gave the confrontation between neighbouring Indochinese States a patron-client character similar to that which existed during earlier phases of the Indochina war.

By 1978, external Powers were again drawn directly into the conflict in Indochina. Vietnam's attempt by armed force to revise the pattern of power in the region triggered a Chinese "punitive" attack in early 1979. Likewise, the United States, concerned that the Soviet Union might secure a strategic advantage in Indochina, became more directly involved in the power politics of the region. The Sino-Vietnamese conflict, along with the American decision to reinforce ties with China in order to counter the Soviet Union, created a new and polarised power alignment in Indochina which left Vietnam little alternative but to further strengthen relations with the Soviet Union. By the early 1980s, the pattern of power in Indochina seemed once again to be governed by the interests of external Powers acting on the basis of traditional balance-of-power considerations.[7]

---

[7] M. Leifer, "Conflict and Regional Order in Southeast Asia," 162 *Adelphi Papers* (1980).

II—INTERESTS AND ROLES
OF EXTERNAL POWERS

The present crisis in Indochina is as terrible and intractable as at any time in the past 35 years. The widening rift within the communist world ensures that the United States, Soviet Union and China assess the significance of the conflict for power in Indochina in terms of a complicated trilateral competition. In the meantime, Vietnam, which for so long had preserved a balance between competing pressures from Moscow and Peking, is in danger of being locked in the Soviet camp by economic, military and diplomatic necessity. The cockpit in which these international rivalries are being played out is Kampuchea. In light of these traditional balance-of-power considerations, we must examine the interests and roles of the major external Powers, namely the People's Republic of China, the Soviet Union and the United States.

(a) *China*

In Indochina, Peking continues to pursue the same strategy of denial that has marked its foreign policy since 1949. Motivated more by national security considerations than by revolutionary aspirations, China has consistently sought to prevent military forces allied to any major Power threatening China to expand into its border areas. Acting on that calculus, China intervened against United States forces in Korea in the 1950s and in the 1950s and in the 1960s sent troops into Laos and North Vietnam.[8] During the American Indochina war, Chinese policy was to provide as much aid as possible to North Vietnam and to act as its rear area of support but to avoid any involvement which could lead to direct military confrontation with the United States or any actions that might provoke American attacks on China.

After 1975, Peking's strategic priorities continued to focus on preventing any hostile major Power from establishing a position of dominance on its southern periphery. In particular, China hoped for friendly and independent successor régimes throughout Indochina. Instead, the Chinese found themselves engaged in intense rivalry with a militarily powerful Vietnam which was intent on establishing its dominance in the region. What was more dangerous, from Peking's point of view, was that Vietnam was becoming more closely aligned with the Soviet Union. As early as June 1975, Teng Hsiao-ping warned that "the other super-Power" was replacing the United States as a threat to the peace and security of Southeast Asia

---

[8] For a full account see: A.S. Whiting, *The Chinese Calculus of Deterrence* (1975).

and that "it insatiably seeks new military bases in Asia."[9] Fearing that "the tiger (the Soviet Union) might be let in through the back door while the wolf (the United States) was expelled through the front gate," Chinese strategy was to reduce Vietnam's military power in the region and to force Vietnam, from weakness, away from Soviet influence.

Between 1976 and 1979, border disputes, controversy over the role of overseas Chinese in Vietnam, and diverging perspectives on international and regional politics served to worsen relations between Peking and Hanoi. However, for both countries the issue of Kampuchea was central to their embittered relationship. In order to counterbalance increasing Soviet aid to Vietnam, China provided material and technical support to Kampuchea. During the course of the next several years, China was drawn into increasing support of the Pol Pot régime. The Vietnamese held Peking responsible for Kampuchea's continued belligerence and were concerned that Peking might succeed in isolating Vietnam and debilitate long-term economic development by forcing on her a long and costly war in Kampuchea.[10]

Vietnamese-Kampuchean hostilities were accompanied by the persecution of large numbers of Chinese residents in Vietnam onwards from early 1978. This policy led to a mass exodus of Chinese from Vietnam and to an even further deterioration in Sino-Vietnamese relations.[11] In May 1978, China terminated all economic aid to Vietnam, withdrew its remaining advisers, and closed several Vietnamese consulates in China, thereby reducing Sino-Vietnamese relations to the bare minimum.

Following this open break in relations, Vietnam declared publicly that its principal enemy was now China[12] and it consolidated its international alignment accordingly. In June 1978, Vietnam joined the Soviet bloc's Council for Mutual Economic Assistance (COMECON). This move was perceived by China as further proof

---

[9] *Peking Review*, July 4, 1975, p. 11.

[10] Vietnamese Central Committee member Hoang Tung described China's policy as directed to "provoke a disease which is not fatal but (which would) keep us always sick." Cited in G. Porter, "Asia's New Cold War," *The Nation*, September 9, 1978, pp. 209–212.

[11] At the same time, however, it was clear that Vietnamese treatment of their ethnic Chinese was not the major issue of contention between the two States. Peking had not protested at the "Socialist transformation" of North Vietnam in the 1950s; neither, more recently, had China done anything to defend ethnic Chinese from persecution by the Khmer Rouge régime in Kampuchea.

[12] The Vietnamese Politbureau, meeting in June 1978, saw Vietnam facing war with China on two fronts. As a result of this new strategic analysis, the Politbureau decided to identify China as its main and immediate enemy and to draw up plans for a military offensive to overthrow the Pol Pot régime and replace it with a client. N. Chanda, "The Timetable for a Takeover," *Far Eastern Economic Review*, February 23, 1979, p. 34.

that Vietnam had sided irrevocably with the Soviet Union, and in turn, China accused Vietnam of pursuing "regional hegemonism" and serving as the "Cuba of the East" and "junior partner" in a Soviet attempt to gain control of Southeast Asia. The conclusion of the 25-year Treaty of Friendship and Co-operation with the Soviet Union in November 1978 confirmed for Peking the establishment of a Vietnam-Soviet anti-China alliance. One month after the signing of the friendship treaty, the Kampuchean National United Front for National Salvation was formed with open Vietnamese support and evident Soviet endorsement. In late December 1978, Vietnamese forces crossed the frontier in a blitzkrieg and replaced the ousted Pol Pot régime with members of the Hanoi-trained United Front. In retaliation, China invaded Vietnam in February 1979, not to challenge the existence of the government in Hanoi but to demonstrate to Vietnam that China also had important strategic interests in the region and was a Power to be reckoned with in Indochina.

China's invasion contributed significantly to the impoverishment of Vietnam's northern border region, but in many respects was counterproductive. Vietnam did not pull its troops out of Kampuchea but, on the contrary, increased its military forces there. In addition, Vietnam was driven even further into the embrace of the Soviet Union who, in turn, gained greater access to Vietnam's military and naval bases.

Despite these setbacks, Peking remained intransigent in its opposition to Vietnam and the Soviet Union. In April 1979, Chinese Deputy Foreign Minister Han Nianlong set out Peking's terms for a settlement of the Sino-Vietnamese conflict and demanded that Vietnam withdraw its troops from Kampuchea and Laos and oppose Soviet hegemony in Asia. Chinese strategy had as its objective keeping the border issue alive by threatening a second invasion and obliging the Vietnamese to maintain a large armed force in the north, not only causing a serious drain on the country's fragile economy but also relieving pressure on the Khmer Rouge who are waging a guerrilla war in Kampuchea with Chinese support.

Of all the parties involved in the current Indochina conflict, Peking seems the most determined to obtain Vietnamese acceptance of the subordination of their own interests within the region to those of China. Although China has been willing to encourage broadening the base of the resistance in Kampuchea in order to make the continuation of the conflict more palatable and provide for a more acceptable political alternative to Pol Pot and the Khmer Rouge, it has refused to contemplate a political settlement to the conflict that does not include Vietnamese withdrawal. Accordingly,

Peking is likely to continue a strategy of diplomatic attrition against Vietnam hoping to cause economic disruption by compelling the Vietnamese to maintain themselves in a perpetual state of military alert.[13]

(b) *Soviet Union*

Although Southeast Asia has not traditionally been one of its vital spheres of influence, Moscow has been drawn into the region as a result of its desire to compete with the United States and China in the Third World and to deny its adversaries the use of strategic regions. During most of the 1950s and 1960s, American dominance in Asia tended to minimise or eliminate Soviet influence in practically all of non-communist Asia. With United States escalation in Vietnam in the decade after 1965, however, Soviet involvement greatly increased. The Soviet Union supported the Democratic Republic of Vietnam in whatever manner it could—military supply, diplomatic and economic support—so long as direct confrontation with the United States was avoided. By the late 1960s, however, growing rivalry with China became more important than competition with the United States.

After 1975, the Soviet Union moved to take advantage of the vacuum in Indochina created by the withdrawal of American forces and the defeat of American clients in the region. Although Hanoi attempted to maintain equidistance between Moscow and Peking, the Soviet Union conducted its relations with Vietnam from a position of considerable advantage. When the war ended, the Soviet Union urged on the Vietnamese the Soviet model for economic development and poured in Russian and Soviet bloc aid.[14] At the same time, the Soviet Union, which was several thousand miles away from Indochina, did not seem to pose as much a direct threat to Vietnamese national interests as did Hanoi's traditional rival, Peking. By 1978, Hanoi responded to considerable pressure from Peking along its border and in Kampuchea by ending its longstanding policy of remaining neutral in the Sino-Soviet dispute. Hanoi unequivocally sided with the Soviet Union by joining COMECON

[13] According to Chinese Foreign Minister Huang Hua, "Vietnam's difficulties at home are not so great that it will withdraw troops from Kampuchea and allow a political settlement. We have to create conditions for the Vietnamese to accept political solutions. We should create conditions for a political settlement now, that is to say, give moral, political, diplomatic as well as material assistance to the patriotic Kampuchean forces" while maintaining economic, political and military pressure on Vietnam. *The Straits Times*, March 20, 1980.
[14] A major Soviet agreement was negotiated in Moscow in October 1975. The USSR agreed to fund 60 per cent. of Vietnam's 1976–1980 Five-Year Plan at a cost of about $3.2 billion. See D. Pike, "The USSR and Vietnam: Into the Swamp," 19 *Asian Survey* (1979), pp. 1164–1166.

and signing a Treaty of Friendship with the Soviet Union. As a consequence, Vietnam became for Moscow the "outpost of the forces of peace and socialism in Southeast Asia."[15]

The Soviet Union, despite its physical distance from the area, now possessed the ability to participate in a major realignment of power in the region. Soviet support for Vietnam included not only diplomatic and political backing at the United Nations but also economic aid to keep the country afloat and military aid to enable Hanoi to maintain its armies in Laos and Kampuchea.[16] Of longer term strategic importance is the extent of Soviet military assistance to Vietnam. The conflict in Indochina is estimted to cost Moscow $2 billion per year. Defence agreements grant the Soviet Union access to Vietnam's military airports and harbours at Da Nang and Cam Ranh Bay and Russian officers train Vietnamese troops and carry out sophisticated surveillance of the region from these bases. The Soviet military presence has also increased in Kampuchea where the port of Kompong Som one day could be of greater strategic value to the Soviet navy than Cam Ranh Bay. Soviet advisers and technicians who now number over 400 are training the Kampuchean army and supplying the Heng Samrin régime with tanks. The Soviet Union has thus established a more solid base for its military operations in the Pacific and Indian Oceans and has acquired a strategic position in Asia, threatening China's southern borders, and facing the important American bases at Clark and Subic Bay in the Philippines.

(c) *The United States*

The communist victories in Indochina in 1975 effectively marked the end of American military intervention in the region. Although the United States continued to maintain a military presence from its bases along the Pacific Rim, extending from Japan and Okinawa, to Guam, the Philippines and Australia, the United States no longer considered it necessary to play a strategic role in mainland Southeast Asia. Shortly thereafter, the Southeast Asia Treaty Organisation (SEATO) ceased to function and the United States military presence in Thailand ended. Preoccupied with other critical issues and areas of the globe, the United States made it plain that the American presence in Southeast Asia was to be an economic, rather than a military or overly political one.

---

[15] *Pravda*, October 16, 1977.
[16] Russian material aid to Vietnam reportedly amounts to $3 million per day. Furthermore, there are about 8,000 Russians working in Vietnam, in addition to several thousand East Europeans and Cubans, and at least 10,000 Vietnamese go to Moscow every year for training of some kind.

During the early years of the Carter Administration, the United States made an attempt to restore relations with Vietnam. These negotiations initially foundered over the Vietnamese demand for war reparations. In July 1978, Vietnam dropped all pre-conditions to the normalisation process and American-Vietnamese talks, broken off in 1977, resumed in September 1978. However, the talks were soon overcome by other events, in particular, America's decision to normalise and strengthen ties with China and Vietnam's subsequent wars with Kampuchea and China. Recognising a new and polarised power alignment in Indochina, Vietnam was left with little alternative but to sign a virtual military alliance with the Soviet Union.

Thereafter American-Vietnamese relations deteriorated irreparably. Negotiations over the establishment of diplomatic relations were suspended, and United States policy-makers loudly condemned the Vietnamese invasion of Kampuchea. The United States, like China, displayed no interest in a negotiated settlement over Kampuchea which did not entail a withdrawal of Vietnamese troops from that country. Washington was principally concerned that Moscow was attempting to alter the military balance in Asia by achieving a preponderance of influence and military superiority in the region. This concern provoked a balance-of-power reaction on the part of the United States in the form of strengthened ties with China.

From 1979 onwards, relations between Washington and Peking were shaped by increasingly close bilateral and strategic considerations. Although the Carter Administration tried to pursue an even-handed policy toward Peking and Moscow, by mid-1979 Washington no longer made any pretence that it intended to remain equidistant between the two. In Peking, Vice President Walter Mondale spoke of the "many parallel strategic and bilateral interests" of China and the United States, and informed the Chinese that "both our political interests are served by your growing strength in all fields."[17] Soon afterwards, the United States granted most-favoured-nation status to China without doing the same for the Soviet Union—a clear sign of departure from the policy of evenhandedness.

Until the Soviet invasion of Afghanistan, the rapid improvement in Sino-American relations had been confined to political and economic fields. After December 1979, however, a body of

---

[17] Vice President Walter Mondale at Peking University, August 27, 1979. *Department of State Bulletin*, October 1979, p. 11.

understandings regarding military co-operation emerged between Washington and Peking. In a dramatic policy shift, Secretary of Defense Harold Brown informed the Chinese in January 1980 that the United States was now willing to sell military support equipment to Peking.[18] At the same time, Brown indicated United States willingness to see China act as a counterbalance to Soviet and Vietnamese ambitions in Southeast Asia and warned that if "others" should "threaten the shared interests of the United States and China, we can respond with complementary actions in the field of defence as well as diplomacy."[19]

Following President Reagan's inauguration in 1981, the United States and China have pursued almost identical policies towards Vietnam. In a statement in Peking in June 1981, Assistant Secretary of State for East Asia and the Pacific, John Holdridge declared: "If you give them (the Vietnamese) what they want, this does not make them change their policy in any way. We will seek, if we can, to find ways to increase the political, economic and yes, military pressures on Vietnam, working with others and in ways which will bring about, we hope, some changes in Hanoi's attitude towards the situation."[20] To this end, the Reagan Administration tried to align several other countries behind its policy to cut their programmes to Vietnam and support American and Chinese attempts to "bleed" Hanoi into submission. Japan cancelled its aid programme in 1979 and has not yet renewed it, while the EEC rejected in 1981 a request from the United Nations Children's Fund (UNICEF) for milk powder, butter, oil and high protein foodstuffs for Vietnamese children. An appeal by the United States Food and Agricultural Organisation for emergency food aid to Vietnam has also been ignored by the West.

For the past several decades the United States has consistently striven, with varying success, to prevent a succession of what were perceived to be hostile powers from controlling the strategically important Indochinese peninsula. Motivated by balance-of-power considerations arising from Vietnam's relationship with the Soviet Union, Washington played the "China card" decisively in late 1978. The United States now feels that it shares a community of interest with Peking in trying to contain a united and expansionist Vietnam.

---

[18] See: "U.S. Discusses Sale of Military Technology," *Department of State Bulletin*, March 1980, p. 45.

[19] *Xinhua News Agency*, January 6, 1980.

[20] D. Davies, "Caught in History's Vice," *Far Eastern Economic Review*, December 25, 1981, p. 20.

III—INTERESTS AND ROLES
OF REGIONAL STATES

The conflict in Kampuchea has engaged the competing interests of China, the Soviet Union and the United States. As a function of their rivalry, the external Powers have imposed patron-client relationships on the Indochinese States which has served to sustain the momentum of the conflict. Thus, although Vietnam and the States of the Association of Southeast Asian Nations (ASEAN) have an interest is working out for themselves a viable structure of mutual relations, this will not prove possible until the external Powers agree to measures which will mitigate their competition in the region.

(a) *Vietnam*

For over three decades, Vietnam symbolised the global conflict for power waged by communist and non-communist Powers in Asia and the Third World. When the government of a united Vietnam commenced power from May 1975 onwards, it faced immense social and economic problems. On the domestic front, the Vietnamese seemed determined to devote their energies to domestic development and consolidation, and Hanoi initially imposed a relatively moderate socialist order on southern Vietnam.[21] Internationally, Vietnam's post-war objectives of economic development and reunification required massive assistance and co-operation from both Eastern and Western bloc countries.[22]

In order to achieve these goals, the Socialist Republic of Vietnam (SRV) sought to broaden its contacts with the non-communist industrial world. The SRV adopted new trade and investment codes and appealed to international financial institutions such as the World Bank for assistance. After an initial period of hostility towards America's former allies, the SRV also sought friendly ties with all non-communist Southeast Asian countries. Stressing its independence and non-alignment, Hanoi adopted a conciliatory stance towards ASEAN nations and pledged to move closer to the ASEAN concept of peace and neutrality for Southeast Asia.

Vietnam's foreign policy, however, met with consistent failure. In particular, the policies and perceptions of Hanoi and Peking continued to differ, especially where the role of the Soviet Union in

---

[21] W.J. Duiker, "Ideology and Nation-Building in the Socialist Republic of Vietnam," 17 *Asian Survey* (1977), pp. 413–431.

[22] Foreign Minister Nguyen Duy Trinh indicated at the Fourth Party Congress that the SRV had to look for aid from sources other than just socialist countries. See the text of his speech in *Nhan Dan*, December 28, 1976.

the region was concerned. Vietnam's refusal to endorse China's anti-hegemony stance resulted in the latter's decision not to respond to Hanoi's pleas for long-term economic aid. When Vietnamese Party Secretary Le Duan turned to Moscow for a five-year economic aid agreement, Peking retaliated by terminating its own grant programme to Vietnam. Hanoi and Peking also had different strategic interests in the region. Apart from the Chinese threat, Hanoi's principal security concern is to prevent Laos and Kampuchea from becoming sanctuaries for insurgent groups among the minorities who straddle its borders. Hanoi believed that this situation could only be prevented by implanting client régimes in these States. Peking, on the other hand, is not easily reconciled to Vietnamese domination in Indochina. A Vietnam-led Indochina with strong links to the Soviet Union posed grave risks to China's security and led Hanoi into direct and open conflict with Peking.

By 1978, Vietnam was diplomatically isolated, militarily under pressure and economically stagnant. In June 1978, after it became clear that China intended to halt all economic aid and, frustrated by its lack of progress in attracting monetary investment, technological aid and a trading relationship with the West, Vietnam joined the Soviet bloc's Council for Mutual Economic Assistance (COMECON). At the same time, there appeared to Hanoi to be mounting evidence of a growing collusion between Chinese "expansionism" and United States "imperialism." The consequence of these events was profound. Vietnam's long-standing efforts to avoid taking sides in the Sino-Soviet dispute were compromised and the SRV now faced a two-front war with China to the north and Kampuchea to the west. Kampuchea's close identification with China's international posture made the situation even more intolerable for Hanoi. In late 1978, Vietnam, buttressed by a friendship treaty with the Soviet Union, took military action which seemed to achieve the goal of a Hanoi-dominated Indochina.

Since its invasion of Kampuchea in December 1978, Vietnam's principal aims have been to eliminate all internal challenges to the Heng Samrin régime and to secure international recognition for its *fait accompli* in Kampuchea. As of 1982, neither of these goals have been achieved. Although the various anti-Pol Pot and anti-Heng Samrin "Free Khmer" groups do not offer a real threat to Vietnamese consolidation of power, the Khmer Rouge guerrilla forces remain intact and are able to frustrate Vietnam's political design in Kampuchea. Likewise, on the diplomatic front, Hanoi has been frustrated in its attempts to persuade the international community and, in particular the ASEAN States, to accept the transfer of power in Phnom Penh. In reaction to a number of diplomatic initiatives which have taken place since 1978, Hanoi has asserted that the situation in Kampuchea is irreversible and that it is prepared to wait and let time decide the outcome of its actions. To this end, Hanoi has rejected ASEAN and United Nations supervised elections in Kampuchea.

Hanoi has outlined its short-term diplomatic strategy in the following terms: "in confronting several enemies at the same time, it is imperative to use flexible tactics to divide them and firmly oppose this power while engaging in détente with other powers, retaining initiatives and avoiding disadvantageous combats. . . . "[23] However, unlike earlier periods, Hanoi is no longer able to play one adversary off against another to its own advantage. Hanoi's adversaries show no intention of wavering from their resolve to draw the line against further Soviet and Vietnamese expansion. Peking appears unlikely to be reconciled to a political *fait accompli* in Kampuchea and is proving to be a formidable enemy. Unlike France and the United States, China lies on Vietnam's doorstep and is not subject to the same vulnerabilities as the West. China is unlikely to tire of protracted war and will never "go home" as Western armies did. The Reagan Administration shares parallel strategic views with Peking and appears determined to play the "China card" in order to bring Vietnam to its knees. Of all its adversaries, the ASEAN States appear willing to recognise that Vietnam's security requires that it play a dominant role in Indochina, but they are unwilling to enter into a political accommodation with Hanoi solely on the basis of recognition of the *fait accompli* in Kampuchea.

A key question concerns the continuing resolve and intentions of the Soviet Union. Vietnam's international isolation has placed the entire burden for its support upon communist economies which have severe problems of their own. Although Russian and Soviet bloc aid has been supplied consistently and in increasing quantities, the volume of aid to Vietnam has created some tension within COMECON States.[24] Some reports indicate that Eastern European members of COMECON are complaining about the disproportionately large assistance extended to Hanoi at their expense.

The costs to Hanoi of its exclusive reliance on the Eastern bloc are not only sacrifice of sovereignty and military dependency but also trade dependence. Vietnam's third Five-Year Plan,

---

[23] *Nhan Dan*, May 19, 1980.

[24] An economic and technological agreement between the Soviet Union and Vietnam was signed on July 24, 1981 to cover the period until 1985. According to Mr. Semyon Shackhov, Chairman of the Soviet State Committee for Foreign Economic Relations, "The Soviet Union will almost quadruple its supply of equipment and machinery to Vietnam."

inaugurated in 1981, calls upon Hanoi to adopt a development model based on the export of unprocessed agricultural goods or light industrial products in exchange for industrial equipment from the Soviet Union. In addition, Vietnam has sent approximately 50,000 "guest workers" to factories in Soviet bloc countries in order to help repay the military and economic loans it receives from the East.[25] Given the shortage of skilled labour within Vietnam, this arrangement can only contribute to further underdevelopment in Vietnam. Moreover, in the past the Soviet Union has only been able to provide its allies in the Third World with military aid and heavy industrial goods, items which are seldom appropriate for indigenous development. In the meantime, economic prospects for the Vietnamese people have steadily declined, giving rise to serious concern within and outside the government.[26]

Presently, Moscow is known to be spending at least $3 million per day on its client and the latter's ever-worsening economy, particularly in the south, would deteriorate further if Soviet aid should stop. But how long Moscow can continue such levels of aid in the interests of containing China is questionable. Even with lavish Soviet aid, Vietnam lacks the means to sustain a long-term enmity with China and industrialise itself successfully at the same time.

(b) *ASEAN States*

Since its founding in 1967, ASEAN (the Association of Southeast Asian Nations, made up of Indonesia, Malaysia, the Philippines, Singapore and Thailand) has had stormy relations with Vietnam. For ASEAN the balance of power in Indochina had been irreversibly altered by the communist victories and the United States defeat in 1975. Although the ASEAN States showed an initial readiness to adjust to this new situation, mutual suspicion born of the war years prevented this from occurring. ASEAN feared that a militarily strong Vietnam would support indigenous insurgents in their own countries. Vietnam, on the other hand, described the ASEAN States as a prop of American policy because of their continued economic and security ties to the West. Disagreements between Vietnam and ASEAN at the non-aligned summit in

---

[25] According to Western diplomats, the workers are paying off Vietnam's debt by receiving only a part of their Eastern European salaries. The rest is set aside for debt servicing. *New York Times*, December 28, 1981.

[26] According to a confidential World Bank Report: " . . . when the war in Vietnam finally ended in 1975, *per capita* production of major commodities had changed little, or fallen, since the 1940s. Except in some parts of the south, the economic infrastructure is less well developed than in most developing countries and the country's standard of living is one of the lowest."

Colombo in August 1976 seemed for a time to make any form of improved relations unlikely.

During 1977 and 1978, however, both sides made a concerted effort to improve relations. The Vietnamese responded to their border war with Kampuchea and pressure from China by seeking to improve relations with ASEAN and the West. To avoid diplomatic isolation which might prove advantageous to its adversaries, Vietnam adopted a conciliatory stance towards ASEAN nations and, like their Chinese counterparts, Vietnamese leaders toured Southeast Asian capitals in search of support. The SRV's primary fear was of collaboration between the United States, China, Kampuchea, and Thailand, directed against Vietnam. In this context, Hanoi made a major effort to improve relations with Thailand which had been a military ally of the United States during the Vietnam war. ASEAN, for its part, wanted no super-Power confrontation in the region and was primarily concerned that it might lose its neutral status in the course of the Sino-Vietnamese conflict. Therefore, ASEAN pushed for a *modus vivendi* with Vietnam based on its own concept for peace and neutrality for Southeast Asia.[27]

Vietnam's diplomatic offensive came to an abrupt halt in December 1978 when the SRV invaded Kampuchea. After a meeting in Bangkok in January 1979, ASEAN foreign ministers "strongly deplored the armed intervention against the independence, sovereignty and territorial integrity of Kampuchea" and called for the withdrawal of Vietnamese forces from Kampuchea.[28] In particular, Thailand, concerned that a partial buffer between itself and its historical enemy Vietnam had been eliminated, came to regard Hanoi as the principal threat to regional stability. Also, other ASEAN States, namely Malaysia and Singapore along with Thailand, were greatly discomforted by the tens of thousands of refugees who fled repression and war in all three Indochinese countries.[29]

Since late 1978, ASEAN strategy has oscillated between a hard-line position which seeks to isolate Vietnam internationally and a more flexible position which attempts to woo the Vietnamese into a negotiated settlement with offers of economic assistance. Singapore Foreign Minister S. Dhanabolan summed up this position

---

[27] ASEAN'S proposal for the creation of a Zone of Peace, Freedom and Neutrality in Southeast Asia was originally made in 1971 in the hope that the concept would serve as an alternative to competitive military buildups within Southeast Asia and the countervailing military activities of such external powers as the United States and Soviet Union.

[28] B. Grant, *The Boat People: An "Age" Investigation* (1979).

[29] The refugee outflow was the reason for further condemnation of Vietnam at the ASEAN foreign ministers' meeting on Bali in July 1979.

in the following manner: "We need to ensure that the situation in Kampuchea continues in such a way that the price the Vietnamese will have to pay will continue to be high, that the price their supporter, the Soviet Union, has to pay will continue to be high. So it's done on two fronts: One, make sure that the situation does not go in favour of the opposition—keep the thing boiling—keep the price high. And two, continue to seek alternatives where we have certain ideas to develop."[30]

Taking a position close to that of China and the United States, some ASEAN States favour continuing pressure on Vietnam by indirect support for anti-Vietnamese Kampuchean resistance groups and refuse to give unilateral concessions without getting anything in return. At the same time, ASEAN has lobbied hard since 1978 for the continued retention of the Kampuchean United Nations seat to the Pol Pot régime and has sponsored various United Nations resolutions calling for the withdrawal of "foreign forces" from Kampuchea. Other ASEAN States, distancing themselves from Chinese and American strategy, favour a negotiated settlement of the Kampuchean problem which would both preserve an independent Kampuchea and reassure Vietnam against attack by China.

The division within ASEAN over what constitutes the most appropriate response to Vietnamese action in Kampuchea results principally from ambivalence within Southeast Asia about the future role of China in the region. Whereas Thailand and Singapore are inclined to see China as a barrier against Vietnamese ambitions in the region, Indonesia and Malaysia cannot fully accept the deeper Chinese involvement in Southeast Asia that long-term confrontation with Vietnam would imply, particularly as Peking is unwilling to drop its support for communist insurgencies in ASEAN countries.

Discomfort with the new power alignment merging in Southeast Asia led ASEAN in 1980 and 1981 to actively seek a political solution to the Kampuchean problem. Initially, these efforts were focused on China and were made by Thai Premier Prem Tinsulanond and Singapore Premir Lee Kuan Yew who visited Peking in October and November 1980. Although they were able to win Chinese agreement in principle for the ASEAN position that a third force must be found in Kampuchea which will be acceptable to all parties involved in the conflict, Prem and Lee were unable to dissuade China from supporting the Khmer Rouge in their long-term war of attrition against the Vietnamese. A second major diplomatic effort to seek a political settlement in Kampuchea was

---

[30] *The Straits Times*, October 1, 1980.

made by ASEAN at the United Nations Conference on Kampuchea in July 1981 which was attended by over ninety countries but boycotted by Vietnam and their communist bloc allies. ASEAN put forward several resolutions which were meant to be conciliatory to the Vietnamese. It called, for example, for the disarming of the Khmer Rouge before any UN-supervised election in Kampuchea. This was opposed by China and the United States who reiterated their position that Vietnam must withdraw all its troops from Kampuchea before negotiations on a settlement can begin.

The most likely source of future diplomatic initiatives on Kampuchea is ASEAN. These States, Thailand included, now seem to be reconsidering their commitment to the Sino-American line. All of these States see Chinese dominance of the region as a long-term threat and they do not view it in their interest to have a permanently weakened Vietnam which is an ineffective buffer between themselves and China. At the same time, ASEAN would like to see Kampuchea be independent of foreign control and Vietnam reduce its dependence on the Soviet Union.

IV—PROSPECTS FOR PEACE

Peace in Indochina cannot be achieved until the issue of who is to rule in Kampuchea is settled with regional and extra-regional acceptance. To date, Vietnam has shown no willingness to compromise on its firmly held position that the situation is irreversible in Kampuchea. As long as Vietnam and China see themselves as implacable foes, the risks of allowing a non-aligned government to develop in Kampuchea, particularly one that reflects Kampuchean nationalist aspirations and is less compliant to the SRV, are too great for Hanoi to accept. The Vietnamese have never before shown any willingness to retreat in face of their enemies, whatever price their people must pay. They have begun to create a federation of Indochina under their control and, given Soviet willingness to sustain Vietnam in its consolidation of power, the Vietnamese are unlikely to be diverted from their long-standing ambition to have a predominant position in Indochina.

Vietnam's enemies, moreover, have helped to ensue that no alternative is possible. For example, the Chinese invasion of northern Vietnam failed to deter closer Soviet-Vietnamese ties and threats from the West and ASEAN countries to cut aid failed to deter Hanoi from further action in Kampuchea. Those countries which are critical of Vietnam need to question whether their interests are best served by punitive sanctions that only lead to Hanoi's further isolation and progressive reliance on the Soviet Union.

Vietnam is unlikely to change its policies overnight in response to any resumption or commencement of aid. However, a diplomatic approach that emphasises positive incentives and has as its objective the restoration of a measure of non-alignment in Vietnamese foreign policy and an acceptable government in Kampuchea is likely to prove more productive than present policy. Positive incentives could include recognition of Vietnamese security interests in Kampuchea along with international recognition of Kampuchea's neutrality and a coalition government in Phnom Penh; normalisation of political relations and the commencement of economic relations with the United States; a security guarantee from China; and improved economic ties with ASEAN, Japan and the other Western industrialised States.[31]

The benefits to Hanoi of such enticements would be peace in Kampuchea, the removal of the Chinese threat, greater opportunity to concentrate on badly needed domestic economic development, increased aid from non-communist sources and, concurrently, a lessened dependence on the Soviet Union. There are already indications that the Soviet-Vietnamese relationship is neither easy nor natural and that the alliance is held together only by the imperatives of the balance of power. The Vietnamese have traditionally resisted close relations with external Powers, and nationalistic impulses are likely to press Vietnam away from an unduly dependent relationship with the Soviet Union in the long run.

Presently, however, the force of circumstances have engaged the complementary interests of Hanoi and Moscow. As long as the Sino-Vietnamese conflict remains unresolved and Vietnam is at the time faced with continuing economic crises at home and unabated war in Kampuchea, Hanoi has no choice but to sacrifice its sovereignty and military independence on account of its close ties with the Soviet Union. A continutation of political polarisation in Southeast Asia will result in an isolated and embittered Vietnam, utterly dependent on the Soviet Union and with little inclination to compromise.

---

[31] These possible initiatives have been outlined in some detail in W. Turley and J. Race, "The Third Indochina War," 41 *Foreign Policy* (1980), pp. 115–116.

DISPUTE-SETTLEMENT
IN AFRICA

By
MALCOLM SHAW

IF there is any necessary prerequisite to the operation of an international system of States of juridical equality, it is that some rules must exist to restrain resort to force, such rules being by and large observed. Coupled with this requirement is the need to provide for the resolution by peaceful means of such problems as may arise between the various parties to that system. In a negative sense, it would suffice if such means were to deter the disputants from resorting to the use of force or at least bring to a speedy end any recourse to violence. Far more preferable, however, would be a situation wherein such means could provide for the satisfactory settlement of important differences and the establishment or restoration of harmonious relations. There are a number of techniques that are available for use by States for the purposes of dispute settlement, while international law provides principles that may be relevant to particular situations. Further, there are now an increasing number of institutional mechanisms aiming at the peaceful resolution of disputes. However, the incidence of inter-State conflicts shows no signs of diminishing. It is in the area of the Third World that the number and ferocity of such conflicts is especially marked and nowhere is this more apparent than on the continent of Africa.

I—Methods of Dispute-Settlement

Article 2(3) of the United Nations Charter declares that "All Members shall settle their international disputes by peaceful means in such a manner that international peace and security, and justice, are not endangered." This provision was elaborated in the Declaration on Principles of International Law Concerning Friendly Relations and Co-operation Among States in Accordance With the Charter of the United Nations, adopted in 1970. It is stipulated that "States shall accordingly seek early and just settlement of their international disputes by negotiation, inquiry, mediation, conciliation, arbitration, judicial settlement, resort to regional agencies or arrangements or other peaceful means of their choice." The same methods of dispute settlement are outlined in Article 33(1) of the United Nations Charter.

The methods of attaining a pacific resolution of international disputes may be conveniently classified in terms of three categories: diplomatic procedures, arbitration and judicial settlement. Diplomatic procedures incorporate negotiations, inquiry, good offices and mediation, and conciliation.

It is of the essence in the two procedures of arbitration and judicial settlement that the parties accept that they will be bound by the verdict of the arbitrators or judges hearing the case. With regard to arbitration,[1] the parties retain considerable control over the process until the moment when the tribunal considers the award, whereas in the case of judicial settlement the format, constitution and procedures involved are in existence before the parties bring their case and the element of flexibility is thus to that extent far less.

II—THE INSTITUTIONAL FRAMEWORK

(a) *The United Nations*

Article 1(1) of the United Nations Charter emphasises that one of the purposes of the Organisation is "to bring about, by peaceful means, and in conformity with the principles of justice and international law, adjustment or settlement of international disputes or situations which might lead to a breach of the peace." The United Nations is in effect primarily concerned with the maintenance of international peace and security and thus with those disputes which are likely to endanger this. Since it is the Security Council that is deemed to be seised of the primary responsibility for the maintenance of international peace and security, it has been given a series of powers under the Charter with regard to the investigation of disputes, the settlement of disputes by calling upon the parties to use one of the means specified in Article 33(1) or indeed by recommending "such terms of settlement as it may consider appropriate," where it deems that the maintenance of international peace and security is likely to be endangered.[2] In certain circumstances, the Security Council may adopt binding decisions imposing sanctions.[3]

The General Assembly may discuss any issues within the scope of

---

[1] Article 15 of the Hague Convention on the Pacific Settlement of Disputes 1899, notes that "international arbitration has for its object the settlement of differences between States by judges of their own choice, and on the basis of a respect for law." See also J. L. Simpson and H. Fox, *International Arbitration: Law and Practice* (1959).

[2] For example, resolution 242(1967) dealing with the Middle East conflict.

[3] Chapter VII, UN Charter. See also article 25.

the Charter and may make recommendations with regard to them, provided that the Security Council is not exercising its functions with respect to a dispute or situation.[4] Subject to the same proviso, the Assembly may recommend measures for the peaceful adjustment of any situation which it deems likely to impair the general welfare or friendly relations among nations and may call the attention of the Security Council to situations which are likely to endanger peace and security.[5]

(b) *The Organisation of African Unity*

The OAU, established in 1963,[6] declared as one of its principles "the peaceful settlement of disputes by negotiation, mediation, conciliation or arbitration," while all member-States pledged themselves in article XIX to settle all disputes[7] among themselves by peaceful means. To this end, a Commission of Mediation, Conciliation and Arbitration was created as one of the four principal institutions through which the organisation was to accomplish its purposes, the other three being the Assembly of Heads of State and Government, the Council of Ministers and the General Secretariat. The jurisdiction of the Commission, however, is not compulsory, and in the event of a refusal by one party to submit to the jurisdiction, the issue would become political. The parties have under the Protocol of the Commission the choice of three modes of settlement: mediation, conciliation and arbitration. It is to be noted that the peaceful settlement of disputes by judicial means is not provided for, nor is any reference at all made to the International Court of Justice. Indeed, a provision in an early draft of the OAU Charter stipulating that the International Court was to be concerned with problems relating to the interpretation of the Charter[8] was replaced by article XXVII, which states that such questions are to be decided by a two-thirds vote of the Assembly of Heads of State and Government. One must also point to the absence of any

---

[4] Articles 10 and 12.

[5] Articles 14 and 11(3). Note, that by resolution 377(V), the Assembly affirmed its right to deal with a situation of breach of the peace or act of aggression where the Security Council fails to act because of the exercise of the veto.

[6] The OAU Charter was adopted at a conference of Heads of State and Government in Addis Ababa on May 25, 1963. See generally C. Legum, *Pan-Africanism* (1962); T. Elias, *Africa and the Development of International Law* (1972); and Cervenka, *The Organisation of African Unity and Its Charter* (1968).

[7] Note that the types of dispute dealt with in the UN Charter in articles 2(3) and 33(1) are not so broadly defined.

[8] CIAS/Sp. Comm,/Charter, May 24, 1963 and CIAS/Comm/Rep.1. See also Tiewul, "Relations Between the United Nations Organisation and the Organisation of African Unity in the Settlement of Secessionist Conflicts," 16 *Harvard International Law Journal* (1975), pp. 259–2.

reference to the United Nations within the context of the peaceful settlement of disputes through the OAU. The 21 members of the Commission were appointed in 1965 and the first meeting took place in 1967. However, significantly, no disputes have been referred to it.

The supreme organ of the OAU is the Assembly of Heads of State and Government, which meets at least once a year and occasionally in emergency session. There is some disagreement as to whether Assembly resolutions are binding or not. Cervenka has suggested that they are not, since the Charter is silent on the matter and since no means of enforcement are provided, although such resolutions "represent the collective consensus of opinion of the Heads of State"[9] Tiewul takes the opposite view.[10]

The Council of Ministers plays a vital role within the OAU. It meets twice a year and additionally in emergency session and has wide-ranging functions, including drafting and adopting resolutions and declarations for submission to the Assembly. On a number of occasions, it has played a part in the settlement of disputes by the appointment of ad hoc commissions.

III—AFRICAN PRACTICE
REGARDING THE MODES OF DISPUTE-SETTLEMENT

African States have demonstrated a marked reluctance to resort to judicial or arbitral methods of dispute settlement. The Charter of the OAU for example, neither established a court nor made any reference to recourse to the International Court of Justice in the Hague. A Commission of Mediation, Conciliation and Arbitration was created, but with optional jurisdiction and indeed it has yet to be activated to resolve any African dispute. Thus, not only have the more structured modes of dispute settlement been virtually ignored in African practice, so also has the one permanent, institutional mechanism for this purpose created on the continent. The means adopted in practice to try and resolve African conflicts have varied somewhat in the light of the particular circumstances. Some of the major disputes will now be briefly surveyed.

(a) *Inter-State Disputes*
    (i) *The Morocco-Algeria Boundary Dispute.*[11] Morocco has laid claim to a large sector of territory within the colonially defined

---

[9] *The Unfinished Quest for Unity* (1977), p. 22.
[10] *Op. cit.* in note 8 above, at p. 276.
[11] An excellent documentary survey of this, as well as other, boundary problems may be found in Brownlie, *African Boundaries* (1979). See, for this dispute, pp. 55–83.

boundaries of Algeria on the basis of the territorial extent of the pre-colonial Moroccan empire. Extensive areas of the border, in fact, were never demarcated, primarily in view of the nature of the territory. Prior to its independence, the provisional Algerian government recognised the existence of a "territorial problem" with Morocco, but after independence Algerian attitudes changed and when French soldiers departed, both Morocco and Algeria sent in soldiers to occupy positions in the disputed areas. Minor clashes precipitated a wider conflict in October 1963. Morocco demanded consideration of its territorial claims, while Algeria called for recognition of the borders as they existed at the moment of Algerian independence. After a series of unsuccessful mediation attempts by the Council of the Arab League and a number of African and Arab States, the Emperor of Ethiopia and the President of Mali managed to persuade the parties to accept what became known as the Bamako Agreement. This incorporated cease-fire, a commission to determine a demilitarisation zone composed of the parties and the mediators, a request to the combatants to observe strictly the principles of non-interference and of settlement of all disputes between African States by negotiation, and a proposed meeting of OAU foreign ministers at Addis Ababa to establish a commission which would *inter alia* put forward suggestions for the settlement of the dispute. This arbitration commission was set up in November 1963 with representatives of Ethiopia, Mali, Ivory Coast, Nigeria, Senegal, Sudan and Tanganyika and the following February an agreement regarding a demilitarised zone, withdrawals, the establishment of a no-man's-land and an exchange of prisoners was signed.[12] In January 1969, Morocco and Algeria signed a Treaty of Solidarity and Co-operation and in 1970 the parties agreed upon a final settlement of the frontier dispute with a joint demarcation commission. The colonial frontier was recognised, while Morocco was to have a share in mineral exploitation regarding the disputed area. In June 1972, a border agreement was signed declaring that the disputed area would remain part of Algeria. This was ratified by Algeria in 1973, but has yet to be ratified by Morocco. The mid-1970s, however, marked a turning point for the worse in relations between the parties on account of the Western Sahara problem. It should be noted that the United Nations played no significant part in the easing of tension during the 1960s.

(ii) *Somali Claims*. Somalia is unique among African States in being a homogeneous nation-State, but large numbers of ethnic

---

[12] See *Keesings Contemporary Archives*, pp. 19939–40.

Somalis live in areas of Ethiopia, Kenya and Djibouti. Somalia has sought to unite all Somali-inhabited areas under its flag and has thus rejected the *status quo* approach adopted by the OAU with regard to the borders bequeathed by the colonial Powers. The Somali case was discussed at a preparatory meeting of foreign ministers at Addis Ababa dealing with the creation of the OAU in 1963. Somalia requested an item to be placed on the agenda dealing with territorial disputes between neighbouring African States and the establishment of machinery to resolve them. It was included under item VII dealing with the creation of a Permanent Conciliation Commission, but never actually dealt with as the establishment of such a commission was subsumed under the general discussion on the setting up of an organisation of African States.[13] At the first OAU Summit Conference, the Somali president put forward his country's case, but was faced with arguments supporting the territorial integrity of States based upon colonial borders advanced by Ethiopia and the representatives of the pre-independent Kenyan African National Union party.

In July 1963, Ethiopia and Kenya signed a mutual defence agreement and in early 1964 incidents in the Ogaden region of Ethiopia claimed by Somalia led to fighting between the regular armies of Ethiopia and Somalia. Somalia informed the OAU Secretariat of the fighting and requested a meeting of the United Nations Security Council. The Secretary-General of the United Nations emphasised that an African framework would be preferable for discussion of the problem and the issue was accordingly placed before an Extraordinary Session of the OAU Council of Ministers at Dar-es-Salaam. Somalia informed the United Nations Secretary-General that it would not raise the matter with the Security Council while the problem was in the hands of the OAU. At the Conference, a resolution was adopted calling for a cease-fire, cessation of hostile propaganda and negotiations for a peaceful settlement of the dispute between Ethiopia and Somalia.[14] A more limited resolution was adopted with regard to Kenya. At the Second Ordinary Session of the Council of Ministers held at Lagos, a further resolution was approved which, while reaffirming the one made at Dar-es-Salaam, called on Ethiopia and Somalia to open direct negotiations and significantly referred to Article III(3) of the OAU Charter, which specifically emphasises respect for the sovereignty and territorial integrity of States. A cease-fire was

---

[13] CIAS/Plenary/3, May 22, 1963. See also Brownlie, *op. cit.* in note 11 above, pp. 826–51 and 888–916.

[14] ECM/Res.3(II). See also Touval, "The Organisation of African Unity and African Borders," 21 *International Organisation* (1967) p. 102.

ultimately agreed through Sudanese mediation in March 1964 and the joint communique issued at the end of the meeting between the parties noted that the talks had taken place in accordance with the recommendations of the OAU.

The OAU kept the problem in view during succeeding years and a minor agreement was signed between Ethiopia and Somalia in 1965. A meeting that year between Somalia and Kenya arranged by Tanzania failed to achieve any results. However, during the fourth OAU Assembly in Kinshasa in 1967, the Zambian president encouraged these parties to meet and following a conference at Arusha under Zambian mediation, an agreement was signed relating to the easing of tension.

The Ethiopian-Somali situation remained quiescent for a number of years. However, the issue was revived in 1973 due to a number of factors ranging from the growing tension between the two with regard to the decolonisation of Djibouti to the discovery of oil and gas in the Ogaden region. Somalia accused Ethiopia of massing troops in the area at the OAU Council of Ministers in May 1973 and insisted on placing the issue on the agenda of the OAU Assembly in terms of a territorial dispute. In the event, the Council decided to appoint a five-man commission and the following month an OAU good offices commission was set up with a Sudanese mediator.[15] As the Ethiopian régime weakened and was ultimately overthrown, infiltration of the Ogaden by the Somali-backed Western Somali Liberation Front (WSLF) increased. By the summer of 1977, it was clear that the WSLF controlled virtually all of the Ogaden plain.

On August 2, 1977, the Ethiopians failed to secure the necessary two-thirds vote for the convening of an emergency session of the OAU Council of Ministers. The OAU Commission set up in 1973 attempted to mediate, but as the WSLF was denied a hearing, Somalia boycotted the closing sessions of the meetings. A resolution was, however, adopted by this commission which reaffirmed the inviolability of African frontiers as at the date of independence and condemned political subversion.

On February 11, 1978, Somalia officially announced that its regular army was being sent into the Ogaden, but Cuban and Soviet assistance to Ethiopia proved decisive and on March 9, 1978, Somalia declared that its forces were being withdrawn. Somalia received no international support for its irredentist activities and it was made clear that military aid would only be sent to Somalia to defend its recognised borders.

---

[15] *Africa Research Bulletin*, May 1973, p. 2845 and *ibid.*, June 1973, pp. 2883–4, and 2850. See also Mayall, "The Battle for the Horn: Somali Irredentism and International Diplomacy," *The World Today* (September 1978), p. 336.

A meeting of the OAU Commission on the dispute took place in Lagos in August 1980 and adopted a six-point resolution. This emphasised *inter alia* "the recognition, affirmation, implementation and application" of the principle of the inviolability of frontiers of member States as attained at the time of independence. The resolution also invoked as a principle the strongest possible opposition to any encouragement of subversion against the government of another country.[16]

The dispute shows no signs of being settled. Somalia has maintained its support for the WSLF guerrillas, while its military efforts have been consistently thwarted. The OAU has continued its efforts, focusing on the territorial issue. At the June 1981 Assembly of Heads of State and Governments of the OAU, a resolution was adopted despite Somali objections reaffirming that the Ogaden was "an integral part of Ethiopia."[17]

(iii) *The Uganda-Tanzania War*.[18] Following a long period of tense relations between the two States, Ugandan troops invaded Tanzanian territory down to the Kagera river. However, following a visit by a delegation from the OAU, President Amin of Uganda declared that he would withdraw his troops provided that Tanzania would not invade Uganda and would not arm Ugandan exiles. Tanzania, on the other hand, took the view that African States and the OAU had to condemn Uganda's occupation of its territory. Towards the end of November, Tanzanian forces entered Uganda having driven out the invaders. The OAU announced that it would set up a special committee to analyse the causes of the border war. The chairman of the OAU, President Numeiry of Sudan, visited the parties and Kenya in December, but Tanzania was highly critical of the OAU failure to condemn Uganda's invasion and rejected any move to set up a special fact-finding committee until this was rectified.

The deteriorating border situation prompted President Amin to call for an immediate Security Council meeting in February 1979, but both the president of the Council and the United Nations Secretary-General held that this call did not constitute a properly worded request and no action was therefore taken. An OAU mediation committee (composed of Central African Empire, Gabon, Gambia, Madagascar, Nigeria, Togo, Tunisia, Zaire and Zambia) met in Kenya to try and achieve a cease-fire. Tanzania laid down four conditions for such a cease-fire: OAU condemnation of

---

[16] *Africa Research Bulletin*, August 1980, pp. 5763–4.

[17] *Keesings Contemporary Archives*, p. 31055.

[18] See *Africa Research Bulletin*, November 1978, pp. 5052–5; *ibid.*, December 1978, p. 5088; *ibid.*, February 1979, pp. 5153–5; and *ibid.*, March 1979, p. 5186.

the Ugandan invasion, Ugandan renunciation of any claim on Tanzanian territory, compensation for loss of life and property during the two-week Ugandan occupation of the Kagera region and a pledge to cease using Tanzania "as a scapegoat for [Amin's] internal problems." The committee decided to send delegations to visit the parties. Tanzania re-emphasised its position and noted that the OAU could not remain neutral since as a result of Uganda's aggression, Tanzania's territorial integrity and the OAU Charter had been violated.

The mediation committee, however, concluded at the beginning of March that it could do no more to settle the conflict. It noted that Amin had accepted all the OAU peace proposals calling for a cease-fire and respect for territorial integrity, while Tanzania reaffirmed its demand that the OAU condemn the Ugandan invasion. The issue was resolved, in the event, by military force. On April 11, 1979, Kampala, the Ugandan capital, fell to the Tanzanian and Ugandan exile forces. The new régime received widespread recognition within a few days.

(b) *Civil Wars*

(i) *Wars of Secession.* Since the advent of the decolonisation era in the later 1950s and early 1960s, Africa has been faced by a series of wars of secession. African emphasis upon State sovereignty and territorial integrity coupled with fears of chaos if the admittedly arbitrarily determined colonial borders were disturbed has conditioned its response in this area. African States have refused to recognise any right in international law of secession in relation to independent States, whether or not as a manifestation of the umbrella principle of self-determination, and this had clearly affected the manner of settlement of such disputes by peaceful means.

The Congo-Katanga dispute of 1960–1963 was marked by extensive United Nations involvement, which ultimately resulted in the use of force by United Nations troops against the Katangan secession, but this was predicated upon Belgian and mercenary control of the secessionist enterprise. Of a different character entirely was the Biafran secessionist attempt of 1967–70.[19]

In this case, the OAU took a strong line condemning secession in any member State at its September 1967 Conference and a mission was sent to Nigeria to emphasise the desire of the OAU Assembly for the territorial integrity, unity and peace of Nigeria. The

---

[19] See generally, Stremlau, *The International Politics of the Nigerian Civil War 1967–70* (1977), and *Africa Research Bulletin*, January 1970, pp. 1642–54.

following year, the Assembly called on member-States of the OAU and the UN to refrain from any action detrimental to the peace, unity and territorial integrity of Nigeria.

In September 1969, at the sixth OAU Assembly a resolution was adopted which called on both sides "to agree to preserve in the overriding interests of Africa the unity of Nigeria." On January 12, 1970, Biafra surrendered, both sides referring to the acceptance of the "OAU Resolution."

The civil war fought in the Sudan for the secession of the three southern provinces was ultimately resolved between the two sides themselves in an agreement in 1972, following a conference in Addis Ababa. Outside interest was sporadic, although an inconclusive round-table conference was held in Khartoum in 1965 attended by representatives from the north and south, with observers from Algeria, the United Arab Republic, Uganda, Kenya, Nigeria and Ghana.[20] Another situation which has attracted relatively few outside mediation attempts concerns the attempted secession of Eritrea from Ethiopia. In this case, a violent war has raged with surprisingly little attention being paid to it by the OAU or other possible mediatory bodies. Relevant factors here would probably include the important status enjoyed in Africa by Ethiopia, at least prior to the revolution, Soviet and Cuban involvement and the complicating Arab dimension, coupled with the anti-secessionist stance adopted by the vast majority of African States.

(ii) *Wars for Control of the Authority Structure.* In such cases, the civil war is centred on control of the State as a whole and its governmental machine, rather than on an effort by one particular area to secede and form a separate, independent State.

The Chad civil war may be dated from 1966.[21] The country is basically divided between a Moslem north and a Christian and animist south, the latter controlling the government since independence, although the divisions are in fact far more complex. French aid for the government was matched by Libyan aid for the rebel Frolinat organisation based in the north. A conference held in February 1978 in Libya, in which Libya, Chad, Niger and Sudan took part, led to further meetings of the participants and Frolinat, which ended in an eight-point agreement between the latter and the Chad government, which recognised Frolinat and called for a

---

[20] See Eprile, *War and Peace in the Sudan 1955–72* (1974); and K. Kyle, "The Southern Problem in the Sudan," *The World Today* (December 1966), p. 512.

[21] *Africa Research Bulletin*, March 1979, pp. 5195–7; *ibid.*, May 1979, p. 5266; *ibid.*, November 1979, pp. 5464–6; *ibid.*, March 1980, pp. 5611–2; *ibid.*, June 1980, p. 5709; *ibid.*, October 1980, p. 5822; *ibid.*, December 1980. pp. 5903–7; *ibid.*, January 1981, pp. 5929–34; and *ibid.*, June 1981, pp. 6068–9.

cease-fire throughout Chad. This agreement, however, was followed by a series of battles as a result of which Frolinat advanced into central Chad, being stopped only by the use of French troops. In August 1978 an agreement was signed between the government and the Hissan Habre branch of Frolinat, by virtue of which Habre became Prime Minister and the country administered by a government of national unity. This arrangement broke down within a few months and the Sudanese president, chairman of the OAU for that year, attempted mediation. This appeared to succeed with the signature on March 15, 1979, of the Kano Agreement by President Malloum, Prime Minister Habre, and the representatives of Frolinat and the Popular Movement for the Liberation of Chad. This agreement was also signed by Niger, Libya, Sudan, Cameroon and Nigeria; and provided for a neutral force of Nigerian troops to work under an independent monitoring commission consisting of a Nigerian chairman plus two delegates from each of the participating countries and one representative from each of the Chadian signatories. A National Transitional Union Government composed of all the Chadian signatories was to be established.

At a further conference consisting of all Chad's neighbours (Niger, Nigeria, Libya, Sudan, Central African Empire and Cameroon), the dissolution of the government established in Chad that April was demanded and more Chadian factions were encouraged to sign the Kano accord. The Libyan Foreign Minister noted that this was the first time that neighbouring States had sought a peaceful solution to the internal conflicts of an African State. Further clashes broke out in Chad between movements in the government and Nigeria withdrew its forces from the country. In August 1979, the Lagos Accord on National Reconciliation in Chad brought together 11 rival groups in a government of national unity with the leader of Frolinat as President and the leader of the southern forces as Vice-President.

The Accord, however, broke down as fighting started between the forces of the President and the Defence Minister, Habre, and Libyan troops intervened on behalf of the former in the spring of 1980. The OAU ad hoc Sub-Committee dealing with the problem organised a conference at home in October 1980 calling for the establishment of a neutral African force in Chad, but this had little effect. Increased Libyan involvement led to the victory of the President's forces and an announcement at the start of January 1981 of the merger of the two countries. This was condemned by the OAU. Various attempts at resolving the crisis on the part of African leaders failed, but a resolution of the June 1981 OAU Assembly called for an OAU peacekeeping force to be sent to Chad. This was supported by France, who offered financial and logistical aid and propelled into reality by Libya's precipitate withdrawal from the country in November 1981.[22]

(c) *The Western Sahara Dispute*

This dispute, neither an inter-State dispute in essence, nor a civil war, is primarily a conflict between Morocco and the Polisario movement representing the inhabitants of the former Spanish colony.

Morocco and Mauritania laid claim to the territory on a variety of historical, cultural and ethnic grounds. In 1975, the UN General Assembly requested an advisory opinion from the International Court of Justice on aspects of the problem and a visiting mission went to the area. The court concluded that it had found no legal ties between the parties on the one hand and the territory on the other at the time of Spanish colonisation of such a nature as to effect the application of UN General Assembly Resolution 1514(XV) in the decolonisation of the Western Sahara and in particular the principle of self-determination.[23] The United Nations Visiting Mission reporting within a few days of the court's opinion, stated that "there was an overwhelming consensus among Saharans within the territory in favour of independence and opposing integration with any neighbouring country."[24]

Morocco, however, organised a "green march" of civilians into the territory. An agreement with Spain and Mauritania soon followed, the essence of which marked the acceptance by the parties of the partition of the Sahara between the two claimants upon Spain's withdrawal, which duly took place in February 1976.[25] In December 1975, the United Nations General Assembly adopted two resolutions dealing with the problem. The first reaffirmed the principle of self-determination and the need to apply it to the territory "within a framework that guarantees and permits them the free and genuine expression of their will," while the second confusingly took note of the tripartite agreement and called only for respect for the aspirations of the population and merely "free consultations" organised by a United Nations representative rather than United Nations supervision of the act of self-determination.[26]

---

[22] *The Guardian*, November 2, 1981, p. 6.
[23] See M. Shaw, "The Western Sahara Case," 49 *British Yearbook of International Law* (1978) p. 119 and I.C.J. Reports, 1975, pp. 12, 33 and 68.
[24] A/10023/Add.1, Annex, paras. 202, 219–20 and 229.
[25] See Franck, "The Stealing of the Sahara," 70 *American Journal of International Law* (1976), p. 694.
[26] Resolutions 3458A (XXX) and 3458B (XXX).

In February 1976, following an increasing number of clashes in the territory, the Polisario independence movement declared the sovereign Saharan Arab Democratic Republic. The United Nations Secretary-General announced that the United Nations would not legitimate the actions of Morocco and Mauritania, which together with the fighting taking place, rendered any consultation impossible. The meeting of the OAU Council of Ministers in June 1976 adopted a resolution proposed by Benin unconditionally supporting the just struggle of the Saharan people and calling for respect for the territorial integrity of Western Sahara and the withdrawal of foreign and occupation forces. As a result of this, Morocco boycotted the subsequent OAU summit meeting and discussion of the issue was accordingly postponed. OAU plans to hold a special session on the problem were put off on a number of occasions. At the July 1978 OAU summit conference a resolution was adopted which reaffirmed the intention of holding a special session on the issue and a committee was established "to find a solution to this question compatible with the right of self-determination."[27] The United Nations General Assembly in Resolution 32/22 reaffirmed its commitment to the principle of self-determination in this case and expressed the hope that a just and lasting solution could be found in accordance with United Nations principles at the proposed OAU summit meeting.

In July 1978, a coup took place in Mauritania which led to the unilateral declaration of a cease-fire by the Polisario with respect to its southern opponent, and ultimately to an agreement whereby Mauritania renounced all claims to the southern part of Western Sahara under its control.

The OAU committee established in July 1978 (the so-called "committee of wise men") set up in December 1978 a subcommittee, consisting of the Heads of State of Nigeria and Mali, to make an on-the-spot investigation of the dispute, and in that month the United Nations General Assembly adopted two resolutions on the issue.[28] The first, Resolution 33/31A, stressed the inalienable right to the Saharan People to self-determination and independence as well as the responsibility of the United Nations in the matter. Resolution 33/31B took note of the decision of the OAU summit in July 1978 to establish an ad hoc committee and expressed support for its efforts. An increase in fighting in the area in 1979 between Morocco and the

---

[27] *Africa Research Bulletin*, June 1976, p. 4047; *ibid.*, June 1976, pp. 4078 and 4081; *ibid.*, July 1977, pp. 4486–7; *ibid.*, August 1977, p. 4523; *ibid.*, September 1977, p. 4554; *ibid.*, March 1978, pp. 4770–1, and *ibid.*, July 1978, p. 4914.
[28] *Ibid.*, July 1979, p. 5330.

Algerian-supported Polisario occurred and a number of towns in the Western Sahara and in southern Morocco were attacked. In addition, a growing number of States recognised the Saharan Republic.

The OAU committee reported to the OAU summit in July 1979, calling for a referendum on self-determination for the Western Sahara, and this report was adopted by the necessary two-thirds majority, after a Moroccan walk-out. This was the first time that OAU Assembly of Heads of State and Government had taken a clear stand on the issue and it reflected a continuing decline in Morocco's influence, by a takeover of the southern region of Western Sahara by Moroccan forces.

The OAU "committee of wise men" dealing with the problem held a meeting in December 1979 at which Morocco was urged to withdraw from the territory and a referendum on self-determination was called for.[29] The OAU summit in July 1980, however, postponed a decision on the question of the admission of the Saharan Arab Democratic Republic to the organisation, despite indications that a clear majority favoured this, in the light of threats to leave the OAU made by Morocco and its supporters.[30] The "committee of wise men" organised a meeting in Sierra Leone in September 1980 of all the parties involved including Morocco, Mauritania, Algeria and Polisario, at which a fair and general referendum was called for to be organised by the United Nations and the OAU together with a cease-fire which would be supervised by United Nations peace-keeping troops.[31] This did not materialise, however, until an apparent Libyan-Moroccan reconciliation at the June 1981 Summit prompted King Hassan of Morocco to accept the need for "a controlled referendum" which would "simultaneously respect the objectives of the latest recommendations of the 'committee of wise men' and the conviction which Morocco has of its legitimate rights."

In the light of this, the OAU established an implementation committee to oversee in essence the carrying out of the September 1980 proposals.[32] It remains to be seen whether this will be successful since a number of problems relating to the plan's provisions have begun to emerge, in particular with regard to the nature of the referendum and the responsibility for its organisation.[33]

[29] *Ibid.*, December 1979, p. 5498
[30] *Ibid.*, July 1980, pp. 5731–2.
[31] *Ibid.*, September 1980, p. 5794.
[32] *Keesings Contemporary Archives*, pp. 31053–5.
[33] *West Africa*, October 26, 1981, p. 2489.

IV—AFRICAN PRACTICE
WITH REGARD TO PRINCIPLES
OF RELEVANCE IN DISPUTE-SETTLEMENT

(a) *Initial Recourse to African Mechanisms*

One of the principles that has evolved over the last two decades or so is that disputing African States should first of all attempt to resolve their differences within an African framework. Based essentially on Articles 33 and 52 which deals with regional organisations of the United Nations Charter, this approach has crystallised in practice. It has been recognised, indeed encouraged, by the United Nations Security Council. In resolution 199(1964), dealing with the Congo crisis, the Council noted its conviction that the OAU "should be able, in the context of article 52 of the Charter, to help find a peaceful solution to all the problems and disputes affecting peace and security in the continent of Africa." Although this clearly indicated that the Security Council viewed the role of the OAU as operating within the general jurisdiction of the UN Charter, and subject to the Council's primary responsibility for the maintenance of international peace and security, it can nevertheless be seen as an early acceptance of the African organisation as an organ of resort with regard to African disputes.

In the case of the Congo crisis, which of course erupted before the OAU came into existence, the intervention of the United Nations can be seen as a direct response to the involvement of non-African elements in the affairs of that country. The efforts of the OAU-established mediation committee in 1964 failed in the light of the intransigence displayed by Tshombe, the former architect of Katanga's secession, and additional foreign intervention in the form of the "Stanleyville Operation." It will be recalled that Somalia first of all called on the United Nations at the time of the 1964 conflict with Ethiopia, but was later convinced not to pursue that course while the issue was being dealt with by the OAU.

The United Nations took virtually no part in efforts to resolve the Nigerian civil war and the action undertaken by the OAU has not sought to establish a primary or superior jurisdiction. On the contrary, it has encouraged United Nations involvement in such matters. This was so even with regard to discussions relating to the decolonisation of the Western Sahara when it had become apparent that serious inter-African disputes were involved.

The general rule relating to the advisability of initial recourse to African efforts can be seen with regard also to the Libyan-Chad boundary dispute. While Chad did bring the issue before the United Nations Security Council in February 1978, it withdrew its complaint later that month as a result of discussions between the parties, held under Sudanese mediation.[34] A mediation committee was set up by the OAU in July 1977 and the issue was discussed at the July 1978 summit. Whether this principle of initial recourse to African mechanisms has proved efficacious is another matter, however. The record has proved to be very mixed. What can be said is that this principle has clearly been seen by African States as central to the evolution of some sort of regional order with respect to the continent. It can indeed be regarded as a vital threshold factor to an effective African system of dispute settlement.

(b) *Respect for the Sovereignty and Territorial Integrity of States*

Article II(3) of the OAU Charter emphasises the adherence of member-States to the principle of respect for the sovereignty and territorial integrity of each State. In 1964, the OAU adopted a resolution in which it solemnly declared that all member-States pledged themselves to respect the frontiers existing on their achievement of national independence. This resolution was not unanimously accepted as both Morocco and Somalia refused to be bound, but it can be said to have marked the acceptance by Africa as a whole of a new and definite territorial régime, one based on the legal validity of the colonially drawn frontiers.

Practice has reaffirmed this position. The OAU has shown that it is firmly opposed to irredentism. Its response to the Somali crises of 1964, 1973, and 1977–81 demonstrates this. Its attitude to the Western Sahara dispute may also be cited in support, since the dominant principle to be applied has been accepted as being that of self-determination, defined as permitting the population a free choice as to its future political status. The OAU has similarly set its face against recognising a right of secession in the case of independent States. This can be seen with respect to the Congo, Nigeria, Sudan and Ethiopia. Resolutions that have been adopted by the OAU have stressed the principles of national unity and territorial integrity.

In colonial and neo-colonial white minority rule situations, the right to self-determination has been firmly emphasised as the applicable principle. But in such decolonisation cases, African States have also stressed the role of the United Nations and such situations have been treated as distinct from inter-African disputes *per se.*

---

[34] *UN Monthly Chronicle*, March 1978, p. 5. Note also that Morocco withdrew its complaint to the UN Security Council in June 1979 regarding alleged Algerian aggression, following an appeal by President Numeiry of Sudan, the OAU Chairman: see *UN Monthly Chronicle*, July 1979, p. 30.

(c) *Non-Intervention*

Both the Charters and practice of the United Nations and the OAU have emphasised that importance of the norm of non-intervention. Article 2(7) provides that nothing contained in the United Nations Charter shall authorise the organisation to intervene in matters essentially within the domestic jurisdiction of any State. In 1965, the General Assembly declared that "no State has the right to intervene, directly or indirectly, for any reason whatever in the internal or external affairs of any other State." The OAU Charter emphasises the principle of non-interference in the internal affairs of States, as well as expressing unreserved condemnation of political assassination and subversive activities on the part of other States. A Declaration on the Problem of Subversion issued by the OAU Assembly in 1965 reiterated these points.

In the case of the Nigerian civil war, the Federal Government only reluctantly permitted OAU involvement, but since the organisation in effect adopted Nigeria's basic position as regards national unity and territorial integrity, no serious problems arose.

In the Uganda-Tanzania conflict of 1978–9, however, the principle of non-interference was clearly breached. The Ugandan invasion and purported annexation of part of neighbouring Tanzania constituted a serious violation of the territorial integrity of the victim State. It offended against both the United Nations and OAU Charters and enabled Tanzania to take action under the self-defence provisions of article 51 of the United Nations Charter to repel the invaders and prevent any immediate recurrence of the invasion threat. Tanzania, however, went further than this. It permitted the former Ugandan leader, Milton Obote, to issue an insurrection appeal from its territory in January 1979 and encouraged Ugandan exiles to form an Ugandan National Liberation Front to fight against Uganda.[35] Such activities on the surface appeared to offend against the OAU stand on subversion and interference. The overthrow of the Amin administration and the successful occupation of the whole of Uganda, however, clearly violated United Nations and OAU norms regarding non-intervention. It went beyond the permitted limits of self-defence under international law.

Tanzania's action was severely criticised by President Numeiry, the OAU chairman and attempted mediator in the dispute, at the July 1979 OAU summit. This issue was ultimately shelved and the President of Liberia, the host leader, concluded that "all of us are convinced the Charter of the OAU needs to be examined and revisions made so that such matters as this can be handled

---

[35] *Africa Research Bulletin*, March 1979, p. 5187, and *ibid.*, April 1979, p. 5222.

appropriately in future."[36] It remains to be seen how far in practice
the principle of non-intervention has been breached and how far
Tanzania's forceful action will serve as an example and a precedent
for other African States.

V—CONCLUSIONS

This survey of practice relating to certain important disputes among
independent African States points to some preliminary conclusions
as regards ways adopted to resolve serious differences. In terms of
the accepted classification of methods of dispute settlement, it is
significant to note the virtually complete rejection of resort to
arbitration or judicial settlement on the basis of rules of international law that many consider not only ambiguous but too Western-
oriented is especially marked.

This distrust of a permanent institutional framework for the
peaceful resolution of disputes has also led to the virtual demise of
the OAU Commission of Conciliation, Mediation and Arbitration.
Of the reasons that may be put forward to explain this, the most
powerful is clearly the emphasis that Third-World States in general
and African States in particular have placed on State sovereignty
and the manifest fear of outside interference. The emphasis,
therefore, with respect to the resolution of inter-State disputes has
been shifted on to the more informal and flexible methods of
negotiation, mediation and good offices, and conciliation.

Negotiation is often the method of first resort and the one that is
usually effective in resolving most disputes of a non-serious nature.
But where the issue is relatively more contentious, third-party
involvement is usually required. This has occurred in many
instances in recent African practice, but without distinctions being
drawn between mediation, good offices and conciliation. Instead,
mediation has been used almost as a generic term for third-party
involvement of a non-binding, informal and flexible manner.

Such mediation has been effected, or attempted, either by a
distinguished individual or by an ad hoc committee comprising
anything from two to 10 States. Emperor Haile Selassie, until his
overthrow in the Ethiopian revolution, was the leading example of
the former with Kenyatta of Kenya, Tubman of Liberia and Gowon
of Nigeria as further instances of leading African personalities
making influential contributions to the resolution of disputes. More
usual, however, is the use of ad hoc commissions composed of a
number of African Heads of State. Examples here would include

---

[36] *Ibid.*, July 1979, pp. 5328–9.

the Moroccan-Algerian conflict of 1964, the Somali disputes, the case of Chad and the Western Saharan problem. In most instances, the commission in question will have been designated through the medium of the OAU. When this has occurred, a greater authoritativeness is generally perceived to be involved. In a number of cases, the OAU Council of Ministers or Assembly of Heads of State and Government has adopted a resolution bearing directly upon the dispute in question, for example in the Congo and Somali crises of 1964 and the Western Sahara dispute. In others, the OAU has merely provided the arena in which attempts at a solution have been made, for example the border dispute between Ghana and Upper Volta in the early 1960s which was eventually solved through bilateral negotiations in June 1966. Such commissions have been ad hoc dealing only with particular disputes, composed of leading personalities and operating in accordance with general political considerations, rather than on the basis of a series of legal rules.

If African States have shied away from dipute settlement by strictly legal criteria and institutional formality, the role of the OAU has been of great importance. It has provided a convenient, valuable and recognised framework within which the ad hoc mediation system has flourished. It has also been instrumental in elucidating a number of relevant principles for use by African States. But its significance should not be exaggerated. The organisation has failed to solve many serious disputes, for example the Somali conflicts with its neighbours, the Nigerian, Sudan, Ethiopian and Chad civil wars and perhaps most forcefully the Angolan war. It has proved hesitant with regard to the Western Sahara conflict and virtually moribund as regards the Uganda-Tanzania war. There are many reasons for these failures, outstanding among them being the extreme reluctance of African States to commit their vital, and perhaps not so vital, interests to outside parties, particularly institutional ones. One must therefore in the light of practice see the role of the OAU in African dispute settlement in terms of providing an existing and flexible framework for the encouragement of acceptable third-party mediation, rather as an active instrument itself for the resolution of such disputes. The OAU may in the course of time evolve into this, but this would not appear to be imminent. It remains as a form of African "sorting-office" for ad hoc mediation.

What the OAU has sought has been the creation of relative harmony rather than the enforcement in an open and effective manner of its own principles. Its strength lies in its capacity to encourage the process of third-party mediation, but to remain a viable force for the future it must progress beyond this.

MULTINATIONALS AT WORK

AN INSIDE ASSESSMENT

By

X.X.

THE worldwide business empires commonly referred to as multi-national enterprises are a phenomenon of the last 30 years, although many of them such as Ford and Exxon, had a number of international subsidiaries before the Second World War. Multi-nationals may be defined as large business corporations controlled predominantly by nationals of the country in which their head-quarters are situated, but with operating activities spread across many different countries, employing tens of thousands of people.

The public image of the multinational enterprise is formed out of prejudice and ignorance. Some of this prejudice is encouraged, even initiated or catalysed, by politicians who wish to shift responsibility for their failures onto others, and find that the blame rests all too credibly on multinationals in the eyes of a gullible public. The main reason why mud sticks so readily to a multinational, whether or not with justification, is the mystery which surrounds the organisation and its decision-making machinery. The closure of a car assembly plant, for example, which may cast a blight over an entire city, perhaps even a region, is seen by the affected community to have been ordered by anonymous directors sitting behind closed doors, perhaps a continent away. The anger of voters with their political overlords finds expression at the polls. Politicians—or at least those who succeed in maintaining their power base—are acutely aware of their precarious position and take care to protect their public image. A multinational, in contrast, is overwhelmingly impersonal, which gives rise to deep frustration amongst those who feel they have been wronged by it, so that the resentment lives on. In these circum-stances it is but a short step to project the blame apparently attributable to one specific corporation to all multinationals.

I—CHARACTERISTICS AND NORMS OF BEHAVIOUR OF MULTINATIONALS

(a) *Absence of Personality*

The apparent absence of personalities at the head of multination-als is partly a function of the limited tenure of office at the very top—the typical top executive reaching the pinnacle at the end of his career—and partly because the prima donna is actively discouraged. Chairman and directors are appointed, and retire, with such frequency that few become publicly known. Occasionally a showman emerges to catch a few headlines before disappearing precipitately from the scene, probably prematurely. Top managers unite swiftly to oppose one of their number who seeks to corner the limelight. As in the Kremlin—witness the fate of Khrushchev—the leader must not be too far above the hierarchy on whom he depends. Very occasionally a talented communicator is chosen as chairman and, assuming he does not have to explain away disasters, becomes an accepted and respected spokesman not only for his company, but perhaps also for the industry in general. Because this can yield benefits to his fellow-directors too—fame for the company, reflected glory for the directors, increased business prospects, better quality staff recruits—such an outstanding individual will be accepted, and attention can then turn to the succession. Even less frequently, an outstanding business mind emerges at an early enough stage in his career for him to remain at the top for a decade or more. Arnold (Lord) Weinstock of General Electric of the United Kingdom is one such example. A radical and dynamic programme to keep that company up with the leaders in its field, coupled with astute and ruthless management, have clearly succeeded to date. He is likely to have made his enemies within the corporation, who have waited in vain for failure to sweep him aside, but who so far have been confounded. In such an exposed position, there is no substitute for success and no excuse for failure.

(b) *Norms of the Promotional Ladder*

In order to appreciate how a multinational functions, it is essential to understand the processes which influence executive behaviour. Certainly every top executive does, or he would not be where he is. Typical senior executives in multinationals take care to be neither too exposed nor too isolated. New ideas have to be canvassed amongst colleagues before they are recommended for further consideration. Only when a quorum of support is available will the responsible executive formally present his case. That support will be duly noted by the as yet uncommitted amongst the directorial decision-takers. It may only have been obtained at some cost: the sponsoring executive's support for another's pet project, or agreement to the transfer of a young high-flier from one division to another. Although the sponsoring executive is partially exposed, his burden is shared by those supporting him, and they cannot all be demoted or sacked in the event of failure of the scheme. The principle of collective support and protection applies. It would be safer not to promote anything, but ultimately the deteriorating results of his sector catch up with the individual who plays it too safe. Furthermore his ambition to rise further in the organisation will be unsatisfied unless he can show some reason why he should rise above the increasingly tough competition surrounding him as his career progresses.

The uncompromisingly ambitious senior executive acknowledges to himself, but probably to no-one else (because the ambitious trusts nobody), a series of precepts for improving his position which can be summarised in the following way:

(1) *Demonstrate success*—where possible by displaying genuine examples of prowess, otherwise by purloining those of rivals or more junior colleagues and by association with the successes of others.

(2) *Disguise failure*—by non-disclosure if this is likely to succeed, or by partial disclosure if the penalties for non-disclosure are too great. An able "politician" can sometimes turn a corporate failure into a personal success through emphasis of the incidental benefits arising from a failed project. This can be dangerous, for his shrewd peers and rivals may see through his scheme and ridicule him, perhaps outside his own hearing. But the safest protection from failure is the collective responsibility of the colleagues who were cajoled into giving their support in the first place. Their complicity must be tactfully exposed if it is not freely offered at the moment of reckoning.

(3) *Denigrate rivals*—through the use of legitimate comment on the plans or results of rivals, and by exposing their managerial weaknesses and therefore their unsuitability for a higher post. This too is dangerous and can back-fire, especially if the rival succeeds in turning the tables on his denigrator. Discretion is the art of this game, although observers of the scene will quickly become aware of the real battle being fought in deadly earnest beneath the superficial skirmishing over the item of business. They will enjoy their role as spectators although they may have a vested interest in the outcome. Their ultimate support may also be sought by both rivals. A choice may have to be made, although if necessary a neutral stance can easily be taken by the use of obfuscatory language which can often be unchallenged by colleagues who recognise the technique but are unwilling to cross-question the individual using it, for they too will make use of it when it suits them.

(4) *Elicit the benediction of the chairman*—or for the chairman, substitute any of the top, or soon to reach the top, dozen or so individuals. This curiously paternal route to promotion can be

remarkably successful, although its utility disappears with the retirement of the father-figure. A series of promotions, however rapid, takes time. So the beneficiary needs to choose his paternity with an eye not only to the influence but also to the future corporate longevity of his promoter. The beneficiary needs also to be able to promote his own cause, and to defend it, to his rivals and superiors on the departure of his promoter, or his fall from grace may be even more rapid than his rise. A curious aspect of this relationship is that the paternal figure usually stands to gain little or nothing from it, and may well lose authority if the recipient of his benediction fails him. Naturally he believes in his prodigy, but his judgment may well owe more to subliminal influences than to dispassionate analysis. The paternal judgment is frequently found lacking. The paternal figure may see in the younger man the qualities he lacks, although the fact that the younger man does not possess his strengths may be overlooked.

(5) *Foster outside connections*—such as an influential father, or marriage to a well-connected daughter. Such links will ensure that the executive is noticed, and may even result in his peers seeking to be approved by him as a means of being favourably reported to those influential connections.

(c) *Battle for Control*

The inner machinations at work in the headquarters of the multinational have little immediate bearing on its numerous affiliates worldwide. Their concern will be the local national manufacturing plan and market. Some may have wider regional interests, but probably few, if any, of the locally recruited staff will find their way into the headquarters organisation. Although increasingly multinationals are encouraging their brighter and more ambitious young executives from the overseas affiliates to seek a career in the main stream of the worldwide organisation, all still have distinctive national emphasis—or bi-national in the case of Shell and Unilever (Dutch/British). Nonetheless the ambitious within the affiliate will seek to curry favour with the powerful in the corporate headquarters in the continuing quest for promotion, for the most powerful control mechanism available to the headquarters over its affiliate is the appointment of its top managers. Such managers should be at once dynamic yet susceptible to central influence and persuasion. These are normally conflicting qualities, so that the appointee usually turns out to have predominantly one or the other. He will have given evidence of both to have obtained the post.

The headquarters organisation of a multinational has a curious sense of unreality about much of its activity. Typically it will be located in, or near to, a large city. Usually the office complex will be some distance from its manufacturing activities in that country, and large distances from its oversea affiliates and their activities. A typical affiliate might itself have a similar, but smaller, headquarters building separated from its factories. Almost inevitably, the abiding interest of the ambitious staff in the worldwide headquarters, and therefore those amongst them who will reach the top, is their own career and how to further it. This is not necessarily to question their dedication to the job, their loyalty, integrity, or ability, which will vary from individual to individual. Nevertheless, headquarters is a world of its own, acutely interested and involved in the worldwide activities of the corporation, but ultimately focusing inwards on itself. Most of those working within it will have been recruited direct from school or university and will work for no other organisation. They are conditioned to the particular organisation and have only a limited awareness of, or indeed interest in, the working of other corporations, government departments, small companies, or indeed the world at large unless there is specific incentive to find out. A potential executive board member of a multinational will not be judged primarily on his acceptability to outside organisations, or on his ability to deal with them, so much as on his internal suitability.

II—Standards of Behaviour

The aspect of a multinational's activities which seems to attract most public and press criticism is its ability to move funds and factories from one country to another. Unions are angered by the undermining of their power to negotiate nationally. Governments are suspicious of tax avoidance (if not evasion), contravention of foreign exchange regulations (in spirit if not legally) and of "fixed" prices between subsidiaries in different countries. The press and public cannot identify with those who decide to move a factory elsewhere, for they are in the corporate headquarters abroad, and the locally-born general manager is believed to be just a mouthpiece. It is felt that a multinational can cross national boundaries with impunity like a migrating bird. The prime aim of multinationals is to maximise their profits. In that respect they are no different from other companies, or from individuals. That the paraphernalia of national boundaries and restrictions should be utilised as far as possible for the benefit of the corporation should hardly be surprising, nor does this represent a dangerous or reprehensible trait. Governments by now are wise to the existence of actual or potential loopholes through which multinationals can, if allowed, achieve excessive profits. Such opportunities are now largely, but not entirely, denied to multinationals, who are quite philosophical about the fact. Flagrant contravention of laws is a rare occurrence, and even where this does happen, can usually be traced to the over-zealous activities of local management anxious to show better results. The international board has more sense, and is altogether too cautious and conservative, to sanction deliberate illegal activity, for the adverse publicity and damage to the corporate image worldwide on discovery far outweighs the gains which can be made. Also the headquarters of a multinational is not all that secure from infiltration, in spite of recent measures to tighten up, nor are all employees necessarily so blindly loyal as to keep sensitive matters secret. The chances of discovery are therefore too high, whatever the temptation may be. In any case the boards of multinationals consist of individuals who on average probably have no lesser standards of moral behaviour than citizens at large, although they have a greater sense of danger and for self-survival than the average citizen.

In many other respects, multinationals set business standards which are the envy of other companies. In relation to the local business environment in which their subsidiaries operate, their pay, conditions and pensions are almost invariably good, and their equipment similarly so. Although a natural reluctance to spend money on pollution control is evident, multinationals are at least as forward, usually much more so than smaller national companies, in introducing new control measures. They will avoid taking pollution control measures whenever local authorities will allow them to, for no executive will present a case for capital expenditure on such measures when there is no overwhelming case for such non-remunerative investment. As regards safety measures, the standards set by multinationals are usually higher than the minimum legal levels, and often many times higher. In general, a board recognises that it is in its own interest for criticism of the corporation's activities to be minimised. Mud cast at a multinational usually sticks, because it is a multinational and regardless of the justification for the allegations. The safest course is therefore to avoid, within reasonable limits, the likelihood of mud being thrown.

One particular allegation does deserve closer analysis: that multinationals move their production to low-wage countries and then pay wages comparable with the local levels. It is alleged that this causes unemployment in the high-wage countries and leads to "exploitation" of the people of low-wage countries. Taken at face value, and stripped of its emotions, this process is logical and arguably even beneficial on balance to the world at large, for the high-wage countries are by-and-large capable of fending for themselves, including re-employing or supporting their unemployed, whereas the poorer countries will remain poor without the injection of capital and expertise from outside. Whether it is in the interests, for example, of Malaysia to attract micro-chip production to its shores, is perhaps debatable in terms of the employment of women and the disruption of the family. Each case must be judged on its own merits as far as the benefits, as against the disbenefits, of a particular project in a less developed country are concerned. It is not for multinationals to set themselves up as international socio-political referees but to get on with the business of business. Politicians and governments must decide what is acceptable in any particular country.

The division between politics and business is not always clearcut, as for example, in the case of South Africa, where racial laws which are anathema to most countries of the world are combined with relatively low wages and the enforced separation of families. Most multinationals have kept out of South Africa, but a significant number, principally with British connections originating from the colonial era, have remained. Probably only one of them—British Petroleum (BP)—has suffered severely in another country because of the existence of its activities in South Africa; its interests in Nigeria were nationalised although it has been compensated by the Nigerian government. It also lost its oil lifting rights from Nigeria at the time when oil was scarce. However, the overall effect on BP's business has been negligible. Until, therefore, significant dissuasive steps are taken, the boards of multinationals will have difficulty in phasing down or pulling out of South Africa except on the grounds of unprofitability. The South African government, meanwhile, is careful to preserve profitable conditions. International governmental action could easily cause the multinationals to pull out of South Africa, but such action has not yet occurred. Until, or unless, it does the multinationals there must continue to view their investments strictly in terms of risk and return. One important factor in this equation, as explained earlier, is the durability of the existing government and the likely attitude of any successor to those companies who have co-operated with it. Arguably a new, even Marxist, régime emerging from the black majority in South Africa would need the continued help of the multinationals as much as does the existing régime, unless it were to turn to Eastern Europe or to China for long-term economic support—which brings with it the prospect of political interference.

There is no absolute answer to the question of multinationals in South Africa. Are they keeping the white Nationalists in power, or are they alleviating the lot of the oppressed blacks? Are they accelerating the process of change to democracy, or are they helping to ensure continued autocracy, whether white or black? The board of a multinational will make its own decision and will have to live with the consequences. Whether the influence of the multinationals in South Africa is in the long-term for good or bad, must be left to the moralists and, ultimately, the historians. Although South Africa is currently the most poignant instance of a régime with which multinationals co-operate, perhaps reluctantly, and at some considerable risk to their business interests elsewhere, there are other lesser instances, and there will no doubt be yet others in future, perhaps an autocratic, rightist régime in South America or communist in Southeast Asia.

III—Strengths of Multinationals

How can a multinational be so successful in a competitive and complex world when its managers are encouraged to become corporation men rather than worldly wise? There are a variety of explanations, all of which compensate handsomely for the inherent inefficiency of an introvert organisation. Success occurs in spite of the organisation, rather than because of it. First amongst the strengths available to a multinational is that of finance. Projects costing $1 billion or more, such as launching a new mass-production car or an aeroplane, can only be attempted by organisations which simultaneously have open lines of credit from dozens of banks. Multinationals are a godsend to banks who, although they will find themselves in competition with other banks and will probably have to concede a slightly lower interest rate than to smaller clients, are able to lend large sums of money at little risk and with minimal overheads. The project may fail, but the multinational will survive. Banks therefore, as a general rule, lend to the company rather than finance a project.

Secondly, much modern-day business is so large—for example oil production and refining—that for most part multinationals are virtually the only organisations able to participate in it. There are numerous exceptions, but domination by the multinationals of big business is widespread. The continued existence of smaller companies in competition with multinationals is in a large measure due to national protective measures, such as those adopted by the French to ensure the survival of their oil, chemical and automobile companies, and to anti-trust legislation prohibiting the reduction of competition through amalgamation (particularly in the United States). Legislation elsewhere ensures that local companies must participate in certain industries or projects—in Australia, for example—thus ensuring that multinationals must seek local partners.

Thirdly, multinationals are able to keep at the forefront of technical development in their particular fields of activity, through investment in research and development, or by buying out the inventions of smaller companies or individuals. Similarly they are able to acquire, by exploration or buying into a discovery, the lion's share of the natural resources not controlled by governments. Again sheer size, and the application of it worldwide, can assure a high market share for a Procter and Gamble or a Unilever in a variety of household products. Either can afford to sit out a long period of cut-price competition in one market through the strength it has obtained from its other markets. A local rival is unlikely to last the pace of outright competition to the finish, although it may be able to achieve a measure of co-existence.

Fourthly, the variety of a multinational's activities ensures as a general rule that the failure of any one project, however large, does not drag down the whole corporation. Shell and Gulf, for example, absorbed vast losses in their joint nuclear business with barely a blip noticeable in the graph of total corporate profits. No doubt other capital investment projects had to be postponed or cancelled as a direct result—for multinationals too have their financial limits, even if these are sometimes rather conservatively applied by the board. Conservatism, however, is an essential element of a successful board, for it ensures the survival of the corporation. The failure of several projects in close succession could indeed lead to the collapse of a multinational, but that is precisely the pitfall of which every board is acutely aware and which above all it seeks to avoid by declining to take on too many large risky ventures at the same time.

Fifthly, the size and importance, and also the relative scarcity of multinationals in any one business, ensure that they are cultivated by governments. Since politicians risk losing votes if their meetings with the heads of multinationals are given publicity, photographs and reports of these occasions are rarely seen in the newspapers. The multinationals themselves are reluctant to become too closely associated with a current government for fear that its successor, whether elected democratically or self-appointed by a less salubrious route, should be prejudiced against them. The chairman and directors of a multinational have ready access to the highest echelons of government in most countries of the world, provided that a subject of mutually important interest is for discussion. This applies to Western, Soviet and Third-World countries alike; democratic, communist or autocratic. This is not to say that the board members of a multinational are necessarily politically astute or even particularly well informed. There is no pressing reason for such political sophistication, partly because of the temporary occupation of the pinnacle of power by national leaders, and the need to have an equally fruitful relationship with their successors; partly because of the insularity of life in a multinational. Political astuteness—directed outwards as opposed to inwards—is not a prerequisite of promotion. Whether it should be is less certain. Multinationals cultivate political connections only in those countries in which they have an actual or immediately prospective business interest. In the organisation somewhere there is usually a small group taking a wider view of the world but it is unlikely that it will take more than a superficial interest in countries which are not currently of immediate business concern.

The sixth strength, to which I shall return later, is the quality of much of its middle management.

IV—Problems and Weaknesses of Multinationals

The case as stated in this paper so far would appear to suggest that the multinationals have survived with their honour intact. It would be over-simplistic, but not unduly unfair, to summarise the argument to date as being that multinationals are creatures of our time, an indispensible part of the modern industrial scene; they are not perfect but their influence by-and-large is for the general good. If a nation does not wish to have them operate within its borders, it can legislate to curb them and even eliminate them. In that event, something would have to replace them, perhaps a government agency, and arguably that could be worse. The antagonism towards multinationals in many parts is therefore largely a prejudice not based on logical thought processes. Most of the damage attributed to multinationals results from the process of technological change and economic reality rather than to any inherently evil nature in the people who work for them.

If most criticism does miss the target, this is not to argue that multinationals have no weaknesses. These are related primarily to the size, the power this affords and to the organisational complexity and inefficiency which result. Also because of their innate conservatism, multinationals tend to be naïve in their assumptions, or lack of them, about economic and political change. This arises perhaps from their essentially pragmatic approach to changing events, so many of which in any case are largely unpredictable. Anyone who attempts to forecast future trends and events will inevitably be wrong some of the time. For an ambitious senior manager in a multinational such exposure is best avoided. Similarly it is best to refrain from supporting a colleague who is so rash as to recommend a project based on certain forecast changes to the economic or political scene. A neutral stance will be safer, for a manager is rarely taken to task for failing to predict future trends or events. They are, after all, outside his control, and if the critics had known better why did they not speak up before? A multinational therefore awaits events rather than anticipates them. For example, General Motors and Ford did not introduce smaller cars into the United States market after the 1973 oil shock until evidence of demand for Japanese cars had become overwhelming. Oil majors similarly have only now begun to reduce their oil refining capacity following the sharp increase in oil product prices and the effect this has had on demand.

(a) *Neurosis of periodic reorganisation*

As with the Roman Empire, a multinational can ultimately over-reach itself and become unmanageable. The way out of this dilemma, which some have followed, is to reorganise the corporation into smaller, more manageable units. Whilst this can work quite satisfactorily for a while, difficulty arises because the different units tend to grow apart and tend to become independent of the corporate headquarters. If a unit is able to finance its growth from cash flow, the links with the centre become even more tenuous. Then the corporate headquarters may have to exert ever more overt pressure to retain control, with the ultimate weapon being replacement of key members of the unit's top management. The corporate headquarters too may then have difficulty in providing an attractive career prospect for bright managers, whereas the increasingly indpendent units may well provide a more enticing opportunity for the young manager languishing in an increasingly irrelevant headquarters system.

The organisational dilemma—of decentralisation versus recentralisation—is a continuing and debilitating neurosis of the multinational, made worse by the political in-fighting which it encourages as each ambitious individual struggles to gain power and influence from a reorganisation. It is by no means unusual for the higher levels of decision-making virtually to grind to a halt during those periods just before and immediately after a reorganisation. The corporation continues to function because the middle and lower echelons continue to do their jobs—purchase orders are placed, invoices are passed for payment, cheques are signed and factories continue to operate. However, at such a time the corporation is vulnerable to technological innovation by competitors, and to continuing or growing losses in difficult business areas. Morale of staff may fall, leading to the departure of some good managers and specialists and to loss of confidence amongst business partners and customers.

(b) *Grooming of Managers*

A further dilemma arises from the need for management training. A lifetime's career working his way up the corporate structure is a wholly inadequate training for a board member of a multinational. He will have to share in taking decisions about businesses of which he has little knowledge, because he may have worked his way up in only one part of the group's activities. If he is moved about from business to business, he may never have done a solid job at any stage. Having led a sheltered business life, he will be ill-fitted to adjust to taking decisions in a hostile, competitive world. He will survive, for he must be a survivor to have got that far, but he will not lead nor will he inspire.

The injection from outside of new blood at a high level seldom works because a new individual, however brilliant, has the enormous disadvantage of being unfamiliar with the complex internal machinations of the corporate system. His arguments will be suspect from the outset, and he will be easily outmanoeuvred by those seeking to discredit or isolate him. He will find it a hopeless task to try to understand an organisation which others have spent two or three decades getting to know intimately. It is akin to the mayor of New York being appointed *Burgomeister* of Hamburg without knowing a word of German.

Although the senior management therefore has had a narrow, cloistered business education, it is largely unaware of the short-comings this creates. Indeed managers of multinationals are inclined to believe that they are an altogether superior breed: after all, the results of the corporation speak for themselves and everbody has heard of the big names such as General Motors, ICI or Renault. In truth, much of the profit arises in spite of top management rather than because of it.

Those who make the corporation function through thick and thin are the unknown, unremarkable middle or lower levels of manage-ment who are the backbone of the organisation and the embodiment of technical and professional expertise. The corporation takes care to ensure that it offers enough incentive to recruit and retain sufficient numbers of competent, sometimes excellent middle managers to develop and carry out the worldwide business of the group. Every large organisation has its share of the hangers-on—those who do just sufficient to stay out of trouble but not enough to contribute anything of any value. But in amongst the thousands of employees—850,000 in the case of General Motors, 400,000 for General Electric (United States) and 325,000 for Siemens—are the real professionals whose achievements are probably not fully recognised within the company and whose bosses are quick to take the credit for progress made or successes proven. Some would make excellent top management and board members, but are denied the opportunity to rise by superiors who are quick to stifle any manifestation of ability lest it should provide a challenge to themselves. Such situations are common-place in all large organisations because it is impossible for the top management to know their staff personally and to separate the wheat from the chaff. As a result, the chaff can all too easily become the top management itself. In a multinational this leads to proposals frustrated before they can be seriously considered; to projects deferred so long that they are outdated by the time they are launched; to simple, unprofessional errors by those more concerned with their next promotion than with dedication of the job in hand.

(c) *Control of Divisions and Subsidiaries*

Whilst these weaknesses are perfectly natural and to be expected in a large organisation, and indeed they manifest themselves in all walks of life, they are a negative force which increases in potency with the size of the organisation. Size however is a mark of success and therefore difficult to curtail. By the very nature of the power struggle within a multinational, the top management will be reluctant to hive off a successful and self-sufficient division as a means of simplifying its control structure. Indeed strong growth in turnover, and preferably profits, can help to stave off the risk of a takeover. Lesser multinationals can be swallowed by greater ones—witness the struggle for the takeover of Conoco and Marathon—and occasionally divisions are sold by one multinational to another, usually for fund-raising reasons or with the removal of losses in mind. But there are few instances of a multinational floating off its own subsidiary as an independent company. Shares in an overseas subsidiary, however, are sometimes sold to the public in that country, but rarely to an extent in excess of 50 per cent. or with separation from the group in mind. It is not in the nature of the men in power at the top of a multinational voluntarily to surrender any of that power even in the interests of efficiency. Yet it is precisely that process which would ensure that multinationals did not become too big for their own good. By keeping a relatively slim, dynamic organisation, a multinational can ensure that it is well suited to keep abreast of developments in its chosen fields. The process of floating off a division which has reached the point of independent viability, need not be too difficult to carry through in practice. New shares in the division in question can be issued to shareholders so that at the moment of hiving off, the new company (formerly the division) and the corporation would have the same shareholders in identical proportions. Thereafter the shareholdings change as new shareholders buy into, and existing shareholders sell out of, one or the other.

The worth of the corporation theoretically declines to take account of the reduced assets, but this would not be to the detriment of the shareholders who would own compensating shares in the new company. It would also make sense, for example, to float a less successful division in a declining industry in order to free the corporation of potential future losses. However, this would have to be done before the stockmarket appreciated that such a decline of fortunes was likely, or the floating could lead to the collapse of the new company.

The most common reasons for multinationals divesting themselves of divisions or overseas subsidiaries are the prospect of continuing losses, and government restrictions. In the latter case, sale to the government may be the best, perhaps the only, course open and this could be engineered by the government as a cheap, back-door form of nationalisation, or of neutralisation of a too-powerful foreign influence. In most cases these divestments are effectively involuntary.

Control of its subsidiaries is one of the abiding and recurring problems facing a multinational, and one which absorbs much valuable top management time and effort which could more usefully be dedicated to furthering the business of the corporation. Because governments prefer to see the important companies in their country owned and run by local people, it is often necessary for a multinational to concede a measure of local autonomy to its subsidiary. The press and public locally are not fooled by this exercise and well understand that the principal power still resides in the corporate headquarters elsewhere. In some cases, however, local management is able to exercise a surprisingly large degree of autonomy, more, often much more, than the headquarters feels to be desirable. This is particularly the case if the subsidiary is involved in joint ventures with local companies or with local subsidiaries of other multinationals which similarly exercise a considerable measure of self-determination. If in addition the country has a hostile climate, uncomfortable hotels, or other disagreeable features which discourage visits from headquarters, or alternatively there are factors which inhibit communications such as a difficult foreign language or a large time difference with corporate headquarters, the stage is set for a high degree of independence for the subsidiary.

Corporate headquarters has the ultimate sanction available to it of removing the chief executive or withholding support for the subsidiary's capital investment programme, but these draconian measures are likely to upset the local government, press and public opinion. A recalcitrant local chief executive would no doubt ensure that due publicity was given to the event, and would use this as a weapon before his dismissal. This would conspire to expose a multinational where it is most vulnerable—its reputation for pursuing its own interests at the expense of the host country's. The local management may also carry support for its independent cause from the top management of the local companies with which it has joint ventures. If the chief executive is a local man, he may have no corporate ambitions outside his own country and therefore be willing to risk his career with the multinational in the knowledge that headquarters would be reluctant to sack him. Even if it did, he could probably count on a number of lucrative offers from other local companies. So can the stage be set for months, perhaps years of limited, but from the point of view of the corporate headquarters, disruptive independence and strife. Ultimately a troublesome subsidiary can be sold off to the local government or public. If the subsidiary's results are good enough, the irritation of its independence would be stoically borne in the interests of corporate profitability. If not, it might be dispensed with.

Some multinationals are unwilling to risk such problems with their overseas subsidiaries, willingly give a high degree of autonomy to them, and tolerate the irritations which result in the belief that local autonomy is ultimately better for efficiency. They may go even further and introduce, say, 25 per cent. local equity into the subsidiary to make it publicly accountable. The disadvantages of such autonomy are, however, substantial. The local management generally has little interest in, or experience of, the business world outside its own country and therefore remains narrowly nationalistic in its outlook. Its main concern will be to maintain its independence of corprate headquarters, an essentially negative aim. Although some cross-fertilisation of staff with corporate headquarters probably will take place, it will not be enough to confer on the subsidiary the advantage of the world-wide experience of the group. At the same time the stigma of being a multinational will still apply to the subsidiary, and this may block its opportunities in certain areas, due to public pressure or governmental edict. More ominously, its desire to remain independent of the centre is likely to cause the subsidiary's technical competence to become lacking, or outdated, or even to fail. In other words such independence has many disadvantages without any significant advantage. In the unlikely event that the subsidiary's efficiency does improve, somebody in corporate HQ will wish to take the credit, and therefore to interfere once again in its activities.

V—SUCCESS OF MULTINATIONALS

(a) *Absence of Effective Alternatives*

Multinationals exist because they fulfil a need. They indulge in large-scale technological innovation and risk-taking, and the production of raw materials and finished goods for which there is widespread demand. If they and the paraphernalia of their existence were to be abolished overnight, the world would be immeasurably poorer. Let us consider probably the only two theoretical alternatives to multinationals: national or nationalised concerns, and smaller international concerns.

Nationalised, *i.e.* State-owned, corporations restricted to their country of origin would in most cases be an inferior alternative as far as effectiveness and efficiency are concerned. Take three examples—cars, oil and computers. Although State-owned concerns exist in the case of cars (Renault in France, British Leyland in the United Kingdom) and oil (ENI in Italy and VEBA in Germany), these represent a relatively small proportion of each industry's operations. All four companies also are themselves multinationals. However, such companies require international markets for their goods and it is only through the stimulus given by international competition that technological development has proceeded so fast. Certainly far less oil would have been found in the world if each country had its own national oil company which searched without competition only within its own boundaries. Likewise IBM would not have been able to play such an important part in revolutionising the computer industry if the world had not been its oyster. The multinationals have been the main means by which developments in one corner of the world have been utilised for the wider benefit of many other parts of the world.

Nationalised concerns restricted to their country of origin are not renowned for their efficiency or for their business acumen. It would not be possible to show that their performance, or their contribution to any nation, exceeded that of a multinational under similar circumstances. Their very monopoly, and therefore security of survival, ensures an absence of urgency and vitality which are prerequisites of progressive activity. National (non-nationalised) companies may escape the dead hand of monopoly and State-supported security, but lack the wider horizons and stimulus which the world market presents to the multinational. Artificial restriction of a company's operations within the country of origin will therefore usually lead to an inferior performance overall. This may be offset somewhat by the nationalistic spirit of employees, a more homogeneous working environment and inspired leadership.

A multinational split into a number of smaller international companies could well represent a step towards greater efficiency provided that each company was allocated a business area within which it had a reasonable propect of survival and development on its own. For example, the coal interests of Exxon might well be able to stand alone providing they had a sufficient capital base from the outset to enable them to borrow further in pursuit of an expansion programme. The wide diversification of some multinationals, especially the oil companies, who see their own industry contracting in future, could lead to organisational indigestion and therefore inefficiency. This need not matter if other companies rise to supplant unsuccessful oil companies in, say, the coal business but more probably the oil companies will take over or neutralise such competitors. The power of multinationals, and the protection this affords them from competition, is therefore also potentially a brake on progress.

(b) *Secrets of Success*

Although multinationals have their weaknesses, and although there exists a seamier side of their everyday life and operations, their influence in a world with largely materialistic ideals has been, and is likely to continue to be, towards improving the living standards of ordinary people in those societies within which they operate. Wherever individual inventions or technological improvements may have been conceived—and many have originated in the research and engineering laboratories of the multinationals—at the forefront of their development, introduction into operation and continued improvement have been the multinationals. Herein lies the secret to the success and growth of these giant organisations, and there is a particular and crucial explanation for it which is almost invariably taken for granted by critics and apologists alike—the high quality of most middle management and specialists. These are the unsung heroes whose imagination, competence, and in many cases, brilliance have led to the jumbo jet, the latter-day motor car, direct-dialling telephone connections across the world, colour television and many other modern-day miracles. We may take issue with the use to which some of these are put—a function of human nature for which multinationals cannot be held responsible—or with the activities of some companies in some circumstances—for instance, Nestle's widespread marketing of powdered milk in Africa and its arguably adverse consequences to the health of children. The overwhelming evidence, however, is in favour of the multinationals who have been in the mainstream of the developments from which the vast majority of people in the world benefit, however marginally in the poorer nations.

The middle managers of the multinationals have organised and carried out the projects, with the vital co-operation of the specialists—scientists, engineers of many disciplines and perhaps unique experience, and professionals (legal, tax, financial, accounting, *etc.*). These people are the power-house of the multinationals. Most of them will not reach the top because they do not have the right characteristics—I will not say qualities. Some do not have the ambition, others are content to concentrate on what they truly enjoy doing, and others again are contemptuous of the scheming, unscrupulous methods, and the unprofessional conduct which they witness amongst some of the top management and which they believe are the necessary traits of success. Perhaps most would be out of their depth at the top, but some at least would make better board members of multinationals than some of those privileged to hold those positions who scorn the selfless dedication and responsibility which that high office demands of them. The unsung heroes are unknown outside their own industrial circles, and their retirement will occur largely unnoticed by the great corporation.

(c) *Ladder of Promotion*

Multinationals are able to pick and choose their recruits from an abundant excess of good applicants. Requirements for qualifications are high, but the pay and conditions are calculated to attract the best talent. In most cases, promotion to middle management and to the top specialist jobs is based on merit. The performance of the younger, more junior staff can be observed over their early years during which promotion of the better ones will be approved by lower and then middle managers. Top management will have ear-marked the high-fliers, from whom they will select their eventual replacements, but the remainder will be of little or no interest to them, except as means to an end. Consequently promotion in the lower and middle ranks is a competitive but largely fair process, supervised by the competent and professional middle managers themselves. Inevitably a small minority of those managers will be imcompetent or barely competent, perhaps because of age, illness, strain or over-promotion through the error of judgment of their superiors. Some of them too will be the failed high-fliers, who may not settle well into a lesser role than the one they had set for themselves. However, by-and-large the multinationals are careful to stock the all-important middle management and specialist jobs with the best people available. It is, after all, in the interests of the whole corporation, including all levels of staff, that this should happen, for ultimately failure drags everybody down. Some mistakes are made and have to be rectified by sideways moves or by promotion into jobs of a less critical kind. Rarely, however, does a young capable executive find himself left on the shelf with no promotion prospects.

CONCLUSIONS

We may be confident of the survival and prosperity of most multinationals, although some will from time to time get into difficulties as one or more loss-making divisions drag down the whole corporation, and as sheer size takes its toll in loss of control and inefficiency. If they did not exist, the Henry Fords or Arnold Weinstocks would have to create them. Their potential for self-improvement is great but this is broadly true for all human activities, and multinationals should not be singled out for exceptional criticism simply because of their power. No one multinational is all powerful on its own, and they are fortunately not very efficient at forming cartels amongst themselves. They can therefore be put to work in the service of any government prepared to make the effort to learn how to deal with them. This is a route few of the less developed countries have bothered to follow, although it could have a major influence on their growth prospects. The rest of us can remain uneasily contented in the knowledge that we need the multinationals as much as they need us, their employees and their customers.

DEVELOPMENT-PLANNING
IN ADVERSITY

By

RAY BROMLEY

IT is generally agreed that development-planning[1] has failed to live
up to the high expectations expressed for it in the 1950s and 1960s.
Since the late sixties it has entered a phase of criticism and crisis,
stemming from the growing realisation that the voluminous output
of documents and employment of technically-skilled personnel is
hardly matched by its impact on economic, social and political
processes.[2] Numerous observers have recognised such planning to
be ineffectual, and many have argued that it exists to serve the
needs of professionals seeking technical prestige, foreign governments and international organisations demanding plans as prerequisites for "aid," and politicians requiring impressive documents to
show off while disguising the ineptitude and impulsive decision-
making of their régimes. As a result, development planning has
been described as "a facade," "a symbolic charade," or just as
"pseudo-planning."[3] In other words, it is seen as merely a cover for
the essentially unplanned nature of governmental activity, or as an
act played out to impress foreign interests and to keep radical
intellectuals "out of mischief" by involving them in government
without giving them any real power or meaningful responsibility.

The criticisms of development-planning which have emerged since
the late 1960s have been severe and often vicious,[4] emphasising the
considerable disparities which exist in most Third-World countries[5]

---

[1] Defined here as "governmental planning for socioeconomic changes which are deemed to
be progressive by the planners themselves, and/or by substantial fractions of the country's
ruling élites, and/or by some electoral system representing a larger proportion of the country's
population."

[2] See, *e.g.*, M. Faber and D. Seers (eds.), *The Crisis in Planning* (1972); A. Wildavsky,
"Does Planning Work?," 24 *Public Interest* (1971), pp. 95–104; *ibid.*, "If Planning is
Everything, Maybe It's Nothing," 4 *Policy Sciences* (1973), pp. 127–153.

[3] See K. Griffin and J.L. Enos, *Planning Development* (1970), pp. 201–203; R. Bromley,
Development and Planning in Ecuador (1977), pp. 67–72; D.Seers, "The Prevalence of
Pseudo-Planning," in Faber and Seers, *op. cit.* in note 2 above, Vol. 1.

[4] See, *e.g.*, Naomi Caiden and A. Wildavsky, *Planning and Budgeting in Poor Countries*
(1974).

[5] The general term "Third World" is used here to group those countries which are
"subordinated to" or "dependent upon" the global capitalist system, but which are not part of
the central "cores" of that system in North America, Western Europe and Japan, or of the
extensions of those cores in Australia, New Zealand and perhaps South Africa. This
definition of the Third World excludes the socialist countries of the COMECON bloc, and
also those formerly Third World countries which have deliberately, and apparently
permanently largely opted out of the capitalist system, *e.g.*, China, Vietnam and Cuba.

between what is specified in the documents described as National Development Plans, and what actually takes place in the periods covered by these plans. The National Development Plans have generally taken the form of books; voluminous and often attractively-produced documents specifying quantitative objectives and listing specific major projects to be accomplished and completed over a fixed-term period ranging from three to 10 years. These documents usually say *what* should be done over the plan period, explaining *why* this should be done through a lengthy "diagnosis" of the country's problems and prospects. In general, however, they give little information on *which* governmental and non-governmental agencies should take the necessary actions *when* and *with what* resources. Thus, though the documents are intellectually sophisticated and set targets to be achieved, they rarely specify in detail *how* the targets are to be reached. When the targets are achieved it may be as much coincidence or good forecasting by the planners as the result of the detailed implementation of a carefully-devised development strategy specified in the plan. Indeed, targets are almost as often overshot as not reached, and the overall pattern of fulfilment of the plan's objectives is usually patchy and inconsistent, more resembling a random walk than a carefully-followed preselected route.

I—THE MAIN DEFICIENCIES
OF NATIONAL DEVELOPMENT-PLANNING

The reasons for the partial or distorted implementation of National Development Plans are numerous and complex. Outstanding, however, are four major factors.

First, most plans are not sufficiently detailed and specific to be implemented like engineers' blueprints or architects' designs. Their implementation calls for considerable intuition and initiative, and for continuing administrative work in specifying responsibilities, allocating resources, and ensuring an adequate flow of funds and materials to the appropriate persons and institutions at the right times. In practice, such follow-up actions rarely take place, and few countries even have the required resources or administrative capacity to implement their plans.

Secondly, the principal planners rarely have the political power to order or enforce the implementation of their plans, and they usually do not command a broad enough consensus within the ruling élites to ensure unanimity or even co-ordinated action in pursuit of planned objectives. Indeed, what little political leverage they have in the first few months after a plan's publication usually dissipates in a welter of intra-governmental rivalries and power struggles.

Thirdly, there is a strong and essentially negative ethic among communities of development-planners that their task is to produce plan documents, and that it is not really their responsibility to involve themselves in implementation, the monitoring of implementation, or even the evaluation of the impact of governmental policies. In many cases they also hide behind a smokescreen of supposed technical neutrality in which their proposals are presented as optimum and politically neutral, effectively avoiding many of the major issues facing the national society and ignoring existing power structures and class alliances. Such planners have been described variously as "paper planners," "armchair planners" and "narrow planners," and their tendency is to focus much more on the intellectual sophistication of the documents that they produce than on the potential for implementation.[6] They are easily excluded from the real decision-making processes of government because they conceive their objectives much more in terms of professional respect, technical skill and intellectual repute, than in terms of building coalitions of interest, mobilising resources, or revitalising the administrative system.

Fourthly—a factor even more damning and comprehensive than the first three—development-planners have often been trying to do the impossible: to specify the future of a whole country over several years, assuming not only that they have the power to enforce what they prescribe, but also that there is continuity in the social and political systems, the absence of major natural disasters, and the accuracy of numerous economic predictions regarding supply, demand and prices in international trade and monetary flows. In practice such factors are normally outside the national planner's control, and they are extremely difficult to forecast in anything but the short term. Within the world economic system, it is the Third-World countries which generally have least access to sophisticated data sources and forecasting techniques, and it is often the same countries which are most intensely vulnerable to unexpected changes. Time and time again, therefore, unexpected changes in the context of national development effectively prevent the implementation of National Development Plans. Though environmental factors underlie some of these changes, for example in the case of crop failure because of prolonged drought, the two most common and crucial factors are political instability and economic dependence. It is on these two factors that much of the remainder of this essay will focus.

---

[6] See, *e.g.*, R. Bromley, "The Planning Process," 9(3) *IDS Bulletin* (1978), p. 45; T. Killick, "The Possibilities of Development Planning," 28 *Oxford Economic Papers*, NS (1976), pp. 161–184.

II—POLITICAL INSTABILITY
AND ECONOMIC DEPENDENCE AS UNDERLYING PROBLEMS

Political instability and the consequent lack of continuity in government policy are usually thought to affect only a relatively limited range of countries, while many others are associated with relatively regular and predictable changes of government, or with "stable" and essentially dictatorial régimes. In reality, however, it is not only the chronically unstable countries such as Bolivia, which has had more different Presidents than years of independence, that fail to fulfil the preconditions for effective national development-planning. Those countries, such as Colombia and India, which have relatively regular and predictable national and local elections, often have notable discrepancies between the phasing of national plans and the phasing of elections. Newly-elected politicians usually repudiate the policies of their predecessors, and though national plans are rarely formally declared inoperative after elections, they are often effectively ignored. Furthermore, the apparent predictability of governmental changes is often less of a limit to political instability than might at first seem the case. Cabinet reshuffles are relatively common, innovative ministers are often moved on or thrown out altogether, and some countries—most notably Colombia—have institutionalised systems of rotation of political offices during government terms.

Wherever governments are chosen by genuinely competitive multi-party elections, the electoral cycle imposes relatively predictable policy changes which are rarely envisaged in national plans. Thus, new governments usually have a "honeymoon phase" when their initial policies seem generous and popular, followed by a phase of increasing criticism and crises, often accompanied by political repression, deflation and economic austerity measures. Towards the end of their electoral terms governments focus much more heavily on vote-catching measures, rapidly reflating the economy, reducing taxes and increasing social benefits. Such political tactics wreak havoc with economic development strategies, confirming to many technocratic planners that politicians are corrupt, self-seeking, incompetent, and impossible to work with.

Any repudiation of political instability and electoral politics may well lead the planner to think that what the country needs is "a good dictator" who has both the power and the longevity to ensure stability and continuity in the political system. In reality, however, "good dictators" are rare by any standards, and many would argue that goodness and dictatorial behaviour are simply incompatible. Furthermore, "stable" dictators do not necessarily have stable governments. Many are the stories of ministers mysteriously disappearing, being assassinated, or simply fleeing the country after internal disagreements within the government. Those countries which have had strongly repressive régimes for sustained periods have usually lost most of their best technical manpower through assassination, imprisonment, expulsion, or most commonly of all, "voluntary" emigration. Such a brain-drain, or in other cases "brain elimination," is hardly conducive to the creation and maintenance of a corps of skilled planners and administrators.

The concept of "dependency" as a basic characteristic of most Third-World countries with essentially capitalist economies, has recently come under sustained attack.[7] Many of the original writings of the *dependentistas* have been shown to be contradictory and incoherent, and it is clear that dependency is neither precisely definable and measurable in mathematical terms, nor exclusively confined to the so-called Third World or to peripheral capitalist economies.[8] All countries are dependent on changing circumstances in the international system, and no governments have total control over national or international affairs. "Dominance" and "dependence" are relative rather than absolute terms, and they are more easily applied to specific contexts and relationships than to general structural relationships. Interdependence is the keynote of the global system and, though relationships are often unbalanced and exploitative, there is no shortage of examples—such as the Vietnam War and the Iranian Hostage Crisis for the United States—to show that massive disparities in power and wealth do not necessarily determine the outcome of specific situations.

Despite all the above caveats, however, the basic concept of "economic dependence" does have a particular significance in the analysis of relatively small and poor Third-World countries which are strongly reliant on international trade and foreign investment. Such countries are extremely vulnerable to changes in the international economic system, and to pressures from foreign governments and multinational companies. As a result, most of the major decisions and circumstances affecting their economic futures are effectively outside the control of their governments. Despite the rapid national economic growth and impact on the world economy

---

[7] See, *e.g.*, B. Warren, "Imperialism and Capitalist Industrialization," 81 *New Left Review* (1973), pp. 3–44; A. Nove, "On Reading André Gunder Frank," 10 *Journal of Development Studies* (1974), pp. 445–455.

[8] See, *e.g.*, H. Brookfield, *Interdependent Development* (1977); Aidan Foster-Carter, "Neo-Marxist Approaches to Development and Underdevelopment," in E. de Kadt and G. Williams (eds.), *Sociology and Development* (1974), pp. 67–105; A.G. Frank, "Dependence is Dead, Long Live Dependence and the Class Struggle," 5 *World Development* (1977), pp. 355–370.

of the Organisation of Petroleum Exporting Countries (OPEC) during the 1970s, there is little evidence to suggest that most Third-World countries have any real chance to control world markets or to impose terms of trade. While oil is certainly a vital, strategic commodity, bananas, peanuts, jute and most other major Third-World exports are not. There is cut-throat competition in the world markets for most tropical agricultural products, and national good fortune is often dependent on the differential international impact of crop diseases and bad weather. Mineral exporters are severely affected by United States government and multinational company decisions to stockpile or to sell-off stockpiles. More generally, international trade is severely affected by the changing global pattern of wars and economic boycotts, as evidenced for example, by the sharply fluctuating world copper market of the 1970s, relating to such factors as partial boycotts of left-leaning régimes in Chile and Peru, and combinations of boycotts, sabotage and liberation army attacks affecting rail communications from the Copperbelt of Zaire and Zambia.

With the proliferation of independent mini-States during the 1960s and 1970s, an increasingly large proportion of Third-World countries lack even the most elemental bases for economic, political or cultural self-reliance. Many Third-World governments have very little bargaining power in world markets and international relations. Not only do they suffer from all the classic problems of economic dependence affecting countries which are heavily reliant on the export of a few primary products, but also they are under continuous threat of infiltration, penetration, invasion, boycott or blockade by powerful neighbouring countries or by one of the world's two super-Powers. Thus, small and once-peaceful countries such as Cambodia, Lebanon, Tibet and Somalia may simply be trodden underfoot in regional military conflicts and changing big-power alliances; or involved as cannon-fodder in bizarre wars by proxy. Some of the smaller countries may even be "taken over" by international racketeers or become staging-posts for the trafficking of narcotics or other forms of contraband, Under such circumstances medium- to long-term national development planning can be little more than a speculative public-relations exercise.

Wherever relative poverty, political instability and economic dependence coincide, the "Paradox of Planning" initially explained by Caiden and Wildavsky, is strongly evident.[9] Planning is intended to ensure greater stability, efficiency, co-ordination, skills, capital resources *etc.*, yet it is often unable to have any significant effect

---

[9] *Op. cit.* in note 4 above, pp. 264–271.

precisely because of the lack of these variables. In other words, many of the objectives of development planning are effectively preconditions for its success. Because of this, planning, as it is currently conceived in most countries, can never succeed. Only a major change in the form of planning under consideration and perhaps also in the context within which planning is conducted, can lead to any meaningful form of planned national development.

III—STATE PLANNING, PRIVATE ENTERPRISE, AND THE POSSIBILITIES OF A "TRANSITION TO SOCIALISM"

It is somewhat ironic that many of the national governments from the rich, capitalist West which have demanded the preparation of integrated, comprehensive development plans as preconditions for the disbursement of economic and technical "aid," do not encourage the preparation of such plans in their own countries of origin. Such attitudes seem to be based on two major assumptions: that Third-World socio-economic systems are relatively simple and therefore easier to plan than their "sophisticated," developed First-World counterparts; and that Third-World economies are in a state of emergency reflected by mass poverty and deprivation, calling for drastic measures modelled on the Soviet Five-Year Plans of the 1920s and 1930s, or on the Marshall Plan for the recuperation of Western Europe after the Second World War.

Both the above assumptions are extremely dubious. There is little *a priori* reason to believe that the Third-World social formations are necessarily simple, and some, most notably India, are remarkably complex. Though many Third-World economies are relatively simple, the shortage of basic statistical information and of local expertise can make them remarkably difficult to plan. Such difficulties are particularly striking in the cases of countries like Turkey, Colombia and Paraguay, where substantial flows of contraband goods, massive international narcotics traffic, undocumented shifts of personal finances in and out of the country, and large-scale emigration of manpower, all contribute to produce an economy which is both little-known and remarkably difficult for governments to control. Also notable in most Third-World countries is the very lack of any sense of emergency in governmental circles. Governments are often based on delicate coalitions of interest and complex patterns of reciprocal assistance between groups sharing access to the fruits of power. Under such circumstances decisive governmental actions are often viewed as "rocking the boat," and there is a strong tendency towards pernicious bureaucracy, profiteering by corrupt minorities, and notable conservatism in policy-making. In most cases the human resources and political will are simply not available to take advantage of a sudden injection of external capital, and there is a notable lack of dynamism in the mobilisation of local resources for capital investment.

In short, most Third-World economies and social formations are neither so simple nor so dynamic as to justify integrated comprehensive medium- to long-term national development-planning. In terms of international comparisons, what is seen to be unsuitable for most of the "rich" (the First World) is equally inappropriate for the "poor" (the Third World). Most of the reasons for such inappropriateness are different in First- and Third-World countries, but one factor is notably similar—the significance of private enterprise. It is difficult for governments to control essentially capitalist economies based mainly on different types and scales of non-governmental enterprises. Only a strong combination of mandatory and indicative planning can achieve a degree of control over such economies, and yet such measures are usually considered to be contradictory to the basic ethics of private enterprise. The alternatives, therefore, are threefold: first, to abandon any attempt at comprehensive national development-planning, considering such planning as an affront to capitalism; secondly to continue national planning as a "facade" or "charade," with many of the more perceptive observers realising that it serves no useful purpose; and, thirdly, to change the bases of the economy so as to facilitate governmental planning—or, in other words, to effect a "transition to socialism."

The very idea that, in order to facilitate national planning, governments might gradually expropriate private enterprise and either hand it over to its workers or convert it into State-controlled enterprise, is somewhat far-fetched. The tail of planners does not wag the governmental dog, and it is hardly likely that a whole power structure and system of accumulation will be changed just to help a small and politically-weak techno-bureaucratic élite. While the practice of planning may be one of the beneficiaries of a transition to socialism, therefore, it is unlikely ever to be a prime force in such a transition. Once such a transition has been effected, however, the practice of national planning is certainly facilitated, both by the increasing State control of many aspects of the economy and by the reduced involvement of multinational corporations and other foreign investors.

Regrettably, even the most democratically-elected and popular governments in the Third World are not free to choose the political, economic and social destinies of their countries. Any major change from the status quo is likely to bring reactions from local élites, the armed forces, the governments of powerful neighbouring countries, multinational corporations, and above all, the world's two super-Powers. The experiences of Chile, Chad and Afghanistan in the 1970s bear ample witness to the extent to which the national destiny is outside the control of many governments. A "transition to socialism" may only be possible through the intervention of a massive external force, or through the assumption of determinedly authoritarian measures by a firmly-established government. For much of the Third World, and however much one might wish the opposite, a decisive transition to socialism is highly unlikely in the 1980s. There will certainly be shifts between the "capitalist" and "socialist" blocs, but there is little immediate prospect of many Third-World countries achieving political stability and overcoming economic dependence through the adoption of some self-reliant, nationalistic, socialist development model. Indeed, some of those that do shift towards socialism may merely follow the examples of Afghanistan and Cambodia, where precarious socialism has brought new forms of political instability and economic dependence, rather than overcoming these problems once and for all.

IV—New Horizons for Development Planning under Peripheral Capitalism

Given the numerous problems described above in achieving a transition to socialism, and given that much of the world's population are either unaware of the potential benefits to be offered by socialism or actively opposed to socialist solutions, it is worth reviewing some of the alternative proposals to "reform" development planning while retaining an essentially "peripheral capitalist" development model. In this section, four inter-related approaches to reforming development planning are considered in turn, beginning with the easiest and most tried and tested, and ranging through to the most difficult and least-experimented possibilities.

(a) *Concentration on Short-Term Planning and a Bank of Projects*

There can be little doubt that the best-known weighty text on development planning is Albert Waterston's *Development Planning: Lessons of Experience*, first published in 1965.[10] This book proposes a line of improvement for national planning which has subsequently been followed by a wide range of authors and aid agencies. The basis of the strategy is to cut the time-scale of planning and to concentrate primarily on short-term planning and

---

[10] For a summary of Waterston's ideas, see also his "An Operational Approach to Development Planning," in Faber and Seers (eds.), *op. cit.* in note 2 above, Vol. 1, pp. 81–107.

the conduct of detailed feasibility and design studies for specific projects. It usually involves a shift from five- or 10-year integrated, comprehensive national plans to one-year outline national plans largely listing and assigning priorities to specific investment projects. At the same time, greatly increased resources are pumped into project planning, creating a "bank" of projects ready for potential financiers.

The "Waterston line" responds to the problems encountered in conventional national development-planning by proposing more realistic forms of planning. To say the least, however, the approach is loaded with ideological implications and vested interests. Waterston wrote as a staff member of the World Bank, and the book was published under the Bank's auspices. The approach is eminently convenient to the Bank and other major international funding agencies because it ensures a ready supply of fundable projects with the sorts of economic analyses required by international financiers seeking to recuperate their loans.

Overall, the Waterston line tends to produce a concentration on relatively large-scale capital investment projects, mainly of an infrastructural type. Correspondingly, it neglects not only smaller-scale projects using less-sophisticated technology, but also post-construction maintenance activities and long-term social programmes requiring relatively little capital investment. Even more worrying may be the loss of any vision of a desired national future framed in anything more than material terms. Social transformation, popular participation and numerous other worthy concerns tend to be swept under the table in a policy-making circle which is increasingly governed by the ruthless logic of cost-benefit analysis. Furthermore, long-term benefits with complex externalities tend to be ruled out altogether or assigned relatively low values through shadow pricing and discounting mechanisms. As a result, emphasis is laid very heavily on shorter-term and more directly monetary benefits likely to impress financiers. In short, the Waterston line tends to produce a continuation and intensification of capitalism in the Third World, often implying increased economic dependence within the global economic system.

(b) *The Integration of Planning with the Annual Budget Cycle*
Following the Waterston line by shifting the emphasis from medium- and long-term planning to short-term planning, the most obvious time scale to retain a vestige of integrated comprehensive planning is one year. Given that most governments conduct their financial affairs according to an annual budgetary cycle, and given that development-planning is heavily involved in allocating invest-

ments, many authors, including Waterston himself, have proposed that one-year plans be co-ordinated directly with the budgetary year.[11] Some authors go rather further in proposing that the plan and the budget should be unified as a single document, prepared and implemented by the same key agency of government.

Few specialists would object to the basic idea of co-ordinating the annual plan with the budget, but there is considerable disagreement as to the utility of one-year integrated comprehensive plans. Those who oppose the Waterston line, but who do not reject the idea of development-planning altogether, tend to argue for medium- to long-term planning, suggesting that one-year plans are short-sighted, disjointed, and lacking in any meaningful development strategy. In contrast, those who adopt more extreme versions of the Waterston line often play down the significance of one-year comprehensive plans in favour of project and sectoral plans.

Co-ordinating the annual plan with the budget not only faces the apathy of those planners who do not assign a high priority to annual plans, but also the differences in style and self-image of "planners" and "accountants," the latter being a general summary term and caricature for the types of specialists conventionally found in Ministries of Finance. Planners tend to have intellectual and visionary perspectives, concentrating on broad questions of prin-ciple and policy rather than on narrow matters of detail. In contrast, accountants tend to be much more concerned with specific matters of detail and with questions of administrative procedure. In reality, therefore, the simple combination of planners and accountants in the same governmental agency or in the execution of a joint task, does not ensure interaction and harmony, let alone productive collaboration. The ideal of joint activity towards common goals requires not only institutional unification or high-level orders to work together on the same document, but also a systematic and co-ordinated approach to give structure to the relationship.

The best-known and most widely-used system for integrating planning with budgeting activities is undoubtedly "Planning-Programming-Budgeting Systems" (PPBS), or simply "Programme Budgeting."[12] Most people would sympathise with its basic inten-tions: to orient government budgeting towards ensuring greater efficiency and cost-effectiveness in programmes providing services to the public, and to facilitate the comparison of alternative policies and programmes. The realities of PPBS, however, are far less

---

[11] See, *e.g.*, Waterston (1972), *op. cit.* in note 10 above, pp. 98–100; Caiden and Wildavsky, *op. cit.* in note 4 above, pp. 300–322.

[12] See, *e.g.*, D. Novick (ed.), *Current Practice in Programme Budgeting (PPBS)* (1973).

convincing, and in the United States where it was comprehensively introduced into the Federal Government under the Johnson Administration in the 1960s, it was formally abandoned by most agencies under the Nixon Administration in the early 1970s. Though PPBS has very laudable objectives, its administrative procedures tend to be costly, time-consuming, repetitive and bureaucratic, creating a series of formalities without a functional collaboration of planners and accountants.[13] Though many attempts have been made to produce a planning and budgeting system which is better integrated than PPBS, no new system has yet been adequately tested in a range of different governments and agencies. To date, therefore, the integration of planning and budgeting, though very desirable in principle, has proved remarkably hard to achieve.

(c) *Demystifying Planning, Adopting an Iterative Approach, and Decentralising the Administrative System*

The most frequently proposed, though not the most widely adopted, schemes to improve development-planning suggest that it should be removed from its present techno-bureaucratic isolation and incorporated more firmly into the activities of all levels of government.[14] Some authors go so far as to recommend the abolition of specialist ministries and departments of planning, giving the responsibility for decision-making firmly to the executive agencies of government. Others simply suggest that planning agencies should consult more widely with different interest groups and executive agencies, and that plans should be phrased in more explicit language, avoiding technical sophistication and specialist jargon. In both cases the aim is to diffuse planning activities more widely in governmental circles, and to ensure a more effective link between planning, the exercise of political power, and the inter-action of different interest groups.

The diffusion of planning activities within government is based on a recognition that planning is nothing more than "defining and achieving objectives for the future" of a given population, economic sector, institution, enterprise, programme, project, and/or geographical area. In other words, planning is seen as a normal governmental activity rather than something new, specialist and highly technical. In such a conception, planning not only involves

---

[13] See, *e.g.*, A. Wildavsky, "The Political Economy of Efficiency," 26 *Public Administration Review* (1966), pp. 292–310; *ibid.*, "Rescuing Policy Analysis from PPBS," 29 *Public Administration Review* (1969), pp. 189–202.

[14] See, *e.g.*, Bromley, *op. cit.* in note 6 above; O. Mehmet, *Economic Planning and Social Justice in Developing Countries* (1978), pp. 175–198; R. Chambers, "Rural Poverty Unperceived: Problems and Remedies," 9 *World Development* (1981), pp. 1–19.

the preparation of documents called development plans, but also the identification of problems, the study of these problems, the consultation involved in selecting policies, the conduct of feasibility and design studies, the approval and implementation of the chosen strategies, and above all, the evaluation of the results of implementation, leading to the identification of new problems and objectives and the selection of new policies. Thus, planning is seen as a continuous and cyclical activity involving a learning process. This learning process is based both on the identification and correction of past errors, and also on the gradual recognition of new potential objectives and means of reaching those objectives.[15] Such an approach leads inevitably to the abandonment of medium- to long-term master plans, usually replacing them with broad strategy documents specifying government objectives in relatively general terms, and with specific policy papers and project plans detailing proposed governmental actions.

A broadly-based, non-technocratic and iterative style of planning is likely to lead to the abandonment of "top-down" planning models based on the progressive disaggregation of an integrated, comprehensive national development strategy, usually derived from specialist macroeconomic modelling and analysis. Instead, national development strategies are likely to be aggregations of specific sectoral, regional and local strategies, with an allocation of resources to each sector, region and locality based on the recognition of their relative political and economic power, and on the opinions of powerful interest groups regarding their potentials and needs. This is not strictly a "bottom-up" planning model in which each community works out its own schemes and these are progressively aggregated in local, regional and national assemblies of representatives to produce the national strategy. Rather it is a "two-way" model in which indications are passed downward from the central policy-making bodies of government regarding resources likely to be available and the rough division of resources between sectors and regions, and in which indications are passed upwards from sectoral, regional and local interest groups regarding possible projects, potentials and needs. The two-way model functions through negotiation, and it is firmly rooted in the workings of the political system with a consequent recognition of power structures, the significance of patronage, and the mobilisation and alliance of specific interest groups to extract concessions from government.

---

[15] See, *e.g.*, L.J. Goodman and R.N. Love (eds.), *Project Planning and Management: An Integrated Approach* (1980); D.A. Rondinelli (ed.), *Planning Development Projects* (1977), pp. 1–25.

In most countries the full benefits of a non-technocratic, iterative approach to development-planning cannot be achieved without a considerable measure of administrative decentralisation, and there is little indication that such decentralisation is likely to be achieved. It has long been argued that decentralisation can decongest the decision-making system at the national level and can encourage popular participation in decision-making and plan implementation at the local level. Such measures require the devolution of power, responsibility, and control over revenues or revenue-raising opportunities. In other words, they require that central government voluntarily relinquishes some of its attributes and functions. Regrettably, such a decision is usually only taken if leading politicians have strong anarchist leanings, or if devolution is seen as the only effective way to keep the country together as a single basic unit. Political centralisation has probably been a stronger force than decentralisation in most countries over the last 30 years, and there is little sign of a counter-movement. Indeed, the technologies of mass media and centralised control seem to be advancing much more rapidly than the reality of popular participation, and there is little beyond the continuing strength of nationalist secessionist movements in a wide range of countries to give any real evidence of pressures for decentralisation.

(d) *Action Planning, Transactive Planning, and Planning as Societal Learning*

The twin recognitions that planning should be a continuous and cyclical activity involving a learning process, and that planning should be a central function of government in consultation with relevant interest groups and powerful élites, has led to some more revolutionary, but also more vacuous, proposals. Academic writers enthused by highly democratic principles, by the rapidity of social change, and by the potential of "futurology" as a means of combining forecasting with planning to achieve a desired future, have produced some idealistic proposals for highly flexible and participative planning. Some proposals—the "action planning school"—have focused on the virtual abandonment of master plans and strategy documents, concentrating instead on creating a capacity to continuously monitor rapidly changing situations and to respond quickly through governmental action.[16] Others—the "transactive planning school"—have concentrated on the interaction and bargaining of different interest groups, with government

[16] See, *e.g.*, O. Koenigsberger, "Planning for Rapid Change," *Report and Proceedings, Town and Country Planning Summer School: Queen's University of Belfast, 1967.*

being reduced to the role of "referee," "implementing agency," or "advocate protecting the more disadvantaged groups."[17] Still others—the "planning as societal learning school"—have envisaged planning as a highly democratic, long-term and futuristic exercise, working out a common, societal value base, a vision of a desired optimum future, and a path towards that future.[18]

Action planning, transactive planning, and planning as societal learning all have two fundamental weaknesses. First, they have little clear specification of roles and tasks, so that it is almost impossible to explain how *in practice* such activities would be conducted. Thus, they appear to be utopian and impractical, and in reality they have rarely been tried. Secondly, they assume a benevolent, stable government which is anxious to promote the general welfare of the population and to hand over as much power as possible. In reality most more stable governments tend to seek and acquire greater powers rather than to voluntarily give them up, and many are in the hands of powerful military, industrial, landowning or trading interests who have little concern for the general welfare.

The three approaches under discussion also have some more specific weaknesses. In the case of action planning, there is a strong tendency for the model to lead towards more centralised and less democratic government through the manipulation of information by a central power élite. In the cases of transactive planning and of planning as societal learning, there is a basic assumption that the population as a whole is highly literate, articulate, informed and participative, without elements of basic ignorance, apathy, anomie or media manipulation. Such conditions are very rare in the world today, and they are certainly not relevant to most of the contemporary Third World. Both transactive planning and societal learning seem optimistic products of the late 1960s—the era of Flower Power and of Danny the Red—when there was a prospect of seemingly limitless economic growth and mass consumption. In the aura of depression, recession and return to Cold War surrounding the late 1970s and early 1980s, they seem far less realistic.

V—The Limits to " Improved Planning"

The various proposals reviewed above to "reform" development planning all have some merit. A transition to socialism with increased State involvement in the economy and the adoption of policies favouring increased national self-reliance, is the most obvious route to improved planning and to national transformation.

---

[17] See, *e.g.* J. Friedmann, *Retracking America: A Theory of Transactive Planning* (1973).
[18] See, *e.g.*, D.N. Michael, *On Learning to Plan and Planning to Learn* (1973).

The principal alternative, the Waterston line, is effectively an ideological opposite contributing to a different sort of national transformation more akin to the Brazilian "miracle" of the late 1960s and early 1970s; not so much a route towards self-sustaining growth as an acceleration of "associated dependent development."[19] Integrating annual plans with the budget cycle, adopting an iterative approach, and achieving a measure of administrative decentralisation, are all commendable improvements to conventional development-planning. They are equally adaptable to socialist and capitalist economic systems and forms of planning, but all are far more easily proposed than truly achieved. Finally, action planning, transactive planning and planning as societal learning are all based on very laudable principles, most notably the encouragement of popular participation in decision-making and the achievement of high levels of flexibility in planning, but these lines of thinking are notably lacking in realism.

Overall, the approach taken to increasing the efficacy of development planning must be closely adapted to the style of government, development policies and ideological characteristics of the country concerned. There is no universal prescription to make planning more effective, and any remedy adopted to solve current problems must be tailored to the nature of the system in which it is to be applied. "Improved planning" can make a contribution to a country's development prospects, but its contribution is likely to be very limited unless there is at least a moderate degree of political stability, governmental political will, administrative competence and economic self-reliance in the country concerned. Indeed, where such stability, will, competence and self-reliance are lacking, there is very little prospect of any "improvement" in planning; the conditions are simply not present to favour the appointment and tenure of capable personnel, or any grants of meaningful powers to facilitate plan implementation.

In conclusion, it is pertinent to consider the fundamental question: Is development-planning an impossible task under conditions of political instability and economic dependence? The answer is "no." Planning is possible and does indeed take place on a limited scale in countries suffering from political instability and economic dependence, but such planning is likely to be relatively constrained and ineffectual, with a far more notable production of documents than achievement in terms of implementation. Even the most chronic cases of instability and dependence, such as the Garcia

---

[19] See the classic work, only recently published in English: F.H. Cardoso and E. Faletto, *Dependency and Development in Latin America* (1980).

Meza régime in Bolivia from July 1980 to August 1981, permit the planning of specific short-term projects handled by semi-autonomous governmental bodies with their own budget. Not surprisingly, however, such chronic cases show little evidence of any coherent ongoing national development strategy. Planning is effectively fractionalised into specific, localised, short-term schemes, without any broader and longer-term co-ordinating strategy. Under such difficult circumstances development-planning can continue with modest effects often accentuating economic and technical dependence, but it has no chance of initiating a shift towards greater political stability and economic self-reliance. The prospects for real improvements which would be highly favourable both to the welfare of the majority of the population and to the efficacy of development planning, depend heavily on political changes which lead to the arrival of more stable, conscientious, efficient and ideologically-coherent régimes. It is to sudden and enduring political changes rather than to national development plans, that the inhabitants of chronically unstable, dependent and misruled countries must look for any form of national salvation. What development-planning cannot achieve, a *coup d'état*, revolution or crushing electoral victory sometimes can.

THE NEW INTERNATIONAL
ECONOMIC ORDER (I)

By

D.H.N. JOHNSON

By the New International Economic Order (NIEO) is usually meant the triad of resolutions adopted by the General Assembly of the United Nations in 1974, namely: (i) Declaration on the Establishment of a New International Economic Order, adopted on May 1, 1974[1]; (ii) Programme of Action on the Establishment of a New International Economic Order, adopted on May 1, 1974[2]; (iii) Charter of Economic Rights and Duties of States (CERDS), adopted on December 12, 1974[3]

This paper will be divided into the following sections: Section 1 will deal with the background to NIEO; Section 2 will include a brief analysis of the NIEO resolutions; Section 3 will examine the legal status of the NIEO resolutions; Section 4 will examine certain arbitrations where NIEO has been an issue; Section 5 will examine the fate of NIEO since the resolutions of 1974 were adopted; and finally, in Section 6 an attempt will be made to assess the future prospects for NIEO.

Before proceeding to the first Section, however, it is desirable to pay some attention to the meaning of the word "order" in this context. In a perceptive article Professor Schwarzenberger has defined "order" as denoting "a, primarily, *de facto* state of affairs," whereas, according to the same author, "law is viewed as including any norms intended to regulate social conduct which, if required, can be authoritatively determined on a basis of consent or compulsion and enforced by the application of external sanctions."[4] This raises the question of the relation between law (normative) and order (*de facto*), a relationship which the commonly used phrase "law and order" tends to confuse rather than to clarify.

As Professor Schwarzenberger has pointed out, there can be various forms of order. They may range from "a negative form of peace, that is effective control of those subject to such a system by an essentially metalegal apparatus of force and power" to a

---

[1] Resolution 3201 (S–VI).
[2] Resolution 3202 (S–VI).
[3] Resolution 3281 (XXIX).
[4] "Law, Order and Legitimation," 23 *Current Legal Problems* 240 (1970), at 242.

situation, admittedly rare, in which there is such a degree of "consensus among those involved" that there is no need for legal rules of behaviour.[5] A frequent function of law is to legitimate—*i.e.* to recognise, confirm and justify—an existing state of affairs or order. This legitimation, which turns a *de facto* order into a *de jure* order, may be achieved either through the exercise of power or through consent, the consent being arrived at on the basis either of mere reciprocity or of a genuine desire to collaborate.

International society offers various examples of the relation between law and order. Before the establishment of the League of Nations in 1920 international society was so little organised that to talk of an international order at that time would, in Professor Schwarzenberger's view, "appear to be unduly euphemistic" and the expression "international quasi-order" would be a more appropriate term.[6] Since 1920, and still more since the foundation of the United Nations in 1945, international society has been in certain respects more organised, although it would still be straining at language to say that anything more than "international quasi-order" exists. The reason for this is that the degree of legitimation that has been achieved, either through the exercise of power or by consensus, is insufficient to justify the use of the term "international order."

Applying this reasoning to the field of international economic relations, Professor Schwarzenberger has referred to the existence in the pre-1914 period of certain *de facto* orders, such as the "international investor-debtor nexus" operated by the City of London, together with "the policing function of the British navy,"[7] and the gold standard.[8] The same author, whilst taking note of certain developments in the period between 1919 and 1939, has said these were "too limited and too fragmentary to constitute an international economic order in any meaningful use of the term."[9] So the question remains whether there have been any developments since 1945 to make it meaningful to speak of an international economic order. This question is relevant because the proponents of "the new international economic order" owe a duty to explain whether, in their view, they are replacing an existing economic order with their "new" version or whether they aim to create an economic order where none—or at any rate nothing more than a "quasi-order"—exists.

---

[5] *Ibid.*
[6] *Ibid.*, p. 251.
[7] *Economic World Order? A Basic Problem of International Economic Law* (1970), p. 8.
[8] *Ibid.*, p. 9.
[9] *Ibid.*, p. 35.

In seeking to answer this question, Professor Schwarzenberger subjects to scrutiny certain resolutions of the General Assembly of the United Nations, especially Resolution 1803(XVII) on Permanent Sovereignty over Natural Resources, adopted on December 14, 1962, which some claim as a precursor of NIEO; the practice of the United Nations in the application of sanctions, especially economic sanctions; and a variety of international treaties, including those dealing with slavery, drugs, the law of the sea, the trade of landlocked countries, Antarctica, outer space, diplomatic and consular relations, nuclear weapons and human rights. On the surface the record since 1945 looks impressive, especially as regards the number of treaties providing for international co-operation that have been concluded. It is necessary, however, to look below the surface. Commenting on some of the treaties, Professor Schwarzenberger notes in them "a tendency to pay even greater attention" than in the time of the League of Nations "to the susceptibilities of the guardians of national sovereignty by a more cautious formulation of international obligations and further provision for renunciation and escape clauses."[10] As for the treaties on economic human rights, his conclusion is that "in so heterogeneous an environment" it has proved impossible to formulate the rules of "a living international economic order."[11]

Of particular significance in the genesis of "the new international economic order" is Resolution 1803(XVII). As already explained, this proclaims "permanent sovereignty over natural resources." However, as Professor Schwarzenberger explains, "nothing could have been worse from the point of view of capital-importing States than an affirmation in legally binding form of the principle of the inalienable character of sovereignty over natural wealth and resources" since such an affirmation "would have destroyed the last vestiges of their rather relative credit-worthiness."[12] So the Resolution declared that this sovereignty, while in principle inalienable, could be alienated in the context of freely negotiated agreements, leaving it open to Western company lawyers, in the guise of naturalist ideologists, to argue that investment agreements between Third-World countries and private corporations came within the protection of the principle of *pacta sunt servanda*, traditionally regarded as the basic norm regulating relations between sovereign States. Thus, "in an international society divided into world blocs, with the "Third World" forming an uneasy and unstable in-between area, the naturalist ideology of inalienable sovereignty over natural

[10] *Ibid.*, p. 56.
[11] *Ibid.*, p. 64.
[12] *Ibid.*, p. 48.

wealth and resources is not," in Professor Schwarzenberger's view, "intended to constitute a new rule of consensual *jus cogens*. It is no more than a convenient para-legal ideology of power economics."[13]

On the basis of Professor Schwarzenberger's analysis, therefore, there was in 1970 no international economic order in a meaningful sense of that term. Whether, as a result of the NIEO resolutions of 1974, such an order now exists will be examined in the following Sections.

I—THE BACKGROUND TO NIEO

The campaign for a New International Economic Order may be said to have had its origin in the Charter of the United Nations of 1945. In the Preamble to that Charter the Peoples of the United Nations expressed their determination "to promote social progress and better standards of life in larger freedom" and "to employ international machinery for the promotion of the economic and social advancement of all peoples." In Article 1 of the Charter one of the Purposes of the United Nations was said to be "to achieve international co-operation in solving international problems of an economic, social, cultural, or humanitarian character . . . ." To that end the General Assembly was enjoined to "initiate studies and make recommendations for the purpose of . . . promoting international co-operation in the economic, social, cultural, educational, and health fields . . . ." [Article 13(1)(*b*)].

The details of United Nations activity in the economic sphere were set out in Chapters IX and X of the Charter. Article 55 laid on the United Nations the duty of promoting "higher standards of living, full employment, and conditions of economic and social progress and development"; in Article 56 all Members pledged themselves "to take joint and separate action in co-operation with the Organisation for the achievement of the purposes set forth in Article 55"; and Article 60 provided that "Responsibility for the discharge of the functions of the Organisation set forth in this Chapter shall be vested in the General Assembly and, under the authority of the General Assembly, in the Economic and Social Council, which shall have for this purpose the powers set forth in Chapter X."

In practice responsibility for achieving the economic goals adumbrated in the Charter was divided between the individual

---

[13] *Ibid.*, p. 49.

Members themselves, the General Assembly, the Economic and Social Council and the specialised agencies. The Economic and Social Council was established as a "principal organ of the United Nations"(Article 7 of the Charter) largely on the strength of the report of a committee under the chairmanship of Mr Stanley Bruce[14] to the Assembly of the League of Nations. This committee, which reported just before the Second World War started in 1939, had recommended that the League (which at that time had no equivalent organ) should establish a Central Committee for Economic and Social Questions. The outbreak of war prevented the implementation of that recommendation. The Dumbarton Oaks Proposals of 1944 provided for an Economic and Social Council, but the decision to raise that Council to the status of a "principal organ of the United Nations" was not taken until the San Francisco Conference of 1945.

The status of the Economic and Social Council, as a "principal organ of the United Nations" and yet as an organ "under the authority of the General Assembly," is and always has been ambiguous. Although enlarged from its original size of 18 members to 27 in 1965, and then to 54 Members in 1973, this Council has not developed as a powerful force. It has not even been very successful in the administrative task it was given by Article 63(2) of the Charter, which was to "co-ordinate the activities of the specialised agencies through consultation with and recommendations to such agencies and through recommendations to the General Assembly and to the Members of the United Nations." These agencies, of which there are now about 20,[15] include bodies of various types. Some, such as the International Telecommunications Union, whose origin can be traced back to a treaty concluded in Paris in 1865, and the Universal Postal Union, which dates from a Postal Convention signed in Berne in 1874, are among the oldest international organisations in existence.

The International Labour Organisation, though remodelled in 1946, owes its origin to the Treaty of Versailles of 1919. Most of the specialised agencies, however, such as the International Bank for Reconstruction and Development—usually known as the World

---

[14] Bruce was Prime Minister of the Commonwealth of Australia from 1923 to 1929. He served as Australian High Commissioner in London from 1933 to 1945 and was created Viscount Melbourne of Westminster Gardens in the City of Westminster in 1947, being the first Australian to sit in the House of Lords.

[15] In some cases there is uncertainty as to whether an agency is or is not a "specialised agency" within the meaning of the Charter. Although the term "specialised agencies" is still widely used, the Secretariat of the United Nations appears to prefer the more cautious expression "inter-governmental organisations related to the United Nations."

Bank—the International Monetary fund, the International Civil Aviation Organisation, the Food and Agriculture Organisation, the United Nations Educational, Scientific and Cultural Organisation, the World Health Organisation and the World Meteorological Organisation came into being at about the same time as the United Nations itself. The Intergovernmental Maritime Consultative Organisation (recently renamed International Maritime Organisation) was a relative latecomer, not beginning to function until 1959.

By 1959 the devastation caused by the Second World War had been largely repaired, and international attention began to focus on a new problem, the so-called "gap" between the "developed" and the "developing" nations (sometimes referred to as the gap between the "rich" and the "poor" or between the "North" and the "South").[16] A number of initiatives were taken. By a treaty of December 14, 1960 the Organisation for European Economic Co-operation (OEEC), which had been established in 1948 to administer aid to European countries under the Marshall Plan, was reconstituted with a wider membership and with much wider objectives, including "the development of the world economy," and came to be known as the Organisation for Economic Co-operation and Development (OECD). Membership of this Organisation is often considered as the hallmark of a "developed" country, organised along basically free enterprise lines. On December 19, 1961 the General Assembly adopted unanimously Resolution 1710 (XVI), in which it *designated* "the current decade as the United Nations Development Decade, in which Member States and their peoples will intensify their efforts to mobilise and to sustain support for the measures required on the part of both developed and developing countries to accelerate progress towards self-sustaining growth of the economy of the individual nations and their social advancement so as to attain in each under-developed country a substantial increase in the rate of growth, with each country setting its own target, taking as the objective a minimum annual rate of growth of aggregate national income of 5 per cent. at the end of the Decade." A similar Resolution—2626(XXV)—was adopted by the General Assembly without vote on October 24, 1970. In this the Second United Nations Development Decade, starting from January 1, 1971, was *proclaimed* and an International Development Strategy for the Decade, consisting of 84 paragraphs, was *adopted*.

Other initiatives followed, including the proclaiming by President Kennedy on March 13, 1961 of the Alliance for Progress, a measure

---

[16] "North" and "South" as used here are political rather than geographical terms as the Antipodean nations, Australia and New Zealand, are considered as belonging to the "North."

designed to promote development of the Latin American countries[17]; the decision of the General Assembly on December 8, 1962 to convene the United Nations Conference on Trade and Development (UNCTAD),[18] followed by a further decision of the General Assembly on December 30, 1964 to establish UNCTAD as an organ of the General Assembly to meet at intervals of not more than three years[19]; and the decision of "The Governments which are contracting parties to the General Agreement on Tariffs and Trade (GATT)," at Geneva on February 8, 1965, to adopt the "Protocol Amending the General Agreement on Tariffs and Trade to Introduce a Part IV on Trade and Development."[20] The effect of the new Part IV was to encourage "developed contracting parties" to give preference to the trade of "less-developed contracting parties" without expecting reciprocity, thus cutting across the basic principle of "general most-favoured nation treatment" set forth in Article 1 of the original GATT.

Therefore, leaving aside the controversies engendered by NIEO, it is clear that well before 1974 there was at least a moral and political commitment by the entire international community to adopt a policy of economic growth and to ignore the warnings of ecologists that such a policy would bring about environmental disaster.[21] It is also clear that there was a strong commitment to improve through collective action the position of "under-developed"—now more usually called "developing"—countries, and that this commitment involved, if not a restructuring, at least a reshaping, of the international economic quasi-order established in 1945.

The most important principle underlying this international economic quasi-order was the principle, enshrined in Article 2(1) of the Charter of the United Nations itself, of "the sovereign equality" of the Members of that organisation, so that not even the United Nations could take decisive action in the economic sphere without the consent of individual countries.[22] There was a faint suggestion that such an organisation might be established, but it came to nothing, when the Havana Charter for an International Trade

---

[17] See F. Parkinson, in this *Year Book*, Vol. 18 (1964), p. 96.

[18] Resolution 1785 (XVII).

[19] Resolution 1995 (XIX).

[20] 572 UNTS 320.

[21] On the distinction between moral and political commitments on the one hand, and legal commitments on the other hand, see the article by the present writer in 32 *British Year Book of International Law* 97 (1955–1956).

[22] The special case of the "complete or partial interruption of economic relations," which the Security Council may call on Members of the United Nations to implement under Article 41 of the Charter need not be considered here.

Organisation, adopted by the United Nations Conference on Trade and Employment at Havana on March 24, 1948, failed to secure ratification.[23]

In the case of the two specifically economic organisations that were established, the World Bank and the International Monetary Fund, the principle of State sovereignty was carefully preserved. True, a country could not expect to utilise the facilities of these organisations without giving some undertakings, but there was no suggestion that membership was compulsory or that the Bank or the Fund could on their own initiative give directions to Members, let alone to non-Members. As a foretaste of what was to come, however, it is interesting to note that, unlike the Bank and the Fund which were established on the basis of "weighted voting," the International Trade Organisation (ITO) proposed by the Havana Charter would, if it had come into existence, have followed the principle of "one State, one vote." This factor may explain, at least in part, why the Havana Charter never entered into force. However, the Havana Conference was not totally without result. Although the ITO never came into existence, the General Agreement on Tariffs and Trade (GATT), which was originally intended to be a subsidiary agreement under the ITO Charter and to be administered by the ITO Secretariat, survived and continues to survive in the form of a "*de facto* if not *de jure* an international trade organisation."[24]

Despite the pressure which led to the inclusion in GATT of Part IV, there remained an impression among the developing countries that GATT had been, and still was, more concerned to reduce trade barriers between the developed countries than to give positive assistance to the developing countries.[25] It was this feeling which generated the pressure to call the United Nations Conference on Trade and Development in 1962, and subsequently to establish UNCTAD as an organ of the General Assembly specifically charged

[23] See J.E.S. Fawcett, in this *Year Book*, Vol. 5 (1951), p. 269.

The name of this Conference, as compared with UNCTAD, is interesting, indicating that just after the Second World War the maintenance of full employment was still considered an attainable goal. By the 1970's such a possibility was considered remote and the emphasis had shifted to the development of the developing countries. However, already in the Havana Charter of 1948, alongside Article 3(1) which referred to the duty of each Member to "take action designed to achieve and maintain full and productive employment" there were several references to the development of "countries which are still in the early stages of industrial development." [See Article 1(2); Article 8; and Article 10(2).]

[24] G. Curzon, *Multilateral Commercial Diplomacy* (1965), p. 34. See also J. H. Jackson, *World Trade and the Law of GATT* (1969).

[25] See G. L. Goodwin, "The United Nations Conference on Trade and Development," in this *Year Book*, Vol. 19 (1965), p. 1, and U. Kirdar, *The Structure of United Nations Economic Aid to Underdeveloped Countries* (1966), pp. 242–258.

with the duty, as stated in General Assembly resolution 1995 (XIX), "to promote international trade, especially with a view to accelerating economic development." Moreover at UNCTAD I, in Geneva from March 23 to June 16, 1964, fifteen 'General Principles' to govern international trade relations were adopted as recommendations of the Conference. These recommendations were without binding force, but similar recommendations were to emerge again in the NIEO resolutions of 1974.

It was a wide variety of factors which brought about the adoption of the 1974 resolutions. First there was the fact that at the time there was a modicum of "détente" between the super-Powers. It would have been politically impossible for instance for such resolutions to be adopted in an atmosphere of intense Cold War, such as prevailed before President Nixon's visit to Moscow in 1972 or has prevailed again since the Soviet invasion of Afghanistan in 1979. Secondly, there was the war between certain Arab States and Israel in 1973, with the concomitant oil embargo imposed by the Arab States. Thirdly, there was the substantial increase in the price of oil imposed by the Organisation of Petroleum Exporting Countries (OPEC). Although almost simultaneous with the oil embargo, this was in fact a quite separate development, not confined to the Arab oil exporters. These two factors, taken together, put the developed countries under certain pressure to make concessions to the developing countries, as well as increasing the confidence with which the latter group put forward their demands. Fourthly, there was the additional pressure, already referred to, from UNCTAD, which in turn derived its impetus from bodies such as the "Non-Aligned Movement" and the Group of 77.[26] At longer remove there was the influence of legal writers, especially in Latin America, such as Alejandro Alvarez[27] and Jorge Castañeda.[28]

The idea of a Charter of Economic Rights and Duties of States,

---

[26] "The key to the concerted action in the United Nations in 1974 on behalf of the new international economic order is the fusion, for that specific purpose, of the main drives of the former non-aligned group and of the Group of 77, now expanded to over a hundred countries." E. McWhinney "The International Law-Making Process and the New International Economic Order," 14 *Canadian Yearbook of International Law* 57 (1976), at 61. As this author has pointed out, the non-aligned group consisted mainly of countries in Africa and Asia, whereas the Group of 77, which emerged at UNCTAD I, had a strong Latin American component. The former group had originally been concerned mainly with political questions, whereas the Group of 77 tended to concentrate on economic issues. The importance of Yugoslavia in promoting the NIEO should also not be overlooked.

[27] Chilean judge on the International Court of Justice from 1946 to 1955; author of *Le droit international nouveau dans ses rapports avec la vie actuelle des peuples* (1959).

[28] Author of *Legal Effects of the United Nations Resolutions* (1970), and the influential article "'Valeur juridique des resolutions des Nations Unies," 129 *Hague Recueil* (1970). At this writing Mr Castañeda is Foreign Minister of Mexico.

such as eventuated in resolution 3281(XXIX) adopted by the General Assembly on December 12, 1974, was first put forward by President Luis Echeverria of Mexico at UNCTAD III at Santiago, Chile, in April 1972, and a Working Group, with Ambassador Castañeda, also of Mexico, as chairman, was set up to prepare a draft. This Working Group was proceeding at a fairly leisurely pace when its labours were overtaken by the dramatic events of 1973 as regards the price and availability of oil. It was these events which produced the Sixth Special Session of the General Assembly of the United Nations in April and May 1974. At this Special Session, which was held to discuss Raw Materials and Development, and where a leading role was played by Algeria, the Declaration on the Establishment of a New International Order and the Programme of Action on the Establishment of a New International Economic Order were adopted. In the Declaration the General Assembly reminded itself that the United Nations "must have an even greater role in the establishment of a new international economic order" and in the very next sentence stated that "The Charter of Economic Rights and Duties of States, for the preparation of which the present Declaration will provide an additional source of inspiration, will constitute a significant contribution in this respect." The Charter of Economic Rights and Duties of States was adopted later in the year at the twenty-ninth regular session of the General Assembly.

It is this series of events which accounts for the somewhat untidy and repetitive nature of the founding documents of NIEO.

II—A BRIEF ANALYSIS OF THE NIEO RESOLUTIONS

Mention has already been made of the untidy and repetitive nature of the NIEO resolutions. In the interests of space, therefore, this analysis will be kept brief. This course is the more acceptable in that the principles of NIEO are now generally well known. Further, this analysis will concentrate on the Charter of Economic Rights and Duties of States (CERDS), as this instrument is the most mature and best prepared of the NIEO documents, as well as being the latest in time. Of the two resolutions adopted on May 1, 1974, emphasis will be placed on the Declaration on the Establishment of a New International Economic Order—which will be referred to simply as "Declaration"—as opposed to the more detailed Programme of Action on the Establishment of a New International Economic Order.

The basic philosophy of NIEO is set out in the preamble to the Declaration. It is there said that there is a "widening gap between the developed and the developing countries" and that this is an "injustice." Stated in such broad terms, without a definition of "developed" and "developing" countries, and without admitting that, as between *some* "developed" and *some* "developing" countries, so far from there being a "widening gap," the reverse is the case, this amounts to little more than a convenient slogan. However, this is followed by the statistical assertion in paragraph 1 of the Declaration that "The developing countries, which constitute 70 per cent. of the world's population, account for only 30 per cent. of the world's income." It is then stated that "it has proved impossible to achieve an even and balanced development under the existing international economic order," and that "the gap between the developed and the developing countries continues to widen in a system which was established at a time when most of the developing countries did not even exist as independent States and which perpetuates inequality."

The blame for this situation is placed on "the remaining vestiges of alien and colonial domination, foreign occupation, racial discrimination, *apartheid* and neo-colonialism" [Declaration paragraph 1]. In the view of the Soviet Union, these are Western phenomena, thus enabling the Soviet Union to argue that it has no responsibility for the present situation and need bear none of the burdens implied by NIEO. In the view of the People's Republic of China, however, the Soviet Union is just as much to blame as the Western countries are for the plight of the developing countries. To return to the Declaration, since these phenomena, whoever is responsible for them, are the cause of the present situation, it follows that one of the principles of NIEO is "the right of all States, territories and peoples under foreign occupation, alien and colonial domination or *apartheid* to restitution and full compensation for the exploitation and depletion of, and damages to, the natural resources and all other resources of those States, territories and peoples." [Declaration, paragraph 4 (f)]. Western commentators have tended to underestimate the extent to which, under NIEO, a transfer of resources from developed to developing countries is claimed not merely as a means of improving the lot of developing countries but also as a redress for past wrongs. Significantly, the Declaration does not allow the colonialists to set off, against the compensation they are expected to pay, any expenditures they may have incurred in building up the infra-structures of the developing countries concerned.

The best known of all the rights claimed under NIEO is the right of every State "to choose its economic system as well as its political, social and cultural systems in accordance with the will of its people, without outside interference, coercion or threat in any form whatsoever." [Charter, Article 1]. This leads to the claim that "every State has and shall freely exercise full sovereignty, including possession, use and disposal, over all its wealth, natural resources and economic activities" [Charter, Article 2(1)]. This leads in turn to the claim that every State has the right to regulate foreign investments and supervise the activities of transnational corporations [Charter, Article 2(2)(a) and (b)], a claim which no State is likely to dispute. There follows, however, the claim that every State has the right "to nationalise, expropriate or transfer ownership of foreign property, in which case appropriate compensation should be paid by the State adopting such measures, taking into account all its relevant laws and regulations and all circumstances that the State considers pertinent." [Charter, Article 2(2)(c)]. What has aroused controversy here is the implication that, in deciding what compensation is "appropriate," only the view of the expropriating State need be considered. The sub-paragraph makes no reference to international law at all, saying rather that "in any case where the question of compensation gives rise to a controversy, it shall be settled under the domestic law of the nationalising State and by its tribunals" unless that State freely agrees to "other peaceful means," by which is presumably meant some kind of international arbitration.

Article 5 of the Charter is no less controversial. It asserts that: "All States have the right to associate in organisations of primary commodity producers in order to develop their national economies, to achieve stable financing for their development and, in pursuance of their aims, to assist in the promotion of sustained growth of the world economy, in particular accelerating the development of developing countries. Correspondingly all States have the duty to respect that right by refraining from applying economic and political measures that would limit it."

This provision was clearly designed to ratify and approve the activities of organisations such as OPEC, and even to stigmatise as illegal any measures which purchasers of the commodities concerned might take by way of retaliation. In Western countries OPEC is widely regarded as a cartel, and as a particularly obnoxious one. The proponents of NIEO, however, seek to draw a distinction between price-raising efforts by States associating "in organisations of primary commodity producers in order to develop their national economies" and restrictive business practices operated by transnational corporations. Section V(b) of Resolution 3202(VI) requires that such practices be "eliminated."

Another controversial principle of NIEO is the claim that: "All States are juridically equal and, as equal members of the international community, have the right to participate fully and effectively in the international decision-making process in the solution of world economic, financial and monetary problems, *inter alia*, through the appropriate international organisations in accordance with their existing and evolving rules, and to share equitably in the benefits resulting therefrom." [Charter, Article 10].

This claim relates in particular to the principle of weighted-voting as applied in the World Bank and the International Monetary Fund. The character of these institutions would be completely changed if they were to be obliged to take decisions on the basis of "one State, one vote": indeed it is doubtful if the principal contributors to them would be prepared to remain in them under such conditions.

Articles 18 and 19 of the Charter both call for an extension of the system whereby developed countries grant to developing countries "generalised preferential, non-reciprocal and non-discriminatory treatment" in matters of trade, especially tariffs. This principle has been accepted by the developed countries, although there may be room for argument as to the extent, speed and duration of its application.

More controversial is Article 28 of the Charter which provides: "All states have the duty to co-operate in achieving adjustments in the prices of exports of developing countries in relation to prices of their imports so as to promote just and equitable terms of trade for them, in a manner which is remunerative for producers and equitable for producers and consumers."

This sounds like an effort to achieve the "just price" recommended by mediaeval theologians. In modern terms it proposes a system of "indexing" one economic variable to another, and such systems of "indexation" are not unknown in national economies. They are not easy to operate but it has to be remembered that it has been a persistent grievance of developing countries that, save in exceptional situations, the "terms of trade" are loaded against them.[29]

Other propositions of NIEO include the duty of developed countries to transfer technology to developing countries [Charter, Article 13]; the duty of developed countries to promote "increased net flows of real resources to the developing countries from all sources," *i.e.* private investment as well as official aid [Charter, Article 22]; recognition of the right of every State "to enjoy fully the benefits of world invisible trade and to engage in the expansion of such trade [Charter, Article 27]; and acceptance of the principle that "the seabed and ocean floor and the subsoil thereof, beyond the limits of national jurisdiction, as well as the resources of the area, are the common heritage of mankind," with the consequence that

---

[29] See Goodwin, *op cit.* in note 25 above, p. 10.

the benefits derived from the exploitation of these resources must be "shared equitably by all States, taking into account the particular interests and needs of developing countries" [Charter, Article 29].[30]

III—THE LEGAL STATUS
OF THE NIEO RESOLUTIONS

As has been pointed out, the NIEO instruments were all resolutions of the General Assembly. A considerable literature has developed on the question of the legal effect of these resolutions.[31] It is not intended to reopen that issue here in a general way. Nor is it necessary to do that, since most commentators agree that, in order to assess the legal effect of a resolution of the General Assembly, it is necessary to consider a number of factors, such as the majority by which the resolution was adopted, the entity to whom it was addressed, the nature of the resolution, the intention (so far as that can be gauged) of the General Assembly in adopting it; the title given to the resolution and the state of the law before the resolution was adopted. It cannot seriously be argued that all resolutions adopted by the General Assembly are legally binding. Nor, however, can it be maintained that such resolutions can never be mandatory.

With regard to the NIEO resolutions, it is possible to narrow the issue somewhat. The two resolutions of May 1, 1974, were adopted "without vote," although "reservations" were entered by the representatives of the United States, the Federal Republic of Germany, France, Japan and the United Kingdom. The delegate of the Federal Republic of Germany also entered some separate "reservations and interpretations" on behalf of the European Economic Community.[32] The Secretary-General of the United Nations has maintained that the concept of reservations is not applicable to the voting of decisions in organs of the United Nations. However, in refutation of this contention, Judge Gros has

---

[30] Here the NIEO resolution was reenacting a principle already foreshadowed in resolution 2749 (XXV) adopted by the General Assembly on December 17, 1970. The implementation of this principle has proved to be one of the most controversial issues in the Third United Nations Conference on the Law of the Sea.

[31] See Sloan, 25 *B.Y.I.L.* 1 (1948); Johnson, 32 *B.Y.I.L.* 97 (1955–56); Skubiszewski, 18 *Int. Org.* 790 (1964); McMahon, 41 *B.Y.I.L.* 1 (1965–66); Skubiszewski, 41 *B.Y.I.L.* 198 (1965–66); Sorensen, 101 *Hague Recueil* 91 (1960, III); Waldock, 106 *Hague Recueil*, 26–35, 96–193 (1962, II); Virally, 2 A.F.D.I. 66 (1956); Castañeda, *Legal Effects of United Nations Resolutions* (1969) and 129 *Hague Recueil* 207 (1970); Arango-Ruiz, 137 *Hague Recueil* 419 (1972, III); Stone, *Israel and Palestine, Assault on the Law of Nations* (1981), especially Chapter 2; Garibaldi, 73 *Proc. Am. Soc. I. L.* 324–327 (1979).

[32] For the reservations of these countries and speeches in support of them, see U.N. Document A/PV 2229 of May 1, 1974. See also 13 *ILM* 744–766.

pointed out: "The practice is a constant one, necessitated through the need to provide States wishing to dissociate themselves from a course of action with a means of making their attitude manifest.

"The consequence of the rejection of this practice and its effects would be to treat the political organs of the United Nations as organs of decision similar to those of a State or of a super-State, which, as the Court once declared in an oft-quoted phrase, is what the United Nations is not. For if a minority of States, which are not in agreement with a proposed decision are to be bound, however they vote, and whatever their reservations may be, the General Assembly would be a federal parliament . . . . The everyday operation of the United Nations would be deprived of all the flexibility made possible by statements of reservation and by abstention."[33]

There is the added difficulty in the case of the two resolutions adopted on May 1, 1974, that there is a dispute as to whether they were adopted by "consensus" or not. For example, the representative of the United States, Mr Scali, spoke as follows: "Some have referred to the procedure by which these documents have been formulated as that of 'consensus'. My delegation believes that the word 'consensus' cannot be applied in this case. The document which will be printed as the written product of this special General Assembly does not, in fact, whatever it is called, represent a consensus in the accepted meaning of that term. My delegation did not choose to voice objection to the resolution presented to us this evening even though, at the last moment, it was presented without mention of the word 'consensus'. The intent, however, was clear. This was intended as a consensus procedure, but our objecting to it at the last second would only have served to exacerbate the divisions that we have worked to the best of our ability to bridge during the last weeks."

On the other hand, the representative of France, Mr Guiringaud, said: "I cannot fail to hail the consensus that has marked the adoption of the basic documents that were discussed. The United Nations has committed itself along the right course by avoiding any final confrontation, which would not have failed to create a difficult atmosphere for future deliberations on topics in the economic field." He then proceeded to congratulate those delegates who were responsible for this happy conclusion including, especially and in the light of subsequent events ironically, "our friend and conciliator the

---

[33] See the Dissenting Opinion of Judge Gros, the French judge, in the case concerning *Legal Consequences for States of the Continued Presence of South Africa in Namibia (South West Africa) notwithstanding Security Council Resolution 276 (1970) I.C.J. Reports 1971*, p. 16 at p. 334.

Ambassador of His Majesty the Emperor of Iran." Then, as if to sound a note of caution, Mr Guiringaud added: "The consensus on which this session is about to conclude does not, however, mean that we have succeeded in reaching an understanding on all issues." And he proceeded to characterise some of the proposals that had been put forward as "unrealistic, because it is all too clear that the structures that serve as the framework for trade among States and economic entities are only what they are—they cannot be changed by simple votes—and that the prestige of our Organisation as well as its possibilities for action would be affected for a long time if an attempt was made here for extreme claims against the will of a considerable minority."[34]

Space does not allow a full discussion of the procedure which has come to be known as "consensus," and on which a considerable literature has by now been developed.[35] Suffice it to say that it is essentially an informal and political device which permits resolutions to be adopted in international bodies without a great deal of commitment being involved. It suits well the situation, which is fairly frequent in practice, where some States, while not in full agreement with a proposal, do not want actually to vote against it. They may adopt this attitude for a number of reasons. They may think they would incur unnecessary political odium by actually voting against the proposal. Or they may think—as appeared to be the view of the French Government in May 1974—that the matter is at a fairly early stage of discussion and that it would be better to try to improve the proposal at a later stage rather than vote against it on a preliminary view. "Consensus," as Vignes has said, "differs from unanimity, even though each requires that there be no dissenting voice. However, while a contrary view prevents consensus, abstention or silence allows it. After the event, all kinds of statements, explanations, interpretations, even reservations are possible, although the last would be only of a partial character."[36]

---

[34] This view accords with that expressed by Professor Werner Levi in this *Year Book*, Vol. 32 (1978), pp. 286, 287–8, where he said: "The attempt of the developing States to begin solving their problem of material inequality by legal means is a reversal of the historical process. In the past, developed States established their superiority *de facto* and thereafter reinforced it by foisting discriminatory, unfavourable and unequal treaties on the dominated States. The law was used to confirm and legalise an existing situation. The developing States want to bring about a desired situation with the help of the law. But their conception of material equality in a very broad sense could hardly be more than a political slogan. Without further definition it could not be operated as a legal obligation."

[35] See especialy Jenks, "Unanimity, the Veto, Weighted Voting, Special and Simple Majorities as Modes of Decision in International Organizations," *Cambridge Essays in International Law, Essays in Honour of Lord McNair*, 448 (1965); de Lacharrière, "Consensus et Nations Unies," 14 *A.F.D.I.* 9 (1968).

[36] "Will the Third Conference on the Law of the Sea work according to the Consensus Rule?", 69 *A.J.I.L.*, 119, 120 (1975).

The legal effect of a consensus is no less difficult to determine than is the question whether a consensus has occurred or not. To quote Vignes again: "At the material level, consensus implies certain rights and obligations. One hesitates to describe it as an instrument, since some think of it as 'general feeling'. In this way its natural result is the resolution of the matter rather than a legally binding act. It sometimes appears that delegations, without opposing or abstaining, nevertheless regard themselves as less closely committed to its detailed wording than if there had been a formal decision for which they had expressly voted."[37]

This language describes the situation perfectly. Delegates at an international gathering are often anxious to resolve the particular matter before them, maybe as amicably as possible, but without incurring long-term commitments.

All things considered, it seems reasonable to conclude that the decisions taken at the General Assembly on May 1, 1974 did not amount to a "consensus" and, even if they did, the degree of commitment to the principles stated in the relevant documents by the delegations who took the trouble to express reservations about them was negligible. In support of this conclusion, it is proposed to cite two further statements—"authorities" might be too strong a term.

In his dissenting opinion, already referred to, Judge Gros expressed the view that a resolution of the General Assembly, which had been adopted by 114 votes in favour, 2 against and 3 abstentions, "was not voted with quasi-unanimity of intention; it was voted by a large majority, clearly under the strong impression that law was not being made." This view was considerably influenced by the following facts: "There were 24 States which, in one way or another, expressed opposition, reservations or doubt. The fact that 19 of these States voted for resolution 2145(XXI) does not in any way diminish the effect of the observations and reservations they made upon the text, for in voting for it the States in question did not withdraw them; thus their votes signified acceptance of a political solution of which some features remained, for each of them, the subject of the opinions expressed."[38]

Although made with reference to a solution where voting took place, these remarks of Judge Gros seem relevant to a situation where there was alleged to be a consensus. Some may object to the distinction he draws between "political solutions" and legally binding acts, but it is only realistic to accept this distinction.

---

[37] *Ibid.*
[38] *Op cit.* in note 33 above, p. 334.

The second statement was also made by a judge of the International Court of Justice, although he was not a judge at the time the statement was made. In a discussion on the legal status of General Assembly resolutions, Professor McDougal had expressed his well-known view that "the key to law was not consent, but expectation" and that "it had to be realised that these expectations were being created all the time, in many different ways." Among these different ways were General Assembly resolutions. Whilst careful to point out that it was necessary to know who voted for the resolution, who voted against it, what was the relative and effective power of the voters and various other factors, Professor McDougal nevertheless asserted that "there didn't have to be 100 per cent. conformity to fact before fundamental policy could be accepted by the international community as a legal norm," and he cited human rights as an area where international law had been changed largely by a series of resolutions.[39] Whereupon Professor (now Judge) Schwebel asserted that "he hoped and believed that Professor McDougal was not correct about the increasing legal significance attributed to the General Assembly's actions. The United States shared the perception with those governments who instructed their delegates on the assumption that how they voted in the United Nations was not law creative and should not give rise to the kind of expectations about which Professor McDougal had spoken. One could not just argue that particular reality away. The widespread attitude of many States in the United Nations, especially those in the West, was: 'So what? It is only a recommendatory resolution of the United Nations, so what does it matter? Why should we offend our friends in the Third World by voting against it?' In the light of this fact, to arrive at a conclusion that would hold these resolutions as binding or law-creating would be at best questionable."[40]

Coming as it did from a person who has held responsible positions in the executive branch of the Government of the United States, and is now the American judge on the International Court of Justice, this was surely an extraordinary statement. It is one thing for governments to vote in a certain way in order to obtain a desirable political solution, as both Mr Guiringaud and Judge Gros suggested governments often do. But it is quite another thing for governments to cast their vote in an opposite sense from what they believe, simply in order not to offend other governments, as Professor Schwebel suggested that his, and apparently some other, governments do. If Professor Schwebel's views are to be taken

---

[39] 73 *Proc. Am. Soc. I.L.* 328–329 (1979).
[40] 73 *Proc. Am. Soc. I.L.* 332–333 (1979).

literally, it becomes a pointless exercise to enumerate and assess the votes of particular governments on particular resolutions. Perhaps that was his intention.

The situation with regard to the Charter of Economic Rights and Duties—Resolution 3281(XXIX)—is different in that that resolution was adopted by the General Assembly on December 12, 1974 by a vote, the figures being 120 in favour, 6 against and 10 abstentions. The States voting against were Belgium, Denmark, Federal Republic of Germany, Luxembourg, United Kingdom and United States, whilst those abstaining were Austria, Canada, France, Ireland, Israel, Italy, Japan, Netherlands, Norway and Spain. It is clear therefore that all the countries opposed to, or at least lukewarm about, the resolution belonged to a definite group, that of the developed countries. Another factor worth noting is that, when a separate vote was taken in the Second Committee on Article 2(2)(c)—the provision concerning nationalisation—there were 16 votes against and 6 abstentions.

Had it not been for these figures, there might have been a stronger case for arguing that the Charter had legal effect than had the resolutions adopted on May 1, 1974. The document had been much longer in preparation,[41] and the words "Charter," "Rights" and "Duties" were at least suggestive of some degree of legal obligation. However, from the fact that 16 States definitely did not support the resolution, whilst as many as 22 States were not satisfied with one of its key provisions, it seems reasonable to conclude that the Charter, like the two earlier resolutions, was "not voted with quasi-unanimity of intention" and "under the strong impression that law was being made," the test applied by Judge Gros, and one which, in the view of the present writer, it is reasonable to apply before it can be maintained that a resolution of the General Assembly of this type becomes a legally binding act.

This conclusion seems also reasonable in the light of the fact that, at any rate by responsible proponents of NIEO, it is not seriously argued that the NIEO resolutions are legally binding in their

---

[41] In Resolution 45 (III), adopted by UNCTAD on May 18, 1972, it was decided, on the proposal of the President of Mexico, to appoint a Working Group of government representatives to draw up a draft Charter of the Economic Rights and Duties of States. In resolution 3037 (XXVII), adopted on December 19, 1972, the General Assembly itself enlarged this Working Group. Further in resolution 3082 (XXVIII), adopted on December 6, 1973, the General Assembly decided in the light of the progress achieved by the Working Group, to extend the latter's mandate, and urged it "to complete, as the first step in the codification and development of the matter, the elaboration of a final draft Charter of Economic Rights and Duties of States, to be considered and approved by the General Assembly at its twenty-ninth session."

entirety. What is, however, maintained, at least by some governments and other authorities, is that not merely does a "new
international economic order" actually exist but that at least the
broad principles of that order are contained in the three resolutions
of 1974. That being so, it becomes relevant to consider some
arbitrations held since 1974 where NIEO has been an issue. This will
be taken up in Part Two in the 1984 Volume of this *Year Book*.

EQUALITY AND DISCRIMINATION IN INTERNATIONAL ECONOMIC LAW (XI):

THE GENERAL AGREEMENT ON TARIFFS AND TRADE

By

JOHN H. JACKSON

THIS is the eleventh contribution to the series on *Equality and Discrimination in International Economic Law*, initiated by Professor Schwarzenberger's paper under this title in the 1971 Volume of this Annual, and continued in the 1972 Volume by G.G. Kaplan on *The UNCTAD Scheme for Generalised Preferences* and B.G. Ramcharan on *The Commonwealth Preferential System*, in the 1974 and 1975 Volumes by P. Goldsmith and F. Sonderkötter on *The European Communities* and *The European Communities in the Wider World*, in the 1977 Volume by A. Sutton on *Trends in the Regulation of International Trade in Textiles* and C. Stoiber on *The Multinational Enterprise* and by B.G. Ramcharan in the 1978 Volume on *The United Nations Economic Commissions*, the 1980 Volume on *The Council for Mutual Economic Assistance*, and the 1981 Volume on *Development and International Economic Co-operation—Managing Editor*, Y.B.W.A.

THE history of non-discrimination obligations concerning international economic matters extends back for centuries, but in recent decades it has become increasingly complex, and in some eyes at least, increasingly "checkered." Although it has been argued that customary international law imposes a non-discrimination obligation on nations in the conduct of their international trading relationships, the prevailing view seems to be that this is not so, that if such an obligation exists it does so by virtue of treaty agreements only.[1] For centuries, various treaties, especially "FCN" (Friendship, Commerce and Navigation) treaties, have contained a variety of non-discrimination clauses, but since the Second World War, the principal non-discrimination norms are those which are

---

[1] G. Schwarzenberger, "Equality and Discrimination in International Economic Law," in this *Yearbook*, Vol. 25 (1971), p. 163–181. J.N. Hazard, "Editorial Comment: Commercial Discrimination and International Law," 52 *American Journal of International Law* (1958), p. 495.

included in the General Agreement on Tariffs and Trade (GATT). This article will focus on these norms as expressed in GATT.

Basically there are two types of non-discrimination norms relating to international economic behaviour. First there is the norm of "Most-Favoured-Nation" ("MFN") treatment. This norm requires nation A to give equal treatment to economic transactions originating in, or destined for, other countries entitled to the benefit of the norm. A second form of non-discrimination requirements is the "National-Treatment" obligation. This norm requires that a nation treat within its own borders, goods, services, persons, *etc.*, originating from outside its borders, in the same manner that it treats those which are of domestic origin.

While the descriptions of these two types of "economic-equality" norms—MFN, and National Treatment—have been stated broadly, to remind readers that they can apply to a variety of contexts (even to "human-rights treatment"), nevertheless the *GATT* only applies to trade in goods.[2] It does not apply to trade in services such as insurance, banking, engineering or technology, nor does it apply to many other matters treated in FCN and other treaties, such as treatment of investment or capital flows, the right of "establishment," *etc.* The remainder of this article will focus on the GATT norms of and thus be confined to the subject of international trade in *goods*.

In addition, this paper will be confined to the first of the two types of non-discrimination mentioned above, namely the MFN obligation.

I—THE BACKGROUND OF GATT AND ITS OBLIGATIONS

The GATT agreement, drafted in 1947, culminated a half century of various international efforts to regulate government conduct which affected international trade.

(a) *History of the GATT*

During the Second World War and the immediate post-war period, important initiatives for economic co-operation reflected two objectives of international economic policy. The first objective was the reduction of tariffs. This objective was pursued by the United States through the negotiation of "reciprocal trade agreements" under authority granted to the President by Congress in the Reciprocal Trade Agreements Act of 1934 and subsequent acts

---

[2] See generally, J.H. Jackson, *World Trade and the Law of GATT* (1969), Chapter 20.

extending his authority.[3] The predecessors of most of the clauses of GATT can be found among the clauses of the 32 such agreements negotiated and accepted by the United States between 1934 and 1945.[4]

The second objective of government international economic policy in this period was the prevention of war. It was felt that the restrictive "beggar-my-neighbour" policies adopted in the 1920s and 1930s, with their disastrous effects on world trade and domestic economies, had been a cause of the rise of dictatorships in the 1930s and of the Second World War.[5]

These two strands of policy began to merge in 1945 when the United States invited other nations to join in multilateral negotiations directed towards the establishment of a multilateral tariff reduction agreement. At the same time, the United Nations Economic and Social Council (ECOSOC) was established by the UN Charter to serve as a co-ordinating body for co-operation in international economic activities, and in February 1946, at its first session, ECOSOC called for a "United Nations Conference on Trade and Employment" to draft a charter for an "International Trade Organisation" (ITO) and to negotiate for the reduction of tariffs on a world-wide basis.[6]

A series of four preparatory conferences were held in 1946 through 1948 to work on a GATT and on a charter for an ITO. The first three of these were "Preparatory Committee" meetings for the "United Nations Conference on Trade and Employment," known as the Havana Conference. These three were held in London in October and November of 1946; at Lake Success, New York in January and February 1947; and in Geneva from April to October of that year. The fourth was the "Havana Conference" itself, from November 1947 through March 1948.[7]

The Geneva Conference in 1947 developed a draft ITO charter, completed tariff negotiations, and drafted a code of conduct—the "GATT"—to protect the benefits expected from the tariff negotiations.

---

[3] *An Act to Extend the Authority of the President Under Section 350 of the Tariff Act of 1930 and for Other Purposes*, 59 Stat. 410, 19 U.S.C. §§ 1351–66, effective July 4, 1945.

[4] See list of the agreements reproduced in the *Hearings on Extension of the Reciprocal Trade Agreements Act Before the House Comm. On Ways and Means*, 79th Cong., 1st Sess. 38, 636, 932 (1945).

[5] *Op. cit.* in note 2 above, at p. 36; W. Brown, *The United States and the Restoration of World Trade* (1950), at p. 29; C. Wilcox, *A Charter for World Trade* (1949), at p. 3.

[6] Executive Branch GATT Studies, No. 9, "The Most-Favoured-Nation Provision," at 134, Committee on Finance, United States Senate, Subcommittee on International Trade, 93d Cong., 2d Sess. (Compilation of 1973 Studies prepared by the Executive Branch: Committee Print, March 1974).

[7] *Op. cit.* in note 2 above, at p. 42.

The 1947 Final Act of the Geneva Conference authenticated the GATT agreement. Governments, however, were reluctant definitively to accept the GATT, because some of them needed additional legislative authority to do so, and they desired to avoid going to their parliaments until the Havana Charter was complete and ready for parliamentary approval also. The solution was to apply GATT under a Protocol of Provisional Application, expecting that after the ITO came into being under the Havana Charter, the GATT would be definitively brought into effect as a special agreement administered by the ITO. The GATT itself has never come into force but is applied only under this Protocol of Provisional Application or later protocols of accession containing substantially similar language.[8]

The Havana Conference completed an ITO charter in 1948. However the ITO met with substantial opposition in the United States Congress and its fate was sealed in December 1950 when the United States announced that the Charter would not be resubmitted for congressional approval.[9] The GATT then began to evolve into an organisation to fill the vacuum left by the demise of the ITO. It has performed this role uneasily, but more satisfactorily than anyone had a right to expect. It has done so, however, without an adequate institutional or constitutional structure of its own. In addition to this institutional weakness, application through the Provisional Protocol has meant that Part II of GATT (the "code of conduct"), was by the terms of the Protocol applied only " . . . to the fullest extent not inconsistent with existing legislation,"[10]; a measure that has given rise to the so-called "grandfather rights" for some countries in GATT.

(b) *The Obligations of the GATT*

The central focus of the GATT is the reduction of tariffs. Almost all of the Contracting Parties have negotiated a schedule of tariff concessions, which are annexed to the GATT and are a part of the GATT obligations.[11]

Apart from the tariff concessions, however, the central obligation of the GATT is that of Most-Favoured-Nation treatment (MFN) contained in Article I. Through the application of the MFN clause,

---

[8] Protocol of Provisional Application of the General Agreement on Tariffs and Trade (1947), 55 United Nations Treaty Series 308. See also *op. cit.* in note 2 above, at p. 60.

[9] U.S. State Dep't. Press Release, December 6, 1950, printed in 23 *Dep't. State Bull.* (1950) at p. 977; see W. Diebold, *The End of the ITO* (Princeton Essays in International Finance No. 16 (1952); R. Gardner, *Sterling-Dollar Diplomacy* (1956), at p. 378.

[10] *Op. cit.* in note 8 above.

[11] *GATT*, Article II, paragraph 7.

tariff commitments are generalised to all GATT parties. Both Article I, the MFN obligation, and Article II, outlining the legal significance of the Tariff Schedules bound in GATT, are included in Part I of the GATT. Unlike those obligations in Part II of the GATT, the Part I obligations take precedence as international legal obligations over pre-existing inconsistent national legislation.[12]

The obligations in Part II of the GATT form a "code of conduct" designed largely to protect the value of the tariff concessions negotiated and bound in GATT from being undermined as the result of non-tariff barriers to trade (NTBs). Part II deals with such subjects as: National Treatment in international taxation and regulation (Art. III); Antidumping and countervailing duties (Art. VI); Export subsidies (Art. XVI); Quotas (Arts. XI–XIV); Customs Valuation (Art. VII); Customs fees and formalities (Art. VIII); Publication of regulations (Art. X); Freedom of transit (Art. V.); Marks of origin (Art. IX); State Trading (Art. XVII); Safeguard measures (Art. XIX); and other barriers to trade (Art. XX, XXI).

The process of multilateral tariff reduction has continued through seven "rounds" of tariff and trade negotiations held under the auspices of GATT,[13] namely: 1–Geneva, Switzerland 1947; 2–Annecy, France 1948; 3–Torquay, England 1950; 4–Geneva 1956; 5–"Dillon Round," Geneva 1960–1961; 6–"Kennedy Round," Geneva 1964–1967; 7–"Tokyo Round," Geneva 1973–1979 (often called the "MTN," Multilateral Trade Negotiation).

All of the rounds have resulted in general cuts in tariffs. The last two, the Kennedy and Tokyo rounds, have also addressed problems caused by non-tariff barriers to trade. The Kennedy Round resulted in an Anti-dumping "code" (which had a checkered career) but little else with respect to non-tariff barriers. By contrast, the Tokyo Round (recently completed and still in the process of implementation) made considerable progress on questions of non-tariff barrier. In addition to two tariff protocols and a plethora of bilateral agreements completed in this round, the negotiation produced seven major multilateral "codes" relating to a variety of government practices which "distort" international trade.[14] These are: Agreement on Technical Barriers to Trade (the "Standards Code"); Agreement on Government Procurement; Agreement on Interpretation and Application of Article VI, XVI and XXIII of GATT

---

[12] *Op. cit.* in note 2 above, at p. 60.

[13] *Op. cit.* in note 2 above, at pp. 221, 223. Ambassador Robert S. Strauss, Forward, in "Symposium on the Multilateral Trade Agreements," 11 *Law and Policy in International Business* (1979), p. 1257.

[14] GATT, *Basic Instruments and Selected Documents*, 26th Supplement (1980), at p. 3.

(regarding subsidies and countervailing duties); Agreement on Implementation of Article VII of the GATT (regarding Customs Valuation); Agreement on Import Licensing Procedures; Agreement on Trade in Civil Aircraft; Agreement on Implementation of Article VI of the GATT (replacing the Kennedy Round Anti-Dumping Code).

The extraordinary scope of the Tokyo Round results, combined with the confused and ambiguous legal relationship to the GATT of some of the Tokyo Round agreements and the multiplication of institutions (committees) and dispute settlement procedures (as contained in many of these agreements) is beginning to have its constitutional impact on the GATT already.[15]

II—THE MOST-FAVOURED-NATION OBLIGATION

(a) *Background and history of the obligation*

Most-Favoured-Nation (MFN) clauses in international commercial matters came into use in the Seventeenth and Eighteenth Centuries. They were used in bilateral treaties as a short-hand means of "incorporating by reference" benefits that had been granted in other agreements.[16] In many cases governments used a conditional MFN clause, by which concessions granted to one country are granted to another on an MFN basis only if that other country grants compensatory or reciprocal concessions. Gradually governments moved to an unconditional MFN. Starting with the Tariff Act of 1922, the United States has pursued a policy of granting MFN treatment on such an "unconditional" basis.[17]

The League of Nations Covenant included a reference to the goal of "equitable treatment for the commerce of all members." A 1936 League-of-Nations standard MFN clause formed the basis for the MFN clause included in an early draft of an ITO Charter, and was an important influence on the MFN clause that was incorporated in the GATT.[18]

(b) *GATT Article I and its application*

Although there are several MFN or non-discrimination clauses in the GATT, the most important MFN clause is that which appears in

---

[15] J.H. Jackson, "The Birth of the GATT-MIN System: A Constitutional Appraisal," 12 *Law and Policy in International Business* (1980), at p. 21.

[16] *Op. cit.* in note 2 above, at p. 250.

[17] Executive Branch GATT Studies, No. 9, "The Most-Favoured-Nation Provision," at 134, Committee on Finance, United States Senate, Subcommittee on International Trade, 93d Cong., 2d Sess. (Compilation of 1973 Studies prepared by the Executive Branch: Committee Print, March 1974).

[18] League of Nations Economic Comm., *Report on the Most-Favoured-Nation Clause*, L.N. Doc. C.379, M.250. 1936 II.B. (Sales No. 1936 II.B.9.).

Article I, paragraph 1. It reads: "With respect to customs duties and charges of any kind imposed on or in connection with importation or exportation or imposed on the international transfer of payments for imports or exports, and with respect to the method of levying such duties and charges, and with respect to all rules and formalities in connection with importation and exportation, and with respect to all matters referred to in paragraphs 2 and 4 of Article III, any advantage, favour, privilege or immunity granted by any contracting party to any product originating in or destined for any other country shall be accorded immediately and unconditionally to the like product originating in or destined for the territories of all other contracting parties."

It will be noted that the application of the clause is limited to matters relating to the importation and exportation of *products*, and that the obligation of this clause is unconditional. Any concession granted by a contracting party to a product of another country "shall be accorded immediately and unconditionally to the like product originating in or destined for the territories of all other contracting parties." For example, if country A, a GATT contracting party, negotiates a bilateral agreement to reduce its tariff on widgets from 20 per cent. ad valorem to 10 per cent., it must apply the new tariff rate to widgets originating in the territory of any GATT contracting party. The obligation to extend any bilaterally negotiated concession to all GATT contracting parties essentially leads members to negotiate tariff reductions on a multilateral basis.

Countries have developed means of avoiding some of the effect of MFN obligations. Tariff classifications can be narrowed so that a tariff rate will be applied only to the product of the country with which the reduction was negotiated. The classic example of such a narrow classification is that appearing in the Swiss-German Treaty of 1904 calling for a reduction of tariffs on " . . . large dapple mountain cattle reared at a spot at least 300 metres above sea level and having at least one month grazing each year at a spot at least 800 metres above sea level."[19]

There are a number of interstitial interpretative questions of GATT Article I that can pose difficulties. For example, in applying a countervailing duty to offset a subsidy enjoyed by goods originating from a particular country, it is clear by practice and custom that the duty may be applied only to the goods from that country, without violating MFN obligations owed to that country.[20]

---

[19] G. Curzon, *Multilateral Commercial Diplomacy: The General Agreement on Tariffs and Trade and Its Impact on National Commercial Policies and Techniques* (1965) at p. 60, note 1.

[20] Practice clearly supports this, but in addition the basic purpose of countervailing duties or anti-dumping duties would be partially undermined if MFN application were required in each situation. See GATT Article VI.

(GATT Article VI is relevant here.) But can a nation consistently follow a policy which exempts subsidised goods from certain countries (*e.g.* less developed countries) from countervailing duty actions, while at the same time applying such duties to subsidised goods from other GATT members?[21]

Likewise it is not always clear what is a "like product" deserving most favourable treatment.[22] Furthermore, the phrase "originating in" can be troublesome.[23] Are goods assembled in B from parts produced in X, to be considered goods of B or goods of X? Often a formula based on percentage of value added is utilised in these cases.

(c) *The policies of MFN*

It is appropriate to ask what are the basic policies of an MFN obligation. A thorough answer will not be attempted here, but a few of the objectives of the MFN clause can be mentioned. Basically, it appears that there are two groups of arguments that buttress the policy of MFN. First, a group we can loosely call "economic reasons," and secondly, a group of political or "not-so-economic" arguments.

With respect to economic arguments for MFN, one can list several: First, a principle of non-discrimination could have a salutary effect of minimising distortions in the "market" principles that motivate some views of economic institutions. By applying government trade restrictions uniformly, without regard for the origin of goods, the market system of allocation of goods and production will have maximum effect. Widgets will tend not to be shipped half way around the world, when widgets just as good, for a comparable price, can be obtained from a neighbouring country. If tariffs are applied more heavily to the neighbouring goods, however, goods from afar may be purchased, and long shipments stimulated, incurring inefficient costs.

Another economic type argument for MFN links the MFN policy to a more general policy of freeing trade from as much government interference as possible. Since MFN has the effect of generalising specific trade liberalising practices, it is argued that more liberalisation *overall* is obtained when MFN prevails than when it does not.

Finally, under this loose grouping of economic arguments, can be mentioned the value of minimising transaction costs. If MFN were

---

[21] Recently this issue was involved in a complaint brought in GATT by India against the United States. This case was subsequently settled before a decision by the panel constituted to hear the case. Bureau of National Affairs, *U.S. Import Weekly* Nr. 97 (1981); p. 5.

[22] *Op. cit.* in note 2 above, at p. 259.

[23] *Op. cit.* in note 2 above, at pp. 257 and 464.

fully applied, customs officials would not need to bother with the "origin of goods" question, and customs procedures would be simplified.

A second group of policies stresses the "political" side of MFN. Without MFN, governments could form trade cliques and groupings more readily. These special groupings can cause rancour, misunderstanding and disputes, as those countries "left out" of favours resent their inferior status. Since special preference "deals" between nations, as well as specifically targeted trade restraining actions, are more easily implemented if MFN does not apply, a world trading system is basically a less stable economic environment. The risk ensues that tensions among nations will be more frequent. Such economic tensions have been instrumental in the past for escalating controversies that lead to military action or other breaches of the peace.

Consequently one can acknowledge some important policies which support an MFN principle, although clearly there may be countervailing policies that would suggest legitimate departures from MFN. The trend in recent years appears to be towards more departures.

(d) *Exceptions to MFN in the GATT agreement*

The combination of the basic MFN clause in Article I, paragraph 1 and the other MFN clauses appearing in the GATT, means that most GATT obligations are subject to the MFN obligation.[24] However, the GATT Agreement itself contains a number of exceptions, and actions taken within the context of GATT or outside of it also establish a number of departures from MFN. During the decades of GATT existence, there has allegedly been an erosion of the rigour of MFN, for one reason or another.[25]

In this and the next few sections, will be discussed some of the exceptions to the MFN principle. Perhaps most significant are the exceptions for Customs Unions and Free Trade areas, and the exception for preferences for developing countries. Each of these will be taken up in later sections.

Article I itself contains exceptions to the MFN obligation, which

---

[24] MFN or similar obligations are found in GATT Article I; Article IV; Article III, paragraph 7; Article V, paragraphs 2, 5, and 6; Article IX, paragraph 1; Article XIII, paragraph 1; Article XVII, paragraph 1 and Article XX, paragraph j. *Op. cit.* in note 2 above, at p. 255.

[25] United States Tariff Commission, *Report to the Committee on Finance of the United States Senate and its Subcommittee on International Trade, Part I*—"Trade Barriers: An Overview," T.C. Publ. 665 (1974) at 110. Quoted in J.H. Jackson, *Legal Problems of International Economic Relations* (1977), p. 544.

were important historically. This article allows exceptions for preferential arrangements listed in Annexes A to F of GATT, many of which arose out of colonial ties. For example, the British Commonwealth preferences are given some exemption from MFN under this exception. Over the decades of GATT existence, with the steady lowering of general MFN levels of tariffs through seven trade negotiation rounds, these historical preferences have tended to become gradually less significant. The formation and enlargement of the European Economic Community (a major "exception" itself), has further altered the meaning of the historical preferences of the GATT annexes. However the Yaoundé and Lomé conventions between the EEC and a number of developing countries,[26] many of which were former colonies of EEC member States, may in some cases be regarded as a form of continuation of these historical preferences, albeit without the explicit legal basis provided in the GATT Annexes.

At the First Session of the Contracting Parties, Article XXXIII of the GATT was amended to allow accession of new members to GATT on the vote of two-thirds of the contracting parties. One logical consequence of this action was to add Article XXXV to permit a contracting party to decide that the GATT will not apply as between it and another contracting party, if a decision to this effect is taken at the time either first joins GATT. This was designed to avoid forcing a country to enter an international trade agreement with another country against its will. The most extensive use of Article XXXV was in connection with Japan. Fifteen contracting parties invoked Article XXXV with respect to Japan at the time of Japan's accession to GATT in 1955, but subsequently most of these invocations have been lifted.[27]

Article XXV of GATT contains a general power of "waiver" by a special (two-thirds) majority of the contracting parties. Although it has been argued that this power should not be used to alter the effects of GATT Article I because amendments to that article require unanimity,[28] nevertheless a number of waivers have been adopted granting exemption from MFN obligations. The most significant of these was the 1971 waiver for the preference system for trade of developing countries (discussed below). Waivers have also been granted for the United States for its part in the Canadian-United States Automotive Products Agreement (providing pre-

---

[26] See GATT Report, *"The ACP-EEC Convention of Lomé,"* Basic Instruments and Selected Documents, 23d Supplement (1977), p. 46.

[27] *Op. cit.* in note 2 above, at p. 100; GATT, *Analytical Index 2d rev.* (1966), pp. 160–162.

[28] GATT Document L/403, (1955).

ferential free trade in auto products), and a number of other specific exemptions from MFN.[29]

Various other articles provide potential exceptions from MFN. For example, Article XX contains exceptions to all GATT obligations for certain health and welfare type government actions, although the article requires that actions "not be applied in a manner which would constitute an unjustified discrimination between countries." Article XXI provides an exception for national security reasons. Articles XII–XIV establish various exceptions to GATT obligations, when quotas are justifiable for balance-of-payments reasons, and these articles, especially Article XIV, can afford some limited exemption from the MFN obligations. Similarly Aticle XVIII offers some balance-of-payments exemptions for developing countries.

Although not made explicit, it is clear by practice and custom that anti-dumping duties or countervailing duties (GATT Article VI) can be applied to certain imports of certain origin, without a need to generalise such duties (which would partly defeat their purpose). It is not clear, as previously mentioned, whether a *policy* of applying such duties could be established which exempted certain countries.

Government procurement practices have traditionally been considered unreached by the language of GATT Article I, and the language of GATT Article III and the preparatory work of GATT seem to support this approach.[30]

The Article XXIII complaints-dispute procedures of GATT provide for the possibility of non-MFN actions in response to an offending nations activity causing "nullification or impairment" of benefits under the agreement. Although many cases have occurred under Article XXIII, only one went so far as to obtain the necessary Contracting Parties' approval for a retaliatory action. In that case Netherlands was authorised to apply a discriminatory quota against exports from the United States.[31]

Finally there are two GATT provisions which at least implicitly touch on the MFN question. First, under the escape clause of Article XIX of GATT, a country which finds that imports are causing serious injury to one of its competing domestic industries is sometimes allowed to temporarily restrain those imports. There is interpretative material suggesting that such import restraints must be imposed on an MFN basis, although this interpretation is

---

[29] *Op. cit.* in note 2 above, at p. 549 (for a list of waivers). GATT, *Basic Instruments and Selected Documents*, 14th Supplement (1966), p. 37.

[30] *Op. cit.* in note 2 above, pp. 254, 360; GATT Article I, and Article III paragraph 8.

[31] GATT, *Basic Instruments and Selected Documents*, 1st Supplement (1953), p. 32.

disputed, and has been one cause of an impasse in the "safeguards" negotiation during the Tokyo Round.[32]

Secondly, Article XVII dealing with State trading enterprises has been interpreted by some to allow departure from MFN. The issue is not yet settled.[33]

(e) *Customs Unions and Free Trade Areas: Article XXIV*

Article XXIV allows an exception to the obligations of GATT for certain regional arrangements. The exception in Article XXIV applies to three types of arrangements: (1) Customs unions; (2) Free trade areas; and (3) "an interim agreement necessary for the formation of a customs union or of a free-trade area."

A free-trade area is a group of customs territories in which customs duties and other restrictive regulations on "substantially all" products originating in the territory are eliminated. A customs union, like a free-trade area, involves the elimination of customs duties between the member States. In addition, in a customs union, the members adopt a common schedule of tariffs and system of regulation of trade with respect to products from the territories of non-members.

The establishment of a customs union or free-trade area requires a departure from the MFN principle. If there were no such exception to the MFN principle, the elimination of customs duties between the participants would have to be generalised to all Contracting parties to GATT with no *quid pro quo*.

The policy underlying the Article XXIV exception as expressed in that article, is a recognition of "the desirability of increasing freedom of trade by the development, through voluntary agreements, of closer integration between the economies of the countries parties to such agreements." While the GATT makes an allowance for regional arrangements, Article XXIV, paragraph 5 provides that regional arrangements shall not have the effect of increasing restrictions on imports from third countries. For customs unions or interim agreements leading thereto, the common tariffs applied by the members of the arrangement to imports from third countries shall not be higher on the whole than the "general incidence" of such tariffs in the territories of the parties prior to the arrangement. Arrangements establishing or leading to the establishment of a free-trade area shall not result in higher tariffs in the constituent territories than those existing prior to the arrangement.

---

[32] *Op. cit.* in note 2 above, at p. 564, GATT, *The Tokyo Round of Multilateral Trade Negotiations, (Report by the Director-General)*, (1979), p. 90.

[33] *Op. cit.* in note 2 above, at p. 346.

Article XXIV allows an exception to MFN treatment for interim agreements leading to the formation of customs unions or free-trade areas. Such agreements must contain a "plan and schedule for the formation of such a customs union or such a free-trade area within a reasonable length of time." None of the arrangements notified to GATT have at the outset satisfied the definitions of a free-trade area or a customs union contained in paragraph 8 of Article XXIV, although some evolved into one of these. A number of regional arrangements have been so loosely drawn as to draw into question whether they even fulfil the requirements for an "interim" agreement. The GATT language is unfortunately ambiguous, and the GATT has allowed some very loose preferential arrangements to exist without effective challenge in the context of GATT. Article XXIV has become, some say, the most significant loophole to the MFN obligation.[34]

(f) *The Generalised System of Preferences*

At the first session of the United Nations Conference on Trade and Development (UNCTAD) in 1964, the developing countries called for a generalised system of preferences (GSP) to be granted by the industrialised countries to all developing countries, partly to replace the mélange of then existing preferential arrangements based primarily on colonial ties. Discussions on the nature of GSP took place in the late 1960s in the contexts of UNCTAD and the Organisation for Economic Co-operation and Development (OECD). The developed countries wanted a system which would allow each developed country to determine the beneficiaries, product coverage, amount of reduction and other aspects of the plan it was to implement.

In 1971, the Contracting Parties to GATT approved a waiver of MFN under Article XXV, paragraph 5 of GATT, for the purpose of instituting GSP. The waiver allows for a departure from Article I obligations for a period of 10 years, but actions resulting from the Tokyo Round negotiation have effectively perpetuated this departure.[35] The waiver of the MFN obligation extends to all developed countries and is for the purpose of allowing them to extend preferential tariff treatment to developing countries without having to generalise such treatment to other GATT contracting parties.

---

[34] K. Dam, "Regional Economic Arrangements and the GATT: The Legacy of a Misconception," 30 U. *Chicago Law Review* (1963), p. 615; *Op. cit.* in note 2 above, p. 575.

[35] GATT waiver (Decision of 25 June, 1971), at GATT, Basic Instruments and Selected Documents, 18th Supplement (1972), p. 24; Tokyo Round Decision, GATT B.I.S.D. 26th Suppl. (1980), p. 203.

The schemes adopted by the individual developed countries to implement GSP vary in their terms. The preference schemes vary in terms of the products covered, the countries benefiting from the schemes, the level of tariff cuts, rules of origin, and whether the products on which the preferences are granted are subject to non-tariff barriers such as quotas or tariff quotas. In addition, all of the schemes include safeguard mechanisms such as escape clause provisions or quantitative limitations on trade under the preference schemes.[36]

The United States was the last major developed country to institute a preference scheme, doing so almost four years after the GATT waiver. Congress delegated authority to the President to implement GSP in the Trade Act of 1974. The Congress provided guidelines for the selection of beneficiaries, expressly excluding certain countries (such as OPEC members), and establishing criteria for inclusion of specific products in the preference list. Such preference goods receive duty free treatment when imported into the United States from a "beneficiary country," unless certain conditions which lift the preference in some cases have occurred.[37]

Several of the codes of conduct negotiated in the Multilateral Trade Negotiations provide for special treatment for developing countries. At the Thirty-Fifth Session of the Contracting Parties to GATT in November 1979, the Contracting Parties adopted four decisions relating to the framework of international trade, which decisions were drafted in the Tokyo Round negotiations. One of these decisions, the Decision of November 28, 1979 on "Differential and More Favourable Treatment and Reciprocity and Fuller Participation of Developing Countries" allows an exception to the Article I obligations to "accord differential and more favourable treatment to developing countries" including preferential tariff treatment under the GSP. Unlike the 1971 waiver, this Decision does not have a time limit.[38]

(g) *The "Voluntary Export Restraint" Problem*

Voluntary Export Restraints (VER) are becoming more frequently used by nations seeking to limit imports into their country. The importing country (or representatives of one of its industries) approaches an exporting country and seeks a formal or merely tacit "arrangement" whereby the exporters limit the amount of products

---

[36] McCulloch, *United States Preferences: The Proposed System*, 8 J. *World Trade Law* 216, 217 (1974).

[37] United States, Trade Act of 1974, Public Law 93–618, Approved January 3, 1975, 19 U.S.C. §§ 2101–2487, 88 Stat. 1978, at Title V.

[38] See note 35 above.

they ship to the importing country. In some cases this practice is justified as an "escape clause" action, but in many other cases it has no legal basis, and often is a technical violation of GATT. Yet no country complains—the exporters fear worse measures if they don't comply; the importing country is hardly interested in complaining.[39] Since a VER can be targeted at a particular country, it operates as an important exception to MFN in practice.

(h) *The Tokyo Round agreements and their effects on MFN*

Other agreements reached in the Tokyo Round, have broadened the GATT system governing international trade relations. The MTN codes provide new rules and new forums for consultation and dispute settlement, and several of these "codes" have a significant relationship to the MFN principle.

The MTN codes deal primarily with non-tariff barriers to trade. Two of the codes, the Subsidies Code and the Government Procurement Code, allow a sort of conditional MFN approach in their substantive obligations. One effect of United States acceptance of the Subsidies Code was to require the introduction of an injury test in United States countervailing duty law. The United States had avoided the GATT obligation of an injury determination as a prerequisite to the imposition of a countervailing duty through the application of the "grandfather clause" of the Protocol of Provisional Application. The United States was unwilling to grant the concession of an injury test to countries that were not willing to make commitments contained in the code to reduce the use of subsidies in international trade. Consequently the United States has taken the position that it will not grant the injury test to subsidised goods from countries which have not accepted the Code or comparable commitments. United States law requires the Executive to carry out this condition,[40] although the Code itself does not require it, and it has been argued that the United States position is contrary to United States obligations under GATT's MFN clause. This raises, *inter alia,* the issue (discussed above) whether a nation can discriminate in establishing its *policy* of applying countervailing duties.

The Government Procurement Code took a similar approach to MFN. Countries were not willing to grant national treatment for their government procurement practices to countries that were not

---

[39] S.D. Metzger, "Injury and Market Disruption from Imports," in Papers Submitted to the Commission on International Trade and Investment Policy (the "Williams Commission"), U.S. Government, July 1971, v.I, p. 168–173.

[40] Trade Agreements Act of 1979, Public Law 96–39, Approved July 26, 1979, 93 Stat. 144, at Section 2 and Section 101.

willing to grant similar treatment reciprocally. In this case it can be argued that the GATT does not impose any MFN obligation.[41]

Another MTN code, the "Technical Barriers" or "Standards" Code is also being implemented by the United States on a partly conditional basis. Only those countries willing to accept this code or its principles, will be accorded the full procedural advantages regarding information about and challenges to the development of certain product standards, under the United States law.[42]

CONCLUSIONS

Although overstatement should be avoided, nevertheless it seems fair to say that the principle of non-discrimination in international trade, as embodied in GATT Article I, has been central to the post-Second World War trading system. It is based upon policies that are both economic and political in nature, and which appear to remain valid for today and the future. Yet there clearly are countervailing policy considerations—the desire to aid developing countries, and the desire to promote deeper trade liberalisation by encouraging customs unions and free trade areas, among others. These countervailing considerations, plus the usual and frequent government motivations of expediency or special "deals," have led over the years to substantial and apparently growing departures from MFN. Whether the advantages of MFN treatment can be retained in the face of such trends, remains to be seen.

---

[41] See note 30 above.
[42] *Op. cit.* in note 40 above, at Section 421.

INTERNATIONAL PROTECTION OF WHALES

By

PATRICIA W. BIRNIE

ALTHOUGH it was seals that first became the subject of international treaties for their conservation[1] in the past decade it is whales that have attracted most attention from conservationists intent on ensuring that the Whaling Convention[2] becomes an instrument for the protection of whales rather than for the regulation of commercial whaling. Recently also there has been growing use of comprehensive instruments, national and international, to protect all marine mammals on an ecological basis, more in accord with scientific knowledge of their special characteristics.

I—SPECIES OF MARINE MAMMALS, AND STATUS OF STOCKS

The United Nations Environment Programme and Food and Agriculture Organisation Draft Global Plan of Action for the Conservation, Management and Utilisation of Marine Mammals defines them as "mammals which spend all or a large part of their time in the sea and obtain all or a large proportion of their food predominantly from it,"[3] including species whose ancestors were marine but which have moved into fresh waters. They fall into three groups:

1. *Cetaceans*: whales and dolphins divided into: (*a*) Mysteceti: baleen whales which filter feed, mainly on krill, a shrimp like crustacean found in Antarctic waters. These include blue, fin, humpback, sei, Bryde's, minke, gray, right and bowhead whales; (*b*) Odontoceti: toothed whales, eating small whales, dolphins, porpoises, fish, seals, squid, etc.; they include sperm whales and smaller whales such as the pilot and killer whales; also porpoises and dolphins;

2. *Pinnipeds*: seals, sea lions and walruses, feeding mainly on fish, squids, crustaceans and some krill;

---

[1] Convention for the Protection of Fur Seals, 104 *British State Papers* (1911), p. 175.
[2] International Convention for the Regulation of Whaling, 1946, printed by direction of the Commission 1964.
[3] *Global Plan of Action for the Conservation, Management and Utilisation of Marine Mammals* (FAO/UNEP Project Nr. 0502–78/02), FAO, Rome 1981, p. 1.

3. *Sirenians*: dugongs, manatees, Steller's sea cow (extinct),[4] found in shallow coastal waters and feeding exclusively on aquatic vegetation, being the only large mammals converting it to meat. For legal purposes, however, the definition can be different depending on the meaning attributed in particular conventions.

Whole species or particular populations of these animals have been greatly depleted by various human activities—hunting, incidental catching in nets used for other fisheries, disturbance of habitats by increasing industrial use of coastal waters and increasing pollution. Status of stocks is a contentious issue in all regulatory commissions in the light of insufficient or contradictory data, scientific knowledge and population dynamics theory, confused by the political and economic implications for harvesting States.[5] Large whales are the most depleted, especially right and bowhead; blue and humpback to a lesser extent. Fin and sei whales are generally well below their most productive levels but the smaller minke and Bryde's are not yet generally seriously affected. Sperm whales' status is controversial; large populations exist but high catches of males give conservationists cause for concern. The status of small cetaceans is generally uncertain in the absence of information on many stocks but an IWC (International Whaling Commission) sub-committee has pointed the threat to some, especially freshwater species.[6]

Several species of pinnipeds have occasionally been grossly over-exploited but following effective conservation agreements have usually recovered; currently the form most endangered is the monk seal. Sirenians, which are not yet subject to any international conventions have been gravely depleted in the tropical coastal and fresh waters they inhabit.[7]

Special Characteristics[8]
Legally marine mammals have always been equated with fish (with the unfortunate consequences outlined herein) but they are in fact different in many respects being warm blooded creatures, giving

---

[4] For details see L. Watson, *Sea Guide to Whales of the World* (1981); E. Mitchell "Review of biology and fisheries for smaller cetaceans," 32 *Journal of the Fisheries Research Board of Canada* (1975), p. 875 *Draft Report of FAO's Advisory Committee on Marine Resources Research (ACMRR) Working Party on Marine Mammals* for La Jolla Meeting, January 1973.

[5] M. McGonigle, "Economics, Ecology and Whales," 9 *Ecology Law Quarterly* (1980), pp. 120–237.

[6] 29 IWC Rep. (1978), pp. 87–89.

[7] *Op. cit.* in note 3 above, Appendix 6B Threatened Marine Mammals—Distribution and Systematic List, pp. 112–123.

[8] "Legal Aspects of Conservation of Marine Mammals," Report of Workshop, Quissac, France, December 10–14, 1979, Center for Environmental Education Monograph Series, pp. 4–5.

live birth after long gestation and suckling their young. Cetaceans are the most atypical with many surprising, unique and often inexplicable aspects of anatomy, biology and physiology. About 12 species have been hunted profitably mainly for oil (formerly used in soap and margarine) and meat (mostly used in pet food and fertilisers), but substitutes now exist for all uses and new uses and values, both non- and low-consumptive, have developed: whale watching, scientific interest, filming, exhibiting, performing. Some people also attribute symbolic, cultural and aesthetic value to marine mammals.

Great whales are remarkable for size (blue whales can reach over 100 feet) and consume vast quantities of food which is important also to other species and the sea's economy; hunters may thus demand culling of these and other marine mammals (*e.g.* seals, dolphins). Whales are highly migratory; feeding in cold waters and moving to warm waters in winter to mate and calve; baleen whales particularly feed in polar waters; all are especially vulnerable to capture as they congregate at these times. Similarly they are air breathers and need to surface and spout which, coupled with their bulk, increases visibility and facilitates capture. Seals spend part of their time on land or ice, particularly to pup, and they too are vulnerable then.

More is now known about whales' biology and social habits, which affect distribution and population structures, than for most other marine species but paradoxically the more that is known the more scientists realise they do not know; for example, about their respiratory system, enabling them to submerge with little oxygen; their alimentary canals enabling processing of krill to protein; their echo-location systems; their alleged intelligence and ability to learn. All these characteristics could be vitally important to man. Without taking an anthropological approach it can be said that whales in particular are remarkable compared to fish. Pointers to the biological differences from available information indicate the need to manage them on the basis of different principles; these include low reproduction and therefore stock recruitment rates; late puberty; single young with 2-year gaps between births; longevity (60–90 years according to species). They can be put to wider uses than fish and there is generally a closer relationship between breeding, stock size and recruitment.

All this requires that management bodies should be constituted on a basis that enables them to take account of these special attributes and to garner the maximum continuing information on biological and behavioural limits, which remain controversial. Some conservationists contend that this very uncertainty calls for a moratorium on all catching. Meanwhile the papers accumulated by the Scientific Committee of the International Whaling Commission (IWC) and the reports of the Advisory Committee on Marine Resources Research Working Party on Marine Mammals of the Food and Agriculture Organisation (FAO) have thrown sufficient light on the problems to bring about radical developments in international law protecting these species and in the practice of the IWC and other bodies which may slowly lead to a more ecologically-minded approach to management taking account of species inter-relationships and linkage to their nutritive organisms, to the extent that this is possible given the conflicting national interests in exploitation and protection, the decentralised and pragmatic orga-nisation of marine mammal management and the prevailing doctrines of international law.

II—THE LEGAL STATUS OF MARINE MAMMALS

International law has never recognised the above distinctions by conferring any special legal status on marine mammals; it regards them as common property resources akin to fish (no single user has a right to them)[9] and subject also to the conflicting doctrine of freedom of fishing on the high seas (no user can prevent others from fishing), a doctrine established following the great doctrinal debates in the sixteenth and seventeenth centuries when extended coastal State jurisdiction over fisheries was rejected in favour of narrow limits for the territorial sea and freedom of fishing beyond, harvesting of marine mammals taking place mainly in the latter. Grotius argued that the Roman property-law principle "that which cannot be occupied ... cannot be the property of anyone"[10] applied and that the inexhaustible resources of the sea were an appropriate common property resource to be used for common benefit; he admitted that fish could be said to be exhaustible but conceived it impossible.

The doctrine was challenged in 1895 in the Bering Fur Seals Arbitration.[11] The doctrine of freedom of the seas led to devastation of seal rookeries. The United States, a participant with Great Britain (Canada), Japan, Sweden, Russia and Norway in the Bering Sea fishery, protected seals pupping on its territory, and tried to prevent the others taking them on the high seas by unilaterally

---

[9] F. Christy and A. Scott, *The Commonwealth in Ocean Fisheries*, Ch. 2, "The Characteristics of Common Property Resources," p. 6.

[10] H. Grotius, *Mare Liberum*, ed. J. Scott (1916), p. 27.

[11] Bering Sea Fur Seal Arbitration, Report of Proceedings (1895); for the history of this dispute see D. Johnston, *The International Law of Fisheries* (1965), pp. 205–212.

asserting rights of ownership over the seals, legislating and arresting Canadian vessels which ignored United States regulations. The United States argued that it had property rights in the herd as the natural product of its soil, that it had industrial interests in them and no part of the high seas should be open to individuals to destroy such national interests; it was trustee of the herd "for the benefit of mankind."[12] Great Britain, however, regarded the seals as *res communis* and not subject to property rights. The United States urged the court to bow to public opinion in the civilised world and apply the moral rule, the general standard of civilised justice "founded on the nature of man and the environment in which he is placed."[13] Great Britain contended that property rights could be established only if related to individual seals identified, returning to the Pribilof Islands, tamed or reclaimed before leaving and intending to return there to their owner's control. The United States contended that the seals did have an *animus revertendi* and the seas were free only for non-injurious use. Britain countered that the law was freedom of the seas including "the right . . . to take at will or pleasure the products of the sea."[14]

The Tribunal found in favour of the British arguments that property rights did not exist in the high seas; the United States could not unilaterally conserve. The arbitrators therefore exercised powers given under the arbitral treaty to recommend international regulations. They proposed a nine-point plan which has since become a framework for many other fishery Commissions including the IWC. Measures recommended included prohibited zones; closed seasons; limitation of types of vessel; national licensing; exchange of data; banning prescribed gear; exemptions for indigenous Indians sealing for traditional purposes, using traditional methods. Enactment of appropriate national laws nationally enforced was also advocated, accompanied by a one-three year ban on all killing.

The award was of historic importance to conservation of marine mammals. It prevented unilateral appropriation, emphasised their international aspects and even took account of their biology and habits in assessing the needs of international conservation but it did not recognise any interest of the international community as such. No international management body with comprehensive powers to protect the *res communis* on the community's behalf was recommended. Conservation had to be based on the doctrine of freedom,

---

[12] *Ibid.*, p. 814.
[13] *Ibid.*, pp. 827–828.
[14] *Ibid.*, p. 845

though the latter should be limited to achieve the former. The proposals failed anyway because they could be directed only to Canada and the United States; other vessels sealed unrestricted and Canadian and United States vessels registered under other flags. The disastrous results finally convinced the sealers that only a multilateral agreement could save the fishery and in 1911 the United States, Canada, Japan, and Russia concluded a Convention for the Preservation and Protection off Fur Seals, the first convention protecting marine mammals, based on the award, extended in various forms to the present day.[15] Others have followed this model.

The status of marine mammals as common property resources and the doctrine of freedom was not changed by the First and Second United Nations Conferences on the Law of the Sea in 1958 and 1960 respectively. The Geneva Convention on the High Seas[16] codifies the customary law: the high seas are "open to all nations" (Article 1). Article 2 includes fishing as a freedom of the seas to be exercised, however, with reasonable regard to the interests of other states exercising their freedoms. Neither it nor the Convention on Conservation of Living Resources of the Sea[17] distinguishes or refers to marine mammals. The latter accepts freedom of fishing coupled with a duty to co-operate in conservation measures aimed at maintaining maximum sustainable yield (Article 1(2)) but it was not widely ratified and has been overtaken by recent declarations of 200-mile fisheries zones.[18] The international law relating to marine mammals remains based on the concept of the "common property resource," which, though it has never been incorporated into any treaty, continues to confuse the Roman concept of *res communis omnium* concerning ownership and distribution of wealth with that of open and free access, making effective conservation virtually impossible. The Roman law implication that things owned in common require community consent to their use has not yet been given fully international manifestation.

The UNCLOS III Official Draft Convention on the Law of the Sea[19] does propose establishment of the necessary international means of consent but only for managing deep seabed resources beyond national jurisdiction. The resources of that area are regarded as "the common heritage of mankind" (Article 136

---

[15] Extended for 4 yers by Protocol in 1981; 19 MAC Newsletter (1981), p. 8.

[16] 450 UNTS p. 11; in force September 30, 1962.

[17] 559 UNTS p. 285; in force March 20, 1966.

[18] *Legislation on Coastal State Requirements for Foreign Fishing*, FAO Legislative Study Nr. 21, FAO (Rome) 1981.

[19] Draft Convention on the Law of the Sea (Informal Text) A/CONF. 62/WP.10/Rev.3, September 26, 1980, Part XI (amended and adopted as Official Draft at 10th UNCLOS Session 1981); convention adopted by 130 votes for, 4 against (17 abstentions), April 30, 1982.

following a General Assembly Resolution to that effect)[20] vested in mankind as a whole (Article 137(2)) on whose behalf an International Seabed Authority (established by Article 156) shall act, equipped with organs including an Assembly, Executive Council, exploitative Enterprise, specialist commissions, Secretariat and dispute settlement procedures. Application to the high seas is specifically disclaimed in Article 135. Until a similar normative UN resolution followed by an effective treaty makes similar provisions for marine mammals it is not possible to regard their legal status as fully internationalised. Nonetheless there is some movement towards creating special categories for them, if not changing their legal status, as the following developments, which include special mention in the UNCLOS text, evidence.

III—GLOBAL WHALING CONVENTIONS

(a) *League of Nations Conventions and Protocols on Whaling*

Following pioneering work by the International Council for the Sea (ICES) established in 1902,[21] the League of Nations considered establishment of international rules concerning exploitation of the products of the sea.[22] The League's rapporteur, Snr. Suarez, took a farsighted view. He considered many species useful to man would become extinct if not regulated and aimed at a "new jurisprudence" taking protective account of "the biological solidarity among denizens of the oceans,"[23] their migrations, and that they "observe not international law but internationalism, the sea for them is a single realm."[24] Whales were "the patrimony of the whole human race;"[25] their gross depletion in Antarctica following technological advances in catching and treating necessitated a treaty to resolve the tensions between community interest and free access.

The 1931 International Convention for the Regulation of Whaling,[26] though innovatory, was based on the Fur Seal Treaty and 1930 Northern Pacific Halibut Convention (NPHC)[27] measures (closed seasons, protected species, vessel licensing, data collection,

---

[20] GAR 2749 (XXV), December 17, 1970.

[21] A. Went, *Seventy Years Agrowing: A History of ICES 1902–1973* (1972), pp. 27–29.

[22] See L. Leonard, "Recent Negotiations Towards Regulation of Whaling," 35 *American Journal of International Law* (1941), pp. 90–113.

[23] League of Nations Committee of Experts for the Progressive Codification of International Law 1925–1928; Annex: *Report of Sub-Committee on the Exploitation of the Products of the Sea*: Vol. 2 (1972), p. 232.

[24] *Op. cit.* in note 17 above, p. 234.

[25] *Ibid.*

[26] *Op. cit.* in note 17 above, p. 235.

[27] CXXI LNTS (1930), p. 45.

etc) and did not establish a commission (though the NPHC had done so) or international inspection: major defects. Amendments, following new data, required the convening of diplomatic conferences to effect Protocols (five between 1937–1945), parties to which varied. The League Convention did apply to "all the waters of the world" (Article 9) and parties had to effect national measures to implement it but whales remained undistinguished from halibut. Private inter-company agreements failed to fill the gaps,[28] since not all exploiters participated; unilateral legislation by Norway did no more than scratch the problem's surface; regulations remained inadequate and data insufficient. Suarez's views were disregarded.

(b) *International Convention for the Regulation of Whaling 1946 (ICRW)*[29]

Whales received a respite from catching during the Second World War and by 1945–46 there were more precedents for fisheries commissions[30] including permanent membership with voting and regulatory powers; specialised committees; international enforcement (limited to mutual inspection and reports to the flag State); scientific research by the organisation; sanctuaries. Based on these models the ICRW was adopted in 1946 following two ad hoc diplomatic conferences, the second attended only by 15 whaling States. The main objective was to get rid of the cumbersome pre-war methods of regulating by establishing permanent machinery for modifying existing regulations. There was no attempt to change the resources' status; freedom of fishing subject to voluntary regulation remained the basic premise. Dean Acheson, opening the conference, however, regarded whales as "a truly international resource . . . wards of the entire world"[31] but the International Whaling Commission (IWC) instituted by the ICRW was given no powers akin to wardship; Acheson's words had no legal significance. Fundamentally the ICRW is a treaty regulating whaling (Article V(1)) by listing in a Schedule species requiring protection, rather than protecting whales, which are not defined in the convention, but in practice it has protected increasing numbers of species.

The ICRW remains a significant advance. The Preamble, laying

---

[28] W. Vamplew, *Salvesen of Leith* (1975), p. 198.

[29] R. Gambell (Secretary of the IWC) gives a good account in "Whale Conservation—Role of the International Whaling Commission," 1 *Marine Policy* (1977), pp. 301–310.

[30] M. Savini, *Report on International and National Legislation for the Conservation of Marine Mammals*, Part I: International Legislation, FIRD/C326, FAO (Rome)(1976) lists and summarises the relevant treaties; see also *Annotated Directory of Inter-Governmental Organisations Concerned with Ocean Affairs*, A/CONF.62/L.14, August 10, 1976, Regional Fisheries Bodies pp. 106–131.

[31] IWC Doc. 11 (1946), p. 1.

down the principles and objectives in light of which the substantive provisions must be interpreted, recognises "the interest of the nations of the world in safeguarding for future generations the great natural resources represented by whale stocks," acknowledges the historic pattern of overfishing and its dire results and the need to protect all species from further over-exploitation. But it also aims in vague terms at achieving an "optimum level of stocks without causing widespread economic and nutritional distress." The ICRW makes no attempt to vest the resources in the commission on behalf of the world as does the UNCLOS treaty for seabed resources. It is left to IWC practice to balance these aims bearing in mind also the parties express desire "to establish a system of regulation for the whale fisheries to ensure proper and effective conservation *and* development of whale stocks" (emphasis added). No dispute settlement procedures are provided.

The substantive articles were more apt to protect the industry's interests as IWC history till recently shows.[32] Nonetheless there are many progressive provisions and the IWC institutionally compares favourably with other commissions of the period. Membership is open to all governments (Article II(4)) without conditions. As a result the composition of the IWC has recently changed radically; there are now 35 members, the majority of them non-whaling States favouring conservation; one is land-locked, several are developing States.[33] The ICRW applies to factory ships, land stations and whale catchers under the jurisdiction of Contracting Governments and to all waters in which these prosecute whaling. Alaskan Eskimos recently contended, however, that their vessels do not come within the convention and instituted proceedings against the United States Government for applying IWC restrictions on their bowhead catch.[34] Canada, which withdrew from membership in 1981, takes the view that the ICRW does not apply within the new 200-mile fisheries zones and seeks revision of the convention.

A permanent body, meeting annually, is established, backed by a

---

[32] See J. Scarff, "The International Management of Whales, Dolphins and Porpoises: An Interdisciplinary Assessment," 6 *Ecology Law Quarterly* (1979), pp. 323–571; 1–30 IWC Reports 1950–1980.

[33] Argentina, Australia, Brazil,* Canada (withdrawing), Chile,* China P.R., Costa Rica, Denmark,* Dominica, France, Iceland,* India, Jamaica, Japan,* Korea (Rep)*; Mexico, Netherlands, New Zealand, Norway,* Oman, Peru,* St. Lucia, St. Vincent and Grenadines; Seychelles, South Africa, Spain,* Sweden, Switzerland, USSR,* UK, USA,* Uruguay. Asterisk denotes whaling States; USA catch is limited to Eskimo bowhead take (cultural subsistence exception); Denmark's catches are similar (Greenland and Faroes). Eight non-whaling States joined at 33rd Meeting, 1981.

[34] *E.g., Adams* v. *Vance* (1977), 8 Environmental Law Reportewr, p. 20160; *Hopson* v. *Kreps* (1979) U.S. District Court of Alaska; *Adams, et al.* v. *Klutznick, et al.*, Civil Nr. A78–184 (1981).

growing Secretariat. The IWC issues regulations by means of a flexible amendable Schedule which is an integral part of the Convention and covers a wide range of topics laid down in Article V(1)—from protection of species to catch returns and methods of inspection. Amendments must be based on the criteria of Article V(2)—simultaneously executing the Convention's objectives, providing for conservation, optimum utilisation and development of resources *and* being based on scientific findings. But since this Article forbids restriction of number and nationality of factory ships and land stations and allocation of specific quotas to them effort cannot be controlled and the Convention's objectives can be thwarted. National quotas have had to be allocated by hard fought agreement *outside* the IWC. The IWC also has to take into account the interests of consumers of whale products and the whaling industry (Article V(2)(*d*)); scientific findings in practice have often been tempered to meet these considerations. IWC meetings are now a battleground between the whaling and non-whaling States; conservationists pressing the global moratorium accepted at the 1972 UN Environment Conference[35] have gained ground remarkably spurred by a strong NGO (non-governmental organisation) lobby: Blue, humpback, grey and right bowhead whales are now all protected from commercial whaling, as are most sei and many fin whales. In 1981 at the 33rd Meeting all except one stock of sperm whales, once the main support of the Soviet Union and Japanese industries, were also protected; only minke whales now sustain them.

The IWC's voting and long objections procedures have been much criticised but are seldom used now to defeat conservation. Instead attempts are made to arrive at a consensus based on bargains and compromises between whaling and non-whaling States (especially when the conservationist USA was embarrassed by its Eskimos' demands for a bowhead quota against Scientific Committee advice, which recommended a zero quota: the solving of this issue in 1980 for the time being considerably reduced tension and dealing). Since 1974, as a means of avoiding the global moratorium pressed after the Stockholm Conference, the IWC has adopted New Management Procedures (NMP)[36] offering better protection than the former block quotas and original single overall catch quota.

---

[35] *Report of the U.N. Conferece on the Human Environment*, June 1972, Stockholm, Sweden, UN DOC. A/CONF.48/14/Rev. 1.

[36] 26 Rep. IWC (1976), pp. 25–26; quotas are set by species and area. The Scientific Committee is required to classify stocks into SMS (Sustained Management Stocks) on which specific catches can be allowed; IMS (Initial Management Stocks) more limited catches allowed; Protection Stocks (PS) no catches.

Even these, however, in the light of unsatisfactory data and theories of stock assessment are proving impossible to apply since they require the Scientific Committee to categorise stocks into Protected Stocks (PS), Initial Management Stocks (IMS) and Sustained Management Stocks (SMS) and frequently this committee cannot agree or give the necessary advice; but even so the NMP are facilitating introduction of selective "creeping moratoria" as more and more stocks are classified as PS with zero quotas.[37]

The ICRW retains potential weaknesses: members can withdraw; some have, most recently Panama and Canada. This undermines the global management increasingly perceived to be necessary. International inspection, not provided for in the original convention, was subsequently introduced in the form of a limited International Observer Scheme by amendment of the Schedule[38]; observers are appointed by the IWC but only following bilateral agreements concluded outside the ICRW. It is weak, limited to reporting to the IWC and the flag State, though the latter is required by Article X of the Convention to ensure punishment of infractions. Although the option was provided in Article III(6), the IWC was never brought within the framework of FAO or other UN specialised agency. FAO has been an active observer, and contributor to the Scientific Committee; UNEP also observes but the United Nations itself has never taken a direct interest in the problem. However, under the pressure of the Stockholm Conference moratorium proposals, prodded also by conservationist NGO's, and faced, in fact, with many rapidly declining stocks, the IWC by use of its flexible Schedule and implied powers exercised through its right under Article VI to make recommendations to all or any Contracting Governments on *any* matters relating to whales or whaling and the Convention's objectives, has adapted remarkably to changing perspectives though not so fast as conservationists think necessary. It has used these powers, for example, to recommend that members should not trade with or transfer vessels, gear or know-how to non-member States. Whaling outside the ICRW has now almost ceased because most whaling States under the influence of these resolutions have recently joined the commission (persuaded partly by Japan which wanted to continue trading with them); remaining "pirates" are increasingly pursued by NGO's. The IWC now discusses, as well as such topics as sanctuaries and aboriginal and subsistence whaling, the issues of small cetaceans, humane killing, cetacean intelligence and the ethics of killing.

---

[37] For 1981 quotas see 19 MAC Newsletter (1981), pp. 4–5.
[38] See ICRW, Schedule, March 1981, Part V, Sec. 22(c).

The problem remains of how far States legitimately exploiting whales within the IWC can be persuaded that the global moratorium demanded by the conservationist States is scientifically necessary without provoking withdrawals among the eight States concerned which would then be outside international regulation. The increasing extent to which NGO's are using both violent and non-violent means to deter unregulated whaling may have some influence on them to stay inside the IWC but it is hard to assess this. Such NGO activities prima facie are contrary to the legal doctrines of freedom of the seas which includes both freedom of fishing and freedom of navigation. Some have even interfered in the taking of IWC regulated catches within the 200-mile fishery zone of the State concerned, an even clearer contravention of international law.[39]

Revision of the ICRW to remove potential weaknesses and replace it with a Cetacean Convention is sought by some. Three ineffectual diplomatic conferences have taken place to discuss this outside the IWC[40] but the spread of 200-mile fisheries zones has led some States (*e.g.* Canada) to insist that revision should provide for coastal-State management of cetaceans in these areas. In the writer's view this would be such a retrogressive step, offsetting the considerable progress under the ICRW, that attempts to revise the convention should be abandoned for the present.

Important developments in international law to protect marine mammals have in any case been taking place outside the IWC, under the impact of the Stockholm Conference principles, taking a different approach and introduction innovatory techniques for enforcement.

IV—INTERNATIONAL PRINCIPLES

(a) *UN Conference on the Human Environment (UNCHE)*

The UNCHE[41] laid down 26 principles and various resolutions. They are non-binding recommendations endorsed by UN-General Assembly Resolution and have had considerable normative effect as evidenced by the conventions described below. Principles 2, 4, 21,

---

[39] *Outlaw Whalers* (1980), *ibid*, (1981), pub. Greenpeace; *Outlaw Whalers* (1979) pub. Whale Protection Fund; "Pirate Whaling: A Report by the People's Trust for Endangered Species on Whaling under Flags of Convenience Outside the Jurisdiction of the International Whaling Commission" PTES, (1979); J. Frizell, The Pirate Whalers, 2 *Oceans* (1981), pp. 25–28.

[40] In Copenhagen, July 1978; Estoril, November 1979; Reykjavik, May 1981.

[41] *Loc. cit.* in note 23 above.

25, 32, 33 and 99(3) are particularly relevant. They require safeguarding of natural resources, including fauna and representatives of ecosystems; recognise man's special responsibility to safeguard the wildlife heritage and habitat; acknowledge States' rights to pursue their own environmental policies in exploiting their resources, whilst ensuring that activities under their jurisdiction damage neither other States environments nor the international areas. Governments were recommended to promote conventions to protect species inhabiting international waters; to strengthen the IWC; and to pursue a treaty on trade in endangered species. UNCHE resolved there should be a 10-year moratorium on whaling. The UNEP (United Nations Environment Programme) was established as a secretariat to promote these aims and has done so.[42] It sends observers to IWC and other relevant meetings.

(b) *UNEP's Guiding Principles for the Conservation and Harmonious Utilisation of Natural Resources Shared by Two or More States*

These 15 principles[43] prepared by an inter-governmental group of experts established by UNEP at the United Nations' request were noted, though not formally approved, by the General Assembly,[44] and circulated to governments for consideration. They develop some Stockholm Principles but are not *per se* binding and are at a high level of generality and compromise. Some States regard some of them as already part of customary law; others disagree; the right of States to provide specific solutions on a regional or bilateral basis is recognised. Further agreements are certainly needed to develop, integrate and apply them. For a start "shared natural resources" are not defined though migratory marine mammals would surely qualify. The principles are referred to as "principles of conduct for the guidance of States."[45] They cover the need for co-operation; harmonious utilisation; control of adverse effects of use; the need for further agreements to apply them legally; joint use of competent international organisations; responsibility and liability. The framework for their elaboration is, however, steadily growing.

---

[42] *Op. cit.*, in note 3 above, p. 9.
[43] UNEP/IG.12/2, February 8, 1978, pp. 11–14; XVII *International Legal Materials* (1978), pp. 1098–99.
[44] GAR 33/87, January 19, 1979 (XXXIII).
[45] *Ibid.*, p. 10.

V—COMPREHENSIVE INTERNATIONAL CONVENTIONS
PROTECTING MARINE MAMMALS

(a) *Washington Convention on International Trade in Endangered Species 1973 (CITES)*

CITES,[46] with over 79 parties, aims at controlling trade in all species of wild fauna and flora threatened in various degrees. Its effectiveness is related to the breadth of participation and national actions. States parties must enact national legislation to enforce it and establish national Management Authorities for issuance of the required export and import permits and certificates, advised by a national Scientific Authority. Species requiring protection are assigned by Article II to one of three appendices according to the degree of threat. Appendix I, requiring the most stringent regulations, now includes grey, blue, humpback, right, sei, fin and sperm whales. Appendix I at first did not fully correspond wih IWC's PS categories. There were problems in keeping the two conventions in line as parties are different and CITES meets only biennially.[47] All other cetaceans have been listed on Appendix II as threatened with extinction if trade in specimens is not strictly regulated. Some pinnipeds and sirenians are also listed on these Appendices. It is, however, possible to make reservations and some states have done so. "Specimen" includes (Article I) "any recognisable part of derivative thereof" of any animal. States' Management Authorities, guided by a vigorous and effective CITES Secretariat, are becoming increasingly vigilant and expert at identifying specimens and exchanging information. Trade is being stopped but CITES will be fully effective only if there is near global participation and all States establish competent authorities. The Secretary-General has a crucial role in the information network, receiving State reports under Article VIII(7).

Amendment requires a two-thirds majority; "trade" is given a restrictive definition but includes "export, import and introduction from the sea" (Article I(c)) covering transportation into a State of species taken in areas of the marine environment "*not* under any State's jurisdiction"—an undefined phrase causing controversy in the present unsettled state of maritime limits and so far not acted upon; nor also is Article III(5)'s requirement that Appendix I species introduced from the sea be regulated. Finally parties can

---

[46] Done at Washington, D.C., U.S.A., March 3, 1973; in force 1975; XII ILM (1975), pp. 1085–1104; for a critical account see G. Coggins, Legal Protection for Marine Mammals: An Overview of Innovative Resource Conservation, 6 *Environmental Law* (1975), pp. 1–59.

[47] Following CITES 5th conference, Delhi, 1981, all cetaceans which are PS in the IWC have been put on Appendix I; all others are on Appendix II.

require "comparable documentation" from non-parties which prevents import from a State and re-export to another but cannot stop trade exclusively between non-parties. In spite, however, of these weaknesses CITES has great potential to protect all threatened species as its membership is growing rapidly.

(b) *Bonn Convention on the Conservation of Migratory Species of Wild Animals 1979 (CCMSWA)*

The CCMSWA[48] also develops UNCHE Principles but it is a framework treaty in very general terms introducing many new concepts which will require much State practice to elaborate. It covers all migratory species throughout the world, specifically including marine mammals. Any effect on UNCLOS developments or States jurisdictional claims is disclaimed. It regards resources that cross national boundaries not as national property but shared and thus requiring international protective agreements. National or international action is required for Appendix I species (needing immediate protection); species can be listed on Appendix II if their conservation status is "unfavourable"; States in whose jurisdiction these are found must conclude agreements *inter se*.

The Preamble recognises that wild animals are an irreplaceable part of the earth's natural system which must be conserved for the good of mankind. It introduces new concepts, defined in the substantive articles, such as the "Range State" (one exercising jurisdiction, including over flag ships catching outside national jurisdiction, over any part of a species range). Such States must conserve migratory species for future generations; obligations to conserve and to use wisely, if used, are recognised and action must be concerted. The "ever-growing value of wild animals from an environmental, ecological, genetic, scientific, aesthetic, recreational, cultural, educational, social and economic" point of view is stressed.

Substantive articles define "migratory species," "conservation status," "favourable and unfavourable status." The convention covers *all* areas within the range of migratory species as listed in the Appendices but the measures to be taken are weakly expressed— the importance of range States taking action must be acknowledged; they must *endeavour* to conclude agreements for Appendix II species or immediately protect endangered Appendix I species; to conserve the habitats of the latter and to prevent obstacles to

---

[48] Done at Bonn, Federal Republic of Germany, June 3, 1979; not in force; IUCN Bull., Special Supplt., January/February (1980); ratified by India, Netherlands, Nigeria, Portugal (1981).

migration. A conference of Range States parties can *recommend* measures to benefit species. Guidelines are laid down for the agreements which can include procedures for co-ordinating action to suppress illegal taking.

National Authorities must be established as in CITES. Cetaceans are given special treatment; parties *should* as a minimum "prohibit . . . any taking that is not permitted for that migratory species under any multi-lateral agreement (*e.g.* the ICRW); access to the Agreement of non-range States should be provided. A Secretariat and Scientific Council of Experts is established.

The Convention is a framework one needing to be brought into effect quickly to enable State practice to develop its hortatory rather than binding terms. The ultimate effect of this novel approach remains uncertain meanwhile; much depends on ratification and effective action by States important to marine mammal protection.

(c) *Convention on the Conservation of Antarctic Marine Living Resources 1980 (CAMLR).*[49]

Antarctica is an area abounding in marine mammals and species ecologically bound to them, such as krill, the staple diet of baleen whales, which were the focus of pelagic whaling until over-exploited. The CAMLR is a very different treaty from those discussed so far: it is based on marine ecosystem conservation but has restricted membership, with the unspoken objective of providing a mechanism for the nascent industry of krill catching. A further convention on conservation of non-living resources is currently under discussion.

The Preamble is a subtle amalgam of objectives: the need to preserve the integrity of the environment and ecosystem is stressed but the increased interest is using Antarctica's concentrated resources is noted; co-operation between *harvesting* States is the objective but parties are cognisant of the interest of all mankind in preserving Antarctica for peaceful purposes. CAMLR defines conservation in terms including "rational use" (Article II). Its membership is limited to the 14 "consultative" States party to the 1959 Antarctic Treaty,[50] States with an interest in the area demonstrated by research or harvesting (which States negotiated it), States which subsequently so qualify, and regional economic organisations while their members are qualified (Articles XXVI and

---

[49] Done at Washington, U.S.A., May 1980; not in force; ECO Vol. XV, Nr. 4, (1980) pp. 13–18; for a history see B. Mitchell "Resources in Antarctica—Potential for Conflict," 1 *Marine Policy* (1977), pp. 124–141; ratified by Australia, Chile, Japan, South Africa and the Soviet Union (1981).

[50] 402 UNTS Nr. 5778, p. 71.

XXIX respectively). The Commission established is similarly restricted in composition and voting is by consensus on substantive issues.

Unlike other treaties CAMLR's geographical scope is carefully defined (Article I) to include the whole area of "the complex relationships of Antarctic marine living resources with each other and their physical environment." "Resources" is not specifically stated to include marine mammals but as the definition includes "all other resources" it effectively does so. Article VI provides that nothing in the convention shall derogate from the rights and obligations of contracting parties under the ICRW (not all CAMLR parties will be ICRW parties) but Article II(3) requires all activities in the area to be conducted in accordance with CAMLR's principles including maintaining ecological relationships and preventing irreversible changes in the ecosystem. The Commission can draw non-party States' attention to any of their activities which defeat CAMLR's objectives and must seek co-operation in conserving common stocks with parties exercising jurisdiction over adjacent marine areas. Parties are required (Article XIII) to "exert appropriate efforts" consistent with the UN Charter "to the end that no-one engages in any activity contrary" to CAMLR's purposes. The Commission must also implement the inspection system prescribed in the Convention.

Required conservation measures are detailed covering the usual fisheries commission measures but adding regulation of effort and any other measures ordered necessary by the Commission, *e.g.*, concerning effects of harvesting and associated activities on other components of the ecosystem. Regulation of whaling is likely to be left to the IWC (all whale stocks are PS (protected) in Antarctica, though the IWC boundaries of the area differ from CAMLR's in order to allow minke whaling) but CAMLR's accumulative regulations are likely to affect future IWC regulations, especially if stocks recover and whaling is ever resumed. Co-operation between the IWC and the CAMLR Commission is not, however, specifically provided for, nor was the IWC Secretary invited to observe the negotiating conference; no organisational linkage of scientific advice is established with the IWC Scientific Committee, but SCAR (Scientific Committee for Antarctic Research) is established as a consultative body to the Commission (Article XII). As the Commission can establish subsidiary bodies (Article XIII(b)) and must take account of regulations *and* recommendations of fisheries commissions interested in the area's species, more informal relationships may thus develop.

The Parties obligation to avoid activities undermining CAMLR's aims is somewhat diluted by the CAMLR's careful refusal to pronounce on parties' jurisdictional claims in the area. It makes no concession to demands of some that Antarctica and its resources be declared "the common heritage of mankind."[51] But all must comply with the 1959 Antarctic Treaty's recommended conservation measures whether party to it or not. Dispute settlement procedures with wide choice are provided but reference to the International Court of Justice or to arbitration still requires the specific consent of disputing parties. CAMLR can, however, be amended if all parties agree; amendments bind only if formally accepted but non-acceptance is deemed to signify a party's withdrawal.

VI—REGIONAL DEVELOPMENTS

Space does not permit detailed discussion of these; it should be noted that they are occurring: existing organisations are developing interests in marine mammal conservation. Major developments are:

(a) *Convention on Nature Protection and Wildlife Preservation in the Western Hemisphere 1940*

This treaty[52] between 21 American States was the first with purely conservatory objectives. Its Preambular aim is to establish national sanctuaries "to protect and preserve in their natural habitat representatives of all species of the native fauna in sufficient numbers and over areas extensive enough to assure them from becoming extinct through any agency within man's control." An Annex listing species needing urgent protection included some blue, right, grey and bowhead whales *inter alia*. At a recent meeting in 1979 the Indian Ocean was designated a whale sanctuary.

(b) *The African Convention on the Conservation of Nature and Natural Habitats 1968*

Negotiated by the OAU, it is now in force and is currently under review.[53] A few marine mammals are listed in its annexes, not including cetaceans. It aims at conservation coupled with rational utilisation, including management of aquatic environments by measures to prevent "mass destruction" (Article VII(2)), trade restrictions, international co-operation and public education. The OAU discharges any necessary administrative functions.

---

[51] B. Mitchell and L. Kimball "Conflict over the Cold Continent," 35 *Foreign Policy* (1979), pp. 124–141.

[52] 161 UNTS. Nr. 485, p. 193.

[53] Savini, *op. cit.* in note 30 above, pp. 58–60, pub. General Secretariat of OAU.

(c) *The Berne Convention on the Conservation of European Wildlife and Natural Habitats 1979*

Negotiated through the Council of Europe, directed to habitats, including those of migratory species, requiring international co-operation to conserve, recognising fauna as a "natural heritage," using the Council of Europe as its Secretariat but with a Standing Committee to amend its Annexes of species, this Convention[54] has considerable potential to develop effective measures. Application is restricted to "territory," but this can be interpreted to cover the territorial sea, and can be applied to parties' overseas territories.

(d) *The European Economic Community: Regulation on Common Rules for Imports of Whales and Other Cetaceans, 1981*

It institutes, conforming to EEC obligations as a CITES party, *binding* measures to restrict international trade in cetacean products (as listed in an Annex) within the Community.[55] From Janury 1982 import licences will be required for introduction of these products into the Community, an important reduction of the whale product market.

VII—UNCLOS III

The UNCLOS[56] Convention, adopted on April 30, 1982 though not yet in force, does distinguish marine mammals from fisheries though without effect on their legal status. Articles 55–75 establish an Exclusive Economic Zone in which coastal States have sovereign rights to exploit and conserve fisheries and require them *inter alia* to promote optimum utilisation of resources. Article 64 concerning "Highly Migratory Species" (listed in an Annex including dolphins and cetaceans) also includes promotion of optimum utilisation thereof but joins this with obligations on States to co-operate in conservation directly or through appropriate international organisations. However, an article on "Marine Mammals" (Article 65) added later, removes them from the optimum utilisation requirement and allows coastal States and international organisations to regulate them more strictly than fisheries, requires that States co-operate to conserve and that "in the case of cetaceans they shall

---

[54] Done at Berne, Switzerland, September 19, 1979; not in force; Council of Europe Treaty Series, Nr. 104 (Ed. (1979)).

[55] Council Regulation (EEC) Nr. 348/81, January 20, 1981 (O.J. Nr. L.391, February 12, 1981).

[56] For a good account of the UNCLOS Text's effect on conservation, including of marine mammals, see C. de Klemm, "Conservation and the New Composite Negotiating Text of the Law of the Sea Conference," 4 *Environmental Policy and Law* (1978), pp. 2–17. Recent amendments do not affect these articles.

in particular work through the appropriate international organisations for their conservation, management and study." For the
purposes of this Article the IWC would be the body used, other
organisations such as ITTC (International Tropical Tuna Commission) being, however, appropriate for incidental catches. Canada,
however, recently put another interpretation on the Article,
regarding (*a*) the obligations as discharged if any one organisation is
used; (*b*) the obligation to "work through" an organisation as
arising only when a stock's status is such that an organisation's
attention is necessary (presumably as determined by the coastal
State); (*c*) the obligation as discharged merely by consulting an
organisation's scientific bodies when developing coastal State
measures in 200-mile zones, final measures being decided by that
State.[57] Such interpretations defeat the objectives of this Article,
since they undermine the IWC's central role in whale conservation;
ignore the migratory habits of whales and other special characteristics more appropriately guarded by one central body and could lead
to coastal States in 200-mile zones regulating less strictly than the
IWC, not more strictly as States otherwise are increasingly
beginning to do. United States national measures, for example,
impose a full moratorium and provide sanctions for ensuring
compliance with the regulations of the IWC and marine mammals
conventions by denying to States which undermine conservation
conventions to which the United States is party both fishing
opportunities in the United States 200-mile zone and entry of fish
and fish products into the United States; other States such as New
Zealand, Australia, the United Kingdom are also introducing more
protective marine mammal laws.[58]

CONCLUSIONS

Although there have been many interesting new developments in
the international law to protect marine mammals, including several
conventions distinguishing marine mammals from fish by including
them on Annexes which require that they be given special
protection related to their differences from fish and referring to

---

[57] A/CONF.62/WS/4 Annex. *Statement of Interpretation, Comments, Reservations and
Proposals*, proposed by Canada; See P. Birnie "Small Cetaceans," 5 *Marine Policy* (1981),
pp. 277–281. Canada's intention is to use the North Atlantic Fishery Organisation, the area of
which comes mainly under Canadian jurisdiction.

[58] For details of these laws see P. Birnie, "Legal Measures which may be used for
Prohibiting or Regulating the Conduct of Whaling Operations outside the Regulations
adopted by the International Convention for the Regulation of Whaling," report for IUCN
(International Union for Conservation of Nature) and WWF (World Wildlife Fund), IUCN
Environmental Policy and Law Nr. 19 (1982).

them as a "natural heritage," these fall short of conferring on them the "common heritage" status according to deep seabed resources implemented by a fully internationalised régime. The UNCLOS text segregates marine mammals from fisheries provisions but their status is left ambiguous and the text is not yet legally binding, though now adopted as a convention.[59]

Treaties are increasingly protective but piecemeal, ad hoc and unlinked institutionally. Most conventions are either framework conventions requiring much future State practice to interpret and develop their wide and ambiguous terms, or are not in force or not sufficiently widely ratified to constitute a fully effective international régime. The same applies to the new principles of the UNCHE and UNEP. Nonetheless considerable if muddled progress has been made towards giving effect to the unique characteristics of marine mammals, especially cetaceans, in terms of new measures under international law. State practice increasingly evidences that the new norms are entering into customary international law.[60] It remains to be seen whether the international community will someday take the further steps proposed by St. Lucia on becoming a member of the IWC in 1981. It suggested amending the ICRW and UNCLOS Draft Convention to declare whales "our common inheritance," accompanied by affiliation of the IWC with the United Nations.[61] Others have proposed a General Assembly Resolution.[62] Both approaches, the normative and the conventional, towards establishing comprehensive international institutional management are needed if the status even of great whales is to be changed to afford complete protection. New norms would have to be incorporated both into treaty and customary law and the taking of whales equated more with slavery and piracy as a universal offence,[63] backed by some system of port State jurisdiction. Until these developments take place it must be concluded that marine mammals remain common property resources—continually exposed to the possibility of over-exploitation because States feel free to leave management bodies if quotas are not acceptable to their national interests—and thus only partially protected, however great the improvements since

---

[59] "Can the Third World Stem the American Tide," *The Guardian*, August 29, 1981, p. 17.

[60] *Op. cit.* in note 18 above; for a detailed account of these see P. Birnie, *op. cit.* in note 58 above; M. Bean, *The Evolution of National Wildlife Law* (1977).

[61] Statement to the International Whaling Commission, at 33rd Meeting (1981) on Thursday, July 23, 1981, by Hon. Peter Josie, Commissioner for St. Lucia.

[62] *Op. cit.*, in note 5 above, at pp. 26–27, provides a Draft Declaration of Principles Governing the Conservation of the Great Whales.

[63] See B. Dubner, *The Law of International Piracy—Developments in International Law* (1980), for the form such developments might take.

1895. Concern must still arise at the embryonic state of measures under recent treaties and the lack of mechanisms for their co-ordination. It cannot be said that there is yet any system or régime for protection of marine mammals; existing legal arrangements fall short of the UNEP/FAO Global Action Plan.[64] It is surely time for all States to give legal effect to the realisation that it is not in their vital interests to over-exploit marine mammals and to provide incrementally an answer, at least for marine mammals, by means of further effective conventions and declarations to the question recently raised: "What is the limit to the variety of animals that can be exploited rationally?"[65] The law, as evidenced in this article, offers means of laying down internationally the threats, criteria of behaviour, *etc.*, which make some more worthy of protection than others thus avoiding the slide down "the slippery slope of irrationality (or to be unkind sentimentality)" feared by that questioner.[66]

---

[64] *Op. cit.* in note 3, Sec. IV(4), Improvement of Law and its Application, pp. 48–55; gaps emphasised include lack of co-ordination, no treaty on sanctuary areas, no treaty covering several species including sirenians.

[65] R.B. Clarke (ed.), "Whales and Men (not forgetting seals and a walrus)," 12 *Marine Pollution Bulletin* (1981), p. 322.

[66] *Ibid.*

THE UNITED NATIONS UNIVERSITY

By

P.K. MENON

IN the aftermath of the cataclysms of the Second World War, the United Nations was founded with an original membership of 51 States. In its early years the United Nations was primarily concerned with the immediate problems relating to the post-war world, in particular the East-West confrontation which came to be known as the Cold War. Since then, the focus and emphasis of work has shifted and broadened.

The United Nations with a membership of 157 nation-States, large and small, has been able to make considerable headway, with occasional failures, in the maintenance of global peace and security, decolonisation, promotion of human rights, and the advancement of economic, social and cultural progress. A new kind of intellectual enterprise undertaken by the United Nations is the establishment of the United Nations University, to pursue "global problems of human survival, development and welfare."[1]

I—HISTORICAL BACKGROUND

The idea of the establishment of an international or world university dates back to the various projects and proposals enunciated after the First World War which aroused in many intellectuals a desire to strengthen the spirit and practice of international solidarity among research scholars.[2] The bitter experiences of the Second World War and the fond hopes generated by the foundation of the United Nations produced a fresh impetus to this idea. Fundamental to this idea has been that the proposed institution should increase international understanding and safeguard world peace while at the same time carrying out research and scholarly studies of global importance requiring an international approach.

Be that as it may, it was essentially the personal initiative of U Thant, the former Secretary-General of the United Nations that changed the idealistic aspiration into a practical reality. A true research scholar as he was, U Thant realised that an international

---

[1] United Nations, Doc.A/9149/Add.2.
[2] See United Nations Educational, Scientific and Cultural Organisation, *Report and Comments of the Director-General on the Results of the Feasibility Study Concerning the International University*, Doc. 88.Ex/6 (September 3, 1971).

community of scholars could serve to strengthen the intellectual bonds which help maintain peace. In the Introduction to the Annual Report submitted by him to the United Nations General Assembly at its twenty-fourth session in 1969, the Secretary-General took up and enlarged the idea of founding an international university.

Introducing the Annual Report, U Thant said: "I feel that the time has come when serious thought may be given to the establishment of a United Nations University . . . . devoted to the Charter objectives of peace and progress." The primary function of the University would be, he continued, "to promote international understanding both at the political and cultural levels."

On the basis of what U Thant proposed, the General Assembly adopted Resolution 2573 (XXIV) inviting the Secretary-General "to undertake, in co-operation with the United Nations Educational, Scientific and Cultural Organisation (UNESCO) and in consultation with the United Nations Institute for Training and Research (UNITAR) and any other agency or organisation he deems necessary and taking into account the views expressed at the twenty-fourth session of the General Assembly, a comprehensive expert study on the feasibility of an international university, including a clear definition of the goals and objectives as well as recommendations as to how it might be organised and financed." Various resolutions adopted by the General Assembly subsequently and several surveys and expert studies undertaken in this regard culminated in the establishment of the University: a new kind of institution, an academic instrument for worldwide scholarly collaboration focused on specific practical world problems.

II—A NEW CONCEPT

The terminology "International University" employed in the initial stages of discussion and consultations aroused misunderstandings and controversies.[3] Universities did not relish the use of the prefix "International" pointing out that the "major universities of the world are international in their outlook and in their intellectual mission and also, in many cases, in the composition of their student body and teaching staff."[4] The name was therefore acceptably altered to United Nations University. This has an additional advantage of emphasising its close links with the United Nations family of organisations and their objectives.

As a clear departure from the traditional functions of a university,

---

[3] See *op. cit.* in note 2 above, paragraph 7.
[4] *Ibid.*

the activities of the United Nations University will not include teaching in the ordinary sense of the term, that is what is known as the "undergraduate level" in English terminology and as "first level of the second cycle" in current French terminology. This kind of teaching would unnecessarily duplicate the work already being done by existing institutions and, moreover, to organise such teaching would raise innumerable technical, political and financial problems.

The University will have no central "campus" and, will neither award degrees or issue diplomas. Its scholars may come from any nation and its activities may be located anywhere in the world. It will have a flexible system of co-operation among scholars and among institutions engaged in higher learning and research. It is not the purpose of the University to train candidates to qualify them for specific jobs in a national context. In other words, it is not going to be a factory where participants are considered raw materials to be processed into saleable commodities.

Conceived as a global decentralised network of centres and programmes of research and training, the main concern of the University will be "action-oriented research with the pressing problems of human survival, development and welfare that are the concern of the United Nations and its agencies, and . . . the postgraduate training of young scholars and research workers for the benefit of the world community."[5] This network will be larger in scope and structure than any existing research or training institution. It will provide with opportunities for research workers from many different backgrounds who could compare and analyse the results of their own work and that of their colleagues, with a view to finding new solutions by means of such co-operation.

The University would therefore not be provided with complex and costly laboratories or scientific equipment for its day-to-day work; rather the University or its various centres would establish affiliation arrangements with national universities and research institutes, which would enable it to draw upon the results obtained with the facilities of these national institutions and, in return, offer a larger audience for the work of the affiliated establishments and increased opportunities for conducting studies and comparing results.

The University does not intend to duplicate or compete with existing institutions but is created to meet important research and advanced training needs in direct collaboration with institutions throughout the world. The United Nations University is different from other universities as it works from a central planning

---

[5] United Nations, *United Nations University* (Background Papers, OPI/541, April 1975).

headquarters through networks of institutions and scholars organised: (a) to identify pressing global problems; (b) to help fill important gaps in knowledge and expertise through internationally co-ordinated research and advanced training; (c) to strengthen applied research and advanced training resources, particularly in developing countries where global problems are most seriously manifested; and (d) to disseminate research results.[6]

The distinctive method of its international operation distinguishes the United Nations University from traditional nationally-oriented universities and provides the basis for the sustained network activities that enable the University to mobilise world-wide scholarly resources and focus them on problems of concern to the international community.

In accordance with its mandate, the University disseminates knowledge generated by its programmes and other sources in a variety of publications and meetings and other media designed to reach scientists, scholars and policy-makers throughout the world. It also explores the possibility of organising one or more data banks for the main problems it is to work on.

III—MAIN OBJECTIVES

The objectives of the University are both humane and utilitarian. In short, the work is to seek new ways to improve the conditions of human existence throughout the world. To achieve this, the University will not be organised on the basis of traditional academic departments. Instead, the University's institutes will employ multidisciplinary approaches to specific major world problems. The University's international connections will enable it to achieve interdisciplinary co-operation more systematically and consistently than many institutions of a national or regional character. Because many of the world's problems are concentrated in developing regions, the University, while serving the whole world, will be strongly oriented towards the needs of developing countries. The principal purposes of the University are research, postgraduate training and dissemination of knowledge.[7]

(a) *Research*
Research will concentrate into the pressing global problems of human survival, development and welfare that are also the concern

---

[6] United Nations, *Report of the Council of the United Nations University* [General Assembly: Official Records; Thirty-Second Session; Supplement Nr. 31 (A/32/31)], p. 6.

[7] *Charter of the University*, Article 1. The Charter of the University was adopted by the General Assembly of the United Nations on December 6, 1973 [Resolution 3081 (XXVIII)].

of the United Nations and its Specialised Agencies. The research will be multidisciplinary in character and it will pay attention to the social sciences and humanities as well as to the natural sciences—both pure and applied.[8]

Among other subjects, the research programme would include: (1) co-existence between peoples having different cultures, languages and social systems; (2) peaceful relations between States and maintenance of peace and security; (3) Human Rights; (4) Economic and social change and development; (5) The Environment and the proper use of resources; (6) Basic scientific research and the application of the results of science and technology in the interest of development; and (7) Universal human values related to the improvement of the quality of life.[9]

The main thrust of this research programme is to promote the growth of vigorous academic and scientific communities everywhere and particularly in the Third-World countries in order to meet with their vital needs in the fields of learning and research. In this respect, the university serves as an anti-brain drain agency that increases the effectiveness of research work in developing countries and the attraction of such work for outstanding researchers from those countries, thus helping to build the intellectual capital on which developing countries can draw.

This function is one of the most characteristic features of the University. Its aim is to help developing countries become more self-reliant, less dependent on institutions and experts from other parts of the world, and better able to define and work on their own problems from the viewpoint of their own values and aspirations. In the choice of the University's associated institutions special emphasis is therefore placed on selecting institutions in developing countries that are examples of the successful organisations of research and advanced training focused on problems in the developing world.

(b) *Postgraduate Training*

In its postgraduate training programmes, the University intends to assist scholars, especially young scholars, to participate in research in order to increase their capability to contribute to the extension, application and diffusion of knowledge.[10]

---

[8] *Ibid.* Article 1 paragraph 2.
[9] *Ibid.* paragraph 3.
[10] *Ibid.* paragraph 7.

(c) *Dissemination of Knowledge*

The University will disseminate the Knowledge it gained in its activities to the United Nations and its various agencies, to scholars and to the public. This may help to increase dynamic interaction in the world-wide community of learning and research.[11]

IV—INSTITUTIONAL MECHANISM

The University consists of (1) a Council; (2) a Rector; (3) a University Centre; and (4) Research and Training Centre and Programmes.

(a) *The Council*

The Council[12] is composed of 24 members appointed on a geographical basis with due regard to major academic, scientific, educational or cultural trends in the world. The members serve in their individual capacity. This means that they are in a position to exercise their functions in complete interdependence and need neither solicit nor accept instructions from their governments or any affiliated organisations. The role of the Council as a function oriented collective enterprise is to represent the common interest of the world community rather than individual national interests.

The term of office of the members of the Council is for six years. This gives a certain amount of stability and continuity. The members are appointed by the Secretary-General of the United Nations and the Director-General of UNESCO in consultation with the UNITAR. The Secretary-General of the United Nations, the Director-General of UNESCO and the Executive Director of UNITAR are *ex-officio* members of the Council.

In order to administer the programmes effectively, the Council must be able to make decisions affecting matters of policy. It is therefore indispensable to endow it with powers that will ensure maximum authority to set priorities and which projects shall be approved and carried out. The functions of the Council therefore include formulating principles and policies concerning the activities and operations of the University and to decide on the setting up of the research and training centres and programme.[13] The Council is the supreme organ with principal decision-making powers.

Decisions of the council are normally by consensus.[14] This provision need not necessarily bar progress; action can be taken to

---

[11] *Ibid*. paragraph 4.
[12] *Ibid*. Article 4.
[13] *Ibid*. paragraph 4.
[14] See *Rules of Procedure of the Council of the United Nations University*, Rule 23.

the extent that the members can agree and are motivated by goodwill and understanding. However, to meet with any contingencies and to overcome any obstructionist activities by means of an exercise of veto rights, provisions have been made to make decisions even in the absence of consensus. In the absence of a consensus, decisions are taken by a majority of the members present. Fifteen members of the Council will constitute a quorum.

(b) *The Rector*

The Rector, who is the chief academic and administrative officer of the University, is appointed by the Secretary-General of the United Nations for a period of five years and is eligible for reappointment for one more term of five years. It seems that the post is of the grade of Under-Secretary General. The first Rector of the University was Dr. James M. Hester of the United States, formerly President of the New York University, whose term ended in August 1980. Since he was not available for reappointment, Mr. Soedjatmoko of Indonesia was appointed as the new Rector and assumed office on September 1, 1980.

The Rector has over-all responsibility for the direction, organisation, administration and programmes of the University. Specifically his duties are[15]: (a) Submit the plan of work and the budget estimates of the University to the Council for its consideration and approval; (b) Direct the activities connected with the execution of the research and training programmes; (c) Appoint the personnel of the University; (d) Direct the staff of the University; (e) Set up advisory bodies; (f) Make arrangements with governments and international organisations with a view to offering and receiving services related to the activities of the University; (g) Accept voluntary contributions from governments, international and national organisations, foundations and other non-governmental sources; (h) Co-ordinate the research and training programmes of the University with the activities of the United Nations and its agencies and with research programmes of the world scholarlistic community; (i) Report to the Council on the activities of the University and the execution of its plans of work; (j) Provide the necessary services to the Council.

As a United Nations official, the Rector is required in the performance of his duties to observe the highest degree of independence, impartiality and objectivity as provided in Article 100, paragraph 1 of the Charter of the United Nations. At the same time, although it is sponsored by the United Nations and UNESCO,

---

[15] *Charter of the University*, Article 5, paragraph 3.

the University is an autonomous academic institution and not an intergovernmental organisation. The Charter guarantees its full academic freedom in the choice of subjects and institutions and individuals through which to work. This enables the Rector to exercise intellectual freedom in recognising diverse experiences that enrich and enliven the University and reduce the impact of political provincialism.

Although the decision-making power is vested in the Council, the Rector takes initiatives in regard to organisational set up, planning, management, policy-making, external collaboration and fund raising. It is important to observe that the Rector's powers, though somewhat limited in regard to putting plans into action, are wide in regard to the making of plans. Even if he is not a practical executor of programmes and activities, he is at least a thought provoker.

(c) *University Centre*

The University Centre assists the Rector in the performance of his tasks including administration of the over-all University programmes, and finances it in accordance with the approved budget.

(d) *Personnel*

The personnel of the University consists of academic administrative and trainees. The basic criteria for selection is highest standards of efficiency, competence and integrity with due regard to appropriate representation in terms of geography, social systems, cultural relations, age and sex. The academic personnel is composed of the Rector, his senior collaborators and the directors of the research and training centres and programmes- and research-personnel.

(e) *Finance*

The University is funded by voluntary contributions only. This provides for its viability, objectivity and the quality of its scholarly and scientific work. The voluntary contributions are received from Governments, non-governmental sources including foundations, universities and individuals, and from the United Nations and its Specialised Agencies. The budget estimates are prepared by the Rector in accordance with the United Nations regulations, rules, policies and procedures. The estimates have to be approved by the Council before transmission to the UN General Assembly.

Expenses of the University are met from two sources: (1) income from an Endowment Fund; and (2) Specific project support. The concept of the Endowment Fund is unique in the United Nations family of institutions. It is not financed by regular annual subventions provided by the General Assembly but basically from income derived from the Endowment Fund made up of voluntary contributions.

In addition to the Endowment Fund, it is expected that specific contributions will be made by Governments and non-governmental sources for the support of particular programme activities. The specific project support will play an increasing role after an adequate base for the University's viability has been established through the Endowment Fund.

A target of US-$500 million has been set for the Endowment Fund. The Government of Japan has made the Fund concept a reality by pledging US-$100 million to be contributed over a five-year period. Annual income from this target amount is estimated to range from US-$25 million to 40 million which is the minimum required for basic financing. It is projected that when the Endowment is fully funded, roughly 12 per cent. of income would be spent on headquarters operations, including programme planning, supervision and evaluation, and 88 per cent. on programme activities throughout the world.

As of June 1979, pledges have been made by 26 countries totalling US-$142.4 million to the Endowment Fund of which $92.3 million has been received. A large part of this money, US-$80 million has been contributed by just one country, Japan.[16]

From the preceding paragraphs it may be observed that the University's fund raising potential has not made considerable headway. The main financial problem is that the present level of Endowment Income does not finance an acceptable balance between the cost of necessary headquarters operations and adequate external programme activities. Since the principal purpose of the University is its programme activities around the world, external programme support should far exceed headquarters expenses. Until that level is reached, the University's financial structure may not stand on a sound footing.

The slackness in the flow of contributions may place serious limitations on the capacity of the University to develop as the Council believes it should. The problem in its fund-raising include initial lack of understanding of the identity of this new institution, ignorance about its true nature and residual opposition to the original concept of the University as a traditional campus-based institution, especially among some of the industrialised countries. Thus, in its fund-raising endeavour the University has a two-fold task before it: (1) To eliminate ignorance and alleviate scepticism

---

[16] United Nations, *Report of the Council of the United Nations University* (General Assembly Official Records: Thirty-fourth Session Supplement, Nr. 31) (A/34/31), p. 6.

among governments and academic leaders, and thereby create general and greater acceptance of the University; (2) To obtain material support from all Member States and especially from the industrialised countries.[17]

To meet with this need, the Rector and Vice-Rector for Planning and Development have visited many countries in explaining the University's activities and soliciting funds. The responses indicate promises for the future.

(f) *Location*

The headquarters of the University is situated in the Tokyo metropolitan area. But in a worldwide system of research and training centres and programmes, the location of each centre or programme will be at an appropriate site.

(g) *Status and Privileges*

The University is an autonomous organ of the General Assembly and enjoys the status, privileges and immunities provided in Articles 104 and 105 of the United Nations Charter.[18] In terms of these Articles, the University will possess international legal personality as may be necessary for the exercise of its functions and the fulfilment of its purposes.

The importance of conferring predictable legal status on the University cannot be overemphasised. This is not without historical precedents. In the advisory opinion given by the International Court of Justice in the case concerning the *Reparation for Injuries Suffered in the Service of the United Nations*, a question referred by the United Nations General Assembly, the Court said: "In the opinion of the Court, the Organisation (United Nations) was intended to exercise and enjoy, and is in fact exercising and enjoying, functions and rights which can only be explained on the basis of the possession of a large measure of international personality and the capacity to operate upon an international plane. It is at present the supreme type of international organisation, and it could not carry out the intentions of its founders if it was devoid of international personality."

By the provisions of its Charter, the University "may acquire and dispose of real and personal property, and may take other legal actions necessary to the performance of its functions."[19] It may also enter into agreements, contracts or arrangements with Governments, organisations, institutions, firms or individuals for the

---

[17] *Ibid*. Thirty-Third Session, p. 59.
[18] See *Charter of the University*, Article 3, 11.
[19] *Ibid*. Article 11 paragraph 2.

purpose of carrying out its activities.[20] As such, the University possesses the right on its own account to institute legal proceedings necessary for the protection of its interests and, whether it occupies the position of a plaintiff or defendant, to enter into desirable settlements. Further, the ability of the University to enter into firm commitments is dependent on the applicability to it of the ordinary legal procedures which private businessmen follow in their contractual and other relations.

Provision has been made in the Charter for persons travelling on the official business of the University to be provided with appropriate United Nations travel documents.[21]

V—PROGRAMME OF ACTIVITIES

In selecting specific programme of activities, the United Nations University considered the following factors; the interest and aspirations of large numbers of people particularly in the developing world; the need to identify and study practical world problems not limited to topical issues but considered in relation to the future of mankind, special attention being paid to the fields and topics which are not covered by conventional universities; the exploration and elucidation of fundamental methodologies, including methodologies of multidisciplinary and interdisciplinary research; and the need for innovation.

After full discussion as far back as 1975, the council accepted three broad priority programmes of activities: (1) World Hunger; (2) Human and Social Development; and (3) Use and Management of Natural Resources.[22]

Each of these Programmes deals with aspects of the human condition. They are interrelated parts of an over-all University effort to achieve better understanding of conditions of life throughout the world in order to help improve them. That is the basic responsibility of the University: and draw on the world's intellectual resources—co-operatively—to increase understanding and to help to solve major human problems, all of which are intricately intertwined. The broad mandate given to the University in its Charter provides the framework for this essential holistic approach to using knowledge to clarify and alleviate major problems.

---

[20] *Ibid.* paragraph 3.
[21] *Ibid.* paragraph 4.
[22] See United Nations, *Report of the Council of the United Nations University* (General Assembly Official Record: Thirtieth Session Supplement, Nr. 31) (A/10031), paragraph 19, p. 6.

(a) *World Hunger Programme*

The World Hunger Programme is focused on the most basic material human need: Adequate nourishment for all human beings. It is concerned with identifying and filling important gaps in knowledge about nourishment and with public policy problems concerning the availability of adequate food to people everywhere.

The major concern of this Programme is the fact that starvation and malnutrition constitute a crisis of great proportions in the world today. A major component of the Programme is therefore national and nutritional policy, a subject widely ignored in the past. Another project deals with staggering losses of food after harvest—food waste—an area in which there has been only little, highly fragmented research and inadequate training efforts. It is estimated that 40 per cent. of the food produced in certain regions is lost to rodents, insects, spoilage, and other storage and handling problems. Another area of concern is with developing comprehensive information on human nutritional requirements in tropical areas of the developing world where there is a heavy burden of intestinal parasites and other infections. Diets in such countries often have substances that interfere with the nutrients they contain.

(b) *Human and Social Development Programme*

The thrust of the Human and Social Development Programme reflects widespread disappointment with the result of past development strategies aimed primarily at economic growth. The programme is providing a global forum for scholarly debate and evaluation of strategy alternatives, thereby bringing scientific objectivity to a subject frequently clouded by political controversy.

The Programme attempts to redefine the conventional development wisdom of the recent past which tended to equate economic growth with improvement in the over-all quality of human life. This has often proved not to the case with respect to the rural villages of the Third-World (developing) countries who comprise the bulk of the population. Thus there is now a widespread realisation that new development concepts need to be evolved and analysed dispassionately in order to understand better the complex interplay of social, cultural, economic and political forces that affect the development process on a world-wide basis.

The two major activities under this Programme—Problems of Development, and Technology and Development—are designed to be complementary and mutually reinforcing. The first activity is a long-term research effort involving social scientists and other scholars around the world and seeks to develop new insights about the nature of development problems. The second is directed at the store of practical knowledge that has built up at the village level over the centuries. It seeks to learn more about how local technologies are developed, how they should be linked with the modern sector, and how transfer of such technologies could help meet national, regional and international needs.

The major components of Problems of Development Programme include socio-cultural development alternatives in a changing world, human rights, peace and international law in the context of development. The Technology part of development includes sharing of traditional technology, research-and-development systems in rural settings, technology transfer, transformation and development.

(c) *Use and Management of Natural Resources*

The Programme on the Use and Management of Natural Resources is concerned with the physical conditions in which we live and the natural resources available for us to improve life. Activities are focused on problems of ecology and energy. Special attention is being given to the humid tropics and to arid lands, huge zones encompassing most of the developing world.

The Programme seeks to develop better understanding of (a) rural energy systems; (b) the mixing of tree crops and livestock in agro-forestry systems; (c) interactions between land and water, especially in the coastal zones, and (d) ecological, social and economic interactions between highland and lowland areas. In the field of energy the focus of the programme is on the potential for alternative energy sources: solar, biogas, wind and others—to meet the growing energy demands of rural areas of the developing countries.

It may be noted at this point that the present Rector, Mr. Soedjatmoko, has proposed that the scope of the University's activities be broadened by adopting five major themes which would incorporate and extend the original three problem areas of world hunger, human and social development, and the use and management of natural resources. These five themes would be: (1) Peace, Security, Conflict Resolution and Global transformation; (2) The Global Economy; (3) Hunger, Poverty, Resources and the Environment; (4) Human and Social Development and Co-existence of Peoples, Cultures and Social Systems; and (5) Science, Technology and their Social and Ethical Implications.[23]

---

[23] *The United Nations University Newsletter*, Vol. 5, Nr. 3 (October 1981), p. 3.

CONCLUSIONS

The United Nations University is a new concept. Abstract exercise of the intellect, without further search for result, is not its functon; on the other hand, work of the University will be programme oriented towards problem-solving. The work of the University is primarily the concern of research scholars rather than national officials and diplomats.

The three compelling reasons for its creation as stated by Dr. Hester, former Rector of the University before the United Nations Economic and Social Council in July 1976, are problem-solving, institution-building, and strengthening the conditions of peace.[24]

The first reason stems from the fact that the international nature of many problems that now confront humanity requires an international or "non-national" approach to their understanding and alleviation. There is no existing research and advanced-training institution to perform this role.

The second reason is to strengthen the capacity of institutions throughout the world to achieve practical results in coping with serious human and natural-resources problems. This function has special reference to developing countries. The University is mandated by its Charter to be particularly concerned with strengthening intellectual resources in developing countries in order to help Third-World institutions be of maximum value to their own societies and to help combat the brain drain.

A third important reason is to give substance to the ideal of an international community of scholars. An institution that enables increased number of scholarly people to share perspectives, knowledge, experience and to engage in collaborative research and training activities may inevitably be an instrument for strengthening understanding, and, one would hope, the conditions of world peace.

Finally, as the former Rector envisaged, "the creation of the University challenges academic people to find ways through which scholars can interact that will help a more stable world order beyond the work of politicians and diplomats."[25]

The fact that the University has been in existence for only a short peiod of time does not permit a full assessment of the success of its three main programmes and most of the projects within them. Each of the programmes is at a different stage of development: World Hunger became operational in early 1976, Human and Social Development in late 1976, and Natural Resources in late 1977.

---

[24] See *Statement by Dr. James Hester Before the Sixty-First Session of the UN Economic and Social Council, Geneva, July 23, 1976,* United Nations, Doc.OPI/CESI/NOTE/373 (July 29, 1976) p. 7.

[25] *Ibid.* p. 8.

Though each of the programmes has devised different methods of operation to suit particular needs, the University has promoted interaction among the programmes while recognising the fact that real problems can only be fully understood and solved as intimately linked aspects of the human condition.

The basic premise of the University is the growing interdependence of issues, nations and regions. This new concept of interdependence requires new intellectual approaches and new forms of organisation of research, advanced training, and dissemination of knowledge. That is what the University is hoping to provide.

THE LEGAL FOUNDATIONS
OF WORLD ORDER

By

ISTVAN POGANY

THE establishment and maintenance of international order has been one of the central tasks of international law. However, politico-legal mechanisms for the maintenance of world order are themselves the product of particular conceptions of the nature of world order and of threats to international stability. Until recently threats to international order have been perceived primarily in military terms. As a consequence institutional and legal developments have reflected the need to establish mechanisms for safeguarding world order from the use of armed force.

There has been increasing recognition, however, of the degree to which threats to world order may also arise from the use of *economic* coercion by States. More fundamentally, it has been argued that the international economic system is itself a primary source of global instability. Consequently it may be questioned whether existing mechanisms for the maintenance of world order are either adequate or appropriate. The purpose of this article is to assess the effectiveness of the present framework for the maintenance of world order in the light of the emergence of new, and non-military, threats to global stability.

I—THE CONCEPT OF WORLD ORDER

The concept of "world order" is itself problematic. It may be taken to refer, at one level, to conditions existing *between* the constituent elements of the international system, *i.e.* States. In this sense, world order may be understood as a condition of peaceful and systematic relations between States. However in addition to this *external* dimension of the concept of world order, which concerns relations *between* States, there is a significant *internal* dimension. Conditions *between* States cannot be divorced from the realities of conditions *within* States. Acute domestic problems *within* a country of an economic, social or political character inevitably affect the *external* policies of that country. Similarly the policies of other governments towards a State will be affected by their assessment of its internal cohesion, economic significance and military capacity. Thus conditions *within* States inevitably impinge on relations *between* States. Ultimately, world order is an indivisible concept embracing both peaceful and systematic relations *between* States, and stable and effective conditions *within* States.

Threats to world order have generally been understood as arising from the use of force by States. Consequently world order has been identified with the *absence* of the use of armed force. However this is a dangerously simplistic notion. Peaceful and systematic relations between States requires more than the proscription of the use of armed force. It requires the elaboration of principles to govern those issues which have been the cause of military conflict. It requires, in addition, an international system which can promote stable and effective conditions *within* States without which world order cannot be assured.

II—THE FRAMEWORK OF WORLD ORDER

The history of efforts to establish and maintain international order, during the nineteenth and twentieth centuries, has been the history of two ideas—balance of power and collective security. The term "balance of power" has been used to describe a number of different concepts. However, as it is generally understood, "balance of power" may be characterised as "a policy of promoting the creation or the preservation of equilibrium."[1] Thus "balance of power" essentially entails a decentralised system in which States endeavour, through a series of shifting alliances, to maintain a rough equilibrium of power as a means of inhibiting the use of armed force.

"Collective security," by contrast, requires States to "join in collective action to put down any aggressive threat by any state, against any other state anywhere."[2] It involves, in addition, "the institutionalization of international relations. It proposes to coordinate the policies of states in accordance with firmly established general principles and to create institutions capable of providing some degree of centralized supervision and management of the system."[3] Although the concepts of "balance of power" and "collective security" are therefore distinct in terms of the methods by which they seek to maintain international order, they are

---

[1] I.L. Claude, *Power and International Relations* (1962), p. 18.
[2] *Ibid*. p. 146.
[3] *Ibid*. p. 148.

identical insofar as they identify threats to world order as arising from the use of armed force.

Throughout the nineteenth century the "balance of power" concept was dominant. It was reflected in the establishment of the Congress system which represented an attempt by the major European States to maintain an equilibrium of power in the European theatre.[4] Moreover the Congress system was a response to the European experience of a disequilibrium of power arising from French military predominance during the early years of the nineteenth century.

After the First World War the principle of "collective security," as embodied in the League of Nations, became the basis of world order. Thus the experience of the First World War confirmed the general belief that the use of armed force remained the primary source of international instability. However the concept of "collective security" was seen as a more effective means of preserving world order from the use of armed force.

Under the League Covenant, the Members undertook "to respect and preserve as against external aggression the territorial integrity and existing political independence of all Members of the League."[5] If a Member of the League went to war in disregard of its obligations under the Covenant, it was deemed to have "committed an act of war against all other Members of the League, which hereby undert[ook] immediately to subject it to the severance of all trade or financial relations. . . . "[6] Moreover, the executive organ of the League, the Council, was empowered to recommend the application of collective enforcement measures involving the use of armed force.[7]

The League of Nations failed to prevent the outbreak of the Second World War. Nevertheless, the experience of the Second World War confirmed rather than undermined the general assumption that the use of armed force remained the major threat to the maintenance of world order. The failure of the League of Nations to avert the war was interpreted not as failure of the principle of collective security but rather as a reflection of the insufficient degree

---

[4] Vagts, "The Balance of Power in International Law: A History of an Idea" 73 *American Journal of International Law* (1979), p. 555 esp. at pp. 564–565.

[5] Art. 10.

[6] Art. 16 (1). Although the League Covenant did not prohibit resort to war, it introduced significant restrictions on the circumstances in which Members could lawfully resort to war. See Arts. 12–15. For an examination of the "gaps" in the Covenant see J. Stone, *Legal Controls of International Conflict* (1954), p. 175.

[7] Art. 16 (2).

to which the principle of collective security had been embodied in the Covenant.[8]

The United Nations Organisation, which constitutes the present framework for the maintenance of world order, was founded out of the experience of the Second World War. Implicit in the provisions of the Charter is the assumption that the use of armed force remains the underlying threat to international order. The overwhelming concern of the United Nations with the preservation of world order from the use of armed force is reflected in Article 1 of the Charter which states that the primary purpose of the United Nations is: "[t]o maintain international peace and security, and to that end: to take effective collective measures for the prevention and removal of threats to the peace, and for the suppression of acts of aggression or other breaches of the peace. . . . " The principle of collective security is realised in the Charter through the acceptance by member States of restrictions on their right to use force, and in their acceptance of obligations to participate in the application of collective enforcement action to maintain international peace and security. In terms of the former, Members are required to "refrain in their international relations from the threat or use of force against the territorial integrity or political independence of any state, or in any other manner inconsistent with the purposes of the United Nations."[9] In terms of the latter, the executive organ of the United Nations, the Security Council, is given significant responsibilities. The Security Council is empowered to "determine the existence of any threat to the peace, breach of the peace, or act of aggression. . . . "[10] The Security Council may, with a view to the maintenance or restoration of international peace and security, decide on the application of collective enforcement action involving either economic or military sanctions (Articles 41, 42). Members of the United Nations may be called upon to assist in the implementation of such collective enforcement action.[11]

There can be little doubt that the United Nations has failed as a

---

[8] Under the terms of the Covenant, the League Council could only *recommend* the imposition of military sanctions against a State which went to war in disregard of its obligations under the Covenant. See Art. 16 (2). Moreover the League Covenant did not prohibit measures of self-help short of war. See I. Brownlie, *International Law and the Use of Force by States* (1963), pp. 59–62. Nor did the Covenant proscribe resort to war in all circumstances. See Stone, *op. cit.* in note 6, above, p. 175. Critically, also, member States were free to decide for themselves whether a State had gone to war in disregard of its obligations under the Covenant, *ibid.*, pp. 176–177.

[9] Art. 2 (4).

[10] Art. 39.

[11] Participation may be mandatory in the case of sanctions not involving the use of armed force. See, generally, Goodrich, Hambro, Simons, *Charter of the United Nations* (3rd rev. ed. 1969), pp. 311–317.

system of collective security. For the principle of collective security to operate effectively states must "identify their national interest so completely with the preservation of the total world order that they stand ready to join in collective action to put down any aggressive threat by any state, against any other state anywhere."[12] Such an identification of national interest with the collective interest in the preservation of world order has not materialised. However, the failure of the United Nations as a system of collective security has had the ironic consequence of a re-emergence of the "balance-of-power" doctrine. Collective security has been discarded, in all but theory, in favour of an uneasy global equilibrium between the Soviet and Western spheres of interest.

III—EMERGENT THREATS TO WORLD ORDER

(a) *Economic Coercion*

Evidently the use of armed force remains a major threat to world order. However, there has been increasing evidence of the emergence of new, and qualitatively distinct, threats to international stability. Developing States who possess control over vital natural resources have come to realise that by regulating the production and distribution of these commodities they can exert significant pressure on developed States. The use of such economic coercion can pose a serious threat to the preservation of world order.

During the Arab-Israeli War of 1973, Saudi Arabia imposed cuts in its oil production in the hope of persuading the United States to abandon its support for Israel.[13] For similar reasons the Netherlands was subjected to a complete oil embargo, while supplies of oil to other EEC countries and to Japan were reduced by 25 per cent. In November 1973, Arab leaders adopted a joint resolution in which they called for the continued "use of oil as an economic weapon" and the maintenance of the oil embargo against States which supported Israel.[14]

The Arab oil embargo led to a rise in oil prices which had an adverse effect on the balance of payments of all oil-importing countries, particularly those of developing States.[15] This contributed to a general trade recession and a consequent loss of productivity and employment.[16] Thus the use of the Arab oil

---

[12] Claude, *op. cit.* in note 1, above, p. 146.
[13] See XIX *Keesing's Contemporary Archives* (1973), pp. 26224–26225.
[14] *Ibid.*
[15] *Ibid.* pp. 26225–26228.
[16] See Paust and Blaustein, 'The Arab Oil Weapon—A Threat to International Peace," 68 *American Journal of International Law* (1974), pp. 433–435.

"weapon" had adverse consequences for international order—international trade patterns were disrupted while the economies of both developed and developing States were placed under increasing strain. In terms of promoting peaceful and systematic relations *between* States and stable and effective conditions *within* States, the Arab oil "weapon" posed a considerable threat to the maintenance of world order.

There has been some discussion amongst lawyers as to whether the Arab boycott constituted a "use of force" within the meaning of Article 2 (4) of the Charter.[17] It seems clear that the Charter was conceived as a means of inhibiting the use of military rather than economic coercion.[18] Nevertheless in its Declaration on Principles of International Law, the General Assembly referred to "the duty of States to refrain in their international relations from military, political, *economic* or any other form of coercion aimed against the political independence or territorial integrity of any State. . . . "[19]

Arguably the imposition of an oil boycott may constitute a "threat to the peace" within the meaning of Article 39. Nevertheless it is doubtful whether the United Nations, as it is presently constituted, could serve as an adequate basis for safeguarding world order from the use of economic coercion by States. The United Nations was established as an instrument of collective security to preserve international order from the use of armed force. Its institutional structure, jurisdiction and powers are a reflection of this overriding objective.

The United Nations was established, moreover, on the assumption of unity amongst the Great Powers. The existence of such unity is vital to the effective functioning of the United Nations system. The United Nations represents a significant shift towards the centralised supervision and management of world order. The pivotal element in this system is the Security Council. However, decisions of the Security Council, on non-procedural matters,

---

[17] See, *e.g.* Paust and Blaustein, *op. cit.* in note 16, above; Shihata, "Destination Embargo of Arab Oil: Its Legality under International Law", 68 *American Journal of International Law* (1974), p. 591.

[18] Goodrich, Hambro, Simons, *op. cit.* in note 11, above, p. 48.

[19] See Annex to G.A. Resolution 2625 (XXV), October 24, 1970 (my emphasis). In its Declaration on the Inadmissibility of Intervention in the Domestic Affairs of States, the General Assembly declared: "No state may use or encourage the use of economic, political or any other type of measures to coerce another state in order to obtain from it the subordination of the exercise of its sovereign rights or to secure from it any advantages of any kind." See G.A. Resolution 2131 (XX), December 21, 1956. See, also, Article 32 of the Charter of Economic Rights and Duties of States: "No State may use or encourage the use of economic, political or any other type of measures to coerce another State in order to obtain from it the subordination of the exercise of its sovereign rights." G.A. Resolution 3281 (XXIX), December 12, 1974.

require the affirmative votes of nine members, including the concurring votes of the permanent members.[20] Thus the unity of purpose of the permanent members is crucial to the effective functioning of the United Nations. However, the practice of the Security Council would suggest that the permanent Members have frequently been preoccupied with their individual political objectives to the exclusion of the collective interest in the maintenance of world order.[21] Consequently the Security Council has been unable to decide on the application of collective enforcement action involving the use of armed force even when dealing with conflicts of a *military* character.[22] It seems improbable, therefore, that the necessary consensus would exist to decide on the adoption of such measures in response to the use of *economic* coercion by States.

The measures available to the Security Council, moreover, are largely inappropriate. The application of economic sanctions against Rhodesia proved of questionable utility because of the lack of compliance of numerous States.[23] However, Rhodesia was of severely limited significance to the economies of most States. The Arab oil-producing countries, by contrast, are of critical importance both as a source of oil and as a market for exports from industrialised countries. Therefore the application of economic sanctions against the Arab oil-producing States could be ruinous for many States.

More generally, it would seem that the States most likely to employ measures of economic coercion are those whose resources are vital to the international economy. Therefore, the imposition of economic sanctions against such States constitutes, at most, a

---

[20] Article 27 (3).

[21] This is substantially a reflection of the fact that both the United States and the Soviet Union, whose interests are often diametrically opposed, are permanent members of the Security Council.

[22] During the Korean conflict the Security Council did authorise Members of the United Nations to provide military assistance to the Republic of Korea in order to repel an armed attack by North Korea. See Security Council resolutions of June 25, June 27, and July 7, 1950. However, there is little consensus amongst international lawyers concerning the constitutional basis of these resolutions. Certain commentators have interpreted them as 'recommendations" under the terms of Article 39 rather than "enforcement action" under Article 42. See, *e.g.* Goodrich, Hambro, Simons, *op. cit.* in note 11, above, pp. 301–315. Professor Higgins has argued, however, that the United Nations action in Korea constituted enforcement action under Articles 39 and 42. See R. Higgins, *United Nations Peacekeeping 1946–1967*, Vol. II (1970), pp. 177–178. Other writers have denied that the Security Council resolutions constituted either recommendations under Article 39 or enforcement action under Article 42. See H. Kelsen, *Recent Trends in the Law of the United Nations* (1951), pp. 927–936; Stone, *op. cit.* in note 6, above, pp. 228–237. Moreover, the Security Council was only able to adopt the resolutions as a result of the absence of the Soviet representative. See, generally, Higgins, *op. cit.* Part 3.

[23] See, *e.g.* L.T. Kapungu, *The United Nations and Economic Sanctions Against Rhodesia* (1973), pp. 123–138.

theoretical possibility the practical application of which would be entirely counter-productive insofar as it would aggravate rather than relieve the threat to world order posed by the use of economic coercion.

The application of military sanctions against States employing economic coercion would be subject to even greater uncertainties. It is generally accepted that the Security Council can only recommend, rather than require, Members to comply with collective enforcement action involving the use of armed force.[24] Moreover, as a consequence of political divisions, the Security Council has never decided on the application of military sanctions even when confronted with acts of armed aggression. It remains improbable, therefore, that the necessary consensus could be achieved to apply such measures in response to economic coercion.

More fundamentally, it may be questioned whether the use of military force would be an effective response to acts of coercion. If applied against developing States it would be interpreted, throughout much of the Third World, as a species of neo-colonialism. Its application against industrialised States, at least those who are permanent members of the Security Council, would be inconceivable because of their power of veto. Thus the United Nations Organisation is largely unsatisfactory as a means of preserving international order from the use of economic coercion.

(b) *The International Economic System*

World order has been assumed to obtain in the *absence* of coercive behaviour by States, and to be endangered as a *consequence* of the coercive behaviour of States. Thus world order has been identified with the *absence* or the use of armed force. This understanding is implicit in Article 1 (1) of the Charter, which states that the purpose of the United Nations is "To *maintain* international peace and security, and to that end: to take effective collective measures for the prevention and removal of threats to the peace, and for the suppression of acts of aggression or other breaches of the peace. . . . "[25]

In the light of the Arab use of the oil "weapon" in 1973/74, it is now clear that *economic* coercion may be as harmful to the maintenance of world order as the use of armed force. However, although economic and military coercion are qualitatively distinct,

---

[24] See, *e.g.* Goodrich, Hambro, Simons, *op. cit.* in note 11, above, p. 316.

[25] My emphasis. Article 1 does enumerate certain other purposes of the United Nations Organisation in the social, economic and humanitarian spheres. However, it is generally accepted that the maintenance of international peace and security is the primary purpose. See, *e.g.* Goodrich, Hambro, Simons, *op. cit.* in note 11, above, pp. 25–26.

they are identical insofar as they involve the deliberate application of particular policies by governments with a view to imposing their will on other nations. Thus economic coercion is largely compatible with the prevailing model of international order which identifies threats to world order as arising from the coercive behaviour of States.

A fundamental reassessment of this proposition and hence of the adequacy of existing mechanisms for the maintenance of world order is required in the light of the growing demand amongst developing States for a New International Economic Order.[26] This demand has been substantially motivated by the belief that the economic and material development of Third-World States is contingent on a fundamental transformation of the norms governing economic relations between developed and developing States. However, it is also based on the conviction that the present character of the international economic system, *irrespective* of the coercive behaviour of States, represents a major source of global instability. Thus the resolution containing the Charter of Economic Rights and Duties of States, adopted by the General Assembly in 1974, declares that "it is not feasible to establish a just order and a stable world as long as a Charter to protect the rights of all countries, and in particular the developing States, is not formulated."[27] Similarly, the preamble to the Manila Declaration, adopted by the Group of 77 in February 1976, affirms that "the implementation of the new international economic order is essential for the preservation of justice and the maintenance of peace and international co-existence. . . . "[28]

The Report of the Brandt Commission has strongly re-affirmed the proposition that the international economic system, quite apart from the coercive behaviour of States, constitutes a major source of global instability[29]: "The crisis through which international relations and the world economy are now passing presents great dangers, and they appear to be growing more serious. We believe that the gap which separates rich and poor countries. . . . has not been sufficiently recognised as a major factor in this crisis. . . . We are satisfied that the world community can have no real stability until it faces up to this basic challenge."

---

[26] See, generally, L. Anell and B. Bygren, *The Developing Countries and the World Economic Order* (1980).

[27] G.A. Resolution 3281 (XXIX) December 12, 1974.

[28] The Manila Declaration and Program of Action was adopted by the Third Ministerial Meeting of the Group of 77 at Manila in February 1976. See UNCTAD Doc. TD/195, February 12, 1976.

[29] See Report of the Independent Commission on International Development Issues, *North-South: A Programme for Survival* (1980), p. 30. (Hereafter cited as: *North-South*).

Although States remain the basic units of political decision-making, in the sense that they are sovereign and therefore possess the capacity to determine their political institutions, social policies and economic structures, they have become increasingly dependent on other States for the realisation of their economic, social and political objectives. Many domestic problems of States are incapable of resolution at the national level insofar as the problems have a significant international dimension. Industrialised States are dependent on developing States for the supply of a wide range of raw materials, and sources of energy such as oil. Increasingly, also, high levels of productivity and employment in industrialised States have come to depend on the establishment of new export markets in developing States.[30] Conversely, developing States cannot achieve a meaningful improvement in their economic conditions in the absence of satisfactory agreements concerning prices for their raw materials, and without systematic financial assistance from the industrialised States to enable them to eradicate poverty and to establish an industrial infrastructure.[31] Moreover, insofar as conditions *within* States inevitably affect relations *between* States, a continuation of the present world economic system could well precipitate a massive deterioration of international order.[32]

The Report argues that in the absence of a new system of economic relations, industrialised States will meet increasing difficulties in maintaining levels of productivity and employment. There is the danger, also, of military conflicts as developed States compete for access to energy and mineral supplies, and seek to impose their control over commodity producers. Developing States, facing rapidly increasing population levels, shortages of food and economic resources, will become increasingly unstable. Moreover, increasing difficulties *within* States will inevitably result in friction and conflict *between* States.

If the arguments of the Brandt Report are accepted, the implications for the maintenance of world order and the utility of the United Nations system are enormous. Indeed our very understanding of the concept of world order may require a fundamental re-examination. World order, as has been seen, has been identified primarily with the *absence* of the use of armed force. Thus threats to world order have been understood as arising from the coercive policies of States. However, it is the fundamental contention of the Brandt Report that the present international system, even in the absence of such coercive behaviour, is

[30] *Ibid*. pp. 68, 70, 278–279.
[31] *Ibid*. pp. 42–43, 71–72, 93, 144–147, Chapter 11.
[32] *Ibid*. pp. 46–47.

inherently unstable and disordered. The Report calls for a broader conception of world order, one which transcends the narrow perspective of military force[33]: "An important task of constructive international policy will have to consist in providing a new, more comprehensive understanding of 'security' which would be less restricted to the purely military aspects. In the global context true security cannot be achieved by a mounting build-up of weapons— defence in the narrow sense—but only by providing basic conditions for peaceful relations between nations, and solving not only the military but also the non-military problems which threaten them. . . . Our survival depends not only on military balance, but on global cooperation to ensure a sustainable biological environment, and sustainable prosperity based on equitably shared resources. Much of the insecurity in the world is connected with the divisions between rich and poor countries—grave injustice and mass starvation causing additional instability. . . . The world needs a more comprehensive understanding of security which would be less restricted to the purely military aspects."

If these arguments are accepted, the United Nations system constitutes an unsatisfactory basis for the maintenance of world order. The United Nations was established on the narrow understanding that world order consists in the absence of the use of armed force and with the principal objective of safeguarding world order from the use of force by States. Thus the Charter requires States to refrain from "any threat or use of force against the territorial integrity or political independence of any state,"[34] and provides a system of collective security, under the control of the Security Council, to maintain or restore international peace and security in the event of a "threat to the peace, breach of the peace, or act of aggression."[35] However if world order is to be understood in the broad sense advocated by the Brandt Report, as a system which can ensure the "basic conditions for peaceful relations between nations"[36] and one which can solve "not only the military but also the non-military problems which threaten them"[37] then the United Nations offers only a partial framework for the maintenance of world order.

It would be misleading to suggest that the United Nations Organisation was established with the *sole* function of regulating the use of force by States. The preamble to the Charter expresses the

---

[33] *Ibid.* pp. 124–125.
[34] Art. 2 (4).
[35] Art. 39.
[36] *North-South, op. cit.* in note 29, above, p. 124.
[37] *Ibid.*

determination of the peoples of the United Nations to "promote social progress and better standards of life in larger freedom" and to "employ international machinery for the promotion of the economic and social advancement of all peoples. . . . " Article 1 states that one of the purposes of the United Nations shall be to "achieve international co-operation in solving international problems of an economic, social, cultural, or humanitarian character, and in promoting and encouraging respect for human rights. . . . " Significantly, also, Article 55 recognises that the creation of conditions of stability and well-being are "necessary for peaceful and friendly relations among nations" and states that the United Nations shall promote: (a) higher standards of living, full employment, and conditions of economic and social progress and development; (b) solutions of international economic, social, health, and related problems; and international cultural and educational co-operation; and (c) universal respect for, and observance of, human rights and fundamental freedoms for all without distinction as to race, sex, language, or religion. In accordance with Article 56, "All Members pledge themselves to take joint and separate action in co-operation with the Organisation for the achievement of the purposes set forth in Article 55."

The Charter also provided for agreements between the United Nations and the various specialised agencies concerned with economic, social, cultural, educational, health and related matters under which the agencies would be brought into relationship with the United Nations.[38] The General Assembly was entrusted with overall responsibility for the discharge of the social and economic functions of the United Nations and, under the authority of the General Assembly, the Economic and Social Council.[39]

Nevertheless, despite this obvious concern of the United Nations with social and economic matters, it is clear from the normative and institutional provisions of the Charter that the Organisation was founded on the belief that the use of military force remains the major threat to international order. This is evident from the specific and legally-binding character of Articles 2 (3) and 2 (4) which are concerned with the prohibition of the use of force by States,[40] as opposed to the general and possibly hortatory character of Articles

---

[38] See Arts. 57–59, 62–64, 66, 70.

[39] See Art. 60.

[40] Article 2 (3) states: "All Members shall settle their international disputes by peaceful means in such a manner that international peace and security, and justice, are not endangered." Article 2 (4) states: "All Members shall refrain in their international relations from the threat or use of force against the territorial integrity or political independence of any State, or in any other manner inconsistent with the Purposes of the United Nations."

55 and 56, in which Members pledge themselves to promote the social and economic objectives of the Organisation.[41] Similarly, if the institutional provisions of the Charter are examined, it is apparent that the United Nations organ entrusted with primary responsibility for the maintenance or restoration of international peace and security, the Security Council, is vested with the most far-reaching powers over the Members of the United Nations. It is the Security Council which may adopt "decisions" which are binding on Members of the United Nations.[42] The powers of the General Assembly and of the economic and Social Council, with respect to the promotion of the social and economic objectives of the United Nations, are merely recommendatory.[43] They are, in the words of Professor Schwarzenberger, "essentially deliberative and policy-initiating or pre-legislative. . . . "[44] Thus the United Nations represents a normative and institutional framework for the preservation of world order from the use of armed force; what is required, in addition, is a mechanism which can resolve the underlying economic problems which may lead to military aggression and endanger peaceful relations between States.

CONCLUSIONS

Conceptions of world order and of threats to international stability are the product of historical experience. In the present century, international order has been threatened by two world wars. Inevitably, threats to world order have been identified with the use of armed force and international order has been equated with the absence of military aggression. Thus the United Nations, the present framework for the maintenance of world order, is the product of its own historical context. It was conceived as a means of safeguarding world order from the type of military aggression that

[41] Article 55 has been cited above. Article 56 states: "All Members pledge themselves to take joint and separate action in co-operation with the Organisation for the achievement of the purposes set forth in Article 55." Professor Brownlie suggests that United Nations organs are gradually investing these provisions with increasing legal authority. See I. Brownlie, *Principles of Public International Law* (3rd ed., 1979), p. 570. In its Advisory Opinion on Namibia, the International Court of Justice, in commenting on the South African administration of Namibia, stated: "To establish. . . . and to enforce distinctions, exclusions, restrictions and limitations exclusively based on grounds of race, colour, descent or national or ethnic origin which constitute a denial of fundamental human rights is a flagrant violation of the purposes and principles of the Charter." I.C.J. Reports 1971, p. 57.
[42] Article 25 states: "Members of the United Nations agree to accept and carry out the decisions of the Security Council in accordance with the present Charter."
[43] See Articles 10, 13, 62, 63.
[44] G. Schwarzenberger, *Economic World Order?* (1970), p. 38.

occurred in 1939[45]: "The Charter . . . was shaped at Dumbarton Oaks in the autumn of 1944, when the issue of the Second World War was still uncertain. . . . It sought to forge a weapon which could be used against just such a danger as then existed if history should ever repeat itself, a security system of irresistible power, and ready, as the Allies in 1939 had not been, for immediate action, and every other consideration was subordinated to this overriding purpose." However, history does not repeat itself. In the post-war period the granting of independence to territories formerly under the control of Western Powers has had a dramatic impact on the international system. Industrialised States can no longer ensure their access to raw materials in developing States nor determine the prices of vital commodities. As the Arab oil boycott of 1973–74 has shown, *economic* coercion by developing States can prove as serious a threat to the maintenance of world order as the use of military force.

In an increasingly interdependent world international order can no longer be equated with the mere *absence* of coercive behaviour by States. World order has been understood in a *negative* sense, as involving the prohibition of certain activities by States. However, while this *negative* conception of world order is of continuing validity in the context of restraining coercive behaviour by States, world order must also be understood in more *positive* terms as requiring the establishment of the "basic conditions for peaceful relations between nations. . . . "[46] As the Brandt Report argues, we must tackle "the causes rather than the symptoms of global problems."[47] Thus world order must now be understood in broader terms, as involving the elaboration of principles to govern those issues which have been the cause of military conflict, and the establishment of an international system which can promote stable and effective conditions *within* States, without which world order cannot be assured.

Law is of vital significance in this process. It is only through the instrumentality of law that the principles of a new system of international order can be realised, and the institutions necessary to regulate a new system of international order can be established. The systems of world order contemplated by both the League of Nations and the United Nations were *legal* systems, in the sense that they were realised through multilateral treaties. The Covenant of the

---

[45] J.L. Brierly, "The Covenant and the Charter," 23 *British Yearbook of International Law* (1946), p. 83 at pp. 90–91.
[46] *North-South op. cit.* in note 29, above, p. 124.
[47] *Ibid.* p. 31.

League and the Charter of the United Nations expressed both the norms of successive systems of international order, which were binding on contracting States as a matter of law, and established the international machinery necessary to ensure compliance with these norms. Similarly, if the arguments of the Brandt Report are accepted, new norms of international behaviour are required and new international machinery must be created if the gap between North and South is to be reduced, and a more comprehensive system of international order is to be established. However, such a transformation of the international economic system must depend on a global consensus which, at the time of writing, seems elusive.[48]

---

[48] The Brandt Report called for a summit meeting of leaders drawn from industrialised and developing States, selected so as to "ensure fair representation of major world groupings." It was hoped that such a meeting could "change the international climate and enlarge the prospects for global agreement." See *North-South, op. cit.* in note 29, above, pp. 281–282. On October 22 and 23, 1981, the leaders of 22 States met at Cancun, Mexico, to discuss North-South economic relations. However, the summit would seem to have accomplished very little, largely due to the profound differences of view that separated the United States from the other participating governments. The Soviet Union, it may be noted, refused to attend. See, generally, *The Times*, October 26, 1981, p.4.

THE CREDIBILITY
OF INTERNATIONAL LAW

By

GEORG SCHWARZENBERGER

Fundamentum est Justitiae Fides
(Credibility is the basis of justice)

Plaque, I.C.J. (New Wing), April 4, 1978

THE object of this paper[1] is to explore the phenomenon of credibility and, by way of illustration, elaborate its usefulness for purposes of International Law.

I—CREDIBILITY AS AN INTER-DISCIPLINARY CRITERION OF EVALUATION

(a) *Delimitation*

The central idea of credibility is the likelihood of the fulfilment of expectations. It demands more than either *acceptability* or *plausibility*.

It is worthwhile also to reflect on the relations between credibility, confidence in good faith, wishful thinking, credulity and gullibility. The demarcation lines between these concepts can hardly be objectively determined. They depend to a large extent on the vantage points chosen and the idiosyncrasies of those applying credibility-tests.

(b) *Constituent Elements*

Credibility has two constituent elements: an empirical component and a future-related calculation of probabilities.

(c) *Objects*

It is the person actively involved in a particular credibility-nexus who decides on the objects of a credibility-judgment. It may relate, for instance, to the truth of a statement or norm, the effectiveness of an organisation or system, or the seriousness of a project.

---

[1] The paper is based on a contribution, entitled *Die Glaubwürdigkeit des Völkerrechts*, to the Bindschedler *Festschrift* (Stämpli, Berne, 1980).

(d) *Functions*

Credibility is based on past experience but oriented towards the present and future. The rationality of any credibility-assessment depends on the strength of the element of experience in the test applied.

The generic function of credibility is to offer a measuring rod based on experience by which to assess, for instance, the future behaviour of persons or the functioning of organisations and systems.

Over and above this, the credibility-test can fulfil two special functions: (1) Credibility may make it supererogatory to produce repetitive evidence of conditions to be fulfilled. (2) Credibility offers a working hypothesis in favour of the object in a credibility-nexus.

The stronger the element of experience is in any credibility-judgment, the greater is its power to persuade critical and impartial observers. In a particular case, credibility may be so strong as to lead to a reversal of the burden of proof.

(e) *Evaluation*

In its summary character, credibility is related to two other tests: the "natural" interpretation of clauses of statutes and treaties, and judgments made by reference to common sense.

These comparisons carry their own warnings. Both national and international courts present a wealth of evidence on the subjectivity in both variants of summary judgment.[2] Yet, legal history also teaches that, notwithstanding the subjectivity of credibility-judgments, at least in one field they are superior to any other test: In the law of evidence, credibility has proved itself as the most reliable test of conflicting testimonies by witnesses in court.

II—THE RELEVANCE OF CREDIBILITY FOR INTERNATIONAL LAW

Within the confines of this paper, it must suffice to demonstrate the usefulness of credibility as a tool of inter-disciplinary studies by two

---

[2] See, for instance, on the "natural and ordinary" meaning of a term, the Advisory Opinion of the International Court of Justice on the *Constitution of the IMCO Maritime Safety Committee* (*I.C.J. Reports 1960,* pp. 159–160) and, on the "rules of common sense and good faith," Judge Sir Hersch Lauterpacht's Sep. Op. in the Court's Advis. Op. on *Admissibility of Hearings* (*ibid. 1956,* pp. 47–48) and, similarly, Judge de Castro's Sep. Op. in the Court's Advis. Op. on *Namibia, ibid. 1971,* p. 174.

illustrations: traditional characterisations of the social environment of international law and the effectiveness of international law.

(a) *The Social Environment*

The description of the existing international system as an international or world community is a favoured cliché of international rhetoric and tame scholarship. Even the International Court of Justice has employed this terminology on more than one occasion—last in its Judgment in the *United States Diplomatic and Consular Staff* case (1980) between the United States and Iran.[3]

Does anybody who describes contemporary international relations in terms of a community think of the billions in (semi-hard) currencies which the world Powers spend year by year on a rearmament race of cosmic proportions and of the proliferation in number and destructive power of nuclear, chemical, biological and physical means of mass extermination in the armouries of "civilised" Powers? Does he recall the wars which, during the present "peace" under the aegis of the United Nations, the world Powers wage against each other by proxy, and others conduct on their own initiative (if not necessarily on their own account), and the "destabilisation" of unfriendly or ideologically unacceptable régimes in the spheres of influence of the world Powers?

Related terms also may claim to be both funny and peculiar: the description of the collectivity of the subjects of international law as a *family of nations* or a community of international law (*Völkerrechtsgemeinschaft*).

The fact that lawyers have been guilty of such inaccuracies is noteworthy. What is more significant is that one inexactitude encourages other misdescriptions and errors. Outstanding among these lapses from grace is the characterisation, on the level of international *customary* law, of areas of binational and multinational rivers as river communities. A primitive type of conceptual jurisprudence is supposed to provide a substitute for evidence in each case of the normative basis for such a construction by reference to the governing treaty-law or international customary law. To cover up the failings of the technique employed, it becomes necessary to invoke spurious notions of natural law and classify areas of bilateral or multilateral rivers as "natural" river communities. In law, they are as natural as "natural" frontiers. The naturalist approach reaches its culmination with misleading analogies, that is, analogies from fluvial regulations and judicial decisions in federal law, to relations on lower levels of social integration such as

---

[3] See, for instance, *ibid. 1980,* p. 19. See also *ibid. 1979,* p. 19.

unorganised and partly organised international societies or societies in confederate frameworks.[4]

To treat argumentations of the type illustrated as lacking in credibility is in accordance with more general experiences: the history of a succession of State systems based on power politics since the third millenium B.C. confirms the inappropriateness of viewing such relations in terms of community relations.

For more than a century, there has been no need to rely on prescientific but ideologically tinged terminologies on the international environment. Henry Sumner Maine and, in his footsteps, sociologists such as Ferdinand Tönnies and Max Weber and philosophers such as R.G. Collingwood and John Macmurray have elaborated the distinction between society and community models and made possible the application of these models to international relations.

Even if the description of international relations prior to 1914 as relations in unorganised or partly organised international societies in the sociological meaning of the term is conceded, attempts continue to be made to view the post-1945 international system as a world community organised in the United Nations.[5]

Against the background of experiences with post-1945 international relations extending over nearly four decades, it should be possible to avoid the illusion that the world confederation of the United Nations amounts to more than a system of power politics in disguise. What is certain is that it is not a world community. Yet if these experiences are ignored, assessments in open conflict with reality fail to comply with even the most lenient standards of credibility.

(b) *The Effectiveness of International Law*

No legal system is or can be absolutely effective. In contrast to the laws of Natural Sciences, which are either valid or invalid, law is based on the assumption (or fiction) of free will. Thus, it is always possible to transgress it but only at a price. So long as the vindication of the law is not unduly delayed, breaches of the law do not impair its validity and credibility.

Nonetheless (or, perhaps, for this very reason), the question must be asked: Why was the credibility of international law in the century

---

[4] The river community accepted as legally relevant by the Permanent Court of International Justice in the case of the *Oder Commission* (1929) was based on the consensual international law of the 1919 Peace Treaty of Versailles (A23, p. 27). See also the *Diversion of Water from the Meuse Case* (1937–A/B 70, p. 20).

[5] See, for instance, Judge Tanaka's Sep. Op. in the *South West Africa Cases* (I.C.J. Reports 1966, p. 274).

between the Vienna Congress and the First World War so much higher than that of international law after the First and Second World Wars?

The strengths and weaknesses of pre-1914 international law can be summarised in seven propositions:

(1) The starting point of pre-1914 international law was the independence of the typical subjects of international law: territorial States. In the absence of demonstrable limitations of their independence, their freedom of action was unlimited, and the exercise of this freedom was as much compliance with international law as respect for limitations imposed by this legal system.

(2) The primary task of international law was to delimit by generally acceptable tests the jurisdiction of the territorial States which were subjects of international law on land, on the high seas and in air space.

(3) Against the background of the political, economic and military predominance of the Western world, these Powers insisted on incorporating into international treaty and customary law substantive standards of civilisation as, for instance, respect for the dignity of States, the inviolability of its representatives and the protection abroad of their nationals, including their investments.

(4) The international customary law of this period was little more than a series of abstractions from a multitude of treaties, the contents of which were treated as self-understood between civilised States, and additional abstractions from national laws as, for instance, legislation on the safety of life on the high seas and codifications of military law.

The general principles of law recognised by civilised nations constituted a further and, like international customary law, subsidiary form of international law. Again, this law-creating process hardly meant more than generalisations from municipal law such as extinctive prescription, moratory interests and *res judicata*.

Beyond this, the enabling rules of international law on Recognition and Consent offered, in principle, unlimited scope for the expansion of international law and organisation.

(5) Like legal rules for equals before the law, international customary law and the general principles of law recognised by civilised nations were based on the principle of reciprocity. Treaties founded on this working principle behind the law shared with the two other forms of international law the high credibility attached to legal rules providing for the mutuality of rights and obligations.

(6) The division of the world between a small number of overland and overseas Powers made possible the creation of a relatively stable international equilibrium. The quasi-orders created on this

footing found their legal expression in the Peace Treaties of 1815 and 1856, the framework- and quasi-constitutional law of pre-1914 international society.

(7) This system of international law was limited by the interpretation in good faith of international obligations, the optional character of the peaceful settlement of disputes, a practically unverifiable discretion in the application of reprisals and an, in State practice, unrestricted *jus ad bellum*. On this basis, even a modest body of laws of war and neutrality came into existence. Again, reciprocity and common standards of civilisation provided the necessary foundations.

The price of the high credibility of pre-1914 international law was its unvarnished subordination to overriding requirements of power politics. So long as an equilibrium acceptable to the international oligarchy as a whole existed, this system of international law could survive even duel wars between some of the greater Powers. When, as in the First World War, the whole quasi-constitution of the pre-1914 world broke down, the continuity of international law depended on an accident of history: which of the two systems of alliances would win the war and organise the inter-war period to come.

In this context, it must suffice to encourage the reader for himself to compare, from the angle of credibility, pre-1914 international law with the international law of the League of Nations period and, in this paper, limit such comparisons to international law since 1945.

The demands made on contemporary international law by doctrine and practice are more exacting than was the case before 1914:

(1) The attempts to expel the devil of sovereignty from international law permitted Beelzebub to return in the shape of a practically unlimited sovereignty of the world Powers and a sharply increasing gradient of "interdependence," comparable with that depicted by Orwell in *Animal Farm*.

The concept of hegemony, introduced and applied by Thucydides to Athens and Sparta as the pre-eminent Powers of his age, continues to explain relations of inequality between equals in law more credibly than "forward"-looking ideologies and forms of wishful thinking.

(2) The attempts made on the universalist plane to equate basic human rights and fundamental freedoms—formulated merely as Purposes in the United Nations Charter—with binding legal norms have hardly contributed to strengthening existing international law. They have, however, done their part to fashion international law as an additional ideological weapon for purposes of intervention in domestic affairs of other sovereign States.

(3) The growing number and severity of breaches of international diplomatic law by authoritarian and totalitarian States and a lamentable lack of solidarity on the part of others with victims of government-tolerated or instigated mob violence are disquieting symptoms of the decline of the minimum standards of any world civilisation and the mounting danger of a worldwide relapse into neo-barbarism.[6]

(4) Postulation of a supposed legal duty under international customary law to recognise new States and the alleged discovery of a non-consensual *jus cogens* are but attempts to introduce surreptitiously legal rules and institutions from areas of higher social integration into the law of a near-anarchic world society. While the former impairs the certainty of international law, the latter facilitates questionable interference with exclusive treaty relations.

Together with, in principle, non-binding resolutions of the General Assembly of the United Nations on matters *de lege ferenda*, such experiments assist in spreading the weeds of an elusive para-international law, with negative effects on the credibility of international law as a whole.

(5) The tendency, especially in international "development"-law, to transform conciliatory policies of capital-exporting States into legal duties to grant unilateral concessions discourages the growth of relations on a sounder basis of reciprocity, not least from the point of view of "developing" countries.

(6) The insouciance with which world Powers and others ignore the consensual *jus cogens*, formulated in Article 2 of the Charter of the United Nations, especially on the threat or use of force, hardly enhances the credibility of this "higher" law. Outrages in these

---

[6] The stockpiling of weapons of mass destruction, including chemical and nuclear weapons with "enhanced" radiation effect, that is, additional amounts of poisonous substances (see, further, the writer's *International Law and Order* (1971), pp. 185 *et seq.*), provides telling insights into the lack of confidence in the observance by potential enemies of less barbarian standards of warfare. This sceptical attitude extends even to treaty relations in periods of *détente* (see this *Year Book*, Vol. 35 (1981), pp. 266 *et seq.*).

It is also relevant to point to an increasing volume of evidence on governments falling back on justifications of actions taken in situations of tension and *de facto* war which are based on concepts of pre-1914 international law and difficult to square with the duty of member States of the United Nations to "fulfil in good faith the obligations assumed by them in accordance with the present Charter" (Article 2(2)).

Application of a hypothetical test may assist readers in obtaining a realistic view of the credibility of international law in a concrete situation: If any reader were condemned to stand in the shoes of a "moderate" diplomatic adviser on any contemplated action which, from the point of view of international law, was questionable or outright illegal, what counsel would he offer "off the record" or secretly to the government concerned?

categories, however, demonstrate dramatically the quasi-character of the United Nations world order and its constitutional law.

(7) What holds this heterogeneous and divided world society together and constitutes the precarious basis of its quasi-order is the fear of the world Powers of co-extermination in another world conflagration. It may be left to a future Thucydides to assess whether Solzhenitsyn's warning is justified that the West has already lost the Third World War and, without realising it, is currently engaged in the Fourth.

Is it astonishing that post-1945 international law can claim but a low credibility? This does not preclude that, nonetheless, some noteworthy and constructive developments of a functional or regional character can be recorded. Yet, they affect the overall picture as little as restful oases that of the desert.

It is possible to argue that, apparently, it makes little difference whether a system of international law in its narrow confines and with its self-effacing limitations has a high credibility or, like contemporary international law, suffers from a serious deficiency in credibility. The objection is justified. The difference between the two systems is merely that between two variants of society law: the one applied in systems of open power politics and the other in systems of power politics in disguise. Whereas the one variant is to be found in unorganised and only partly organised international societies, the other is applied on a confederate level. Yet both have to operate in social environments verging chronically on international anarchy.

III—THE RELEVANCE OF CREDIBILITY
de lege ferenda

For the understanding of the post-1945 experiments with the codification and development of international law, the measuring rod of credibility is perhaps even more significant than for the evaluation of *lex lata*.

As with any other products of treaty law, it is advisable, in analysing codification- and development-conventions, first, to examine carefully whether and for whom such drafts or treaties are legally binding and subject to what reservations, counter-reservations, declarations and counter-declarations of participating States. In this context, any assertion of the "largely" declaratory character of codification- and development-conventions requires thorough and, primarily, sceptical analysis.

In both respects, the 1969 Vienna Convention on the Law of Treaties is instructive. It took over a decade to transfer the Convention from the border zone of 35 participants required to transform it into *lex lata*, at least between the under a quarter of sovereign States bound by the Convention.

To assess the credibility of claims to the largely declaratory character of the Convention, readily verifiable tests are available: beyond close and independent examination of the text of each and every one of its provisions, research into the identity of the contracting parties and, more revealing, the non-participants, as well as the scope and contents of the multitude of reservations and counter-reservations. Application of these tests suggests a high degree of scepticism on the part of the majority of States on the value of this "modernisation" of international treaty-law.

Other relevant instruments, like the Helsinki Final Act (1975), provide their own clues of credibility as agreements under international law. An ingeniously formulated and modestly hidden clause in the Helsinki Final Act contains the expected reservation: the Parties are in agreement that the Final Act is not to be regarded as "eligible for registration under Article 102 of the Charter of the United Nations."[7] With this limitation, the legal relevance of the Final Act is discreetly negatived and, in any case, Parties are precluded from relying on the Act before any organ of the United Nations, including the International Court of Justice.

Another method appears appropriate to test the credibility of texts subject to further consultation and negotiation such as the Draft Convention on the Law of the Sea.[8] It is advisable to distinguish between two groups of clauses: the multitude of rules which openly or covertly modify existing international law in favour of coastal States, and those drafted for the benefit of a non-structured mankind and the creation of an international sea-bed authority for the protection and exploitation of the "heritage of mankind."

While the first group of rules is highly attractive to the majority of conference-participants, the chances of the second for a strong and effective sea-bed authority are slight. Irrespective of whether the draft rules will be on offer only as an inseparable package deal or will be available in bits and pieces, texts of this type fulfil a tactical function o their own. Relying on such proposals, the "largely" declaratory character of which is retrospectively asserted, exagger-

---

[7] Cmnd. 6198 (1975), p. 52. On the tragic consequences of attributing an exaggerated credibility to the Helsinki Final Act, see, for instance, the reports on the criminal and administrative proceedings against Russian "monitors" of the compliance of their country with the obligations of the Act (*The Times*, December 27, 1979, and *The Guardian*, December 28, 1979) and, on the varying records of performance by parties to *legally binding* agreements on human rights in relation to prisoners of conscience, see *Amnesty International Report 1981*.

[8] U.N. Doc. A/CONF. 62/L.78—August 28, 1981.

ated claims based on such "law in the making" obtain through codification a degree of unmerited credibility which would otherwise be denied to them.

Finally, three concrete tests of the credibility of projects for the development of international law which, empirically, have proved themselves as essential law-conditioning factors may, at least, be sketched:

(1) *The Degree of Integration of the Environment of Treaties*: Can any particular draft be squared with an existing international environment, or does its realisation presuppose a far-reaching change in the structure of this environment?

(2) *Homogeneity of the Contracting Parties*: Does the realisation of the draft depend on far-reaching homogeneity of the participants, for instance, in constitutional or cultural spheres?

(3) *The Minimal Ethical Common Denominator*: What is the minimal ethical common denominator between the contemplated contracting parties that is required to assure a relatively smooth operation of the treaty?

The more proposals for the codification and development of international law correspond to all three of these criteria, the higher is their credibility. Conversely, the more readily they fit into an existing social environment, the less they are able to ameliorate the shortcomings of an existing *status quo*.

What these criteria and the credibility-test itself cannot accomplish is to assess positively undertakings which purport to bring about community law inside an almost anarchic society. Yet, they can stimulate reflection on the minimum of structural changes required to give credibility to any particular proposal. Potentially, this is their constructive function.

INDEX

303